Christianity and Sexuality in the Early Modern World

The book surveys the ways in which Christian ideas and institutions shaped sexual norms and conduct from the time of Luther and Columbus to that of Thomas Jefferson. It is global in scope and geographic in organization, with chapters on Protestant, Catholic, and Orthodox Europe, Latin America, Africa and Asia, and North America. All the key topics are covered, including marriage and divorce, fornication and illegitimacy, clerical sexuality, same-sex relations, witchcraft and love magic, moral crimes, and inter-racial relationships.

Each chapter in this second edition has been fully updated to reflect new scholarship, with expanded coverage of many of the key issues, particularly in areas outside of Europe. Other updates include extra analysis of the religious ideas and activities of ordinary people in Europe, and new material on the colonial world.

The book sets its findings within the context of many historical fields – the history of sexuality and the body, women's history, legal and religious history, queer theory, and colonial studies – and provides readers with an introduction to key theoretical and methodological issues in each of these areas. Each chapter includes an extensive section on further reading, surveying and commenting on the newest English-language secondary literature.

Merry Wiesner-Hanks is a Distinguished Professor of History at the University of Wisconsin-Milwaukee. Her most recent publications include *Early Modern Europe, 1450–1750* (2006) and *The Marvelous Hairy Girls: The Gonzales Sisters and their Worlds* (2009).

Christianity and society in the modern world
Series editor: Hugh McLeod

Christianity and Sexuality in the Early Modern World

Regulating Desire, Reforming Practice

Second Edition

Merry Wiesner-Hanks

Routledge
Taylor & Francis Group

LONDON AND NEW YORK

In memory of Bob Scribner (1941–98)
great scholar, great editor, great friend

First edition published 2000
by Routledge

Second edition published 2010
by Routledge
2 Park Square, Milton Park, Abingdon, OX14 4RN

Simultaneously published in the USA and Canada
by Routledge
270 Madison Ave, New York, NY 10016

Routledge is an imprint of the Taylor & Francis Group, an informa business

© 2000, 2010 Merry Wiesner-Hanks

Typeset in Bell Gothic and Perpetua by
Florence Production Ltd, Stoodleigh, Devon
Printed and bound in Great Britain by
TJ International Ltd, Padstow, Cornwall

British Library Cataloguing in Publication Data
A catalogue record for this book is available from the British Library

Library of Congress Cataloging in Publication Data
Wiesner, Merry E., 1952–.
  Christianity and sexuality in the early modern world: regulating desire,
  reforming practice/Merry Wiesner-Hanks. – 2nd ed.
      p. cm. – (Christianity and society in the modern world)
  1. Sex – Religious aspects – Christianity.   2. Sex – History.
  3. Sex customs – History.   I. Title.
  BT708.W467 2010
  261.8'3570903 – dc22   2009044045

ISBN 10: 0–415–49188–6 (hbk)
ISBN 10: 0–415–49189–4 (pbk)

ISBN 13: 978–0–415–49188–4 (hbk)
ISBN 13: 978–0–415–49189–1 (pbk)

CONTENTS

ACKNOWLEDGMENTS

In writing any book, an author incurs many debts; in writing this one, which attempts to span the globe, my debts are both enormous and far-flung. Some of these are financial: I would like to thank the John Simon Guggenheim Foundation for its support, which provided me with a year off to research and write, and also the funds to spend part of that year in the Hawaiian sun instead of the Wisconsin mud. A good chunk of the research for the first edition of this book was accomplished during the year that I held the Association of Marquette University Women (AMUW) Chair in Humanistic Studies, which gave me excellent access to Catholic materials, and I would like to thank AMUW for its support.

More of my debts are scholarly. I would first like to give special thanks to four people: the late Robert Scribner, who as editor of this series first asked me to write something on Christianity and sexuality, taught me (and many others) to see religion as "a matter of continually contested under-standings," and did not blanch when I suggested the book be worldwide in perspective; Barbara Andaya, who invited me to be the comparative voice in a workshop on gender in early modern Southeast Asia, inspired me to move beyond Europe for this study, and arranged for me to have visiting faculty status at the University of Hawaii; Samantha McLoughlin, my student assistant at Marquette, who bore much of the brunt of my decision to go global and plowed through massive amounts of original source materials, including nearly all of the 73 volumes of the *Jesuit Relations,* searching for references to sex and marriage; Cameron Bradley, my student assistant at UWM, who searched the library and the web for new materials as I set out to write the second edition, and whose work was so thorough I nearly despaired.

Choosing to look at the world rather than my more familiar Europe meant that I had to rely on a vast network of friends and colleagues to advise me. I had already discovered, when writing *Women and Gender in Early Modern Europe,* how gracious people were in sharing their expertise, and for this book I shamelessly turned to an even wider circle. JoAnn McNamara, Susan Stuard, Judith Bennett, Susan Karant-Nunn, Scott Hendrix, Ulinka Rublack, Jeffrey Merrick, Susan Burgess, Eve Levin, Mary Elizabeth Perry, Anne Schutte, Larissa Taylor, Allyson Poska, Linda Hall, Asuncion Lavrin, Barbara Andaya, Carolyn Brewer, Ellen Langill, Elizabeth Hitz, Bea Greene, Linda Kealey, and Edward Behrend-Martínez all read and commented on drafts of chapters, and my dear friend Gwynne Kennedy read the entire manuscript.

Women's history has taught us that the axes of difference in history may not simply be reduced to race, class, and gender, but are almost too numerous to list. I was faced with a similar conundrum when thinking of all the people with whom I have discussed the issues in these pages over the years and whose thoughts as well as their published works are thus reflected here. I initially planned simply to thank them as a group lest I risk leaving someone out, but then decided that names are important (another insight of women's history). Thus, in addition to the people I have listed already, and with apologies to anyone I may omit, I would like to thank: Darlene Abreu-Ferreira, Margo Anderson, Jodi Bilinkoff, Renate Bridenthal, Judith Brown, Martha Carlin, Elizabeth Cohen, Natalie Zemon Davis, Lisa Di Caprio, Gisela Engel, James Farr, Evelyn Brooks Higginbotham, Grethe Jacobsen, Margaret Jolly, Amy Leonard, Mary Lindemann, Deirdre McChrystal, Jean O'Brien, Beth Plummer, Catherine Pomerleau, Helmut Puff, Elizabeth Rhodes, Diana Robin, Lyndal Roper, Hilda Smith, Ulrike Strasser, B. Ann Tlusty, Haruko Narata Ward, Gerhild Scholz Williams, and Heide Wunder. Finally, I would like to thank my husband Neil and my sons Kai and Tyr for their patience during the long process of this book in both of its editions, and for sharing in its benefits and its detriments.

INTRODUCTION

A S A HISTORIAN OF A PERIOD LONG AGO, I often encounter
skepticism about the relevance of my research in the contemporary
world. When I began to work on the first edition of this book, I was struck
by how different the responses were to the project. People I met at community
meetings, soccer games, or my hair salon were extremely interested, even
when I told them the book stops in 1750. I could, of course, attribute this
to their "prurient" interests in anything having to do with sex, and see it as
proof that the French philosopher, Michel Foucault, and the American radio
host, Howard Stern, are right: modern people want to talk about sex more
than anything else. But it was not merely the sex part they were interested
in, it was also the connection of sex to Christianity, a connection that they
saw as both self-evident and extremely relevant. As I finish the second edition
of this book, over a decade later, this has not changed.

This book explores Christianity and the regulation of sexual attitudes and
activities from roughly 1500 to 1750, both in Europe and in areas of the
world being colonized by European powers. Although in many ways Christian
treatment of sex during this period continued patterns and practices that had
begun centuries earlier, this was also an era of significant change, caused by
two developments that mark the beginning point of the book. The first was
the splintering of Christianity within much of Europe with the Protestant and
Catholic Reformations. The second was the increasing spread of Christianity
beyond Europe, especially after the Treaty of Tordesillas (1494) gave papal
approval to European appropriation of the rest of the world for colonization.
Both developments had important implications for Christian ideas about and
patterns of sexuality.

The ending point of the book acknowledges the rough chronological juncture of three trends: the emergence of secular governments as more authoritative regulators of sexuality than the church in many parts of the world; the onset of a new wave of exploration and colonialism, which brought different issues and colonial powers to the fore; and the beginning of what scholars of sexuality usually call "modern sexuality." That shift in thinking generated new ideas about the body, changes in marriage patterns, new concepts of gender differences, greater symbolic importance attached to sexuality, and new methods of controlling people's sexual lives. Although scholars disagree about exactly when "modern" sexuality started and how sharply it differed from what came before, the notion of a turning point is nonetheless very powerful. I have therefore chosen to end my study at what most scholars see as the beginning of modern sexuality.

The period covered by the book, roughly 1500–1750, is generally termed "early modern," a phrase developed by historians seeking to refine an intellectual model first devised during this very period, which saw European history as divided into three parts: ancient (to the end of the Roman Empire in the west in the fifth century), medieval (from the fifth century to the fifteenth), and modern (from the fifteenth century to their own time). As the modern era grew longer and longer, historians began to divide it into "early modern" – from the Reformation or Columbus to the French Revolution in 1789 – and what we might call "truly modern" – from the French Revolution to whenever they happened to be writing. This periodization has many critics, however, who point out that both "medieval" and "modern" are not simply chronological designations, but contain value judgements. The thinkers who first conceived of themselves as "modern" saw modernity as positive and "medieval" as negative, but contemporary commentators wonder whether modernity is necessarily a good thing. And what exactly makes something "modern"? Do some parts of the world become "modern" before others? Further questions surround "early modern." For example, how can "early modern" be the first part of "modernity," if "modern" sexuality didn't develop until after "early modern" was over? Is this era therefore modern in some aspects and not in others? As you can tell from this book's title, such questions have not led historians – myself included – to stop using the phrase, but we are more conscious about issues in our choice of terminology.

The same consciousness about terminology applies to the other words of my title. I use the term "Christianity" very broadly, for Christianity had an impact on the regulation of sexuality not only through the actions of church officials and the ideas of theologians, but also through the actions and ideas of lay people, from monarchs to ordinary individuals. If individuals or groups described their actions as Christian or held a position of authority either within a Christian denomination or a state where the official religion was Christianity, I include them here. I am not using "Christian" in a moral sense, and some of the attitudes and activities discussed here may be viewed by people today – and in fact *were* viewed by some early modern people – as being antithetical to what they feel is the true message of Christianity.

"Sexuality" is even more problematic, because no one in the centuries I am discussing used it. "Sexuality," defined as "the constitution or life of the individual as related to sex" or "the possession or exercise of sexual functions, desires, etc.," first appeared in English only in 1800, and to many its invention signals the beginning of "modern sexuality." The ideas of the Austrian psycho-analyst Sigmund Freud were particularly important in this. Freud proposed that everyone had a sexuality as a permanent aspect of their personhood, whether or not they ever engaged in sexual relations. Sexuality was the organizing principle of the self, although many people "repressed" their sexual urges, which led to psychological trauma. Freud's notions have been widely debated in the century since he wrote, but the idea that there is something called "sexuality" and that we all have one is now widely accepted. This was not true in earlier centuries, however. People had sexual desires and engaged in sexual actions that they talked and wrote about, but they did not think of these as expressions of their sexuality, and they defined what was "sexual" in ways that are different than we do. Thus some historians choose to avoid the word "sexuality" when discussing earlier periods, arguing that is anachronistic.

Investigations of the past are always informed by more recent understandings and concerns, however, and using modern concepts can often provide great insights. Thus most historians use "sexuality" in their investigations, though a central part of their research is studying changes in the meanings and boundaries of what was considered sexual. The editors of the central journal in the field therefore chose the title *Journal of the History of Sexuality* when it began publication in 1990, and I use the word as well.

Exploring all aspects of the relationship between Christianity and sexuality over roughly two and a half centuries throughout the world would be impossible to do in a single book. I have chosen to focus on the ways in which people used Christian ideas and institutions to regulate and shape (or attempt to regulate and shape) sexual norms and conduct. Except for an introductory chapter, which traces these issues from the beginning of Christianity to about 1500, the chapters are primarily geographical: Protestant Europe, Catholic and Orthodox Europe, Latin America, Africa and Asia, North America. Each of these chapters surveys learned and popular notions of sexuality, both Christian, and, in areas beyond Europe, non-Christian. Each chapter then discusses the development and operation of Christian institutions, such as law codes, courts, prisons, and marital regulations, as well as actual changes in such areas as marriage, divorce, illegitimacy, sanctioned and unsanctioned sexual relations, witchcraft, relations between Christians and non-Christians and between different denominations of Christians, and moral crimes. Though the book is oriented toward intellectual and institutional change and its social consequences, rather than toward social change alone, I do not see Christianity as an abstract force or regulation as something imposed in a vacuum or simply from the top down. Ordinary men and women as well as religious officials and political elites shaped Christianity's ideas and institutional structures and their impact in matters of sex. As Christianity split into numerous denominations and expanded beyond Europe, the dialectic between official theology and the responses of practitioners grew ever more complex.

For this second edition, there was a staggering amount of important new scholarship, providing insights I have integrated into each chapter. This has resulted in expanded coverage of nearly every issue, and particularly of masculinity, notions of the body, gendered religious symbols and language, and the intersection of sex and race. The chapters on Europe include more extensive analysis of the religious ideas and activities of ordinary people, and the chapters on the colonial world of the ways in which indigenous people and immigrants (including slaves and other coerced migrants) shaped Christian traditions and practices.

Histories and theories of sexuality

This study draws on research and analysis from many fields of history, fields that sometimes overlap or interact, yet that at other times are hostile to one another. Prime among these is the history of sexuality, which, until the last several decades, was viewed as a questionable or at best marginal area of scholarly inquiry. Vern Bullough, one of the first investigators of medieval sexuality, reports that throughout the 1960s – that decade of the "Sexual Revolution" – his research on such topics as homosexuality, prostitution, and transvestism was rejected by historical journals as unsuitable, while books that avoided any discussion of sex, such as Edith Hamilton's *The Greek Way*, were best-sellers.[1] This attitude began to change in the 1970s for a number of reasons. Historians became more interested in the lives of ordinary people rather than simply political or intellectual elites, and they used methodologies from other disciplines such as anthropology and economics to create what they termed the New Social History. These changes combined with the feminist movement to create an enormous interest in women's history, of which the history of women's bodies and sexual lives was a significant part. The gay liberation movement encouraged both public discussion of sexual matters in general and the study of homosexuality in the past and present.

The feminist movement of the 1960s – often termed the "second wave" to set it apart from the "first wave" of feminism that began in the nineteenth century – included a wide range of political beliefs, with various groups working for a broad spectrum of goals. One of these was to understand more about the lives of women in the past, as scholars and activists asserted that history as it had been studied and taught was really "men's history," though it had not been identified as such. This led to an explosive growth in women's history. Historians of women have demonstrated that there is really no historical change that does not affect the lives of women in some way, though often very differently than it affects the lives of men of the same class or social group. Over the last several decades, women's historians have examined many aspects of women's sexuality, along with every other aspect of their lives.

In the 1980s, an increasing number of historians familiar with studying women began to discuss the ways in which systems of sexual differentiation affected both women and men, and used the word "gender" to describe these systems. They differentiated primarily between "sex," by which they meant physical, morphological, and anatomical differences (what are often called "biological differences") and "gender," by which they meant a culturally constructed and historically changing system of differences. Since then, gender historians have turned their attention to men's experiences *as men*, rather than as an unacknowledged universal. Historians interested in this new perspective asserted that gender was an appropriate category of analysis when looking at *all* historical developments, not simply those involving women or the family. *Every* political, intellectual, religious, economic, social, and even military change had an impact on the actions and roles of men and women, and, conversely, a culture's gender structures influenced every other structure or development. People's notions of gender shaped not only the way they thought about men and women, but about their society in general. As the historian Joan Scott put it: "gender is a primary way of signifying relationships of power." Thus hierarchies in other realms of life were often expressed in terms of gender, with dominant individuals or groups described in masculine terms and dependent ones in feminine. These ideas in turn affected the way people acted, though explicit and symbolic ideas of gender could also conflict with the way men and women chose or were forced to operate in the world.

Both women's history and gender history have had a major influence on the history of sexuality, which has also, not surprisingly, been strongly shaped by ideas that originated in gay and lesbian studies. Just as interest in women's history has been part of feminist political movements, interest in the history of sexuality has been part of the gay liberation movement that began in the 1970s. Historians and activists studied same-sex relations in many periods, initially focusing primarily on men – whose lives have everywhere left more sources than those of women – but then also on women. Some put emphasis on continuities and similarities in the experiences of individuals and groups across time, and supported efforts to discover physical bases for same-sex attraction in the brain or genetic code. Others emphasized differences. In the same way that the growth of women's history led scholars to start exploring men's experiences as men, gay and lesbian studies has led some scholars to explore the way in which heterosexual relationships were structured, explicitly labeling these as such rather than simply as marriage or family.

A key feature in these histories was the notion of "sexual identity" or "sexual orientation." During the course of the late nineteenth and twentieth century, physicians, psychiatrists, and scholars in other fields posited that sexuality – that central feature of the psyche – was defined by sexual object choice. Those who desired those of the same sex were "homosexuals," a word devised in 1869 by the Hungarian jurist K.M. Benkert, and those who desired those of the opposite sex were "heterosexuals," a word originally used to describe individuals of different sexes who regularly engaged in non-procreative sex simply for fun, but increasingly used for all those who were sexually attracted to the "opposite" sex. Like sexuality, sexual orientation came to be widely viewed as a permanent part of the self, an idea that now shapes legal decisions and self-descriptions on Internet dating services as well as history and psychiatry.

Historians recognized that the idea of sexual identity developed at a particular point, and this became a marker of "modern" sexuality. Before then there were sexual acts, but not sexual identities. The timing of this change has been hotly debated, however. Some scholars argue for the nineteenth century, others for the eighteenth, and others put the break even earlier as they discover same-sex subcultures or descriptions of individuals as "being" or "having" a certain type of sexuality (rather than simply "doing" certain acts) as early as the fifteenth century. Some scholars have also criticized the idea that there was one dramatic break, however, what the American theorist Eve Kosofksy Sedgwick has ironically labeled the search for "The Great Paradigm Shift."[2]

Sedgwick's comment is part of a broad questioning about systems of both sexuality and gender that posit only two dichotomous categories: heterosexual and homosexual, men and women. (These two systems are related, of course, for only if there are only two genders could everyone be divided into those attracted to "the same" or "the opposite.") This questioning has a number of bases, one of which is the experience of intersexed persons – termed "hermaphrodites" in the early modern era – those whose external genitalia or internal chromosomes and hormones do not allow them to be easily categorized as "male" or "female." If "cultural" gender is based on "biological" sex differences, how is their gender to be determined? In general, the gender polarity man/woman has been so strong that intersexed persons were usually simply assigned to the sex they most closely resembled. Since the nineteenth century this assignment has been reinforced by surgical procedures modifying or removing the inappropriate body parts, generally shortly after birth. Thus dichotomous cultural norms about gender (that everyone *should* be a man or a woman) determine "biological" sex in such cases, rather than the other way around.

The arbitrary nature of the two-gender, two-sexuality system has also been challenged by transsexual, bisexual, and transgender individuals. In the 1950s, sex-change operations became available for people whose external genitalia and even chromosomal and hormonal patterns marked them as male or female, but who mentally understood themselves to be the other. Transsexual surgery could make the body fit more closely with the mind, but it also led to challenging questions: At what point in this process does a "man" become a "woman," or vice versa? With the loss or acquisition of a penis? Breasts? From the beginning? What does the answer to this imply about notions of what is the essence of being a man or woman? If "sexual identity" is based on the choice of one's partner, did such individuals also change from being "homosexual" to "heterosexual" or vice versa? And what about the many people who were attracted to both men and women? In the 1980s such questions began to be made even more complex by individuals who described themselves as "transgendered," that is, as neither male nor female or both male and female. Should such individuals be allowed in spaces designated "women only" or "men only"? Should they have to choose between them, or should there be more than two choices? All of these groups posed challenges to the feminist and gay rights movements, although many groups adapted to include them, reflected in the LGBT acronym. As had been true with the women's and gay-rights movement, people involved in the transmovement also began historical study of people they identified as sharing their experiences.

Anthropologists have provided further demonstrations of the limitations of a two-gender or two-sexuality system, pointing out that many of the world's cultures have a third or even a fourth gender – that is, people understood to be neither men nor women, who often have (or had) specialized religious or ceremonial roles. Such individuals sometimes abstain from sexual activity, but not always; their sexual relations cannot be understood as with the "same" or "opposite" sex, however, but instead something else. The contemporary transmovement points to these examples, and highlights limitations in any dichotomous system of gender *or* sexuality, instead favoring a continuum.

Historians have also been part of this critique, and are decreasingly concerned with the acts vs. identities debate. They have discovered wide variety in gender roles and sexual attitudes and practices across time, and within one culture based on class, nationality, ethnicity, religion, and other factors. These were not simply outgrowths of "biological differences," but culturally constructed and historically changing. Some historians, in fact, came to assert that everything regarding gender and sexuality is determined by culture, a position often labeled "social constructionist." The idea that everyone had a fixed "sexual identity" based on something internal was not only wrong for the past, it was also wrong for the present. Sexual identities – and perhaps even "gender identities" as men or women – were "performative," that is, roles that can be taken on or changed at will. For social constructionists, those who sought physical bases for gender difference or sexual orientation were naïve "essentialists." In addition, argued some, anatomical and genetic tests currently used by medical researchers to explore gender and sexual differences are not applicable for populations long dead, excepting those few tests that can be performed on skeletal remains. Thus the only thing historians *can* explore about past sexuality, they assert, is its social construction, its meaning, because that is what the historical record contains.

Interest in the meaning of sexuality and emphasis on its social construction reflects a more general trend in historical studies over the last several decades, usually labeled the "linguistic turn" or the "New Cultural History." Historians have long recognized that documents and other types of evidence are produced by particular individuals with particular interests and biases that consciously and unconsciously shape their content. Most historians thus attempted to keep the limitations of their sources in mind as they reconstructed events and tried to determine causation, though sometimes these got lost in the narrative. During the 1980s, some historians began to assert that because historical sources always present a biased and partial picture, we can never fully determine what happened or why; to try to do so is foolish or misguided. What historians should do instead is to analyze the written and visuals materials of the past – what is often termed "discourse" – to determine the way various things are "represented" in them and their possible meanings. This heightened interest in discourse among historians drew on the ideas of literary and linguistic theory – often loosely termed "deconstruction" or "post-structuralism" – about the power of language. Language is so powerful, argued some theorists, that it determines, rather than simply describes, our understanding of the world.

In examining sexuality, some historians have concentrated on the words of intellectual, religious, and political authorities, who were usually men. In its attention to discourse and meaning, such scholarship reflects history's linguistic/cultural turn. Other historians have turned their attention to people's actual sexual experiences, including marriage, prostitution, same-sex relations, sexual violence, and many other topics, and attempted to learn what both men and women thought about their own bodies and sexual lives. Such scholarship often considers women's ability to shape their world – what is usually termed "agency" – and sometimes criticizes scholarship that emphasizes the power of linguistic structures, arguing that this denies women agency. In the 1980s the debate among women's and gender historians – not only those who focused on sexuality, but also those who studied many other topics – about the linguistic/cultural turn was very acrimonious, but a quarter-century later it has become less so. Cultural historians now tend less often to focus solely on discourse, but treat their sources as referring to something beyond the sources themselves. In analyzing sexuality, they still emphasize the social construction of sexual and gender categories, but may also talk about actual physical experiences. Historians who were initially suspicious of the linguistic turn use a wider range of literary and artistic sources than they did earlier, thus paying more attention to discourse.

Foucault and his critics

In the study of sexuality, the emphasis on the power of discourse was heightened by the influence of the French philosopher Michel Foucault. In 1976, Foucault began publication of a multi-volume *History of Sexuality*, intended to cover the subject in the West from antiquity to the present. Though only three volumes were published before his death in 1984, the first book, along with Foucault's other works on prisons, insanity, and medicine, greatly influenced later historians.

Foucault asserted that the history of sexuality in the West was not characterized by the increasing repression of an innate biological drive – as Freud and others argued – but instead by the "transformation of sex into discourse." This process began with the Christian practice of confessing one's sins to a priest, during which first acts and then thoughts and desires had to be described in language. This practice expanded after the Reformation as Catholics required more extensive and frequent confession and Protestants substituted the personal examination of conscience for oral confession to a priest. During the late eighteenth and nineteenth centuries, Foucault argued, sexuality began to be a matter of concern for authorities outside religious institutions: political authorities tried to encourage steady population growth; educational authorities worried about masturbation and children's sexuality; and medical authorities both identified and pathologized sexual "deviance" and made fertility the most significant aspect of women's lives. Foucault traced this expansion of discourses about sex into the present, when "we talk more about sex than about anything else."[3] Discourse created sexuality, according to Foucault; before people learned to talk about sex so thoroughly, there was sex, but not sexuality. Modern sexuality is closely related to power, not simply the power of authorities to define and regulate it, but also the power inherent in every sexual relationship. This power – in fact, all power, in Foucault's opinion – is intimately related to knowledge and to "the will to know," the original subtitle of the first volume of his *History of Sexuality*.

Historians of sexuality after Foucault have elaborated on his insights by defining what is specific to modern Western sexuality, exploring the mechanisms that regulate sexuality, and investigating the ways in which individuals and groups described and understood their sexual lives. Other scholars have pointed out gaps or weaknesses in Foucault's theories, and address issues that he largely ignored, among them the relationship between race and European notions of sexuality and the ways in which economic power structures shaped sexual ideas and practices. Despite the various critiques of Foucault, however, he remains the field's most important individual theorist.

Many ideas central to women's and gender history, such as the arguments that culture shapes sexuality and that sexual relationships are power relation-ships (captured in the slogan "the personal is political"), not only parallel Foucault's ideas, but, in fact, pre-date his work on sexuality. Others are quite different, particularly the emphasis on the dissimilar experiences of men and women, and on the ways in which societies create gender distinctions between men and women. Feminist analysts point out that Foucault's studies of sexuality are, in fact, studies of *male* sexuality (though he does not state this explicitly) despite the fact that *female* sexuality has generally been of greater concern to authorities throughout history. Some feminist scholars have reinvigorated ideas drawn from Freud and other psychoanalysts in their work; the repression model has not returned, but the role played by deep psychic structures that may not always be expressed through words has. Lyndal Roper, for example, analyzes the way deep-seated emotions and fantasies about witchcraft provided evidence of its diabolic nature to individuals and communities, combining with worries about marriage, fertility, and sexuality in a deadly mixture, as we will see in more detail in several chapters.

In the early 1990s, during a period of intense AIDS activism, cultural theorists combined elements of gay and lesbian studies with Foucault's ideas and others originating in literary and feminist analysis to create queer theory. Queer theorists argued that sexual notions were central to all aspects of culture, and called for greater attention to sexuality that was at odds with whatever was defined as "normal." They asserted that the line between "normal" and "abnormal" was always socially constructed, however, and that, in fact, all gender and sexual categories were artificial and changing. Some theorists celebrated all efforts at blurring or bending categories, viewing any sort of identity as both false and oppressive and celebrating hybridity and performance. Others had doubts about this, wondering whether one can work to end discrimination against homosexuals, women, African Americans, or any other group, if one denies that the group has an essential identity, something that makes its members clearly homosexual or women or African-American. (A similar debate can be found within the contemporary transmovement, with some people arguing that gender and sexual orientation are fundamental aspects of identity and others that they are not or should not be.) In the last decade, queer theory has been widely applied, as scholars have "queered" — that is, called into question the categories used to describe and analyze — the nation, race, religion, and other topics along with gender and sexuality. This broadening has led some, including a few of the founders of the field, to wonder whether queer theory loses its punch when everything is queer, but it continues to be an influential theoretical perspective.

Histories and theories of colonialism

Along with the history of sexuality, this book also draws many of its ideas from the history of colonialism and its theoretical branch, post-colonial theory, in which questions of identity, agency, and the cultural construction of difference have also been central areas of inquiry. Many recent studies demonstrate that imperial power is explicitly and implicitly linked with sexuality; imperial powers shaped cultural constructions of masculinity and femininity, and images of colonial peoples were gendered and sexualized. This work is often interdisciplinary in nature, combining artistic and literary evidence with more traditional historical documents; its emphasis on discourse and representation frequently align it with the New Cultural History.

An important theme in much post-colonial theory has been the notion of hegemony, initially developed by the Italian political theorist Antonio Gramsci. Hegemony differs from domination because it involves convincing dominated groups to acquiesce to the desires and systems of the dominators through cultural as well as military and political means. Generally this was accomplished by granting special powers and privileges to some individuals and groups from among the subordinated population, or by convincing them through education or other forms of socialization that the new system was beneficial or preferable. The notion of hegemony explains why small groups of people have been able to maintain control over much larger populations without constant rebellion and protest, though some scholars have argued that the emphasis on hegemony downplays the ability of subjugated peoples to recognize the power realities in which they are enmeshed and to shape their own history. The Australian sociologist R.W. Connell has applied the idea of hegemony to studies of masculinity, noting that in every culture one form of masculinity is hegemonic, but men who are excluded from that particular form still benefit from male privilege.

One group of historians, those associated with the book series Subaltern Studies, has been particularly influential in calling for historical research that focuses on people who have been subordinated by virtue of their race, class, culture, gender, or language. Subaltern (the word is drawn from Gramsci's writings) Studies began among South Asian historians, who investigated such topics as Indian peasant revolts and the development of Indian nationalism; it is becoming increasingly influential among historians of other parts of the formerly colonial world, such as Latin America and Africa. Historians of Europe and the United States are also applying insights drawn from Subaltern Studies to their own work, particularly as they investigate "subaltern" groups such as racial and ethnic minorities. They pay special attention to the language of hierarchy and domination, noting that subordinated groups often developed their own distinctive and more liberating meanings for such language in a process the Russian linguist M.M. Bakhtin calls "double-voiced discourse."[4] Thus in the cultural construction of difference and identity, the meanings and implications of words depends on who is using them.

In the contemporary world, the most significant category of difference is often judged to be race. Suspicion and hatred of people with darker skin has a very long history in many parts of the world, but the contemporary meaning of "race" as a system dividing people into very large groups by skin color and other physical characteristics is primarily a product of the nineteenth century. The word "Caucasian" was first used by the German anatomist and naturalist Johann Friedrich Blumenbach (1752–1840) to describe light-skinned people of Europe and western Asia because he thought that the Caucasus Mountains on the border between Russia and Georgia were most likely their original home. He thought that they were the first humans, and the most attractive. (His judgement about Caucasian attractiveness came through studying a large collection of skulls, as he measured all other skulls against one from Georgia that he judged to be "the most beautiful form of the skull.") This meaning of "race" has had a long life, though biologists and anthropologists today do not use it, as it has no scientific meaning or explanatory value.

Identity and sexuality in the early modern period

Many of the issues raised by the newer scholarship on sexuality and colonialism – most of which focuses on the last two hundred years – may seem to be quite contemporary and hence anachronistic in the early modern world. Issues of difference and identity, and the role of sexuality in these, emerge

Figure 0.1

In this gory manuscript illumination of a scene from the book of Numbers (25:7–8), Phineas the priest drives a long spear into a couple having sex. The man was an Israelite and the woman a Midianite, and in killing them Phineas lessened God's wrath with Israel for "playing the harlot," the standard Old Testament phrase for accepting the beliefs of other groups or intermarrying with them. This painting was one of hundreds in the Alba Bible, a translation of the Old Testament from Hebrew into Castilian made under the direction of Rabbi Moses Arragel in Spain in 1430, a period of growing hostility toward Jews. Intermarriage between Jews and Christians was punishable by execution in Christian Spain, which may have been why the Franciscan friars who painted the illuminations chose this particular text to illustrate.

much earlier, however, even before the period covered in this book. For example, English forces conquered much of Ireland in the twelfth century, transforming it into what many see as England's first colony and establishing patterns they would later use throughout the huge British Empire. Those of Irish birth were discriminated against in all realms of life; they had no access to law courts, could not make a legal will or become church officials, and were declared "unfree." As medieval Germans moved eastward into Slavic areas, they prohibited Slavs from joining craft guilds in the towns they founded. Ethnic purity can only be maintained across generations by prohibiting marriage among groups, and laws did just this. Officials in the German-founded cities of eastern Europe, for example, were required to have four German grandparents. The most extensive attempt to prevent intermarriage was Ireland's Statute of Kilkenny from 1366, which states flatly that there were to be no marriages between the descendents of English immigrants and native Irish.

Late medieval European chroniclers and lawmakers writing in Latin used words such as *gens* and *natio* to refer to groups that differed according to language, traditions, customs, family line, kindred, and laws. "Nation" and "people" continued to be commonly used words to describe human differences in the early modern period, though "color" and "complexion" were used as well. In English, the word "race" was also used to describe national groupings – the French race, the Spanish race – or other social groups, such as "the race of learned gentlemen" or "the race of mankind," though it was not linked specifically to skin color until the late eighteenth century.

Commentators recognized that traditions, language, and customs could change, however, and some began to describe differences also in terms of "blood" – "German blood," "English blood," and so on – which made difference heritable. Blood was also used as a way to talk about social differences, especially for nobles. Just as Irish and English were prohibited from marrying each other, those of "noble blood" were prohibited from marrying commoners in many parts of Europe.

Religious beliefs also came to be conceptualized as blood in late medieval Europe, with people regarded as having Jewish blood, Muslim blood, or Christian blood. The most dramatic expression of this in Europe was in the Iberian peninsula, where "purity of blood" – having no Muslim or Jewish ancestors – became an obsession, particularly because there was no way to tell visually whether a person was descended from Jewish or Muslim converts to Christianity. Laws restricted the activities of converts and their children, termed "New Christians," and attempted to differentiate between them and "Old Christians," though in practice this was very difficult. In the sixteenth century, Iberian notions of "purity of blood" were carried to Spanish and Portuguese colonies, where they were used in disadvantaging different types of "New Christians," those of African, Asian, and American ancestry.

After the Reformation, Christian blood was further subdivided into Protestant and Catholic blood. Fathers choosing a wetnurse for their children took care to make sure she was of the same denomination, lest, if he was a Catholic, her Protestant blood turn into Protestant milk and thus infect the child with heretical ideas. Children born of religiously mixed marriages were often slightly mistrusted, for one never knew whether their Protestant or Catholic blood would ultimately triumph. Describing differences as blood naturalized them, making them appear as if they were created by God in nature.

Ideas about differences created by social status, nation, religion, and ethnicity in the early modern period were often understood – sometimes by the same person – to be both culturally created and inherent in the person. Thus the same religious reformers who warned against choosing the wrong wetnurse also worked for conversions, and did not think about whether adopting a new religion would also change a woman's milk. Rulers who supported nobles' privileges because of their distinction from commoners regularly ennobled able commoners who had served as generals and officials. French royal officials with authority over colonies spoke about the superiority of "French blood" but also advocated assimilation, in which indigenous peoples would "become French." Catholic authorities in colonial areas limited entrance to certain convents to "pure-blooded" white or native women, thus excluding mixed-race people, but were more willing to allow a light-skinned mixed-race person than a "full-blooded" native marry a white person. Such contradictions did not generally lessen people's convictions about racial, social, or religious hierarchies, however.

Changing concepts of identity and difference are central to understanding the topic of this book: the ways in which Christianity regulated the sexual lives of Europeans and colonial subjects, and the ways in which individual men and women, Christian and non-Christian, responded to and shaped these attempts at regulation. Though they used different terminology than do contemporary theorists, early modern theologians, lawmakers, rulers, courts and private individuals all wrestled with issues of identity and difference in sexual matters: Should a Jew be allowed to marry a Christian, a Protestant a Catholic, a native American a Spaniard? What were the children of such unions' ethnic, religious, or racial identities? (The answer determined their access to education, property, government positions and marital partners.) Should everyone marry? Should hermaphrodites marry? What about those who vowed to God never to marry: were they holy or was this a misguided attempt to repress a basic human drive that was uncontrollable? Which sexual practices were "normal" (the usual word for this was "natural") and which were unnatural? What sexual practices made one a sinner (a common "identity" in Christianity) – prostitution, masturbation, homosexuality, bigamy, premarital sex, lust for one's spouse – and which were the more serious sins? Early modern individuals also addressed questions about the power of discourse: Should people confess their sexual (as well as other) sins to another person, or was this for God alone? Did talking about (or thinking about) sex matter, or were actions all that counted?

Social discipline

In addition to questions arising from general theories about sexuality and colonialism, this study also engages theories that have been developed specifically about the early modern period. One of these is the notion of social discipline, a concept that originated with the German historian Gerard Oestreich and has more recently been especially associated with the German historian Heinz Schilling. These historians point out that almost all religious authorities in the early modern period, whether Catholic, Lutheran, Anglican (the Protestant church in England), or Calvinist, were engaged in a process of social disciplining, by which they mean working with secular political authorities in an attempt to get people to live a proper, godly life. This process began before the Reformation especially in cities, when, as we will see in more detail in Chapter 1, political leaders regulated prostitution, made sodomy a capital crime, and increased the penalties for illegitimacy. After the Reformation, religious and political leaders of all denominations expanded and sharpened their efforts at social discipline, usually combining them with an increased interest in teaching people the basics of their particular version of Christianity, a process known as confessionalization. Officials began to keep registers of marriages, births, baptisms, and deaths, and these records allowed them better to monitor the behavior and status of individuals. They restricted gambling and drinking, increased the punishments for adultery and fornication, forbade certain books and encouraged the reading of others, prohibited popular celebrations (such as Carnival and parish fairs), and preached and published pamphlets against immoral behavior. In England and New England these measures are especially associated with the Puritans, Calvinist-inspired individuals who thought the reforms instituted by the Anglican Church had not gone far enough and who wanted to "purify" the English church of any remaining Catholic practices and immorality.

This process of social disciplining has been linked to, or seen as part of, a more general social change that is often called the "reform of popular culture" or "the reformation of manners" or the "reformation of lifestyle." The English historian Peter Burke has described the process of social discipline as a "triumph of Lent," in which popular culture was restricted by moral and clerical reformers bent on making people's behavior more pious, somber, and sober.

While Burke concentrates on external agents of control, the German sociologist Norbert Elias focuses on internal agents: that is, on the ways people internalized more controlled social behavior and habits which they learned from their parents or superiors or from reading books of manners and conduct. Elias traces long-term changes in habits of eating, washing, blowing one's nose, and urinating from the fourteenth century through the nineteenth. He notes that these natural functions were increasingly regarded as inappropriate in public, and that polished manners came to be regarded as a sign both of civility and civilization. He links this "civilizing process" to changes in the structures of power and state formation in Europe; to Elias, it explains why Europeans by the nineteenth century could view themselves as "civilized" and superior to the "savages" in areas being colonized. Elias's supporters stress that he was critical of such value judgements. A few of his opponents argue on that contrary that the civilizing process itself is a "myth," that reticence about the public display of nakedness and bodily functions can be found around the world. They point out that taboos about certain behaviors have existed throughout history, and cite the work of Mary Douglas and other cultural anthropologists to support their position.

Cross-cultural encounters

Several theories developed by scholars working in non-European areas during the early modern period have also had an impact on this book. Prime among these is the concept that relations between Europeans and non-Europeans were primarily "encounters" rather than discoveries or conquests, with cross-cultural exchanges in terms of material goods and intellectual concepts in both directions. Early modern encounters not only involved Europeans and non-Europeans, of course, but also Chinese and Southeast Asians, Arabs and Indonesians, and other pairs. In these encounters, people confronted others of different ethnicity, race, language, and/or religion, and they had to develop ways of understanding this alterity. In no instance was that understanding based simply on actual encounters; it was also shaped by preconceptions about other peoples and about themselves. Some scholars describe this process as "creating the Other" or "constructing the Other" or sometimes even "Othering."

Though confronting or constructing the Other occurred throughout the world and was a many-sided process, European responses to non-Europeans have received the most scholarly attention. The greater availability of source materials from Europeans partly accounts for this emphasis. Europe was also establishing political and economic hegemony over much of the world at this time, so that many scholars consider this line of encounter to be the most significant. Some argue, as well, that Europeans both created and utilized more radical distinctions between self and other than other people did.

Studies of European constructions or inventions of the Other include encounters with both the East and the West. Those that focus on European ideas about Asia, such as the works of Edward Said, tend to concentrate on the period since the eighteenth century, whereas those which focus on the New World start, for obvious reasons, with Columbus. European response to the New World was first analyzed by the Mexican historian and philosopher Edmundo O'Gorman, who coined the phrase the "invention of America" to describe the ways in which Columbus's cultural assumptions shaped both his own and subsequent commentators' descriptions of his voyages and the New World. More recently, European writings about the New World have been a central topic for literary critics and historians influenced by theories of the centrality of language. These scholars assert that colonial discourse is so shaped by preconceptions that it can reveal little about the people described; the proper – indeed the only possible – focus of study is simply the discourse itself. Others (myself included) find this approach limiting and unsatisfying, and consider European observations, imperfect and biased as they are, as nonetheless valuable for analyzing other cultures.

Much of the newest scholarship on cultural encounters in the Atlantic has traced the process forward in time, and highlighted the ways in which African and American peoples not only reacted to and fought against European ideas and practice s, but also transformed them in a process of blending and syncretism. Scholars often refer to this process as "creolization," taking this word from *Crioulo,* the mixture of Portuguese and African languages spoken first in the Atlantic islands. ("Creole" now means any language that has evolved as a mixture of languages, as well as a person of European, African, or mixed Eurafrican descent born in the Americas.) Creolization occurred not simply in the early modern Atlantic, of course, but throughout the world, and continues today as people adapt and modify concepts, rituals, and routines coming from elsewhere to better fit with their own traditions, creating new cultural forms in the process.

The range of approaches informing this book may seem quite dizzying, and it may be tempting here at the outset to try to link all of these various theories, or to claim that they are simply different words to describe the same processes: Isn't social discipline really cultural hegemony by another name? Weren't prostitutes and homosexuals, like Native Americans and Asians, constructed as the Other? Weren't popular beliefs and practices in regard to sexual matters restricted similarly throughout the world? The temptation is especially great because the geographical scope of my study is so large, and the precedent for grand theories regarding sex is so well-established; it includes not only Freud and Foucault (and, as we will see Aristotle and Thomas Aquinas) but also the latest pop psychology books on gender differences.

I want to resist that temptation, or at least hold my discussion of unifying themes until the conclusion. A stress on commonalities does help to avoid what Edward Said has termed "orientalizing" (making other cultures appear overly exotic and bizarre), but it also risks creating an artificial sameness, that renders every other culture more or less like "us." Because most theory about sexuality has been developed in reference to Europe (actually only a small part of Europe, England and France) there is a risk of importing western European theory into areas where it is not appropriate. Thus the chapters that follow each address the same topics – ideas, institutions, effects – but the material they present may be even more dizzying in its variety than the theories discussed in this introduction. I hope this variety reinforces rather than negates the expectations of my friends and neighbors, and that it strengthens their assumptions about the continued importance of connections between Christianity and sex.

Further reading

This book is designed for students and general readers as well as more specialized scholars. Because of its audience, and because the materials for a broad study like this are so numerous, I have included only English-language works in this and subsequent chapter bibliographies. Most of the more specialized works included here will lead interested readers to the appropriate primary and secondary materials in other languages.

A good place to begin for overviews of sexual issues are the books of Vern and Bonnie Bullough, including *Cross-Dressing, Sex, and Gender* (Philadelphia: University of Pennsylvania, 1993) and *Sexual Attitudes: Myths and Realities* (New York: Prometheus, 1995). Robert Nye, *Sexuality* (Oxford: Oxford University Press, 1999) and Anna Clark, *Desire: A History of European Sexuality* (London: Routledge, 2008) both survey ideas about sexuality from the ancient world through the present; Nye includes key original sources. For discussions of modern western sexuality, see Carolyn Dean, *Sexuality and Modern Western Culture* (New York: Twayne, 1996); Arnold I. Davidson, *The Emergence of Sexuality* (Cambridge, Mass.: Harvard University Press, 2001); Harry Cocks and Matt Houlbrook, eds, *Palgrave Advances in the Modern History of Sexuality* (New York: Palgrave Macmillan, 2006). The notion of a divide between modern sexuality and earlier ideas can be seen as well in the increasing use of the term "premodern" in recent collections on sexuality, such as that edited by Eisenbichler and Murray in note 1, or Louise Fradenburg and Carla Freccero, eds, *Premodern Sexualities* (New York: Routledge, 1996).

There are countless books that explore issues of Christianity and sexuality in contemporary society, written to provide guidance and advice for clergy and lay people or to address contentious issues such as homosexuality, abortion, or divorce. One of the more academic of these, which does explore historical developments along with contemporary concerns, is Elizabeth Stuart and Adrian Thatcher, eds, *Christian Perspectives on Sexuality and Gender* (Leominster: Gracewing/Grand Rapids: Eerdmans, 1996). Many of the materials included in the section entitled "Sexuality, Spirituality, and Power," from Eugenia C. DeLamotte, Natania Meeker, and Jean F. O'Barr, eds, *Women Imagine Change: A Global Anthology of Women's Resistance from 600 BCE to the Present* (New York:

Routledge, 1997) are from Christian authors, and the section as a whole provides a good comparison of links between sexuality and spirituality in many religious traditions.

There is an excellent survey of the development of the history of sexuality in the introduction to Domna Stanton, ed., *The Discourses of Sexuality: From Aristotle to AIDS* (Ann Arbor: University of Michigan Press, 1992). A summary of the history of the body may be found in the chapter by Ray Porter in Peter Burke, ed., *New Perspectives on Historical Writing* (London: Polity Press, 1991); this book also contains a survey of women's history by Joan Scott. Several other useful essay collections are: Sherry B. Ortner and Harriet Whitehead, *Sexual Meanings: The Cultural Construction of Gender and Sexuality* (Cambridge: Cambridge University Press, 1981); Pat Caplan, ed., *The Cultural Construction of Sexuality* (London: Tavistock, 1987); Kathy Peiss and Christian Simmons, eds, *Passion and Power: Sexuality in History* (Philadelphia: University of Pennsylvania Press, 1989).

Theoretical discussions of the constructed nature of gender and sexual identity include Teresa de Lauretis, *Technologies of Gender* (Bloomington: Indiana University Press, 1987); Judith Butler, *Gender Trouble: Feminism and the Subversion of Identity* (New York: Routledge, 1990) and *Bodies That Matter: On the Discursive Limits of Sex* (New York: Routledge, 1993); Donna Haraway, *Simians, Cyborgs and Women: The Reinvention of Nature* (New York: Routledge, 1991). A key article in the use of gender in historical analysis is: Joan Scott, "Gender: A Useful Category of Historical Analysis," *American Historical Review* 91 (1986): 1053–75.

Important studies of homosexuality over a long time period include: David Greenburg, *The Construction of Homosexuality* (Chicago: University of Chicago Press, 1988) which takes a strongly social constructionist position and has a bibliography of more than 100 pages; Martin Duberman, Martha Vicinus and George Chauncey Jr., eds, *Hidden From History: Reclaiming the Gay and Lesbian Past* (London: Meridian, 1989); Allen J. Frantzen, *Before the Closet: Same-Sex Love from "Beowulf" to "Angels in America"* (Chicago: University of Chicago Press, 1998); Louis Crompton, *Homosexuality & Civilization* (Cambridge, Mass.: Belknap Press of Harvard University Press, 2003). Edward Stein, ed., *Forms of Desire: Sexual Orientation and the Social Constructionist Controversy* (New York: Garland, 1990) traces the whole social constructionist debate, and Scott Bravman, *Queer Fictions of the Past: History, Culture and Difference* (New York: Cambridge University Press, 1997) looks at the state of gay and lesbian studies, especially history. The bibliographies that follow each chapter contain additional works on same-sex relationships relevant to the chapter's focus.

Foucault's impact on the history of the body is explored in several of the essays in Colin Jones and Roy Porter, eds, *Reassessing Foucault: Power, Medicine and the Body* (London: Routledge, 1994), which also contains a select bibliography of works on Foucault. Karma Lochrie, "Desiring Foucault," *Journal of Medieval and Early Modern Studies* 27 (Winter 1997): 3–16 addresses the use of Foucault's work by medievalists and early modern scholars. An excellent summary of Foucault's thought is Alan Sheridan, *Michel Foucault: The Will to Truth* (London: Routledge, 1990) and a good collection of his writings is David Couzens Hoy, ed., *Foucault: A Critical Reader* (Oxford: Blackwell, 1986). An insightful discussion of the intersections between Foucault and colonial studies is Ann Laura Stoler, *Race and the Education of Desire: Foucault's History of Sexuality and the Colonial Order of Things* (Durham, N.C.: Duke University Press, 1995).

Several of the essays in Lynn Hunt, ed., *The New Cultural History* (Berkeley: University of California Press, 1989) discuss the impact of Foucault's thought on history more generally; this collection is also a very helpful introduction to the field of cultural history as a whole. More recent discussions of the impact of the linguistic/cultural turn include: Elizabeth A. Clark, *History, Theory, Text: Historians and the Linguistic Turn* (Cambridge, Mass: Harvard University Press, 2004); Gabrielle M. Spiegel, ed., *Practicing History: New Directions in Historical Writing after the Linguistic Turn* (New York: Routledge, 2005).

Discussions of the relationship between Foucault and feminism have included many collections of articles, such as Caroline Ramazanoglu, ed., *Up Against Foucault: Explorations of Some Tensions Between Foucault and Feminism* (New York: Routledge, 1993), Susan Hekman, ed., *Feminist Interpretations of Michel Foucault* (University Park, Penn.: Penn State University Press, 1996), and Dianna Taylor and Karen Vintges, eds, *Feminism and the Final Foucault* (Urbana: University of Illinois Press, 2004). More detailed analyses of specific issues include Lois McNay, *Foucault and Feminism: Power, Gender and the Self* (Boston: Northeastern University Press, 1993) and Margaret A. McLaren, *Feminism, Foucault, and Embodied Subjectivity* (Albany: State University of New York Press, 2002). Lyndal Roper's book on the witch hunts is: *Witch Craze: Fantasy and Terror in Baroque Germany* (New Haven: Yale University Press, 2006).

Basic works in queer theory include: Eve Kosofsky Sedgwick, *Epistemology of the Closet* (Berkeley: University of California Press, 1990); Julia Epstein and Kristina Straub, eds, *Body Guards: The Cultural Politics of Gender Ambiguity* (New York: Routledge, 1991); a special issue on "Queer Theory: Gay and Lesbian Sexualities," *differences* 3(2) (Summer 1991); Michael Warner, ed., *Fear of a Queer Planet: Queer Politics and Social Theory* (Minneapolis: University of Minnesota Press, 1993); Peggy Phelan, *Unmarked: The Politics of Performance* (New York: Routledge, 1993). For a recent overview designed for students, see Annamarie Jagose, *Queer Theory: An Introduction* (Washington Square, N.Y.: New York

University Press, 1996), and for essays linking feminist and queer theory, see Elizabeth Weed and Naomi Schor, eds, *Feminism Meets Queer Theory* (Bloomington: Indiana University Press, 1997). For very recent considerations of the state of queer theory, see: David L. Eng, Judith Halberstam, and Jose Esteban Munoz, eds, special issue, "What's Queer about Queer Studies Now?" *Social Text* 84/85 (Fall/Winter 2005); Janet Halley and Andrew Parker, eds., "After Sex? On Writing since Queer Theory," *The South Atlantic Quarterly* 106.3 (Summer 2007): 421–642. For applications of queer theory to the early modern period, see Jonathan Goldberg, ed., *Queering the Renaissance* (Durham, N.C.: Duke University Press, 1993), Carla Freccero, *Queer/Early/Modern* (Durham, N.C.: Duke University Press, 2005) and Katherine O'Donnell and Michael O'Rourke, eds, *Queer Masculinities, 1550–1800* (New York: Palgrave Macmillan, 2006).

Robert J.C. Young, *Postcolonialism: An Historical Introduction* (Oxford: Blackwell Publishers, 2001) and Ania Loomba, *Colonialism/postcolonialism*, 2nd edn, (London: Routledge, 2005) both provide good introductory surveys of the main ideas in post-colonial theory. The writings of Edward Said, *Orientalism* (New York: Pantheon, 1978) and *Culture and Imperialism* (New York: Knopf, 1993) are central in the field. Two works that bring together feminist and post-colonial analysis are Trin T. Minh-ha, *Woman, Native, Other: Writing Postcoloniality and Feminism* (Bloomington: Indiana University Press, 1989) and Chandra Talpade Mohanty, Ann Russo, and Lourdes Torres, eds, *Third World Women and the Politics of Feminism* (Bloomington: Indiana University Press, 1991).

The work of the Subaltern Studies group may best be seen in its ongoing series of essay collections, *Subaltern Studies*, which began publication in 1982 in Delhi. Two additional important theoretical works by Indian scholars associated with Subaltern Studies are Partha Chatterjee, *Nationalist Thought and the Colonial World: A Derivative Discourse* (London: Zed, 1986) and Gayatri Chakravorty Spivak, *In Other Worlds: Essays in Cultural Politics* (London and New York: Metheun, 1987). Debates about issues raised by Subaltern Studies may be found in a series of articles by Gyan Prakash, Florencia Mallon, and Frederick Cooper in *The American Historical Review* 99 (1994): 1475–545 and in Mabel Moraña, Enrique Dussel, and Carlos Jaurequi, eds, *Latin America and the Postcolonial Debate* (Durham, N.C.: Duke University Press, 2008).

A good introduction to Antonio Gramsci's notion of hegemony is Joseph V. Femia, *Gramsci's Political Thought: Hegemony, Consciousness and the Revolutionary Process* (Oxford: Clarendon, 1981) or Gramsci's own work, *Selections from the Prison Notebooks of Antonio Gramsci* (New York: International Publishers, 1971). Steve Stern, *Peru's Indian Peoples and the Challenge of Spanish Conquest: Huamanga to 1640* (Madison: University of Wisconsin Press, 1982) discusses hegemony in a colonial Latin American context. For ideas about hegemonic masculinity, see R.W. Connell, *Masculinities* (London: Allen and Unwin, 1995).

Most studies of the links between sexuality and empire focus on the British experience in the modern period, including: Ronald Hyam, *Empire and Sexuality: The British Experience* (Manchester: Manchester University Press, 1990); Anne McClintock, *Imperial Leather: Race, Gender and Sexuality in the Colonial Contest* (London: Routledge, 1995); Felicity Nussbaum, *Torrid Zones: Maternity, Sexuality and Empire in Eighteenth-Century English Narratives* (Baltimore: Johns Hopkins University Press, 1995); Mrinalini Sinha, *Colonial Masculinity: The "Manly Englishman" and the "Effeminate Bengali" in the Late Nineteenth Century* (Manchester: Manchester University Press, 1995); Revathi Krishnaswamy, *Effeminism: The Economy of Colonial Desire* (Ann Arbor: University of Michigan Press, 1998). Gyan Prakash, ed., *After Colonialism: Imperial Histories and Postcolonial Displacements* (Princeton: Princeton University Press, 1995), Lenore Masterson and Margaret Jolly, eds, *Sites of Desire, Economies of Pleasure: Sexualities in Asia and the Pacific* (Chicago: University of Chicago Press, 1997), Ruth Roach Pierson and Nupur Chaudhuri, eds, *Nation, Empire, Colony: Historicizing Gender and Race* (Indianapolis: Indiana University Press, 1998), and Ann Laura Stoler, *Carnal Knowledge and Imperial Power: Race and the Intimate in Colonial Rule* (Berkeley: University of California Press, 2002) discuss other colonial powers. See below and the bibliographical essays that follow Chapters 4 and 6 for readings about the colonial Americas.

Two solid introductions to changing ideas about race are Ivan Hannaford, *Race: The History of an Idea in the West* (Baltimore: Johns Hopkins University Press, 1996) and Brian Niro, *Race* (New York: Palgrave Macmillan, 2003). Robert Bartlett considers medieval European idea of race in *The Making of Europe: Conquest, Colonialism, and Cultural Change* (Princeton: Princeton University Press, 1993). For analyses of early modern ideas of race, see Roxann Wheeler, *The Complexion of Race: Categories of Difference in Eighteenth-century British Culture* (Philadelphia: University of Pennsylvania Press, 2000), Sujata Iyengar, *Shades of Difference: Mythologies of Skin Color in Early Modern England* (Philadelphia: University of Pennsylvania Press, 2004), and Ania Loomba, "Periodization, Race, and Global Contact," *Journal of Medieval and Early Modern Studies* 37(3) (Fall 2007): 595–620. Ania Loomba and Jonathan Burtin, eds, *Race in Early Modern England: A Documentary Companion* (New York: Palgrave Macmillan) provides a wide selection of original sources on the topic. Colin Kidd, *The Forging of Races: Race and Scripture in the Protestant Atlantic World, 1600–2000* (Cambridge: Cambridge University Press, 2006) and David Whitford *From Serf to Slave: The Curse of Ham in the Early Modern Era* (Aldershot: Ashgate, 2010) focus on how religious texts contributed to ideas of race. Considerations of the role of early modern Spain in creating modern racial ideas include: Jerome Friedman, "Jewish Conversion, the Spanish Pure Blood Laws, and Religious Anti-Semitism," *Sixteenth Century Journal* 18 (1987): 3–29, James Sweet, "The Iberian Roots of American Racist Thought," *William*

and Mary Quarterly, third series, 54 (1997): 143–66, and George Mariscal, "The Role of Spain in Contemporary Race Theory," *Arizona Journal of Hispanic Cultural Studies* 2 (1998): 7–23.

Two articles are especially helpful for understanding links between gender and race, and have been widely reprinted in various collections: Tessie Liu, "Teaching the Differences Among Women from a Historical Perspective: Rethinking Race and Gender as Social Categories," *Women's Studies International Forum* 14 (1991): 265–76 and Evelyn Brooks Higginbotham, "African-American Women's History and the Metalanguage of Race," *Signs* 17 (1992): 251–74.

The concept of "social discipline" was first discussed by the German historian Gerhard Oestreich, and his major work has now been translated into English: *Neostoicism and the Early Modern State* (Cambridge: Cambridge University Press, 1982). For Heinz Schilling's work translated into English, see *Religion, Political Culture and the Emergence of Early Modern Society* (Leiden: Brill, 1992). Most of the studies of specific areas are in German, for which there is a good bibliography in R. Po-Chia Hsia, *Social Discipline in the Reformation: Central Europe 1550–1750* (London: Routledge, 1989); this book also provides a good overview of the whole issue.

The notion of a reform of popular culture was set out most influentially by Peter Burke, *Popular Culture in Early Modern Europe* (London: Temple Smith,1978) and Robert Muchembled, *Popular Culture and Elite Culture in France, 1400–1750* (Baton Rouge: Louisiana State University Press, 1985). Norbert Elias's major work, *The Civilizing Process,* was first published in German in 1939, but the first English translation of the first volume on manners was not published until 1978 (New York: Urizen Books). A good introduction to his thought is Norbert Elias, *On Civilization, Power, and Knowledge*, ed. Stephen Mennell and Johan Goudsblom (Chicago: University of Chicago Press, 1998). The classic study of taboos cross-culturally is Mary Douglas, *Purity and Danger: An Analysis of the Concepts of Pollution and Taboo* (New York: Praeger, 1966).

The many works of James Axtell have been especially influential in developing the notion of "encounters" as central to colonial history in North America. See, for example, his *Beyond 1492: Encounters in Colonial North America* (New York: Oxford University Press, 1992) and *Natives and Newcomers: The Cultural Origins of North America* (New York: Oxford University Press, 2000). Colin G. Calloway also has a number of significant books, most recently *White People, Indians, and Highlanders: Tribal People and Colonial Encounters in Scotland and America* (New York: Oxford University Press, 2008). Both Axtell and Calloway, along with other scholars, use the word "Indians" rather than "Amerindians," "Native Americans," or "First Peoples" when discussing the indigenous residents of the Americas. This usage is also favored by many native scholars in their writing and teaching, and I have generally adopted it here.

Edmundo O'Gorman's pioneering study of European colonial discourse was published in Spanish as *La invención de América; El universalismo de la Cultura del Occidente* (Mexico City: Fondo de Cultura Económica, 1958); an expanded and modified version appeared in English as *The Invention of America: An Inquiry into the Historical Nature of the New World and the Meaning of its History* (Bloomington: Indiana University Press, 1961). In the last several decades, it has been joined by numerous others: Tzvetan Todorov, *The Conquest of America: The Question of the Other,* trans. Richard Howard (New York: Harper and Row, 1984); Peter Hulme, *Colonial Encounters: Europe and the Native Caribbean, 1492–1797* (London: Methuen, 1986); Urs Bitterli, *Cultures in Conflict: Encounters Between European and Non-European Cultures, 1492–1800,* trans. Ritchie Robertson (New York: Polity Press, 1989); Peter Mason, *Deconstructing America: Representations of the Other* (London: Routledge, 1990); Stephen Greenblatt, *Marvelous Possessions: The Wonder of the New World* (Chicago: University of Chicago Press, 1991); Anthony Pagden, *European Encounters with the New World: From Renaissance to Romanticism* (New Haven: Yale, 1993); O.R. Dathorne, *Imagining the World: Mythical Belief versus Reality in Global Encounters* (Westport, Conn.: Bergin and Garvey, 1994) and *Asian Voyages: Two Thousand Years of Constructing the Other* (Westport, Conn.: Bergin and Garvey, 1996); John F. Moffitt and Santiago Sebastián, *O Brave New People: The European Invention of the American Indian* (Albuquerque: University of New Mexico Press, 1996). Encounters with and representations of Africans have been the focus of fewer studies; the best introduction to this issue from a European perspective is Kim F. Hall, *Things of Darkness: Economies of Race and Gender in Early Modern England* (Ithaca: Cornell University Press, 1995) and from an American perspective Winthrop D. Jordan's classic *White Over Black: American Attitudes Toward the Negro, 1550–1812* (Chapel Hill: University of North Carolina Press, 1968).

There are numerous essay collections dealing with colonial encounters, some of which do not include discussion of issues of gender and/or sexuality; among those that do are: Francisco Javier Cevallos-Candau, *et al.,* eds., *Coded Encounters: Writing, Gender, and Ethnicity in Colonial Latin America* (Amherst: University of Massachusetts Press, 1994); Stuart Schwarz, ed., *Implicit Understandings: Observing, Reporting and Reflecting on the Encounters between Europeans and Other Peoples in the Early Modern Era* (Cambridge: Cambridge University Press, 1994); Kenneth J. Adrien and Rolena Adorno, eds, *Transatlantic Encounters: Europeans and Andeans in the Sixteenth Century* (Berkeley: University of California Press, 1991); Tony Ballantyne and Antoinette Burton, eds, *Bodies in Contact: Rethinking Colonial Encounters in World History* (Durham, N.C.: Duke University Press, 2005); Ann Laura Stoler, ed., *Haunted by Empire: Geographies of Intimacy in North American History* (Durham, N.C.: Duke University Press, 2006).

Chapter 1

CHRISTIANITY TO 1500

M ANY FACTORS SHAPED ANCIENT and medieval Christian ideas about sex, the institutions that resulted from these ideas and in turn influenced them, and the actual sexual practices of Near Eastern, African, and European Christians. Of these factors, the words of Jesus of Nazareth as recorded in Christian Scriptures were probably the least important, for Jesus seems to have said very little about sex, and his recorded words are contradictory. Jesus describes marriage as ordained by God (Matthew 19:4–5), yet later in the same discussion appears to approve of those "who have made themselves eunuchs for the sake of the kingdom of heaven" (Matthew 19:12). He also characterizes those who remained unmarried as "equal to angels . . . and sons of the resurrection" (Luke 20:36). Jesus clearly opposes adultery and divorce, and seems to have condemned sex with "harlots" (the Biblical term for women who had sex with many men or sold sex for money), though he made friends with individual harlots and shocked priests who challenged him by commenting that repentant "tax collectors and harlots" would get into heaven before they would (Matthew 21:31–32). While Jesus was himself a man, the centrality of the male disciples may have been less evident during his lifetime than it later became; women were present at many of the key events of his life and were the first to discover the empty tomb after the crucifixion (Mark 16:1–8).

For New Testament roots of Christian ideas about sex, the letters of Paul and those attributed to Paul are far more important than the Gospels containing the words of Jesus. A convert from Judaism, Paul never met Jesus, but became an important early Christian missionary. His letters to many Christian groups around the Mediterranean became part of Christian Scripture, and his reputation was so great that works probably written by others were also attributed to him. The Epistles of 1 and 2 Timothy and of Titus are now considered by almost all Biblical scholars not to be Paul's words, though they were considered Pauline for most of Christian history. The majority of modern scholars view Ephesians, Colossians and 2 Thessalonians also as deutero-Pauline, this is, as written by someone other than Paul. Many of the most restrictive comments about women in the New Testament occur in these books, and have carried the weight of Paul's authority.

Like all early Christians, Paul expected Jesus to return to earth very soon, and so regarded sex as one of the earthly concerns that should not be important for Christians. To him, the virgin life was best, but if people could not "exercise self-control, they should marry. For it is better to marry than to be aflame with passion" (1 Corinthians 7:9). Paul warned against those who prohibited marriage and emphasized the importance of spousal love and respect. Like Jesus, Paul opposed divorce, and he even suggested that widows and widowers would be happier if they did not remarry. He condemned all extramarital sex, singling out adulterers and masturbators, along with thieves and drunkards, as people who were unworthy of heaven (1 Corinthians 6:9). This list also includes words that most historians and many Bible translators interpret as referring to homosexuals, although the original Greek is somewhat ambiguous and has occasioned scholarly controversy. Elsewhere Paul condemns male/male sexual activity (Romans 1:27) though his parallel condemnation of some female sexual activity (Romans 1:26) does not explicitly mention female/female sex.

Along with discussing acceptable and unacceptable sexual activities, the letters of Paul introduce a gendered and sexualized metaphor for the Christian community: the bride of Christ. Human marriage is equated with the union between Christ and the church; husbands are admonished to love their wives as Christ loved the church, and wives to be subject to their husbands as the church is subject to Christ (Ephesians 5:21–33). Later authors elaborated on this analogy (as well as on the call for wifely subjection), and extended it to individual Christians, not simply the church as a whole. Christian women, said King Alfonso the Wise of Castile, are all "spiritually espoused to Our lord Jesus Christ by virtue of the faith and baptism they received in His name." Men, too, were occasionally described explicitly as "brides of Christ," and also as children of Jesus understood in sexual terms. As the Spanish theologian Vincent of Ferrar put it: "Jesus every day impregnates the Church, and the womb is the baptismal font, and he sends there his semen from heaven."[1]

Sexuality in Judaism

Because most Christians came to accept Hebrew Scripture as part of their tradition – designating certain books of the Hebrew Bible the "Old Testament" to parallel specific Christian writings termed the "New Testament" – Jewish writings on sex also influenced the development of Christian thinking. Jewish ideas about human sexuality were rooted in Jewish concepts of the divine. In contrast to other ancient cultures, Judaism held to a strict monotheism, with a God (Yahweh), conceptualized as masculine but who did not have sexual relations like Greek or Egyptian male deities did. Yahweh's masculinity was affirmed by the words used to describe him – Lord, King, Father – and not by any progeny or penis. In Hebrew Scripture Yahweh's sexuality was spiritualized, not described physically. Thus human sexual relations, though basically good because they were part of Yahweh's creation, could also be a source of ritual impurity. Nocturnal emissions in men made them and anything they touched unclean, as did menstruation and childbirth in women; sexual relations made both partners impure (Leviticus 12 and 15). Other sexual practices created more than ritual impurity (which was removed by baths or temple sacrifices) and were termed "abominations"; violators were liable to the death penalty. Leviticus 20 specifies as abominations adultery with a married woman, incest with a variety of relatives, bestiality on the part of men or women, and male same-sex relations. (Female same-sex relations are not mentioned anywhere in the Old Testament, and sexual relations between a married man and an unmarried woman were not considered adultery.)

Despite the ritual impurity it created, sex itself was not regarded as intrinsically evil, and husbands were religiously obligated to have sex with their wives. Women were expected to have sex with their husbands – though not religiously obligated – and the bearing of children was seen in some ways as a religious function, for this would keep Judaism alive. Sexual relations were viewed as an important part of marriage even when procreation was impossible, such as after menopause. As the definition of adultery in Leviticus makes clear, men were free to have sexual relations with concubines, servants, and slaves; polygamous marriage was acceptable and occurred often among Jewish leaders in the Old Testament. Theoretically unmarried women were also quite free sexually, for Hebrew Scripture nowhere forbade sex between unmarried individuals, though the harsh treatment of children born out of wedlock undoubtedly acted as a deterrent to such relationships. Selling sex for money was officially prohibited to Jewish women, but the many references to women who did in the Old Testament and other sources indicate that it was tolerated. The usual English translation for such a woman is "harlot," a word that is used frequently to describe the Jewish people's turning away from their single god to worship numerous other deities, a usage that equates polytheism with a woman's having many lovers (e.g., Leviticus 20:5–6; Jeremiah 3). Because many of these deities were the fertility gods and goddesses common to the Israelites' neighbors, their worship sometimes did involve a stress on divine sexuality that was not part of the worship of Yahweh;

the prophet Jeremiah condemns this practice as "committing adultery with stone and tree" (Jeremiah 3:9).

Judaism influenced Christian sexuality not only through the writings of the Old Testament, but also through its actual sexual practices. By the time of Jesus and Paul, most Jewish couples were monogamous, though polygamy was sometimes promoted as an expression of Jewish identity in contrast to the monogamous Romans. Marriage was arranged by the families of the spouses, and involved the transfer of goods or money from the husband's family to the wife's or from the husband to the wife; this would assure her support in the event of his death or divorce. Unilateral divorce on the husband's part was permissible, though community norms frowned on divorce for frivolous reasons. A wife could not divorce her husband, even for desertion, though the desperate situation this created for some women led rabbinical authorities to relax the rules in actuality. Traditionally, Judaism frowned on celibacy – "chastity" is defined in Jewish law as refraining from illicit sexual activities, not from sex itself – and almost all major Jewish thinkers and rabbis were married. In the centuries immediately before the development of Christianity, there was some change in these views, however, and a few Jewish groups such as the Essenes began to advocate abstinence from sexual relations for their members.

Greek and Roman traditions

The Essenes' rejection of sexuality, new to Judaism, came in part from Greek and Roman schools of thought which also influenced Christian ideas directly. Plato and Aristotle, the two most important philosophers of ancient Athens, were both suspicious of the power of sexual passion, warning that it distracted men from reason and the search for knowledge. Both men praised a love that was intellectualized and nonsexual, the type of attachment we still term "platonic." (Neither Plato nor Aristotle was concerned about what sex does to women except as this affects men.) Plato developed a dualistic view of both humans and the world, arguing that the unseen realm of ideas was far superior to the visible material world, and that the human mind or soul was trapped in a material body. This mind/body split did not originate with Plato, but his acceptance and elaboration of it helped to make this concept an important part of Western philosophy from that time on, and led some groups (though not Plato) to reject sexual activity completely. In Aristotle the mind/body split is reflected in the process of procreation (what he termed "generation"), with the male providing the "active principle" and the female simply the "material." (The Greek physician and medical writer Galen disagreed with this formulation, however, and regarded both parents as providing "active principles.") The categories male and female were not completely dichotomous according to Aristotle or Plato, however, but part of a hierarchical continuum, what historians have since termed the "one-sex model." Males resulted when conditions during sexual intercourse were optimal, and females when they were somehow faulty, with heat viewed as the most important force in the creation of sexual difference. Because both women and men were located along the same continuum, certain women could be more "manly" than some men, and exhibit the qualities that were expected of men such as authority or self-control. Accidents might also cause a woman to turn into a man, with her sexual organs emerging later in life the way a boy's did in the womb. (Female sex organs were generally viewed as equivalent to the male's, but simply turned inside out, an idea that lasted well into the seventeenth century.)

Stoic philosophy, which was very influential in Rome, agreed with Plato that sexual passion was disruptive. Stoics viewed sexual relationships as an important area of government concern; government should oversee the family, which they considered the basis of the social order, as well as other types of sexual activities, in order to promote public order and civic harmony. Stoic opinion on sexual matters was widely shared, and Roman lawmakers frequently enacted statutes dealing with sexual offenses. The most serious transgressions were those which might upset the social order: adultery (again limited only to married women); sexual relationships involving young upper-class unmarried women (particularly if the man was from a lower social group); marriages that crossed social boundaries; and rape or abduction of girls or boys.

Most Romans considered marriage a positive good, viewing procreation and the education of children as part of their duty to the state; in fact, Roman law required a man to have children by a legal wife if he wanted to inherit property. Fathers had great power over their children; they could decide whether to accept them into the family at birth and choose who they would marry or if they could divorce. The Stoic notion that spouses should feel "marital affection" (*affectio maritalis*) toward one another gained popularity in the first and second centuries CE; if this affection ceased, formal divorce or less formal separation could end the marriage. Despite the general support for marriage, some marriages were prohibited – such as those between a free man and a prostitute, an actress, a slave or freed slave, or a woman over fifty years of age – though Roman law recognized concubinage as a formal relationship in those cases or in other cases where the individuals did not wish to marry. Roman concubinage was an alternative to marriage, not an addition to it as it was in many other parts of the world; Romans were monogamous, and a man could have either a wife or a concubine, but not both. Being a concubine was generally regarded as honorable and concubines had some legal rights, though not as many as wives. Slaves were not allowed to marry under

Roman law, and relationships which they had with one another created no legally recognized ties.

Roman law increasingly drew a distinction between concubines and women who were sexually available to a large number of people, whether or not they charged for their services. Selling sex for money was not forbidden, however, and the pagan religious calendar had special feast days dedicated to female and male prostitutes. Roman literature also celebrated sexual relationships of all types in a way Roman law did not. The only two sexual activities uniformly condemned in literature were men taking the passive role in same-sex acts – viewed as unmanly and unworthy of a Roman citizen, and suitable only for slaves and prostitutes – and women taking the active role, which was seen as usurping a masculine privilege. Thus gender norms shaped ideas about sexual actions. For Romans, the key distinction in sex was not object choice – as it is in modern understandings of sexual orientation – but whether one took the part of a properly dominant man or a properly subservient woman.

The Romans based their ideas about sex, as about many other things, on the ideas of the ancient Athenians, whose same-sex relationships have been the focus of many historical studies. In Athens, part of an adolescent citizen's training in adulthood entailed a hierarchical sexual and tutorial relationship with an older man, who most likely was married and may have had other female sexual partners as well. For Athenians, as later for Romans, the key distinction was between active and passive, between penetrator and penetrated, with the latter appropriate only for slaves, women, and boys. (There is some dispute about whether penetration was involved in male/male sex involving free men, or whether sex was generally intercrural – that is, between the thighs.) These pederastic relations between adolescents and men were often celebrated in literature and art, in part because the Athenians regarded perfection as possible only in the male. The perfect body was that of the young male, which is why even Aphrodite, the goddess of beauty, is always shown with clothing on in classical Athenian sculpture. The perfect love was that between an adolescent and an older man, although this was supposed to become intellectualized and "platonic" once the adolescent became an adult.

Along with philosophy and law, religion was also connected to sexual issues in ancient Greece and Rome. The classical Mediterranean was home to a wide range of religious beliefs and practices. These spread from one area to another with the conquests first of Alexander the Great and then Rome; individuals frequently honored a number of gods and goddesses through rituals and ceremonies, both public and private. Traditional Roman religion was a civic or state religion akin to patriotism, in which honoring the gods was viewed as essential to the health and well-being of the state. Aside from their immortality, Roman gods were just like humans, so that they, too, experienced sexual passion. Male gods acted in ways that would have been unacceptable had they been mortal; stories of seductions and rapes by Zeus (called Jupiter in the Roman pantheon) and other gods and heroes form a central part of classical mythology. Though several of the most important goddesses, such as Athena (Minerva), Hestia (Vesta), and Artemis (Diana), were virgins, no male gods abstained from sexual relationships. Male priests in some Mediterranean religions did abstain, however, and occasionally even castrated themselves for cultic purposes; such religions in general were strongly dualistic, with self-castration regarded as proof of a priest's rejection of the body and devotion to the spirit. These religions, usually termed "mystery religions" because they offered their adherents secret powers or personal immortality, were gaining followers in the Roman Empire at the time of Jesus, even though Roman authorities were often very suspicious of them.

Early Christianity

In the first several centuries after Jesus, Christianity was spread by individuals and groups acting as missionaries throughout the Mediterranean area. Early converts developed their own ideas about sex, mixing together the teachings of Jesus and Paul, Jewish writings, Greek and Roman philosophy, non-Christian mystery religions, and other religious traditions in highly individualistic ways. There was no central authority in these first centuries, and even bishops were only loosely in control of beliefs and activities in their dioceses; consequently there was an enormous range of ideas and practices.

The ideas that were most influential in the subsequent development of Christianity were those of literate men who corresponded with and advised converts and who often became officials in the growing church. These men, subsequently termed the Church Fathers, held differing views, although the degree of variation was smaller than among the Christian community as a whole. Many of these men agreed with Clement of Alexandria (ca. 150–ca. 200), who accepted marriage – including its sexual activity – as appropriate for Christians and taught, following the Stoics, that husbands and wives should feel affection for one another: "So there is every reason to marry – for patriotic reasons, for the succession of children, for the fulfillment of the universe . . . For the rest of humankind, marriage finds concord in the experience of pleasure, but the marriage of true lovers of wisdom [i.e., Christians] leads to a concord derived from the Logos [i.e. the Word of God, or Christ]."[2] Many church leaders gradually came to consider concubinage and the slave relationships in Rome as marriages in terms of sexual morality, and to advocate for the rights of all classes of people to marry.

Other early Church Fathers were more ambivalent. Tertullian (ca. 150–ca. 240) married and was careful to say that marriages were not prohibited to Christians. Even so, he regarded virginity as preferable; because marriage involved the "commixture of the flesh," it "consists of that which is the essence of fornication." He was particularly opposed to second marriages, which he termed "no other than a species of fornication," and wrote against them in an open letter to his wife and in several other works. Tertullian also railed against women who wore fancy clothing and unmarried women who did not wear veils. For them, he recommended "meanness of appearance, walking around as Eve mourning and repentant, in order that by every garb of penitence she might more fully expiate that which she derives from Eve, – the ignominy, I mean, of the first sin, and the odium (attached to her as the cause) of human perdition."[3]

Sex was not simply a matter for learned treatises during the early centuries of Christianity, although actual practices are harder to trace than theoretical opinions. Sporadic persecution of Christians by Roman authorities led to spectacular martyrdoms, but also led people to conduct many of their ceremonies in private, so that few historical sources remain. Most converts to Christianity or those born into Christian families married, in ceremonies that differed little from those of other Romans. Divorce in the case of adultery was permitted, though remarriage while both original spouses were alive was prohibited, and the remarriage of widows and widowers was frowned upon. Older women whose husbands had died could become part of the "order of widows," assisting in women's baptisms and praying for the group. It appears that most clergy also married, for the first attempt to prohibit clerical marriage was not made until the early fourth century.

Some converts took another path, however. They took Paul's metaphor that Christians were "brides of Christ" literally, and rejected the married life that their families expected of them. Instead they lived singly or in communities, devoting themselves to contemplation or to the charity that was an important aspect of Christianity from the beginning. Their decision to renounce sexuality, though in one sense a rejection of the body, also paradoxically allowed them to claim their own bodies, to decide for themselves what their bodies would do and resist the procreative ethic of Roman society. Stories circulated about men such as St. Anthony (251?–ca. 350), who went out into the Egyptian desert as a hermit and became famous for withstanding sexual temptations, or women such as Mary of Egypt and Thaïs who had been harlots but gave up their sinful life for one of Christian devotion and bodily neglect. Women's choice of virginity was seen as especially threatening to the social and gender order, because it put them in opposition to their fathers (and occasionally husbands) whom they were expected to obey. Some patriotic commentators argued that women's decisions to remain virgins might eventually affect the birth rate, and lead to a decline in the number of Romans at the very moment that the Empire was being attacked and infiltrated by members of "less worthy" groups, such as Germanic tribes. Men choosing a life of virginity could also have been viewed as threatening, for Jesus' statement about becoming "eunuchs for the kingdom of heaven" suggests gender and sexual ambiguity. Christian writers and thinkers instead created a new ideal of masculinity, not based – as earlier Roman ideals had been – on service in the Roman army and being a head of household, but instead on being a "soldier of Christ," a role open to both married and unmarried men.

Many accounts of women's martyrdoms stress sexual aspects of their lives in ways that descriptions of male martyrs do not. In women, preservation of their virginity and chastity at all costs is praised as the ultimate sacrifice. Some saints' lives (accounts of saints' lives are called *hagiography*) from this period describe women who cut their hair and lived dressed as men for much of their lives; only at death was their true sex revealed, with their successful cross-dressing viewed as miraculous rather than scandalous. According to her fifth-century biographer, Saint Pelagia of Antioch was both a repentant harlot and a cross-dresser. Originally "bare of head and shoulder and limb, in pomp so splendid . . . so decked that naught could be seen upon her but gold and pearls and precious stones" she later "lived for these many years shut up and in solitude [as] brother Pelagius, a monk and a eunuch . . . wasted and haggard with fasting." Pelagius died, "and when the good fathers set about anointing the body with myrrh, they found that it was a woman . . . and they cried aloud with a shout, 'Glory to Thee, Lord Christ, who has many treasures on the earth, and not men only, but women also.'"[4] Hagiography cannot be taken as an objective life story, of course, as its purpose is to prove the spiritual merit of an individual, but for that very reason we can tell that Pelagia's biographer approved of her actions. He (almost all saints' lives were written down by men) did not praise her – as we might – as a woman who had escaped the normal restrictions on women or as a gender-bending transvestite, however, but as an example of God working through so lowly a creature.

Stories of heroic virginity were popular among converts (and remained so for centuries), but many church leaders were uncomfortable with such a clear rejection of Roman family models, particularly as they were attempting to make Christianity more socially acceptable. They asserted that women who chose a life of virginity were not to use this as a reason for escaping the normal restrictions on women. They were, after all, "brides of Christ," dependents in a figurative marital relationship; the title that some women chose for themselves, "virgins in the service of Christ," was not acceptable.

The church after Constantine

During the fourth century, the Emperor Constantine first legalized Christianity and then became a Christian himself, and Christianity gradually became a privileged institution in the Roman system. Christian bishops were given greater power within their dioceses, and Christian ideas came to shape imperial law and judicial practice. Gradually, for example, the informal arrangements of slaves came to be considered marriage, and a blessing by a priest came to be a normal part of Christian wedding ceremonies. Christian emperors extended the rules against the marriage of close relatives, so that people were forced to cast wider nets for an acceptable marriage partner.

At the same time, the most prominent Church Fathers became stronger proponents of asceticism than those of earlier centuries had been. This fourth-century movement in part grew out of the earlier movement rejecting marriage, as some of its most vocal proponents, such as St. Jerome (ca. 347–419/20), the translator of the Bible into Latin, came to embrace ideals of sexual renunciation developed by their wealthy female supporters. Jerome's repeated comments that virginity is gold and marriage silver, or that marriage fills the earth while virginity fills paradise, would have not been unwelcome or novel to the Roman women to whom he directed them. By choosing virginity, in the opinion of Jerome and his patrons, a woman could move up the gender hierarchy: "As long as woman is for birth and children, she is as different from man as body is from soul. But when she wishes to serve Christ more than the world, then she will cease to be a woman and will be called man."[5] This gender transformation was to remain a spiritual one, however, for in contrast to the admirers of cross-dressing saints, Jerome did not approve of women who "change their garb to male attire, cut their hair short and blush to be seen as they were born – women."[6]

Non-Christian ideas about sexuality also shaped the fourth-century ascetic movement; this can be seen most clearly in St. Augustine of Hippo (354–430), whose importance in the development of western Christian thought is second only to Paul's. Augustine, the bishop of the north African city of Hippo during the time when the Roman Empire in the west was slowly disintegrating, came to Christianity somewhat late in life after a career as a teacher of rhetoric. Augustine had always been troubled spiritually, and before he became a Christian he had joined the Manicheans, a dualistic religion begun by the Persian prophet Mani (216–77 CE) that combined Christianity, Platonism, Gnosticism, and several other schools of thought. The Manicheans taught that procreation imprisoned the soul, and that sexual desire was also innately evil; the most advanced believers – called the Adepts – were those who could renounce both sexual activity and sexual thoughts. Augustine was never able to reach this stage, however, but lived with a concubine for many years until he became a Christian.

Though he later attacked Manicheanism viciously, Augustine retained much of its suspicion of both sexual activity and desire when he became a Christian. Sexual desire was the "sharpest joy" (*summa voluptas*) in human experience, but it was also the one human craving, in Augustine's view, that overcame both reason and will. The truth of this was made evident to him, as he comments, by the fact that he could not control his erections nor give up his concubine, though he desperately wanted to do so. He uses powerful images to talk about sexual acts and desires, describing the way he battled them with metaphors of war. (In his emphasis on the power of sexual desire, Augustine in some ways prefigured Freud's stress on sexuality as a key element of the self; in continually talking about sex, he is also a very early example of Foucault's "transformation of sex into discourse.") Augustine spoke often about the resurrection of the body, a central doctrine of Christianity; those post-resurrection bodies would be gendered male and female and they would "enjoy one another's beauty" as well as experience the extreme pleasure of seeing God "face to face . . . by means of bodies."[7] They would not feel desire, however, for desire was the result of human sinfulness and disobedience to God, and had no place in paradise.

For Augustine, only God's grace could allow one to overcome sexual desire or any other human weakness. His attitude toward sexuality was thus connected to his very negative view of human nature. In his view, no one after Adam and Eve had free will; original sin was transmitted to all humans through semen emitted in sexual acts motivated by desire, and was thus inescapable. Augustine also saw female subordination as intrinsic in God's original creation, for only men were fully created in the image of God. He considered women intellectually, morally, and even physically inferior: "The body of a man is as superior to that of a woman as the soul is to the body."[8] Their lesser status was to be demonstrated in the only permissible position for intercourse, the woman on the bottom facing up and the man on the top. (This later came to be called the "missionary position.")

Despite his deep suspicion of desire, Augustine viewed marriage more positively than Jerome, and set out what became known as the "three goods" of marriage. These were adopted by most Christian writers after him, including both Catholics and Protestants after the Reformation. To Augustine, marriage was good because it produced children, promoted fidelity between spouses, and provided for a permanent union between two individuals and their families. Divorce was therefore unthinkable, for marriage symbolized Christ's union with the church. Sex within marriage was acceptable as long as the couple desired children and the spouses respected one another. This respect should outweigh lust, for as Jerome warned: "Nothing is filthier than to have sex with your wife as you might do with another woman . . . Every too ardent lover of his own wife is an adulterer."[9] Any coital position or sexual activity that would lessen the chances or not allow for procreation was sinful, another reason for favoring the missionary position, as this was regarded as the most likely to lead to pregnancy. The Church Fathers disagreed about whether a partner seeking sex within marriage for procreation nevertheless sinned, but most agreed that the partner agreeing to sex did not; that partner was simply fulfilling the "conjugal debt," an obligation to have sex when one's spouse wanted it. The "conjugal debt" (what later came to be termed "conjugal rights") applied to both husbands and wives, though husbands were warned their wives might be reticent about expressing sexual needs and might need some encouragement.

During this period, a few men and women decided to blend marriage and virginity, living in what were termed "chaste" or "spiritual" marriages in which the spouses either rejected sexual activity from the start or else renounced it sometime during the course of the marriage. Though Augustine apparently approved of such marriages, most church leaders did not, stating that the power of sexual desire was so great that no one could live with a spouse without sex. This formal disapproval of chaste marriage – Jerome called women who lived in this way "one-man harlots" – contradicted the steady stream of praise for virginity and for overcoming sexual temptation, however, and many accounts of early saints' lives include favorable discussions of their chaste marriages.

Church policy on sexual and related issues was not simply a matter of learned treatises, but was debated and sometimes decided upon at church councils, meetings of large numbers of bishops and other leaders, and at smaller regional meetings known as synods. Councils and synods also acted as courts, for they heard complaints from individuals and groups about the ideas and activities of other Christians. Their decisions, usually called *canons*, gradually created a body of church law and rulings on sexual matters. Because Constantine and later rulers in Europe regarded themselves as the head of the church as well as the state, they sometimes attended church councils and in other ways shaped the development of Christian doctrine and law; secular law and church law (known as *canon law*), though distinct in theory, were very closely related in practice.

Constantine and later emperors sought to restrict the grounds for divorce, and most church leaders followed Augustine in discouraging divorce and remarriage after divorce. Nevertheless, it is clear that many Christians in the centuries after Constantine received official ecclesiastical approval for a divorce and then remarried; many more simply separated, declaring divorce by mutual consent. Widows and widowers also remarried, though Augustine and others encouraged them to devote themselves to prayer or charitable activities instead. The issue of clerical marriage was much discussed and debated; although celibacy was suggested as the most appropriate life, it was never required, and most priests continued to be married. Sexual offenses were gradually taken more seriously: in the fourth century imperial decrees forbade any sexual activity between husband and wife that did not involve penetration of the vagina by the penis, and church councils forbade women and men from dressing in the clothes of the other sex; in the fifth century adultery became a crime for men as well as women, with death as the prescribed punishment, although actual penalties were much milder; in the sixth century the emperor Justinian condemned homosexual activity between men in harsh language, and called for the death penalty for all repeat offenders, although again actual cases were rare. Prostitution largely escaped imperial or church prohibition, despite all the denunciations of "harlots," although Justinian did call for punishments of brothel-keepers and pimps. This toleration of prostitution had the backing of Augustine, who regarded the sale of sex as a necessary evil that should be permitted to keep "honorable" women and girls safe from male lust.

From the fourth through the sixth centuries, when Christian ideas were slowly shaping imperial policy, the Roman Empire itself was changing. Under Constantine, the Empire was divided into two parts, a western part with a capital at Rome and an eastern part with a capital at the old city of Byzantium, which Constantine renamed Constantinople. Gradually the western part of the Empire disintegrated politically, because of internal weaknesses and migration and invasion by groups of people coming from northern and central Europe. After the late fifth century there was no longer any Roman Empire in the west, but instead smaller territories ruled by kings and chieftains who gradually came to accept Christianity and blend Christian attitudes toward sex with their own traditions.

The end of the Roman Empire in the west is the conventional dividing line between the ancient period and the Middle Ages, although many historians in recent decades have stressed that the break was not as dramatic as it is usually portrayed to be and that many institutions – including Christianity – continued unbroken lines of development. Historians of eastern Europe also point out that the eastern part of the Roman Empire, usually termed the Byzantine Empire, remained as a governmental unit a thousand years longer than the western Empire. Nevertheless, Christianity did change its shape during this period. Beginning in the seventh century, Muslims, adherents of the religion begun in Arabia by Muhammad, took over much of the Near East, north Africa and most of the Iberian peninsula, cutting off African and Asian Christians from Christians in Europe. In Europe itself, Christianity became increasingly divided between Christians in western and central Europe who were under the authority of the pope in Rome, and who came to be termed Roman Catholic or simply Catholic, and those in eastern Europe, who came to be called Orthodox. Sexual regulations as well as many other matters separated the two traditions. The remainder of this chapter thus will look first at Catholic Europe in the period roughly 500–1500, and then at eastern Europe and Christians outside of Europe.

The Early Middle Ages in Catholic Europe

The groups of people who migrated into the Roman Empire or lived in what is now western Europe beyond the borders of the old Roman Empire are often referred to as "Germans" and "Celts," but they actually belonged to many different groups who had a variety of sexual customs. (It is difficult to get accurate information on Germanic and Celtic customs before contact with the Romans or conversion to Christianity, as most of these people had no written language; available sources are thus the reports of outsiders or laws and literature written much later.) There are a few common elements: marriage was generally monogamous, though powerful men often had more than one wife or a wife and several concubines and mistresses, what anthropologists term "resource polygyny"; the most important part of marriage was consummation, with no formal marriage ceremony required; adultery was strictly a female offense and could be harshly punished, though often it was not; extended families and clans were important social units, with marriage among the powerful considered a means to ally two clans. Same-sex relationships are mentioned in only one Germanic law code, that of the Visigoths in Spain, while literary works provide contradictory attitudes toward them.

During the fifth through the ninth centuries (a period usually called the Early Middle Ages), the peoples of central and northern Europe gradually adopted Roman Christianity, and church leaders attempted to bring together Germanic tradition and Christian teachings. The Germanic Emperor Charlemagne (ruled 771–814) forbade remarriage after divorce, though he did not practice this in his youth and had a number of concubines in addition to a succession of wives. Archbishop Hincmar of Reims (845–82) first suggested that unconsummated marriages were not fully binding, thereby introducing a concept unknown in the Roman world, though the official church position on the exact requirements for a legal marriage remained ambiguous. Many priests married while others lived with concubines, and reports of an unchaste life were no bar to advancement in the church hierarchy.

During the Early Middle Ages several institutions developed within Roman Catholic Christianity that would eventually have a major effect on the regulation of sexuality. Even before the end of the Roman Empire in the west, the bishop of Rome began to build up the power of his office compared with that of all other western bishops, and gradually used the title "Pope" as well as bishop. With the end of the Empire, the pope gained even more power by taking over political authority in and around the city of Rome as well as continuing to assert his superior spiritual authority. Popes sent many of the missionaries who converted the Celtic and Germanic peoples, thus building up loyalty between newly converted Christians and the papacy. They slowly transformed the Roman Church into a clear hierarchy ranging from local parish priests up through bishops and archbishops to the pope. Letters from the pope conveying his opinion on various issues (termed *decretals*) joined the decisions of church councils in the western church as part of canon law; some of these letters responded to actual cases brought before him, so the pope, like the councils and synods, also served as a judge. As the church expanded, so did its personnel, all of whom were supported by a variety of fees, taxes, tithes, and direct landownership, and eventually the church became one of the largest landholders in all of Europe.

At the same time that parishes were established and most of western and central Europe became at least nominally Christian, monasteries were set up where men and women lived according to certain rules which prescribed stricter standards of conduct than those expected of most Christians. Monasteries were in theory for the spiritual elite, and required their residents to be chaste and obedient to a superior, and to devote themselves to spiritual concerns such as prayer, meditation, and copying Christian manuscripts. They thus institutionalized what had been the more individualistic ascetic movement in the early church, and women who chose not to marry were particularly expected to join a monastery rather than devise their own pattern of spiritual life. Monasteries gave women opportunities for leadership; although every female monastery had to have a priest available to say mass and hear confessions because the church ruled these were functions that no woman could perform, all of the other administrative and teaching duties and much of the spiritual counseling of novices and residents were carried out by women. Some of these early medieval monasteries were double-houses, in which men and women lived in separate sections, with both sexes under the direction of an abbess.

The residents of early medieval monasteries often viewed themselves as religious athletes, controlling all of their appetites – for food, drink, and sex – as a sign of their spiritual vigor. They were encouraged to do so by their fellow monastic residents, who by the tenth century were also putting their exhortations to chastity and control into writing, creating what we might think of as a "sexual identity" – that is, a quality understood to be inherent in a *person*, not simply in sexual acts: chaste virgin. There are only a few extant works of this nature by women religious, such as the plays of Hrosvit of Gandersheim (ca. 930–ca. 990), relating the lives of heroic virgin martyrs in a vigorous and sometimes humorous style. In *Dulcitius*, for example, the soldiers who attempt to strip the valiant virgins before torture find: "We labor in vain; we sweat without gain. Behold, their garments remain on their virginal bodies, sticking to them like skin. But he who ordered us to strip them snores in his seat, and cannot be woken from his sleep."[10] Hagiography from the Early Middle Ages describes with approval the tribulations women endured to preserve their virginity, hiding for years in small places or cutting off their noses and lips so that men intent on raping or capturing them would simply kill them instead. Saints' lives were often part of sermons and were frequently depicted in church windows, so that people came to know these stories very well; later they also became popular reading material.

Works written by monks for their monastic brothers are much more numerous than those by female monastics for their sisters, and were circulated more widely. Some of these contain the most harshly anti-sexual comments in Christian literature, and they are also virulently misogynist. Monks who achieved the status of saints are often praised for never looking at a woman or even allowing a woman's shadow to touch them. Same-sex attachments are a lesser theme in this type of literature, with "special friendships" warned against primarily because they created factions and were disruptive of the monastic community. Monks were encouraged to control not only their actions, but also their conscious and unconscious desires; full continence included control over nocturnal emissions, with extreme fasting suggested as an effective technique to accomplish this end.

The idealization of abstinence and the general suspicion of sexual relations and desires were communicated not only to monks in the Early Middle Ages, but also to lay people through the practice of confession and penance. In the early church, Christians appear to have confessed their sins publicly in front of all believers, but by the sixth century this practice was replaced by private confession to a priest, who then forgave the sin and set a penance that the believer had to perform. As private penance was introduced, guides were written for priests that set out lists of sins and the penances for each one. These guides, called "penitentials," include many sexual activities among their listed sins, and, though some historians see the lists primarily as reflecting the imaginations of their clerical authors, most scholars see them as describing what at least some people actually did. Though the penitentials vary, oral sex, incest, adultery, and bestiality generally received the stiffest penance, with sex between two unmarried persons ("simple fornication"), masturbation (termed "fornicating by himself"), and seminal emissions viewed as less serious.

Clerics and adults generally received a harsher penalty than lay people and younger people. Sex between men and anal intercourse by anyone generally brought a stiff penance, and a few penitentials specifically condemned sex between women, especially if it involved the use of "instruments," because then one of the women was taking the role that properly belonged to men. Sexual relations with one's spouse were also to be kept within strict bounds, and were prohibited when the wife was menstruating, pregnant, or nursing a child, and during certain periods in the church calendar, such as Sundays and Fridays and most major saints' days, plus all of Lent and Advent. This left about fifty days a year when a married couple could legitimately have sexual intercourse, and even this was hemmed in by restrictions as to position (prone, man on top), time of day (night only), and proper dress (at least partially clothed). Following the rules did not free one from ritual defilement, however, for couples were expected to wash after sex before coming to church. Lustful thoughts (termed "adultery in the heart") also merited penance, even if they resulted in no activity, for sinfulness was in one's mind and will as well as one's body. This attention to the individual's mental and moral state also resulted in different penances set for acts that were premeditated, impulsive, accidental, or forced – intentionally seducing someone was far more serious than being swept away by passion or being seduced oneself.

It is extremely difficult to assess whether the system of penance actually affected sexual behavior in early medieval Europe, for measuring that would require sources such as detailed demographic statistics (to see if there was a dip in birth rates nine months after Lent and Advent, for example) that simply do not exist. Because confession is a private matter, there are no lists of sins *actually* confessed to match those of *possible* sins, nor are there diaries from this period that might indicate whether people really felt guilty about what they were supposed to. What is clear is that certain teachings of the church, especially in regard to marriage, did begin to win acceptance; even at the highest levels, monogamy came to be the established household pattern, and divorce became more difficult. This was also increasingly true for slaves and serfs, with the result that households and families across all social levels came to look more like one another than they had in the Roman Empire.

Reforms of the High Middle Ages

The close relationship between church and state that began under Constantine was often beneficial to the church, as it put secular power behind Christian doctrine, but it also created problems. By the tenth century, parish priests, bishops, abbots of monasteries, and other church officials were often chosen by secular rulers and nobles, who expected their appointees to follow their wishes. Many priests took their examples of proper masculine behavior from the secular world, and married or had long-standing relations with women; their families lived with them.

There were various attempts to reform this situation in the Carolingian period, and beginning in the eleventh century, a broad-ranging movement grew over the next two centuries; it is usually termed the "Gregorian reform" after one of its most vocal proponents, Pope Gregory VII (pontificate 1073–85). This movement transformed the church into an institution much more free of secular control than it had been earlier, and it brought with it a number of dramatic changes in the regulation of sexuality. Gregory adopted the ideas of a viciously anti-sexual monk, St. Peter Damian (1007?–72), who argued that clerical marriage was heresy, that priests' wives were "harlots" and their children "bastards." Only if the clergy were freed from the worldly concerns created by families would the church be freed from secular control, argued Damian. In 1059, the church passed a decree ordering clerical celibacy, though officials hesitated to break up existing families. By the next century they were less reluctant, and two church councils (First and Second Lateran Councils, 1123 and 1139) explicitly forbade all priests to marry and declared marriages that did exist invalid.

Reform-minded officials began a campaign against clerical families, driving women and children from their homes. They sought to convince parish clergy not to model themselves on secular nobles, proclaiming that the (unmarried) clerical version of masculinity provided more authority. (In 1215, the Fourth Lateran Council declared that priests had the power to turn bread and wine into the body and blood of Christ, a bold statement of the superiority of clerical authority over all lay people, even rulers.) There were protests against this change in policy, but they were not effective, and clerical celibacy became the policy of the western church from that point on. Other contacts between male clergy and women were also restricted: priests were ordered to live separately from their female relatives, and links between monks and nuns in double monasteries were restricted.

For church officials, the sexuality of female religious was to be controlled primarily by cutting them off from the world, a practice known as enclosure. This became official policy in the papal decree *Periculoso* promulgated in 1298 by Pope Boniface VIII, which ordered all women's convents to enclose. The policy was difficult to enforce, however. Along with women who had entered willingly, medieval convents housed girls and women who had been placed there by their families because the cost of a dowry for marriage was too high; the entrance fees demanded by convents were generally lower than the dowry that a husband of one's own social class would expect. Such nuns often continued to live as they would outside the convent and frequently left the

Figure 1.1
A couple gives each other their hands in marriage, with a priest blessing the union and another couple looking on, in this fifteenth-century wall painting from a church in Risinge in southern Sweden. In the Middle Ages, a priestly blessing and witnesses were encouraged but not required for a valid Christian marriage, because canon law held that the freely given consent of the spouses was all that mattered. By permission of Antikvarisk-Topografiska Arkivet, Stockholm.

convent to visit family or friends. In addition, a number of women lived in less structured religious communities without taking the vows that nuns did, supporting themselves by weaving, sewing, caring for the sick and poor, or performing religious functions such as praying at funerals. Some women who felt a special religious calling remained with their families, devoting themselves to helping others or to prayer, and perhaps attaching themselves to the Dominicans or Franciscans as lay followers called tertiaries. Church officials were often troubled by these women who did fit neatly into the category of "religious" or "secular," and accused them of both heresy and sexual crimes. Strong feelings of piety among many lay women, the realities of the marriage market, and the support of neighbors who relied on their social and spiritual services combined to prevent the elimination of these quasi-religious options for women, however.

The campaign for clerical celibacy extended to same-sex relationships as well. Peter Damian denounced what he termed sodomy (*sodomia*) among clergy, arguing that God's destruction of the Biblical cities of Sodom and Gomorrah resulted from the cities' residents engaging in same-sex intercourse, and that the same could happen to the church. (Whether the Hebrew text says this, or instead says that the cities were destroyed because they refused to extend hospitality to strangers, is debated by Biblical scholars; the disagreement hinges on the interpretation of one Hebrew word.) Damian linked sodomy – by which he meant any sex in which procreation was not possible – with blasphemy (*blasphemia*); both were not simply sins, but denials of God. Damian's words and ideas were picked up by many other authors. The French Dominican William Peraldus (ca. 1190–1271) worried that warning people about sodomy might spread the practice rather than limit it, however, and termed sodomy "the sin that cannot be named." Sodomy was something that pervaded one's whole being, in his view, so there were "sodomites" as well as sodomy. (Thus we might view "sodomite" – along with chaste virgin – as another type of "sexual identity.") It was also unforgivable. When sodomites appeared before God at the Last Judgement: "They cannot speak to excuse themselves on account of ignorance since nature itself taught the law they transgress to brute animals."[11]

Opinions became law. The Third Lateran Council (1179) held that clerics who could not give up same-sex relations were to give up their clerical status, and laymen were to be excommunicated – that is, cut off from church rituals and services, including burial. Church and secular authorities increasingly agreed with Peraldus that same-sex relations were a "crime against nature," and particularly reprehensible because they did not occur anywhere else in creation. (Biologists and people who live in close proximity to animals know that this view is not accurate.) After about 1250 secular jurisdictions in particular sharpened their penalties, although it is difficult to know exactly what actions were being prohibited, as the meaning of "sodomy" was not stable. Sometimes it appears to have meant male–male sex only, sometimes female–female as well, and sometimes any sex that was non-procreative, including masturbation. The fact that sodomy was "the sin that cannot be named" only added to the uncertainty, both for today's historians trying to figure out what people meant, and for people at the time trying to figure out what exactly it was they weren't supposed to do.

The reform movement also brought changes in the marriages and sexual lives of lay persons. In their efforts to assert the independence and primacy of religious authority, church leaders supported the compilation of collections of canon law, the writing of new laws, and the expansion of the jurisdiction of bishops' and other church courts. This continued over several centuries, and so by the thirteenth century, canon law and church courts controlled almost all aspects of marriage (except for property matters) and sexual conduct, including both civil and criminal issues, which, incidentally, brought the church a great deal of revenue through fees and fines. The church developed a definition of marriage that was very different from that of secular society. In contrast to prevailing secular norms, in which people often married their relatives to keep property in the family, fathers had a great deal of control over their children's marriages, and wives were easily repudiated, canon law regarded the free consent of the spouses as the essence of marriage. At the Fourth Lateran Council in 1215, marriage was defined as a *sacrament*, a ceremony that provided visible evidence of God's grace, and as the expected norm for all lay Christians. As such, it was indissoluble. Weddings did not have to take place in a church; in southern Europe they were usually held at home, whereas in northern Europe, they were often held at the church door. The Fourth Lateran Council also ruled on *consanguinity*, or the degree to which blood or marital kinship would prohibit people from marrying each other. Prohibitions of marriage based on consanguinity were later extended to individuals who had had sex with their relatives outside of marriage, and to the relatives of their godparents, termed *spiritual consanguinity*.

Passage of these rules always occasioned debate, and canon lawyers also argued about such issues as whether rapists who persuaded their victims to marry them should be liable for their crime, whether impotence was a valid grounds for annuling a marriage, how that impotence was to be proved, and how often spouses had the right to demand the "conjugal debt" from each other. Disagreement among authorities and confusion among average people about church policy on marriage were two main reasons that sexual and marital cases constituted a large percentage of the business of church courts. Courts regularly granted *dispensations* allowing marriages that were officially prohibited, and many people came to regard the church's rules on marriage as primarily a money-making scheme.

Innovations in the control of sexuality were not just imposed from the top down, but were also spread by lay men and women. One of these was the ritual of churching, a ceremony during which women were purified after childbirth. Churching generally happened about forty days after the birth, and until a woman was churched she did not engage in sex with her husband, appear in public, or take part in religious rituals. It was briefly mentioned by various church officials in the Early Middle Ages, but appears to have spread largely by word of mouth. By the twelfth century women in many parts of Europe were regularly churched in rituals that involved being led to the church by a group of female friends and relatives, and then blessed by the priest and welcomed back into the parish community. For male theologians, churching (which they discussed only rarely) was primarily about ridding women of the corruption of intercourse, but for women themselves its meaning appears to have revolved primarily around the honor due to married women. (Unmarried mothers were regularly denied churching.)

Church courts and legal procedures

Reform measures to increase church power over the laity and centralize papal control within the church led to new types of criminal procedure in church courts. Like most other medieval courts, church courts had traditionally operated with an accusatory procedure, in which an individual accusing someone of a crime confronted the defendant openly in court, produced witnesses (two were usually required), and then a judge or judges (or occasionally jury) decided the case. This procedure protected defendants against frivolous cases, a protection extended further by the fact that the accuser had to bear all costs of the case until there was a verdict, and all costs in cases when the verdict went against him or her; a negative verdict might also lead the original defendant to sue the accuser, which worked as a further deterrent against frivolous cases. Increasingly, however, canon lawyers realized the difficulty of finding two witnesses to certain types of crimes, and saw how reluctant accusers often were to state their case openly in court, so around 1200, they began to devise other sorts of procedures for certain type of cases.

One of these, procedure *per notorium* or *per denunciationem*, authorized a court to proceed against someone whose actions were so notorious that the whole community knew them. No accuser was necessary, and witnesses were only required to testify that people generally believed the accused to be guilty and not that they had actually seen the crime. Procedures *per notorium* were often used against priests who lived with a concubine or patronized prostitutes, although many jurists had reservations about such procedures because they left the defendant with little protection and could be based simply on rumors. Defendants had even less protection in a second type of procedure devised initially by Pope Innocent III (pontificate 1198–1216), proceedings *per inquisitionem*. As in proceedings *per notorium*, the inquisitorial process began with a judge's decision to investigate a person suspected of a crime. The judge called witnesses, heard testimony, made a judgement, and passed sentence, thus combining the roles of judge, investigator, and prosecutor in one. The defendant did have the right to answer the general charges and to deny guilt, but in particularly heinous cases judges were allowed to use torture to provoke a confession. The judge determined when a case was heinous and also had great leeway in choosing the appropriate punishment. That could be penance, fines, imprisonment, and excommunication, or the party judged guilty could be handed over to secular authorities for more stringent punishments such as beating and execution. (Medieval church courts themselves did not carry out the death penalty.)

Inquisitorial procedures became the preferred method of handling those accused of what were dubbed "occult crimes," which included both heresy and sodomy. (The word "occult" comes from the Latin word for hidden from sight, and only gradually acquired its current associations with magic and witchcraft.) In the early thirteenth century, the papacy grew increasingly alarmed by the spread of ideas it judged heretical, and it established a formal tribunal, the papal Inquisition, to investigate and try people accused of heresy. Judges were sent to areas of what is now France and Italy, where a dualist group called the Albigensians had won many people from Christianity with vigorous preaching and charismatic leaders. Albigensians preached that the material world was evil, created by a second divine power, and that the body was a prison for the soul. Not surprisingly, they thus rejected reproduction, and were accused by church authorities of engaging in "unnatural" (i.e., non-reproductive) sex; inquisitorial legal proceedings combined with a military campaign wiped them out.

Secular authorities also recognized that linking heresy and sexual deviance could be a very effective strategy against their enemies. The most spectacular example was the French King Philip IV's trial of the Knights Templars, a military order that had been founded during the Crusades to fight Muslims, but which had also grown extremely wealthy from its landholding and moneylending. In 1307, Philip arrested about 2,000 Templars in France and used the inquisitorial procedure, including torture, to force them to confess to worshipping Muhammad and the devil, parodying the mass, and engaging in anal intercourse with one another. He claimed they had learned the latter from Muslims in the east, who Europeans believed were particularly prone to same-sex desire. He then executed many Templars, confiscated their property and began to persecute other moneylenders, such as wealthy Jews and Italians. It is impossible to tell whether the Templars did any of the things they were accused of, but "heretic and sodomite" thereafter became a standard charge to level at one's political or religious opponents. (This linkage is also the origin of the word "bugger," which comes from "Bulgarian," because Bulgaria was regarded as the home of dualist beliefs such as Albigensianism; it was first used in English in a clearly sexual sense in a 1533 law of Henry VIII.)

Though the Templars most likely never worshipped Muhammad or converted to Islam, the Crusades and the reconquest of the Iberian peninsula from the Muslims did mean that Christian authorities in these areas were confronted with issues regarding marriage and other sexual relations between Christians and non-Christians. Canon law prohibited all such relations, and Christian theologians described them as the worst form of adultery because they involved a non-Christian "defiling" a bride of Christ. (Jewish rabbis and Muslim jurists also prohibited them, but they did not use this marital imagery.) Penalties for sexual relations between Christians and non-Christians could be severe; laws in some areas prescribed death for both partners, and there are examples of this occuring in cases involving Christian women and Muslim or Jewish men. The reverse pairing was much less likely to be punished, particularly if it involved Christian men and Muslim women. In the Kingdom of Valencia, for example, where there was a significant Muslim population, Christian men caught in sexual relations with Muslim women were not penalized, but the women were often enslaved to the Crown, which then sold them for cash, gave them to royal favorites, or licensed them as prostitutes. Nobles and occasionally even monks profited from this system, ordering Muslim women under their jurisdiction to have sex with them and then denouncing them for that sex so they could receive them as slaves; the Crown altered the law slightly to prevent such glaring abuses, but did not revoke it.

The possibility of sexual relations across religious lines was used as a justification for requiring Jews to wear distinctive markers on their clothing, first imposed at the Fourth Lateran Council of 1215. Fear of sex between Christians and non-Christians led the rulers of Castile and Aragon, as well as city governments in the Iberian peninsula, to order Jews and Muslims to live in segregated neighborhoods, and to prohibit non-Christians from eating or trading with Christians. Such actions, as well as periodic riots against Jews, led many to convert to Christianity, which was initially greeted as miraculous, but increasingly viewed with suspicion. Might Jews be converting simply to gain the privileges of Christians, among them the ability to have sex with Christian women? Doubts about the sincerity of Jewish (and to a lesser extent, Muslim) conversions led to increasing restrictions on these "New Christians," and would be one reason that the rulers of Spain established a separate Inquisition in the late fifteenth century, whose actions we will examine in detail in Chapter 3.

Most of the business of church courts did not involve high drama like the Knights Templars or even serious cases such as Christian/Jewish sex, but more prosaic matters: How closely related were two individuals who intended to marry or who had married? Had a promise of marriage in front of one's friends in a tavern involved the proper words of consent so that it was a marriage (such cases generally were brought by a pregnant woman)? Had consent been freely given or been gained by force or threats of force? Was someone correct in calling their neighbor a slut or a bastard? In such matters, church courts paid attention not only to what had happened, the "facts" of the case, but also to what the parties intended. They thus brought into

western criminal law a notion deriving from the church's ritual of penance
– that the mental and moral state of an offender determined the level of guilt
and appropriate punishment. This idea is now fully engrained in most secular
law codes, where, for example, the punishment for premeditated murder is
very different from that for killing someone accidentally in a car accident.
Thus much of the business of church courts involved an examination of
conscience on the part of the parties concerned: Did you think you were
married when you had sex with him? Did you mean to force her into marriage,
and if not, why were you carrying a stick? Did you know she was your cousin
but decided to marry her anyway? Did you know it was wrong to marry again
when you weren't sure your first husband was dead? Punishments were set
according to the nature of the specific crime and the attitude of the defendant.
They could involve fines, exclusion from church rituals, or rituals of humiliation,
such as walking around the church carrying a candle.

Church courts thus not only penalized actions in the Middle Ages, but also
shaped conscience. The church accomplished this objective through a variety
of other means as well. The Fourth Lateran Council commanded all Christians
to make a complete confession at least once a year, preceded by an examination
of conscience in which they were to pay special attention to those sins judged
"mortal," that is, those which, if unconfessed, would make them liable to
damnation. Sexual actions and thoughts were prominent among the mortal
sins, although theologians differed about the precise dividing line between
mortal and venial (lesser) sins in matters of sexuality.

Sermons were also an increasingly important means of communicating
church teachings about sex. Church services continued to be held in Latin –
a language that by the Middle Ages was no longer spoken in Europe outside
of university or ecclesiastical circles – but beginning in the thirteenth century
several new religious orders were founded that preached in the languages that
people spoke. Prime among these orders were the Dominicans, founded by
St. Dominic (1170?–1221), who was sent by Pope Innocent III to preach to
the Albigensians. (The timing and circumstances of their founding and their
dedication to spreading correct doctrine resulted in the Dominicans becoming
the order principally in charge of the Inquisition.) Dominicans and members
of other religious orders such as the Franciscans often went from town to
town gathering large crowds to hear their sermons, which they held in
marketplaces as well as churches. The sermons of the most popular preachers
were later written down and copies made for others to use; sermon collections
are thus a good source for the teachings on sex that people heard regularly.
What they heard were frequent denunciations of harlots and adulterers,
attacks on lascivious monks and adulterous wives, and other condemnations
of a range of sexual sins. St. Vincent Ferrer (1350–1419), for example, a

Dominican preacher who traveled widely in Spain, France and Italy, thundered, "Today the law is not obeyed. [Christian men] want to taste everything: Muslims and Jews, animals, men with men; there is no limit."[12]

Along with such attacks, sermon audiences also heard glorifications of love between husband and wife, which was praised as a model of the love between God and humanity, central to the divine plan for the world and thus "natural." (The link between human and divine love was also becoming increasingly popular in secular chivalric romances at the same time, though these stories often focus more on extramarital love.) Such love was to continue even beyond the grave, especially for women. Twelfth-century preachers spread the idea of purgatory – a place where souls on their way to heaven went after death to do penance for sins they had not done penance for on earth – and taught that widows had a special spiritual duty to say prayers and pay for masses that would shorten their husband's time there. Those who instead gave in to their urges for sex or companionship and looked for a new husband failed in their role as a wife and to some degree shared responsibility for the sins that were keeping their husband's soul in purgatory.

Scholastics and mystics

Theological discussions of sexuality did not end with Augustine, but were continued throughout the Middle Ages by members of various religious orders. In the thirteenth century they were given added impetus in the course of attempts to integrate the ideas of Aristotle with Christian teachings by philosophers termed *scholastics*. These efforts at synthesis appear especially in the writings of St. Thomas Aquinas (1225–74), a Dominican who was not very popular in his own time but whose philosophical system was later declared the official philosophy of the Roman Catholic Church. Though much of Aristotelian and Christian thought is difficult to reconcile – Aristotle does not believe in the immortality of the individual soul, for example – in terms of sexuality they were compatible and largely reinforced one another. Aquinas and most of the scholastics viewed sexual desire as both sinful and irrational, dangerous to the spirit, and – an idea picked up from Greek and Roman medical theory – particularly dangerous to the male body. They classified sexual sins according to their relation to reason and nature: least serious (although still sins) were acts that respected both, which were limited to intercourse between a husband and wife desiring children; more serious were those that were irrational, primarily those that were outside of marriage but could still result in procreation; worst were vices "against nature, which attaches to every venereal act from which generation cannot follow."[13] In this hierarchy, rape – which could lead to conception – is a less serious sin than oral sex between husband and wife. Aquinas also regarded rape of someone else's wife as more serious than rape of an unmarried woman, as the rapist was usurping the sexual role that properly belonged only to the woman's husband. Contraception was included among the worst vices as a "sin against nature," whether attempted through *coitus interruptus* or chemically through herbs and drugs. This included measures taken during the first few months of pregnancy, which medieval authors classified as contraception rather than abortion. In their opinion, not until the fetus quickened (that is, until the mother felt movement) did it acquire a soul, and only after quickening was ending a pregnancy regarded as abortion. (This opinion lasted for centuries; Pope Pius IX declared that ensoulment begins at conception only in 1869.)

Aquinas accepted Aristotle's idea that in procreation "the active power of generation belongs to the male sex, and the passive power to the female," but rejected his views that women were misbegotten men; he and the other scholastics viewed the creation of women as part of God's plan, though they were often puzzled by God's motives.[14] The scholastics believed women had a stronger sex drive than men as well as a lesser capacity for reason; both made them, in Aquinas's words, "naturally subject to man." Any attempt to overcome the divinely ordained and "natural" inequality between men and women was regarded as both unnatural and unChristian, particularly if men sank to the level of women. Men who dressed as women, except during plays and festivals, were suspected of trying to gain sexual access to women. Men who became sexually aroused too often and too easily, especially if this led to intercourse, were not regarded as manly and macho as they often are in contemporary culture, but as feminine because they were ruled by their bodies rather than their minds. In the western church, eunuchs were prohibited from becoming priests because they were not fully men; the practice of intentionally castrating boys or adult men to serve as administrators or servants declined. (Castration continued to be used occasionally as punishment for crimes such as homosexuality and rape, and in the sixteenth century men who had been castrated as boys – whose voices thus did not change – began to perform in Italian and Spanish church choirs.)

At the same time that the scholastics were emphasizing reason as the best way to know God, other Christian thinkers elaborated on mystical traditions of the early church to develop an understanding that involved the body as well as the mind. Literature written by mystics often portrays union with God in very sensual and bodily terms, as tasting or kissing God, bathing in Christ's blood or becoming one with God. Though most mystical visions were not sexual, some male mystics envisioned their souls as feminine, uniting with Christ as a bride with a bridegroom in language full of sexual imagery, or they described the body of Christ in female terms, as Jesus who "suckles us with his blessed breast." By bridging body and soul, mysticism thus provided a kind of counter-discourse within Christianity to the much more common disparagement of the body and the senses.

The virgin body as well as the sensual body was often part of mystics' visions, who connected their own virginity and choice of an ascetic life to the virgin birth of Christ and Christ's own virginity. Female mystics often identified with the Virgin Mary, and saw visions of her that were graphically physical, as is this one by St. Bridget of Sweden (1303–73): "The Virgin Mary appeared again to me, in the same place, and said . . . I showed you . . . the way I was standing when I gave birth to my son, you still should know for sure that I stood and gave birth such as you have seen it now – my knees were bent and I was alone in the stable, praying."[15] Statues of Mary portrayed her as a nursing mother whose body opened up to reveal the Trinity. Given official church attitudes about the greater worth of virginity, motherhood often troubled women who felt they had a special religious calling, but they took heart in the example of the Virgin Mary. Margery Kempe, a fifteenth-century English mystic who had fourteen children, despaired about being pregnant again, but was relieved by a vision of Christ saying to her, "Forasmuch as thou art a maiden in thy soul, I shall take thee by the one hand, and my Mother by the other hand, and so shalt thou dance in Heaven with other maidens and virgins."[16]

Mystics were not the only ones who were devoted to the Virgin Mary. She was depicted so often in the images and stories through which people learned about Christianity that many people believed she was one member of the Trinity. More and more churches and cathedrals were dedicated to her, and special prayers, chants, and devotional activities were developed to honor various aspects of her nature: spotless virgin, loving mother, gifted teacher, queen of heaven, mother of God, compassionate intercessor, grief-stricken mourner. Hundreds of religious confraternities – organizations of men or more rarely of women that sponsored funerals, memorial masses, processions, and altars – were established with Mary as their patron. New ideas about her life and status developed, among them that of her "immaculate conception," which held that, alone of all people born since the Fall of Adam and Eve, Mary was sinless from the moment she was conceived and remained so throughout her life. She was conceived through normal sex between her father and mother – who according to tradition were named Anne and Joachim – but through God's grace this one sexual act did not pass down original sin. The immaculate conception of Mary was hotly debated by medieval theologians, and it became a bone of contention between religious orders. (The immaculate conception of Mary was adopted as official Catholic dogma only in 1854.) Many lay people apparently accepted the idea, however, which put Mary's purity at the center of their veneration.

For other Christians, Mary's motherhood was more important than her virginity. Women in labor often wrapped a sash or girdle that had been wrapped around a statue of the Virgin around their own bodies to protect them, and after a successful delivery gave candles, wax seals, clothing, or jewelry to statues of the Virgin in local churches. Mary was thought not to have experienced labor pains during Jesus' birth, but instead during his crucifixion, when she, by extension, gave birth to human salvation. She was often shown swooning with pain at the foot of the cross. Mary's pain was linked to Christ's Passion, which became an increasing focus of Christian devotional practices in the later Middle Ages. Christians, male and female, were encouraged to contemplate Christ's bleeding body – depicted in ever more excruciating detail in sermons, paintings, and statues – and embrace physical suffering as a way of imitating Christ. Thus women in childbirth – or any Christian in pain – could consider the bodily experiences of either the Virgin Mary or her son when seeking consolation.

The Late Middle Ages and Renaissance in Catholic Europe

The fourteenth and fifteenth centuries (conventionally called the "Late Middle Ages") was a period of crisis in Europe, with war, famines, and plagues, but also a time of cultural change spreading out from Italy that contemporaries called the "re-birth" or Renaissance. The era brought ambivalence in terms of Christian attitudes toward and handling of sexual issues.

The most popular late medieval saint after the Virgin Mary was Mary Magdalene, a figure who in Catholic Christianity combined three different New Testament women and about whom an enormous number of legends had grown up. In the New Testament she was simply described as a woman possessed by a demon whom Jesus exorcized, but the story developed that she was a beautiful wealthy woman who was promiscuous sexually, but who abandoned her previous life on meeting Christ. She thus became the prime example of a repentant "holy harlot." In a story that was first told in the tenth century, Mary and some companions, set adrift by heartless non-believers in a boat without a rudder, landed in southern France. (That she was pregnant with Jesus' baby at the time is a story that is much newer than the tenth century.) She preached to the local people, winning many converts, and then lived alone in a cave, doing penance for her formerly sinful life. The barren surroundings offered no food, but Mary was miraculously taken up to heaven seven times a day by angels, an experience that replaced her need for earthly food. To protect her from the elements, Mary's body became covered with hair, sometimes shown in painting and sculpture as beautiful flowing strands and sometimes as rough fur. Like the Virgin, Mary Magdalene provided an ambiguous message about female sexuality, and by extension male sexuality as well; yes, it was possible for someone who had been sexually active to be saved, but only by renouncing sexual desire and activity.

Real women who sold sex, as opposed to those of tradition and legend, were not made saints. By the Late Middle Ages, most major cities in Europe and many of the smaller ones had an official brothel or an area of the city in which selling sex was permitted. In cities ruled by bishops, the bishop sometimes owned the brothel, and in some cities monasteries and the groups that governed cathedrals (termed cathedral chapters) also owned brothels. Women selling sex outside these areas would be ordered to move, as cities attempted to make a sharper distinction between respectable, married women and the "common women" or "whores" who distributed their sexual favors more widely. ("Whore" may have been a third type of sexual identity in the Middle Ages.) Visiting brothels was associated with achieving manhood in the eyes of young men, though for the women themselves their activities were work. Indeed, in some cases the women had no choice, for they had been traded to the brothel manager by their parents or other people in payment for debt, or had quickly become indebted to him (or, more rarely, her) for the clothes and other finery regarded as essential to their occupation.

City and church authorities taxed brothel residents and managers, and in the fifteenth century set down rules for the women and their customers. They justified the existence of municipal brothels with the comment that such women protected honorable girls and women from the uncontrollable lust of young men, an argument at least as old as Augustine. In a few cities, such as Florence, authorities also noted that brothels might keep young men from same-sex relations, another far worse alternative in their eyes. Officially brothels in most parts of Europe were closed to priests, Jews, and married men, although usually this ban was enforced only in the case of Jews; priests who openly visited brothels were occasionally reprimanded by the church, but rarely received any stronger punishment. In parts of Europe with significant numbers of Muslims, Christian prostitutes were prohibited from having Muslim patrons and were exempt from severe penalties only if they could prove they did not know the religious affiliation of their customers.

During the thirteenth century a special religious order had been set up for repentant prostitutes – named, not surprisingly, the Order of St. Mary Magdalene – which established houses in a number of cities, but by the fifteenth century the movement to reform such women lost its steam. The public and clerical acceptance of municipal brothels in the fourteenth and fifteenth centuries did not result from a change of heart about sexual desire – sex was still regarded as polluting and sinful – but from a sort of resigned acceptance of its power. This attitude also affected the treatment of clerics who continued their relationships with women, for though they were forbidden to marry, many priests lived in stable relationships with concubines and children or had casual relationships with many women. Church councils and synods set stringent punishments for clerical concubinage and fornication, but local church authorities generally enforced these only in cases that involved public scandal, such as rape or abduction. A similar pattern emerged in cases of divorce and separation; church courts allowed separation for reasons not specified in canon law – including cruelty, mistreatment, drunkenness, and financial irresponsibility – although they consented to a true divorce with rights of remarriage only on very rare occasions. While fornication between unmarried persons was officially prohibited, actual prosecutions are very rare, and confessors reported that most of their parishioners did not even consider fornication a sin worthy of penance, much less a crime.

Secular courts run by cities, kings, and nobles became more active in handling marriage issues and sexual offenses, though church courts also continued to hear a large number of cases. (The decision about exactly who had jurisdiction over what types of cases was often a matter of dispute, with plaintiffs often choosing whichever type of court they felt would give them a sympathetic judgement.) Secular courts took particular interest in cases in which an actual crime was involved, such as rape, abduction, or adultery, or where property was at stake, such as disputes over dowries. City governments also passed draconian laws about certain types of sexual behavior: sex between Christians and non-Christians merited death by burning alive in some Italian cities, as did certain types of same-sex acts. The enforcement of these statutes tended to be sporadic and localized, however, and some scholars have noted that male homosexual networks developed in Italian and perhaps other cities during this time. During periods of enforcement punishment could be severe, with death sentences actually carried out and not simply threatened.

By the late Middle Ages, secular authorities in many place became more rigorous than church courts in trying to make people's sexual and marital lives follow a prescribed pattern and drawing a sharp line between acceptable and unacceptable behavior. In 1484, for example, the city council of Cologne asked priests hearing confessions in the city to reveal the extent of those involving sodomy; most of the priests were reluctant to reply, and appear not to have shared the council's concerns about the presence of sodomites. In many places city authorities barred illegitimate children from membership in craft guilds or city government and refused to recognize the church's right to confer legitimacy. Occupational groups such as craft and journeymen's guilds also became increasingly moralistic. They denied membership to those born too soon after their parents' wedding (canonical authorities generally recommended that all children born to married women be considered legitimate, no matter when that marriage had occured), and by the early sixteenth century ejected those known to frequent brothels. They enforced their views through formal actions such as banning individuals from working, and also through informal means, such as public insults or rumors. Sometimes these cases ended up in church or secular courts, as when the person accused of immoral acts attempted to clear his or her name, usually by finding a number of people to testify to his or her good character, a process known as compurgation.

The medieval courts that dealt with slander and rumor provide a good source for the epithets people called one another and can give insight into popular ideas about sexuality. Women were almost always called something sexual, usually a variant of "whore," while men were called names related to their honesty, such as "thief," or to the sexual actions of the women with whom they were involved, such as "whoreson," "whoremaster," or "cuckold." In certain circles "sodomite" was also a common term of abuse, often – as earlier in the twelfth century – used against religious or political enemies; the term frequently appears, for example, in slanderous poetry about New Christian officials in Spain.

Court records, then or now, only provide evidence about things that people judge to be outside the accepted norm, of course. Other sorts of sources indicate that writers and even some preachers presented people with examples of what they *should* do, as well as what they should not. They praised marriage in wedding sermons and orations, going beyond the "three goods" set out by Augustine to note its value to society and to individuals. Jesus himself had shown his approval of marriage by turning water into wine at the wedding at Cana (John 2:1–11), they asserted, a wedding that parishioners could also see depicted in paintings and stained-glass windows. Christ instituted the sacraments, marriage among them, at the crucifixion – an idea shown visually by blood spurting out of Christ's side onto depictions of the sacraments – so that harmonious and orderly marriages merited eternal bliss, though bad marriages also intensified Christ's suffering and merited eternal punishment. These texts and images tended to present women in a positive light, and some even defended physical beauty and sexual pleasure, drawing on classical as well as Christian sources for their examples. Yes, God prized virginity, but he also prized marital households where husband and wife felt mutual affection, proper family hierarchy was maintained, and children were taught how to live an upright life. Sexual desire and activities could disrupt public order, but if properly channeled, they could also be a force for stability, and even merit divine approval. The championing of marriage is, as we will see, a central theme in the Protestant Reformation, but it was not a new idea. Decades earlier learned humanists and city leaders also asserted that just as God would punish those communities that tolerated certain sexual activities, he would also looked favorably on those where sex helped to create stable families and moral order.

Eastern Orthodoxy

Regulation of sexuality in eastern Europe during the Middle Ages followed a slightly different path than that in western and central Europe, in large part because the political and institutional situation was very different. The Roman Empire collapsed in the west in the fifth century, and the pope became a territorial ruler as well as a religious leader; the eastern Roman (or Byzantine) Empire survived until the fifteenth century, although over time it gradually shrank, particularly after the rise of Islam in the seventh century. Christian missionaries traveled north and east from the Byzantine Empire into what would later become Russia and other states; as the rulers of these areas became Christian, they adopted Orthodoxy as the state religion. Within the Byzantine Empire, tradition accorded the emperor a special role ideologically and administratively, holding that the emperor ruled the earthly kingdom in the way that Christ ruled the heavenly kingdom. Orthodox societies recognized distinct spheres of influence for church and state and had separate codes of law and courts of law for each. The Byzantine ideal was harmony (*symphonia*) between church and state; the church defended the faith and the Christian people spiritually, and the state defended them physically. In practical terms the emperor presided at the church councils that formed the apex of Orthodox church structure, and often had the final say in who became patriarch – the title of the bishop of Constantinople. The church councils, composed of all Orthodox bishops who were willing and able to attend periodic meetings, set dogma and general policy. Unlike the Catholic pope, the patriarch was merely the first among equals, and had little more than moral suasion to exercise over other bishops, especially outside the boundaries of the Byzantine Empire. The heads of the Orthodox Churches in Bulgaria, Serbia, and later Russia, titled in various periods as "metropolitan" or "patriarch," generally sought pro-forma confirmation of their appointment from the patriarch of Constantinople, but operated autonomously in their decision making. The lack of a unified code of canon law, a single administrative structure, and even a single language of operation (Greek, Syriac, and Slavonic were all in use) allowed for considerable local autonomy and diversity in Orthodox practices.

The final, formal break between Orthodoxy and Catholicism did not occur until 1054, but eastern and western Christianity were already distinct enough in the fourth century that the thought of St. Augustine had little impact on Orthodox ideas about sexuality. Augustine's linkage of sexual intercourse and original sin and his concept of the "conjugal debt" were never accepted in the Orthodox east, though this did not mean that the eastern church had more favorable views on sex. The most important of the Greek Church Fathers and bishop of Antioch, St. John Chrysostom (ca. 347–407), was ascetic in his own habits and extremely moralistic, frequently preaching against what he viewed as the decadence of the emperor's court and warning against anything that led even to thoughts of sex, such as theater, dancing, or artistic representations of the human body. Although he did not regard original sin as transmitted through sexual intercourse (the Orthodox church tended to pay less attention to original sin in general than the Catholic church), he did see sex as the disgraceful result of Adam's and Eve's disobedience and commented that: "The passions in fact are all dishonorable."[17] Those who had given in to sexual desire and married should never marry again if their spouse died, according to Chrysostom, but spend their remaining years in prayer and penance.

Chrysostom was particularly disturbed by same-sex acts and wrote more about them than any other Church Father. What bothered him most was that sex between males upset gender norms, "for I maintain that not only are you made [by it] into a woman, but you also cease to be a man." As we saw earlier, women who became men by remaining virgins were praiseworthy to St. Jerome, but men who became women were, for Chrysostom, "demented . . . noxious . . . worthy of being driven out and stoned . . . changed from men not into dogs but into a much more loathsome animal than this." In the same sermon, Chrysostom made a few veiled references to sex between women as unnatural and a disease.

Chrysostom's hostility to sexuality and the body comes very close to that of dualist groups like the Manicheans, but he ultimately and grudgingly accepted marital sex and procreation as necessary. Later Byzantine writers were more moderate, viewing marriage as a positive good and the ideal life not as one of virginity, but of loyalty and attachment to one's spouse. A few went so far as to approve of sexual pleasure, as long as the parties were married. This endorsement of marriage extended in some degree to the clergy, for married men could become priests. Acceptance of clerical marriage was limited only to those already in their first marriage, however, for a widowed priest was forbidden to remarry if he wanted to remain a priest, and a man who was unmarried when ordained was expected to remain unmarried. Married priests also could not become bishops. Monks and nuns in the Orthodox church were expected to be unmarried, although married persons could also enter monasteries with their spouse's approval. Many monastery residents were widows or widowers who entered monasteries late in life, rather than life-long celibates. Upper-class widows and, more rarely, unmarried daughters, regarded the establishment of a convent as the perfect way to demonstrate both their devotion and authority, and joint monasteries in which abbesses had authority over both women and men persisted in the east, despite official prohibitions.

Along with its acceptance of clerical marriage, most Orthodox churches also accepted eunuchs as priests; although Byzantine emperors forbade castration, the practice continued from ancient times into the medieval period and there were enough eunuch priests available in Byzantium for the founders of some convents to require all clergy who had contact with their nuns to be eunuchs. Eunuchs were prominent in the imperial court as well as the church, because their inability to father children meant they were considered less likely to use their position for family advantage. Eunuchs were not used among the Slavs; priests there who ministered to convents were supposed to be married men, though often they were not.

Veneration of the Virgin Mary was perhaps even stronger in Orthodoxy than it was in Catholicism. In the course of defining the exact relationship between the divine and human natures in Christ, the Council of Ephesus in 431 affirmed that Mary was *Theotokos*, a Greek word meaning "the one who gives birth to God." In the official decisions of the council, Christ was held to be fully human and fully God united in one person, making Mary the bearer of both, not simply his human nature. The council declared that those who believed otherwise – primarily a group known as Nestorians – were heretics, and the acceptance of Mary as *Theotokos* became an official dogma in Orthodox churches. (The idea of Mary's immaculate conception was later accepted by many in the east as well, but never became official dogma.) Mary's virginity was an official dogma as well, but icons of Mary from Orthodox churches almost always show her holding an infant Christ, making her powerful position as *Theotokos* more important than her sexual status.

As in the western church, church courts developed within Orthodoxy to handle marriage and sexual cases, although there was even more diversity in their rulings than in the west. After the ninth century, Orthodoxy generally required an ecclesiastical ceremony for a marriage to be valid, with consent of both the parents and the couple viewed as desirable. In Slavic areas, marriages among the elite involved a ceremony in church as well as elaborate rituals at home, though for the peasants church weddings were not common until later. In some countries consent of the parents alone was enough for first marriages, and consent of the couple enough for subsequent marriages. Unions between close relatives were prohibited, as were those with relatives of godparents. Second marriages were frowned upon, with the parties required to do penance before the ceremony; some laws prohibited third or fourth marriages altogether, although demographic realities such as early death and frequent widowhood meant that dispensations to overcome this prohibition were sought and often granted. Because nobody – neither parish priests nor state officials – kept records of births, marriages, and baptisms, observance of the restrictions on consanguinity could not be enforced with any regularity, except among the aristocracy, whose bloodlines were common knowledge. Should political ambitions dictate, noble families could generally persuade clerics to overlook violations of the canons.

Grounds for divorce were gradually extended in Orthodox countries. A husband could divorce his wife for adultery or for going to questionable places such as horse-races or bathhouses; if the divorce was granted, he received the right to remarry, whereas the wife could be confined to a convent, although usually she was not. Adultery by a husband was not grounds for divorce – it was not technically "adultery," but rather fornication – but courts did permit divorce in cases where it was blatant and upset community standards, and allowed the wife to remarry. Serious physical abuse, abandonment, impotence, and barrenness were all grounds for divorce; in all of these instances, remarriage was usually permitted. This meant that the eastern churches, though they disapproved of remarriage after the death of a spouse, actually offered more opportunities for unhappy spouses to separate completely and start a new marriage than did the western church. In addition, if a spouse wished to terminate a marriage in order to take monastic vows, the other spouse was expected to agree to it and to promise not to remarry. In actuality, unhappy wives sometimes used the convent as a respectable escape from their marriages, and unhappy husbands hounded or forced their wives to enter; in such cases, the prohibition on remarriage was generally ignored.

Orthodox teachings generally matched western teachings about the limits of sexual activity within marriage – it was to be restricted to certain times and certain positions, and never to involve hindrances to procreation, so contraception was forbidden. Outside of marriage all sexual activity was sin, though there were gradations of sinfulness according to canon law. Unmarried men were rarely punished for fornication unless it involved an upper-class woman or a young girl. Rape was punishable by mutilation in Byzantium and the Balkans or by the rapist being forced to marry his victim; in Russia, rape was punishable by fines. Taking its cue from Chrysostom, Byzantine law set severe penalties for same-sex acts, including death, castration, and imprisonment, though there is little evidence that such penalties were actually carried out. Slavic law was milder, regarding sex between men as no worse than adultery, and often as a minor transgression; secular governments in Slavic lands also did not outlaw sex between men the way western governments did, but treated them simply as a violation of church law.

The Slavic treatment of sex between men was not motivated by liberality on sexual matters, but by an extremely negative opinion of all sexual relations.

Although Byzantine writers sometimes spoke positively about sex (as long as it was within marriage), Russian and other Slavic didactic tracts cast all sexual relations as unnatural and desire as coming from the devil. Church officials communicated these attitudes to the general population through confession, sermons, and stories about saints, all of which described sex as sin and praised virginity and chastity. In contrast to Western theory in which consummation was an important part of marriage and each spouse owed the other the conjugal debt, in Russia the best marriage was an unconsummated one. This belief led to a motif common in Russian saints' lives, that of a saint being conceived of a pious and abstinent mother, and born of a miracle rather than normal marital intercourse. It also led to the popular idea that Jesus was born out of Mary's ear, not polluting himself with passage through the birth canal. Children were viewed as the result of God's will rather than intercourse itself, and the failure to conceive was taken as a sign of God's disfavor. Menstruation thus marked a woman, and menstruating women could not enter churches or take communion; women were also expected to do penance if they miscarried. Whether people actually accepted church teachings is difficult to ascertain, for while penitentials and church law set out official church positions, they do not give insight into how faithfully people followed church prescriptions. Letters written on birchbark that have survived from medieval Russia do contain occasional expressions of passionate love between individuals, so that church teachings about sexuality and the body were in some cases clearly not internalized.

The Orthodox churches in Russia and much of eastern Europe built on Byzantine traditions and accepted the decisions of most church councils called by the emperor or the patriarch of Constantinople, but this was not true for all Christians in the east. The churches in Assyria and Persia split with Constantinople in the early fourth century, and after the Council of Ephesus they welcomed the Nestorians who had been declared heretics. Assyrian Christians (who are often referred to as "Nestorians" although theologically they are distinct) took Christianity to China and Mongolia in the seventh century, and gained large numbers of converts over the next several centuries. Other eastern groups, including the Coptic church of Egypt, split off after the Council of Chalcedon in 451, again primarily because of disagreements about the nature of Christ. These groups also spread Christianity into Central Asia, converting Mongols, Uighurs, and others. Christian churches were established in southwest India by the fourth century at the latest and perhaps even earlier, for by tradition St. Thomas the apostle is regarded as the founder of these communities. This group is thus often referred to as "St. Thomas Christians." They combined Christian with Hindu practices, following many of the same birth, puberty, marriage, and death rituals as their Hindu neighbors.

Though they had a loose affiliation with patriarchs in Persia, each church was largely independent, led by married hereditary archdeacons rather than celibate priests.

As Christianity spread beyond the northern and eastern borders of the Roman Empire, it also spread south up the Nile River. The rulers of the Aksum kingdom in what is now Ethiopia adopted Christianity in the fourth century during the rule of emperor Ezana who, like his contemporary Constantine, realized that Christianity offered a way to cement the various peoples in his realm together. Ezana put crosses on Aksumite coins, and he and his successors sponsored the building of churches, some carved directly out of rock. As in Orthodoxy, married men could be accepted into the priesthood in Ethiopian Christianity, and priests could not marry after ordination. Monks were expected to be celibate and ascetic, and it was these monks, rather than priests, that provided the intellectual and political leadership in the Ethiopian church. Monasteries produced illuminated manuscripts and painted icons, in which the Virgin Mary became an increasingly important figure, honored at most of the thirty feast days of the religious calendar.

The spread of Islam split Asian and African Christians from European Christians, and in many parts of Africa and Asia Christian communities came to live under Muslim rule. Muslims generally allowed them to maintain their traditions and leaders, regarding Christians – and Jews – as *dhimmis,* or "protected people," because they were People of the Book – that is, people who had received holy texts from God before the time of Muhammad. First Arabic and then Turkish Muslims gradually took over more and more of the Byzantine Empire; in 1453 the Ottoman Turks conquered Constantinople and the Byzantine Empire officially ceased to exist. The patriarch of Constantinople was given civil and religious jurisdiction over all the Orthodox Christians within the Ottoman Empire, so that church courts continued to operate, but these were now within a Muslim state. Orthodox attitudes toward and treatment of marriage and sexual issues could not help but be influenced by this situation, as we will see in Chapter 3.

This chapter has focused primarily on the western Christian Church because it is from this church that both the Reformation and European colonialism took their impetus. It is also this church that has been studied most intensely in terms of sexual attitudes and practices and the institutions designed to shape and control these. Throughout the Middle Ages, European Christians knew there were Christians in Asia and Africa, and fantasized about uniting with them against the Muslims. When western Europeans actually made contact with the Christians of India and Ethiopia in the sixteenth century, however, their aims were submission rather than alliance, as we will see in Chapter 5.

Selected further reading

One of the most thought-provoking discussions of sexuality in Judaism is Howard Eilberg-Schwartz, *God's Phallus* (Boston: Beacon Press, 1994). See also David Biale, *Eros and the Jews from Biblical Israel to Contemporary America* (New York: Basic Books, 1992); Judith Baskin, *Jewish Women in Historical Perspective* (Detroit: Wayne State University Press, 1991); Daniel Boyarin, *Carnal Israel: Reading Sex in Talmudic Culture* (Berkeley: University of California Press, 1993); Michael L. Satlow, *Tasting the Dish: Rabbinic Rhetorics of Sexuality* (Atlanta: Scholar's Press, 1995); Howard Eilberg-Schwartz, ed., *People of the Body: Jews and Judaism from an Embodied Perspective* (Binghamton, N.Y.: SUNY Press, 1992). For Jewish law see: Louis Epstein, *Marriage Laws in the Bible and the Talmud* (Cambridge, Mass.: Harvard University Press, 1942) and *Sex Laws and Customs in Judaism* (New York: Ktav Publishing House, 1948); Rachel Biale, *Women in Jewish Law: An Exploration of Women's Issues in Halakhic Sources* (New York: Schocken, 1984).

Several good collections and studies on sex in the ancient world are: Eva Keuls, *The Reign of the Phallus: Sexual Politics in Ancient Athens* (New York: Harper and Row, 1985); David M. Halperin, John J. Winkler, and Froma I. Zeitlin, eds, *Before Sexuality: The Construction of Erotic Experience in the Ancient Greek World* (Princeton, N.J.: Princeton University Press, 1990); John J. Winkler, *The Constraints of Desire: The Anthropology of Sex and Gender in Ancient Greece* (New York: Routledge, 1990); Dominic Monstserrat, ed., *Changing Bodies, Changing Meanings: Studies on the Human Body in Antiquity* (London: Routledge, 1998); *Journal of the History of Sexuality*, special issue on sexuality in late antiquity, 10(3/4) (July/October 2001); Thomas A.J. McGinn, *Prostitution, Sexuality, and the Law in Ancient Rome* (New York: Oxford University Press, 2003); Mark Golden and Peter Toohey, eds, *Sex and Difference in Ancient Greece and Rome* (Edinburgh: Edinburgh University Press, 2004); Christopher A. Faraone and Laura McClure, eds, *Prostitutes and Courtesans in the Ancient World* (Madison: University of Wisconsin Press, 2006). On marriage, see Beryl Rawson, ed., *Marriage, Divorce and Children in Ancient Rome* (New York: Oxford University Press, 1991); Susan Treggiari, *Roman Marriage* (New York: Oxford University Press, 1991); Cynthia B. Patterson, *The Family in Greek History* (Cambridge, Mass.: Harvard University Press, 2001). For works that compare pagan and Christian ideas, see Aline Rouselle, *Porneia: On Desire and the Body in Antiquity*, trans. Felicia Pheasant (London: Basil Blackwell, 1988); Kate Cooper, *The Virgin and the Bride: Idealized Womanhood in Late Antiquity* (Cambridge, Mass.: Harvard University Press, 1996); Deborah Sawyer, *Women and Religion in the First Christian Centuries* (London: Routledge, 1996); Bernadette J. Brooton, *Love Between Women: Early Christian Responses to Female Homoeroticism* (Chicago: University of Chicago Press, 1996). There is a special forum that discusses Brooten's book, with a response by the author, in *GLQ* 4(4) (1998): 559–630. See also Martti Nissinen, *Homoeroticism in the Biblical World: A Historical Perspective*, trans. Kirsi Stjerna (Minneapolis: Augsburg Fortress, 2004). Ross Kraemer, *Maenads* (note 4 to Chapter 1; see "Notes") is a wonderful collection of original sources in translation about women and religion in the ancient world, including pagan, Jewish, and Christian material.

A brief but solid survey of Christian ideas about sexual ethics, arranged by topic, is Mark D. Jordan, *The Ethics of Sex* (New York: Wiley-Blackwell, 2002). Other studies that cover broad time frames include Frank Bottomley, *Attitudes to the Body in Western Christendom* (London: Lepus Books, 1979) and Margaret R. Miles, *Carnal Knowing: Female Nakedness and Religious Meaning in the Christian West* (Boston: Beacon Press, 1989). For more specialized research on the early church, see Robin Scroggs, *The New Testament and Homosexuality* (Philadelphia: Fortress Press, 1983); Peter Brown, *The Body and Society: Men, Women and Sexual Renunciation in Early Christianity* (New York: Columbia University Press, 1988); Wayne A. Meeks, *The Origins of Christian Morality: The First Two Centuries* (New Haven, Conn.: Yale University Press, 1994); Mathew Kuefler, *The Manly Eunuch: Masculinity, Gender Ambiguity, and Christian Ideology in Late Antiquity* (Chicago: University of Chicago Press, 2001); Virginia Burrus, *The Sex Lives of Saints: An Erotics of Ancient Hagiography* (Philadelphia: University of Pennsylvania Press, 2004).

For the ideas and influence of Augustine, see: Margaret R. Miles, *Augustine on the Body*, American Academy of Religion Dissertation Series, no. 31 (Missoula, Mont.: Scholars Press, 1979) and her more recent article cited in note 7; Kari Elisabeth Børresen, *Subordination and Equivalence: The Nature and Role of Women in Augustine and Thomas Aquinas* (Washington, DC: University Press of America, 1981); Elaine Pagels, *Adam, Eve, and the Serpent* (New York: Random House, 1988); Erin Sawyer, "Celibate Pleasures: Masculinity, Desire, and Asceticism in Augustine," *Journal of the History of Sexuality* 6 (July 1995): 1–29. Elizabeth A. Clark, *St. Augustine on Marriage and Sexuality* (Washington, DC Catholic University of America Press, 1996) contains selections from Augustine's writings and a long introduction by Clark.

Ancient and medieval church attitudes toward contraception have been covered thoroughly in John T. Noonan, *Contraception: A History of Its Treatment by the Catholic Theologians and Canonists* (New York: New American Library, 1965), which also covers the period up to 1965. See also John M. Riddle, *Contraception and Abortion from the Ancient World to the Renaissance* (Cambridge, Mass.: Harvard University Press, 1992) and Angus McLaren, *A History of Contraception from Antiquity to the Present Day* (London: Basil Blackwell, 1990), which come to very different conclusions about the effectiveness of contraceptive techniques before the eighteenth century.

On women's actions and ideas about gender in early Christianity, see Joyce Salisbury, *Church Fathers, Independent Virgins* (New York: Verso, 1991); JoAnn McNamara, *A New Song: Celibate Women in the First Three Christian Centuries* (New York: Haworth Press, 1983); Elizabeth Clark, *Ascetic Piety and Women's Faith* (Lewiston, N.Y.: Edwin Mellen, 1988); David M. Scholer, ed., *Women in Early Christianity* (New York: Garland Press, 1993).

For medieval sexuality, a good place to start for a very brief overview is: Jacqueline Murray, "Historicizing Sex, Sexualizing History," in *Writing Medieval History*, edited by Nancy Partner (London: Hodder Arnold, 2005), 133–52. A helpful introduction, designed for students, is Ruth Mazo Karras, *Sexuality in Medieval Europe: Doing Unto Others* (New York: Routledge, 2005). For bibliographical suggestions arranged by topic see Joyce E. Salisbury, *Medieval Sexuality: A Research Guide* (New York: Garland, 1990) and Vern L. Bullough and James A. Brundage, *Handbook of Medieval Sexuality* (New York: Garland, 1996). Conor McCarthy, ed., *Love, Sex and Marriage in the Middle Ages: A Sourcebook* (London: Routledge, 2004) and Martha Brozyna, ed., *Gender and Sexuality in the Middle Ages: A Medieval Source Documents Reader* (Jefferson, N.C.: McFarland & Company, 2005) provide primary source material. Several good general essay collections are: Vern L. Bullough and James A. Brundage, eds, *Sexual Practices and the Medieval Church* (Buffalo, N.Y.: Prometheus Books, 1982); Joyce Salisbury, ed., *Sex in the Middle Ages: A Book of Essays* (New York: Garland, 1991); Karma Lochrie, Peggy McCracken, and James A. Schulz, eds, *Constructing Medieval Sexuality* (Minneapolis: University of Minnesota Press, 1996); Lisa M. Bitel and Felice Lifshitz, eds, *Gender and Christianity in Medieval Europe: New Perspectives* (Philadelphia: University of Pennsylvania Press, 2008). See also the collections by Murray/Eisenbichler and Fradenburg/Freccero noted in the Introduction.

For the early Middle Ages, see Suzanne Wemple, *Women in Frankish Society: Marriage and the Cloister, 500 to 900* (Philadelphia: University of Pennsylvania Press, 1981); Pierre Payer, *Sex and the Penitentials: The Development of a Sexual Code, 550–1150* (Toronto: University of Toronto Press, 1984); Mary Condren, *The Serpent and the Goddess: Women, Religion and Power in Celtic Ireland* (San Franciso: Harper and Row, 1989); Paul Veyne, ed., *A History of Private Life I: From Pagan Rome to Byzantium*, trans. Arthur Goldhammer (Cambridge, Mass.: Harvard University Press, 1987); Clare A. Lees, "Engendering Religious Desire: Sex, Knowledge, and Christian Identity in Anglo-Saxon England," *Journal of Medieval and Early Modern Studies* 27 (Winter 1997): 32–45; Jane Tibbetts Schulenburg, *Forgetful of their Sex; Female Sanctity and Society, ca. 500–1100* (Chicago: University of Chicago Press, 1998); Lisa M. Bitel, *Women in Early Medieval Europe* (Cambridge: Cambridge University Press, 2002). Leslie Brubaker and Julia M. H. Smith, eds, *Gender in the Early Medieval World: East and West, 300–900* (Cambridge: Cambridge University Press, 2004) includes essays on Byzantium and Islam as well as western Europe.

The most important work regarding canon law and sex is James A. Brundage, *Law, Sex, and Christian Society in Medieval Europe* (Chicago: University of Chicago, 1987). Brundage has also written a concise history of the development of canon law, *Medieval Canon Law* (London: Longman, 1995) and many of his most important articles have been collected in *Sex, Law and Marriage in the Middle Ages* (London: Variorum, 1993). On canon law and marriage, see Charles J. Reid, *Power Over the Body, Equality in the Family: Rights and Domestic Relations in Medieval Canon Law* (Grand Rapids, Mich.: Eerdmans, 2004). For detailed analysis of the canonists on issues of women's enclosure and religious life, see Elizabeth Makowski, *Canon Law and Cloistered Women:* Periculoso *and Its Commentators 1298–1545* (Washington, DC: Catholic University of America Press, 1997) and her *A Pernicious Sort of Woman: Quasi-Religious Women and Canon Lawyers in the Later Middle Ages* (Washington, DC: Catholic University of America Press, 2005).

On the actual workings of church courts, see Richard Helmholz, *Marriage Litigation in Medieval England* (Cambridge: Cambridge University Press, 1974); Richard M. Wunderli, *London Church Courts and Society on the Eve of the Reformation* (Cambridge, Mass.: Harvard University Press, 1981); Michael M. Sheehan, *Marriage, Family and Law in Medieval Europe: Collected Studies*, ed. James K. Farge (Toronto: University of Toronto Press, 1996); Sara M. Butler, "'I Will Never Consent to be Wedded with You!': Coerced Marriage in the Courts of Medieval England," *Canadian Journal of History/Annales Canadiennes d'Histoire* 39(2) (2004): 247–70; Sara M. Butler, "The Law as a Weapon in Marital Disputes: Evidence from the Late Medieval Court of Chancery, 1424–1529," *Journal of British Studies* 43(3) (July 2004): 291–316; P.J.P. Goldberg, "Gender and Matrimonial Litigation in the Church Courts in the Later Middle Ages: The Evidence of the Court of York," *Gender & History* 19(1) (April 2007): 43–59; Cordelia Beattie, "'Living as a Single Person': Marital Status, Performance and the Law in Late Medieval England," *Women's History Review* 17(3) (July 2008): 327–40. Sheehan and others have addressed issues regarding the relationship between canon law and medieval European marital patterns in "Legal Systems and Family Systems: Jack Goody Revisited," in *Continuity and Change* 6(3) (1991): 293–364. Their essays generally criticize a widely debated thesis put forward by the anthropologist Jack Goody in *The Development of the Family and Marriage in Europe* (Cambridge: Cambridge University Press, 1983), which proposes that the church encouraged a greater circle of prohibited marriage partners in order to break apart large landed families who had often intermarried, thus making them more likely to give their land and wealth to the church.

On attitudes toward sexuality, see Pierre Payer, *The Bridling of Desire: Views of Sex in the Later Middle Ages* (Toronto: University of Toronto Press, 1993); John Baldwin, *The Language of Sex: Five Voices from Northern France around 1200* (Chicago: University of Chicago Press, 1994); Cindy L. Carlson and Angela Jane Weisl, eds, *Constructions of Widowhood and Virginity in the Middle Ages* (London: Palgrave Macmillan, 1998); Sarah Salih, *Versions of Virginity in Late Medieval England* (Woodbridge, Suffolk, UK: D.S. Brewer, 2001).

On marriage, see Christopher N.L. Brooke, *The Medieval Idea of Marriage* (Oxford: Clarendon Press, 1994); Dyan Eliott, *Spiritual Marriage: Sexual Abstinence in Medieval Wedlock* (Princeton: Princeton University Press, 1993); George Duby, *Love and Marriage in the Middle Ages*, trans. Jane Dunnett (Chicago: University of Chicago Press, 1994); A.J. Finch, "Sexual Relations and Marriage in Later Medieval Normandy," *The Journal of Ecclesiastical History* 47 (April 1996): 236–56; Constance M. Rousseau and Joel T. Rosenthal, eds, *Women, Marriage, and Family in Medieval Christendom: Essays in Memory of Michael M. Sheehan, C.S.B.*, (Kalamazoo, Mich.: Medieval Institute Publications, 1998); Irven M. Resnick, "Marriage in Medieval Culture: Consent Theory and the Case of Joseph and Mary," *Church History* 69(2) (June 2000): 350–71; Anthony F. D'Elia, *The Renaissance of Marriage in Fifteenth-Century Italy* (Cambridge, Mass.: Harvard University Press, 2004); D.L. d'Avray, *Medieval Marriage: Symbolism and Society* (Oxford: Oxford University Press, 2005); Lindsay Bryan, "Marriage and Morals in the Fourteenth Century: The Evidence of Bishop Hamo's Register," *English Historical Review* 121(491) (2006): 467–86; Sara Butler, "Runaway Wives: Husband Desertion in Medieval England," *Journal of Social History* 40(2) (Winter 2006): 337–59; Catherine Clark, "Purgatory, Punishment, and the Discourse of Holy Widowhood in the High and Later Middle Ages," *Journal of the History of Sexuality* 16(2) (May 2007): 169–203; Philip L. Reynold and John Witte Jr., eds, *To Have and to Hold: Marrying and its Documentation in Western Christendom, 400–1600* (Cambridge: Cambridge University Press, 2007).

The impact of the reforms of the High Middle Ages on such issues as clerical sexuality have been analyzed in: Michael Frassetto, ed., *Medieval Purity and Piety: Essays on Medieval Clerical Celibacy and Religious Reform* (New York: Garland, 1998); Jennifer D. Thibodeaux, "Man of the Church, or Man of the Village? Gender and the Parish Clergy in Medieval Normandy," *Gender & History* 18(2) (August 2006): 380–99; Laura Wertheimer, "Children of Disorder: Clerical Parentage, Illegitimacy, and Reform in the Middle Ages," *Journal of the History of Sexuality* 15(3) (2006): 382–407.

Christian attitudes toward same-sex relations in the ancient and medieval periods have been hotly debated since the publication of John Boswell's *Christianity, Social Tolerance and Homosexuality* (note 8) in 1981, which argued that neither the Bible nor the early church was as hostile to same-sex attraction as had been assumed. Mathew Kuefler, ed., *The Boswell Thesis: Essays on Christianity, Social Tolerance, and Homosexuality* (Chicago: University of Chicago Press, 2006), includes essays that build on Boswell's work and a discussion of the book's impact. Boswell's second book on the topic, *Same-Sex Unions in Pre-Modern Europe* (New York: Villard Books, 1994) argued that there were Christian ceremonies blessing same-sex unions in the eastern Church. This work was highly criticized, although very recently some scholars have found other suggestions of such ceremonies in both Judaism and Christianity. See Mark D. Jordan, ed., *Authorizing Marriage?: Canon, Tradition, and Critique in the Blessing of Same-Sex Unions* (Princeton, N.J.: Princeton University Press, 2006).

Studies of same-sex relations in the Middle Ages all touch on the church to some degree. See: Barisa Krekic, "'Abominandum crimen': Punishment of Homosexuals in Renaissance Dubrovnik," *Viator* 18 (1987): 337–45; Michael Rocke, *Friendly Affection, Nefarious Vices: Homosexuality, Male Culture and the Policing of Sex in Renaissance Florence* (Oxford: Oxford University Press, 1995); Anne Gilmour-Bryson, "Sodomy and the Knights Templar," *Journal of the History of Sexuality* 7(2) (1996): 151–83; Mark D. Jordan, *The Invention of Sodomy in Christian Theology* (Chicago: University of Chicago Press, 1997); Glenn Burger and Steven F. Kruger, eds, *Queering the Middle Ages* (Minneapolis: University of Minnesota Press, 2001); Francesca Canadé Sautman and Pamela Sheingorn, eds, *Same Sex Love and Desire among Women in the Middle Ages* (New York: Palgrave, 2001).

Karma Lochrie, *Covert Operations: The Medieval Uses of Secrecy* (Philadelphia: University of Pennsylvania Press, 1999) includes discussion of confession, marriage, and the discourses of sodomy and her *Heterosyncrasies: Female Sexuality When Normal Wasn't* (Minneapolis: University of Minnesota Press, 2005) argues that medieval categorization of sexuality was more diverse than modern scholars have recognized; Carolyn Dinshaw, *Getting Medieval: Sexuality and Communities, Pre- and Postmodern* (Durham, N.C.: Duke University Press, 1999) investigates how certain sexual practices were normalized and others proscribed in late medieval England; Glenn Burger, *Chaucer's Queer Nation* (Minneapolis: University of Minnesota Press, 2003) looks at the way Chaucer developed new ideas of sexual and communal identity; all of these use queer theory in their analyses.

The new history of medieval masculinity often highlights distinctions and conflicts between clerical and lay ideas of what made a man. See: Clare Lees, ed., *Medieval Masculinities: Regarding Men in the Middle Ages* (Minneapolis: University of Minnesota Press, 1994); Jeffrey Jerome Cohen and Bonnie Wheeler, eds, *Becoming Male in the Middle Ages* (New York: Garland, 1997);

Jacqueline Murray, ed., *Conflicted Identities and Multiple Masculinities: Men in the Medieval West* (New York: Garland, 1999); Ruth Karras, *From Boys to Men: Formations of Masculinity in Late Medieval Europe* (Philadelphia: University of Pennsylvania Press, 2002); Katherine Allen Smith, "Saints in Shining Armor: Martial Asceticism and Masculine Models of Sanctity, ca. 1050–1250," *Speculum* 83(3) (July 2008): 572–602.

On sexual relations between Christians and non-Christians, see James Brundage, "Intermarriage between Christians and Jews in Medieval Canon Law," *Jewish History* 3 (1988): 25–40 and "Prostitution, Miscegenation and Sexual Purity in the First Crusade," in P. Edbury, ed., *Crusade and Settlement* (Cardiff: University College Cardiff Press, 1985), 57–65; Mark Meyerson, *The Muslims of Valencia in the Age of Fernando and Isabel: Between Coexistance and Crusade* (Berkeley: University of California Press, 1991), 221–23, 250–51; David Nirenberg, "Conversion, Sex" (note 1) and *Communities of Violence* (note 12).

On women who sold sex, see: Leah Lydia Otis, *Prostitution in Medieval Society: The History of an Urban Institution in Languedoc* (Chicago: University of Chicago Press, 1985); Jacques Rossiaud, *Medieval Prostitution,* trans. Lydia G. Cochrane (Oxford: Basil Blackwell, 1988); Ruth Mazo Karras, *Common Women: Prostitution and Sexuality in Medieval England* (New York: Oxford University Press, 1996) and her "Prostitution and the Question of Sexual Identity in Medieval Europe," *Journal of Women's History* 11(2) (Summer 1999): 159–98; Joelle Rollo-Koster, "From Prostitutes to Brides of Christ: The Avignonese Repenties in the Late Middle Ages," *Journal of Medieval and Early Modern Studies* 32(1) (Winter 2002): 109–44. For Muslim prostitution in Christian Spain, see Mark D. Meyerson, "Prostitution of Muslim Women in the Kingdom of Valencia: Religious and Sexual Discrimination in a Medieval Plural Society," in M. Chiat and Katherine Reyerson, eds, *The Medieval Mediterranean: Cross-Cultural Contacts* (St. Cloud, Minn.: North Star Press of St. Cloud, 1988), 87–96.

Miri Rubin, *Mother of God: A History of the Virgin Mary* (New Haven, Conn.: Yale University Press, 2009), provides an excellent introduction to the changing veneration of Mary. On Mary in medieval culture, see Donna Spivey Ellington, "Impassioned Mother or Passive Icon: The Virgin's Role in Late Medieval and Early Modern Passion Sermons," *Renaissance Quarterly* 48 (Summer 1995): 227–61; Barbara Sella, "Northern Italian Confraternities and the Immaculate Conception in the Fourteenth Century," *The Journal of Ecclesiastical History* 49(4) (October 1998): 599–619; Anne L. Clark, "The Priesthood of the Virgin Mary: Gender Trouble in the Twelfth Century," *Journal of Feminist Studies in Religion* 18(1) (Spring 2002): 5–24. On Mary Magdalene, see Theresa Coletti, *Mary Magdalene and the Drama of Saints: Theater, Gender, and Religion in Late Medieval England* (Philadelphia: University of Pennsylvania, 2004).

Two excellent books that focus on late medieval developments are: Shannon McSheffrey, *Marriage, Sex and Civic Culture in Late Medieval London* (Philadelphia: University of Pennsylvania Press, 2006) and Katherine French, *The Good Women of the Parish: Gender and Religion After the Black Death* (Philadelphia: University of Pennsylvania Press, 2007).

Studies that relate medieval restrictions of sexuality to other types of marginalization include: R.I. Moore, *The Formation of a Persecuting Society: Power and Deviance in Western Europe, 950–1250* (London: Basil Blackwell, 1987); Jeffrey Richards, *Sex, Dissidence and Damnation: Minority Groups in the Middle Ages* (London: Routledge, 1990); Barbara Hanawalt, ed., *Of Good and Ill Repute: Gender and Social Control in Medieval England* (Oxford: Oxford University Press, 1998); Jeffrey Jerome Cohen, *Medieval Identity Machines* (Minneapolis: University of Minnesota Press, 2003); Sharon Farmer and Carol Braun Pasternak, eds, *Gender and Difference in the Middle Ages* (Minneapolis: University of Minnesota Press, 2003); Barbara Hanawalt and Anna A. Grotans, eds, *Living Dangerously: On the Margins in Medieval and Early Modern Europe* (Notre Dame, Ind.: University of Notre Dame Press, 2007).

For studies of related issues that have implications for the control of sexuality in western Europe, see: Georges Duby, ed., *A History of Private Life: II Revelations of the Medieval World*, trans. Arthur Goldhammer (Cambridge, Mass.: Harvard University Press, 1988); Joan Cadden, *Meanings of Sex Differences in the Middle Ages: Medicine, Science, and Culture* (Cambridge: Cambridge University Press, 1993); Caroline Walker Bynum, *Jesus as Mother: Studies in the Spirituality of the High Middle Ages* (Berkeley: University of California Press, 1982) and *Fragmentation and Redemption: Essays on Gender and the Human Body in Medieval Religion* (New York: Zone Books, 1991); Thomas N. Tentler, *Sin and Confession on the Eve of the Reformation* (Princeton: Princeton University Press, 1977); JoAnn Kay McNamara, *Sisters in Arms: Catholic Nuns Through Two Millenia* (Cambridge, Mass.: Harvard University Press, 1996).

Sexuality in Byzantium and in Eastern Orthodoxy has been studied far less than that in western Europe. Works in English include: Eve Levin, *Sex and Society in the World of the Orthodox Slavs, 900–1700* (Ithaca, N.Y.: Cornell University Press, 1989) and "Sexual Vocabulary in Medieval Russia," in Jane T. Costlow, Stephanie Sandler, and Judith Vowles, eds, *Sexuality and the Body in Russian Culture* (Stanford: Stanford University Press, 1993), 41–52; Angeliki E. Laiou, *Gender, Society, and Economic Life in Byzantium* (London: Variorum, 1992) and *Consent and Coercion to Sex and Marriage in Ancient and Medieval Societies* (Washington, DC: Dumbarton Oaks Resarch Library, 1993); Liz James, ed., *Women, Men and Eunuchs: Gender in Byzantium* (London: Routledge, 1997); Marie Theres Fögen, "Unto the Pure all Things are Pure: The Byzantine Canonist Zonaras on Nocturnal Pollution," in *Obscenity: Social Control and Artistic*

Creation in the European Middle Ages, edited by Jan M. Ziolkowski (Leiden: Brill, 1998); Liz James, ed., *Desire and Denial in Byzantium* (Aldershot: Ashgate, 1999). Kathryn M. Ringrose, *The Perfect Servant: Eunuchs and the Social Construction of Gender in Byzantium* (Chicago: University of Chicago Press, 2003) looks at the role of eunuchs in the imperial court and the church, and argues that they were a distinct third gender because they lived outside the normal patterns of procreation. A survey of Russian women's history that includes discussion of sexual issues is Natalia Pushkareva, *Women in Russian History: From the Tenth to the Twentieth Century,* trans. Eve Levin (Armonk, N.Y.: M.E. Sharpe, 1997).

Work in English on the history of Christianity outside of Europe in the millennium from 500 to 1500 is beginning to appear, but this focuses primarily on theological and political issues and contains very little discussion of sexuality or gender. For a recent overview, see Philip Jenkins, *The Lost History of Christianity: The Thousand-Year Golden Age of the Church in the Middle East, Africa, and Asia – and How It Died* (New York: Harper One, 2009). More focused studies include: Elizabeth Isichei, *A History of Christianity in Africa: From Antiquity to the Present* (Grand Rapids, Mich.: Eerdmans, 1995); Otto Friedrich August Meinardus, *Two Thousand Years of Coptic Christianity* (Cairo: American University in Cairo Press, 2002); Christoph Baumer, *The Church of the East: An Illustrated History of Assyrian Christianity* (London: Tauris, 2003); Samuel Hugh Moffett, *A History of Christianity in Asia: Beginnings to 1500* (New York: Orbis Books, 1998).

PROTESTANT EUROPE

DURING THE LATER MIDDLE AGES, a number of groups and individuals increasingly criticized many aspects of western Christianity, including doctrines they judged to have no Biblical basis, institutions such as the papacy or church courts, the tax collection methods and fiscal policies of the church, the ways in which priests and higher officials were chosen, and the worldliness and morals of priests, monks, nuns, bishops, and the pope. Various measures were suggested to reform institutions, improve clerical education and behavior, and even alter basic doctrines, and occasionally these reform efforts were successful on a local level; in several instances reform movements led to dissident groups breaking with the Roman church.

All of this dissatisfaction did not lead to dramatic changes in the structure of western Christianity, however, until about 1520, when the criticisms of Martin Luther, a professor of theology at the German university of Wittenberg, sparked a widespread revolt against the Roman church. Luther and other thinkers in German-speaking Europe, such as Ulrich Zwingli at Zurich in Switzerland, developed a different understanding of essential Christian doctrines. This understanding is often codified as "faith alone, grace alone, Scripture alone." For them, salvation and justification come through faith, not good works, although true faith leads to love and to the active expression of faith in helping others. Faith is a free gift of God's grace, not the result of human effort. God's word is revealed only in Scripture, not in the traditions of the church, although earlier decisions and written works could be used as aids to interpret Scripture. In addition, they taught that both popes and church councils had abused their power and made mistakes, and that there should be no distinction between clergy and lay people (an idea often described as "the priesthood of believers.")

These ideas were attractive to individuals of many different types, but both Luther and Zwingli recognized that if reforms were going to be permanent, political authorities as well as concerned individuals and religious leaders would have to accept them. They worked closely with political leaders, and in the 1520s many of the cities and states of the Holy Roman Empire – what is now Germany – broke with the Roman church and established their own local churches. These churches came to be labeled "Protestant" after a 1529 document issued by princes who followed Luther protesting an order to give up their religious innovations. Religious war between Catholics and Protestants flared up in Germany for several decades, ended by the uneasy Peace of Augsburg in 1555 that allowed the ruler of each of the hundreds of different states in the Empire to decide whether that state would be Catholic or Protestant.

Protestant ideas spread beyond Germany, and by the 1530s much of northern Europe, including England and the Scandinavian countries, had broken with Catholicism. The Reformation in England initially came about because of personal and dynastic issues involving King Henry VIII, but eventually England adopted doctrines and institutions that were similar to those of Lutheran Germany and Scandinavia. In the 1530s, the ideas of John Calvin, the Protestant reformer of Geneva in Switzerland, began to spread to France and eastern Europe, and significant Protestant minorities developed in France, the Netherlands, Hungary, and Poland. Calvin's ideas also influenced John Knox, the reformer of Scotland, and Scotland adopted a Calvinist version of Protestantism in the 1550s, which Scottish settlers took to Ireland later in the century. Calvinist ideas were one of the influences on those in England who saw the English Protestant church as still too close to Catholicism. Called "Puritans" because they wanted to "purify" the English church of what they saw as vestiges of Catholicism, this group grew increasingly powerful in the late sixteenth century and in the seventeenth overthrew the English monarchy. Calvinist Protestants battled Catholics in many parts of continental Europe, and religion was an important factor in the Thirty Years' War which ultimately involved almost every state in Europe. Among its various provisions, the 1648 Peace of Westphalia, which ended the war, attempted to freeze the religious boundaries of the Holy Roman Empire, declaring certain states Catholic, others Evangelical (Lutheran Protestant), and others Reformed (Calvinist Protestant).

The Protestant Reformation is more than the story of Luther and Calvin, for a great many other individuals and groups also developed their own versions of Christianity, some of which included radical doctrines such as communal ownership of property or a rejection of infant baptism. Both Catholics and more conservative Lutherans and Calvinists opposed these radicals and at times suppressed and persecuted them, cooperating with secular authorities, who saw them as a threat to political and social order.

The Protestant Reformation was not simply a theological movement, however, but also one that involved political, economic, and social issues. Many of the leaders who accepted Lutheran or Calvinist teachings did so in part out of desires to end the economic and political power of the papacy in their territories, or, in Germany, to oppose the power of the Holy Roman Emperor, who remained a Catholic. Leaders who rejected Catholicism generally took over church lands and closed monasteries and convents, adding to their economic power. Peasants in Germany in the 1520s attached Lutheran demands for the local election of clergy and preaching the "pure Gospel" to their economic grievances, and were bitter when Luther opposed them in the subsequent Peasants' War. Nobles in France who accepted Calvinism saw this as a way to combat the power of the monarchy as well as the papacy, and in England Henry VIII clearly recognized that a confiscation of church property would swell the royal treasury.

Along with power and money, sex was an integral part of the Protestant Reformation from its beginning. One of Luther's earliest treatises attacked the value of vows of celibacy, and argued that marriage was the best Christian life; Luther followed his words by deeds and in 1525 married a nun who had fled her convent, Katherine von Bora. Although they denied that good works would lead to salvation, both Zwingli and Calvin regarded moral order in households and communities as important, and established special courts to handle cases concerning marriage and morals. The motto of one of these courts was "discipline is the sinews of the church," and they came to have wide powers.[1] Many of the radical groups developed distinctive ideas of the proper sexual life for their members, and punished those who did not follow their rules with complete social ostracization, termed shunning or banning. Since Protestant theology expected good works as the fruit of saving faith, one's sexual activities – and those of one's neighbors – continued to be important in God's eyes, and order and morality were a mark of divine favor.

In a number of matters regarding sexuality, Protestants did not break sharply with medieval tradition. They differed little from Catholics in regard to basic concepts such as the roots and proper consequences of gender differences, or the differences between "natural" and "unnatural" sexual practices. Though Luther flamboyantly rejected canon law – publicly burning canon law books before the students of the University of Wittenberg at one point – it eventually formed the legal basis of much Protestant law regarding marriage and sex. Breaking with tradition in terms of the power of the papacy or the meaning of key rituals turned out to be easier than breaking with tradition in terms of sexual and gender relations. Protestants also did not reject, and in some cases strengthened, the intellectual authority of early Church Fathers such as Augustine, who had been most influential in establishing hostility to or ambivalence about sexuality in western Christianity. Both Protestants and Catholics tried and executed thousands of people, mostly women, for witchcraft, a tragedy resulting in part from notions of human and demonic sexuality shared by most people.

This Protestant continuity with medieval Catholicism, combined with the actions of the Catholic Church after the Protestant Reformation, has led some scholars of sex in post-Reformation Europe to emphasize the similarities rather than differences among Christian denominations. The processes of social disciplining and confessionalization discussed in the Introduction included Catholic, Lutheran, Anglican, and Calvinist authorities, who generally worked with secular political authorities in an attempt to teach people the basics of their version of Christianity and get them to live a pious and moral life.

The recent scholarly emphasis on the similarities between Protestants and Catholics in the twin processes of social disciplining and confessional-ization is in part a reaction against older scholarship that highlighted denominational differences. It is also a result of the many centuries since the Reformation, for in hindsight long-term continuities become more visible. Despite similarities and continuities between Protestants and Catholics, however, and also despite wide variety among Protestants in regard to certain aspects of sexuality, Protestant ideas and institutions did differ from those of Catholic and Orthodox Europe. This chapter thus looks only at Protestant Europe – that is, at England, Scotland, and Scandinavia, along with parts of Germany, Switzerland, France, and the Low Countries. Changes within Catholicism in regard to sexuality after the Protestant Reformation were to some degree a response to Protestantism, so Catholicism, along with Orthodoxy (which saw less dramatic change in this period as it did not experience a Reformation) is the focus of the following chapter.

Protestant ideas

The Protestant Reformation is no longer told as the story of Martin Luther standing alone against the world, but Luther's ideas are still central to an understanding of basic Protestant concepts, because his writings were so influential and voluminous. This is particularly true for his ideas about sexuality, for Luther wrote and spoke about sex and related issues such as marriage and women continually throughout his long career. Because he said so much, however, his words often appear contradictory, and there is sharp debate among scholars about how to interpret them.

About some things there is little disagreement. Luther was faithful to Augustine's idea of the link between original sin and sexual desire, but saw desire as so powerful that the truly chaste life was impossible for all but a handful of individuals. Thus the best Christian life was not one that fruitlessly attempted ascetic celibacy, but one in which sexual activity was channeled into marriage. Vows of celibacy for monks, nuns, and priests should be rendered void, and monasteries and convents should be closed or much reduced in size. A few reformers, such as Andreas von Karlstadt, argued that the clergy should be compelled to marry, though Luther never went this far. Luther understood the sacraments as signs of God's promise of the forgiveness of sins, and regarded baptism and the Eucharist as the only true sacraments. Marriage was thus not a sacrament, but it was the ideal state for almost everyone. Marriage was ordained by God in Paradise when he brought Eve to Adam, making it the first "estate" – what we might term social institution – created by God. Restrictions on marriage that had developed in the Middle Ages should be done away with, and everyone should marry, the sooner after puberty the better.

Because sexual desire was natural and created by God, it was a central part of marriage, and marriages in which it could not be satisfied – such as those to impotent persons – were not truly marriages. The centrality of sex to marriage led Luther to advocate divorce in the case of impotence, adultery, desertion, absolute incompatibility, or the refusal of a spouse to have sex; reconciliation was preferable both for social stability and because Christians should be willing to forgive, but if this could not be effected, the innocent party should be granted a divorce with the right to remarry. An even better solution might be bigamy, which Luther recommended to resolve the marital difficulties of both King Henry VIII of England and Philipp of Hesse, a prominent Protestant nobleman. Luther's advocacy of bigamy grew out of his harsh condemnation of all sex outside of marriage, including prostitution, one of the few issues on which he explicitly broke with Augustine. (Many people were scandalized by this advocacy, and actual bigamists were harshly punished throughout Europe.)

Those who view Luther in a positive light point out that his championing of marriage and denial of the value of celibacy raised the status of married people – the vast majority of the population – and made them no longer second-class Christians. For Luther, marital sex was a positive good in itself; sex increased affection between spouses, and promoted harmony in domestic life. It should not be governed by the church calendar: "although Christian married folk should not permit themselves to be governed by their bodies in the passion of lust . . . neither should [they] pay attention to holy days or work days, or other physical considerations."[2] Marital sex led to bearing children, which Luther saw as women's God-given vocation and a "precious and godly task." He advised those who cared for women in childbirth to "comfort and strengthen the woman who is in labor" by reminding her "that this work of yours [giving birth] is pleasing to God. Bring that child forth, and do it with all your might!"[3] Fatherhood was also pleasing to God: "Now you tell me, when a father goes ahead and washes diapers or performs some other mean task for his child, and someone ridicules him as an effeminate fool – though that father is acting in Christian faith – which of the two is most keenly ridiculing the other? God, with all His angels and creatures, is smiling."[4]

Those who view Luther in a negative light point out that his praise of childbearing as a godly vocation was accompanied by apparent callousness; those caring for women in labor were also to say: "If you die in the process, so pass on over, good for you! For you actually die in a noble work and in obedience to God."[5] Motherhood was also women's *only* vocation, while fatherhood was not a vocation, but simply one of many tasks expected of godly men. (The word "vocation" is based on the Latin word *vocare*, meaning call, and in the sixteenth century meant what God has called one to be; God called men to preach, teach, govern, or work, in the writings of Protestant thinkers, but not to be fathers.) Luther's emphasis on marriage may also have contributed to the suspicion of unmarried persons – always a significant minority in Europe – and particularly of unmarried women, whom he and many other sixteenth-century commentators saw as tempting men to give in to sexual desire:

> For girls, too, are aware of this evil [lust] and if they spend time in the company of young men, they turn the hearts of these young men in various directions to entice them to love, especially if the youths are outstanding because of their good looks and strength of body. Therefore it is often more difficult for the latter to withstand such enticements than to resist their own lusts.[6]

Luther's ideas were repeated and enhanced by later Protestant writers, and formed the basis of marriage ordinances passed by almost all Protestant states. Although marriage was not a sacrament, it was the cornerstone of society, the institution on which all other institutions were based. As such, it was not to be entered into lightly. Most Protestant thinkers regarded the consent of parents and a public ceremony as required for a valid marriage, and broke with Catholic doctrine that the consent of the parties alone could be sufficient; these requirements were written into law. Weddings themselves were to be celebrated solemnly and reverently, without wild drinking or jokes and rituals that celebrated and satirized the sexual aspects of marriage. Wedding sermons should stress the duties of the spouses toward one another and toward God.

Though Luther himself blessed several wedding beds, this practice was generally discouraged by Protestants, as were "superstitious" practices involving fertility, such as throwing grain or untying knots. (Tying knots was a common magical practice thought to create impotence in men.) Joint prayer should replace friendly toasting and singing as the final activity of the spouses before entering the marriage bed for the first time.

After the wedding, the couple were to settle into quiet domesticity, with the husband the clear household head, exercising authority over his wife, children, and servants. In this role as the head of society's smallest unit of government (later Puritan Protestants termed the household the "little commonwealth"), men were guided by a flood of literature describing the ideal male head of household (termed in German *Hausväterliteratur*) that poured from the pens of Protestant pastors. In their sermons and published works, those pastors also spoke often about reproduction, for "fertility is God's blessing and children are God's gifts," enjoined in the creation story, when God's first words to Adam and Eve were "be fruitful and multiply." Mothers, wrote a Prussian church ordinance from 1568, are "the workshop and tool of our lord God since the first creation of the world." As had late medieval preachers, Lutheran pastors often encouraged women to think of their sufferings as similar to those of Christ, and explicitly referred to labor pains as women's "cross." "When a woman is in labor," wrote the Lutheran pastor Thomas Günther in 1546, "she provides faithful Christians with a public sermon on the cross."[7] Thomas Bentley's 1582 *The Monument of Matrones*, the first English prayer book specifically directed at women, also connects the pains of childbirth with those of Christ. It mentions Eve more than it does the Virgin Mary, reflecting a common Protestant view that women should call on Christ rather than on the Virgin Mary for support during childbirth or other tribulations. Mary was not to be an intercessor, but she still provided an example of faith, obedience, purity, and proper conduct in women. She was "home-loving and secluded," commented the Lutheran pastor Caspar Huberinus, "for the angel came inside [the house] to her, not in the streets or at a dance."[8]

In most of his teachings on sexuality and marriage, Calvin largely agreed with Luther. He also rejected the sacramentality of marriage, yet praised its God-given nature. Calvin increasingly came to regard marriage as a covenant, however, a sacred contract like that between God and the church. Thus he insisted that properly contracted engagements be carried through to marriage even if the couple was incompatible, a stricter position than that held by canon law. He also allowed divorce for adultery and desertion (which he saw as a type of adultery), both of which involved one party breaking the covenant, though he advocated attempts at reconciliation first. Like Luther, he based his acceptance of divorce on the words of Jesus in Matthew (19:9 and 4:26),

"Every one who divorces his wife, except on the ground of adultery, makes her an adultress." (His legal logic appears to have trumped common sense here, for fiancés forced to marry seem particularly likely to later seek other partners or leave.)

Calvin was more guarded than Luther on the virtue of marital sex; married persons should "be recalled to measure and modesty so as not to wallow in extreme lewdness," an idea that later English Puritans referred to as "matrimonial chastity."[9] The Puritan writer Robert Cleaver warned of the consequences of such behavior:

> Christians therefore must know that when men and women raging with boiling lust meet together as brute beasts, having no other respect than to satisfy their carnal concupiscence, when they make no conscience to sanctify the marital bed with prayer, when they have no care to increase the church of Christ . . . it is the just judgment of God to send them either monsters or fools, or else . . . most wicked, graceless and profane persons.[10]

As Cleaver makes clear, procreation was not the only reason for marital sex, but in no case should partners practice active contraception; Calvin agreed, terming *coitus interruptus* "monstrous" in his commentary on Genesis. He also stringently opposed all extramarital sex, though his language in regard to prostitution is milder than Luther's; while Luther termed prostitutes "stinking . . . tools of the devil," Calvin thought they might be useful as negative examples for pious Christians who might be inspired after seeing prostitutes to reform their own lives.

Luther, Zwingli, and Calvin, along with a number of other reformers throughout Europe, are usually termed "magisterials" because they believed that the church should work with the state and its officials. ("Magistrates" was the common term for rulers and officials of all types.) As noted above, the Protestant Reformation also had a radical wing, individuals and groups who taught that church and state should be separate and who sought to create a voluntary community of believers as they understood it to have existed in New Testament times. These radical groups, most of which were quite small, developed widely differing ideas on a number of things, but they generally rejected anything they claimed was not Biblical. Thus marriage was not a sacrament to the radicals – some of them rejected the idea of sacraments completely – but many of them placed more emphasis on its spiritual nature than Luther had. Marriage was a covenant between a man and a woman based not only on the covenant between believers and God, as it was for many Calvinist thinkers, but also on the covenant between members of the body of believers. Because of this, the group as a whole or at least its leaders should have a say in marital choice, taught some radical thinkers, broadening the circle of consent far beyond the parental consent required by the magisterials.

The relationship between this marital covenant and the covenant believers had with Christ was a tricky one for radicals, however, who were sometimes confronted with the very real problem of one spouse deciding to leave the group or not living up to expected standards of behavior while the other was faithful. Did a spouse's deviation, either in terms of conduct or doctrine, give the other spouse the right of divorce? This was a question that the magisterials also addressed, and their answer was uniformly no – even if a spouse became a Muslim or a Jew (to say nothing of a different denomination of Christian) all one could do was pray and attempt to convert him or her. Some of the radicals, however, used Paul's words in Corinthians to advocate divorce of non-believers, a position termed the Pauline Privilege. (1 Corinthians 7:15: "But if the unbelieving partner desires to separate, let it be so; in such a case the brother or sister is not bound.")

This divorce was to be followed by a quick remarriage to a believer, however, a policy that in one case led to enforced polygamy. In 1534–35, a group of Anabaptist radicals assumed power in the German city of Münster. Large numbers of Lutheran and Calvinist men left the city, leaving their wives to guard their possessions, and more Anabaptist women than men immigrated. The city's religious leaders decided that God's command to be fruitful and multiply justified polygamy and ordered all women to marry Anabaptists, nullifying earlier marriages; those who resisted were imprisoned and some executed, as was a woman who proposed a corresponding polyandry. The Münsterites emphasized the importance of the male seed in procreation – an idea they linked to their understanding of the nature of Christ, which denied that Mary had any role in creating even his human nature – and of male dominance on earth; in the words of Bernhard Rothmann, one of their leaders, "God wants to create something new on earth, the men shall no longer be to women [effeminate] . . . so here among us he put all women in obedience to men, so that all of them, young and old, must let themselves be ruled by men according to God's word."[11]

Some radical groups spiritualized sexuality along with marriage, emphasizing the goodness of all aspects of human sexuality, including the sexual organs and intercourse. A small German group called the Dreamers, for example, saw intercourse simply as obedience to God's command to "be fruitful and multiply," rather than linking it to disobedience and sin. In the eighteenth century, the Moravian Brethren believed that married couples could experience union with Christ through their sexual relations, and praised the Virgin Mary's physical body in language that was similar to that of medieval mystics. (They thus differed sharply from the Münsterites in their ideas about Mary's role, a good example of the diversity within the radical Reformation.) They sang hymns to Jesus' penis and Mary's breasts and uterus, which their leader, Count Nikolaus Zinzendorf (1700–760), defended by asserting that shame about Jesus' or Mary's sexual organs was a denial of the full humanity of Christ. He approved of language in which union with Christ was described in very physical terms, though he reprimanded congregations where this idea appeared to have led to same-sex kissing among single men.

A few radicals regarded the Christian message as giving them an inner light that freed them from existing religious and secular law. This position, termed *antinomianism,* occasionally led groups such as Ranters in seventeenth-century England to proclaim, "What act soever is done by thee in light and love, is light and lovely, though it be that act called adultery . . . No matter what Scripture, saints, or churches say, if that within thee do not condemn thee, thou shalt not be condemned."[12]

The ideas of the radicals seem very different than those of the magisterials, but in only a few instances in Europe did they lead to any long-term sexual experimentation or break with traditional marriage patterns. (Radical groups that developed slightly later in North America did institute major changes, as we will see in Chapter 6, but these were generally *more* stringent rather than freer in terms of sexual and moral rules.) In Europe the few sexual deviations of the radicals were primarily significant for the propaganda material they provided for both Catholics and magisterial Protestants. The single incident at Münster, for example, was used for decades as a justification for grisly torture and executions of radicals of all types, and groups such as the Ranters caused those in power in England during the Civil War period to pass stringent laws about adultery, profanity, and religious nonconformity.

Protestant institutions

The ideas of the radicals evoked harsh response on the part of magisterial reformers, but the actual failings of their own parishioners and neighbors were a far greater problem. Luther's very early writings emphasize throwing off the shackles of canon law (it is at this point that he burned law books), but by 1525 it was clear to him and other reformers that simply preaching the Gospel was not going to get people to change their ways or create a godly society. They advocated the establishment of courts that would regulate marriage and morals, wrote ordinances regulating marriage and other matters of sexual conduct, and worked closely with the secular rulers in their area, whether city councils or princes. In order to make sure the ordinances were being followed and determine what other measures were necessary, church and state officials often conducted joint investigations, termed visitations, in which they questioned pastors, teachers, and lay people about their religious and moral life. These institutions and activities reflected the values and aims of both religious and political elites, who both regarded marriage and moral order (*Zucht*) as essential to a stable society.

The first Protestant court was the marriage court (*Ehegericht*) in Zurich, established by Zwingli in 1525, which served as a model for similar courts in many other Swiss and German cities. In Zurich and elsewhere, some of the judges were clergy and some of them were members of the city council; none of them were professional jurists. Most cases were brought by private parties, with the judges gathering evidence and examining witnesses, and then arriving at a decision by majority vote. In their early years, the majority of cases in Protestant marriage courts involved disputed marriage agreements, with the majority of plaintiffs unmarried women who wanted to enforce a marital agreement. In making their decisions, judges slowly applied the new Protestant ideas about marriage: Was there parental consent? Was the wedding in a church? Were there witnesses? They also no longer applied the canonical impediments that rendered certain marriages invalid in Catholicism, such as spiritual consanguinity or a previous agreement to marry someone else.

The new courts in Zurich and elsewhere were called "marriage courts," and cases involving marriage formed the bulk of their business, but they also began to hear cases involving other matters that had been heard by Catholic church courts before the Reformation. These included such things as gambling, non-attendance at church, blasphemy, and sexual matters not involving marriage such as fornication and prostitution. In some areas, officials recognized from the beginning that the new courts would have a broader purview than simply marriage, and so used other titles for them, such as consistory. Secular rulers such as those in Saxony and Württemberg in Germany appointed consistories made up of clergy, lay officials, and sometimes professional lawyers. In some areas, such as the city of Strasbourg, the city council refused to allow the clergy to have a voice on these courts, transforming the handling of marriage and morals into a secular matter as early as the sixteenth century. (Strasbourg did allow ministers publicly to shame those they judged guilty of moral lapses.)

The most famous Protestant consistory was that established in Geneva under Calvin's leadership in 1541. Even before the Reformation, the city council of Geneva had jurisdiction over morals cases, though the court of Geneva's bishop could overturn its decisions. The bishop was deposed in the process of the Reformation, but Calvin insisted that a body of both clergy and laymen be established as the guarantor of morals and doctrine, and that it have the power to excommunicate. The Genevan consistory was made up of the city's pastors and twelve lay elders chosen annually by the city's voters from a list approved by the ministers. Its formal charge was to "oversee the life of everyone, admonish amicably those whom they see to be in error or living a disordered life, and, where it is required, enjoin fraternal correction."[13] That "fraternal correction" ranged from scoldings to excommunication; in serious cases the offender could be turned over to the city council, which could use torture and had a wider range of punishments, including execution. (This practice of handing serious offenders over to secular authorities for punishment was generally followed by all religious courts, including the Inquisition, as we will see in the following chapter.) Each of the elders was in charge of one specific district of the city, and could require those simply suspected of moral infractions or doctrinal deviation to appear before the consistory. The consistory thus acted as a social agency as well as a court, and cases were not limited to those brought by the parties involved. These included blasphemy, divorce, Catholic practices, magic, witchcraft, heresy, and sodomy. In this it was not much different from Lutheran consistories; what made it distinctive was the amount of independent power held by the pastors, and the level of its activities. One estimate finds that in many years one out of every fifteen adults in Geneva was ordered to appear before the consistory.

As Calvinism spread into France, Germany, Scotland, the Low Countries, and northern Ireland, ordinances were adopted regulating marriage for Calvinist Protestants and consistories were established to oversee doctrine and morals, which followed various patterns in terms of appointment and membership. In many parts of Germany the consistory was appointed by the ruler, just as Lutheran consistories were, with the pastors and lay members serving only as long as the ruler approved. In France, the Low Countries and some parts of Germany, the consistories were made up of pastors and elected lay elders – as in Geneva – but they often did not have the power to excommunicate and had to rely on voluntary compliance. In many of these areas, only a part of the population was Calvinist, so that the consistory did not have jurisdiction over the whole population as it did in Geneva, but only over church members. Consistories outside of Geneva were often arranged in a hierarchy, ranging from those with jurisdiction over only a single congregation to those with jurisdiction over a larger area (often called a synod, presbytery, or classis) that also served as a court of appeal; in some areas, such as Scotland and northern Ireland, there was also a national body that served as the ultimate court of appeal. These courts heard a wide range of cases and their focus varied over the years, but in general between 30 and 80 percent of their cases involved sex. Consistories took male sexual misconduct more seriously than did secular courts, so a greater share of those brought before them for sexual offenses were male than was true in other types of courts. Both male and female offenders were required to confess openly before the consistory, and often before their home congregations as well; those who professed innocence were rare, and were generally subject to elaborate oaths of compurgation before the court or the entire congregation.

Calvinist consistories everywhere vied with secular courts in asserting jurisdiction over certain types of cases, particularly those that involved property or serious crimes; their authority slowly shrank in many places during the seventeenth century. In Scotland, for example, secular commissary courts increasingly heard marriage and divorce cases, with church courts only providing advice. Though this might seem a clear example of secularization, it was balanced in many places by the criminalization of religious offenses, what historians have called the "criminalization of sin." To again use Scotland as an example, although the Scots Parliament in 1560 refused to adopt the whole Calvinist Book of Discipline as the law of the land, over the next century or so, because of the influence of church leaders, incest, witchcraft, and adultery were made capital crimes, and blasphemy and doing anything on Sunday except going to church were made illegal. (Traces of the last restriction may still be seen in Sunday closing laws that are part of many secular law codes.) Fresh statutes in the later seventeenth century in Scotland encouraged the strict enforcement of all Scottish laws against "filthiness, adulteries, and other abominations." Secular courts in many other parts of Protestant Europe as well imposed punishments for ecclesiastical offenses such as blasphemy, and used methods of punishment for many offenses that were outgrowths of religious rituals of confession, although increasingly punitive in nature. Malefactors had to sit on "stools of repentance" listening to sermons directed at them, apologize and confess before their congregations as well as the court, or wear special signs or garments that proclaimed their status as both sinner and law-breaker. Thus as sins were made crimes, crimes were also made sins. As in Catholic confession, courts took the intent of the individual as well as the actual action into account when assessing the appropriate level of punishment.

Most Protestant areas, whether Lutheran or Calvinist, went through at least a brief period of disorder and uncertainty during which the authority of the old bishop's courts was no longer accepted, but no new institutions had yet been established. In some areas, such as Scandinavia, this could last for decades. This did not happen in England, where the church courts were not disbanded when Henry VIII broke with the papacy, but simply continued as bodies for which the ultimate authority was the king rather than the pope. Because most of the English clergy became Protestant when their king did, many of the men who had been judges in church courts before the Reformation stayed on. England also explicitly retained canon law, slowly reforming it to fit with royal wishes and English statutes. English ecclesiastical courts ranged from local to national, with the Courts of High Commission run by England's two archbishops given the power to fine and imprison as well as impose religious sanctions such as excommunication. In London, the governors of Bridewell and Christ's Hospitals, which housed illegitimate children and the poor, heard cases involving sexual offenses; the governors handled all types of cases they felt had something to do with poverty, such as prostitution and fornication, and thus had wide powers over all Londoners, not simply the poor.

Ecclesiastical courts, along with other church institutions, were disbanded during the period of the Civil War in England and reestablished with the restoration of the monarchy in 1660, but they lost some of their control over sexual matters to secular courts at that time. When Christian denominations other than the Church of England were granted limited toleration after James II was overthrown in 1688 and William and Mary came to power, the power of ecclesiastical courts was further eroded. English clerics and moral reformers, however, interpreted the events of 1688 – in which the Protestant William and Mary replaced the Catholic James – in apocalyptic terms, as God giving England one last chance to truly change its ways. They pressured Parliament to pass new legislation similar to the laws of Scotland against "the notorious sins and vices of this nation," and to enforce existing laws more stringently. Hundreds of cases involving illicit sex were brought forward each year in the common-law courts in London during the 1690s, and many in other cities as well.

Numerous private grassroots societies dedicated to the suppression of vice and the promotion of moral virtue – often calling themselves "Society for the Reformation of Manners" – were founded in the cities and towns of the British Isles in the late seventeenth century, and in some North American colonies as well. Members raised money, employed lawyers, and patrolled the streets themselves or hired constables to arrest prostitutes, close brothels, and bring complaints regarding drunkenness, swearing, fornication, and other moral offenses to the attention of authorities. One society in London posted and distributed a list of the names of everyone it had brought to justice, including customers as well as residents of "houses of lewdness and bawdery." Streetwalkers and brothel-keepers were fined, whipped, and imprisoned, but also – as with those brought before the consistory in Calvin's Geneva – lectured, admonished, and shamed. In the first decade of the eighteenth century more than a thousand prosecutions a year for sexual offenses were brought by such societies in London alone, but this period also marks the beginning of their decline. Criticism grew that debauchery was punished only among the poor, and that the groups relied too much on paid informants. Judges increasingly wanted proof of specific illegal actions, not just suspicion that a person was thought to be "lewd, idle, and disorderly."[14] By the 1740s most of these groups had disbanded, although periodic calls for their reestablishment continued into the nineteenth century.

On the continent in the seventeenth century, the Thirty Years' War convinced most people that religious unity was not possible in Europe as a whole, but it did not convince many religious or political leaders of the virtues of toleration within one territory. Nearly every state had one state church, which rulers saw not simply as an institution for sustaining and expressing faith, but also as an agency of public policy. Loyalty to the state church was a matter of secular law as well as religious practice. This included following established rules regarding marriage and moral conduct, so that matters handled by marriage courts and consistories in the sixteenth century often moved to secular courts in the seventeenth.

Magisterial reformers such as Luther and Calvin and their heirs were not the only ones to develop institutions to regulate sexual and moral behavior, for the many radical Protestant groups that developed in early modern Europe did so as well. In some cases these were bodies of elders to whom accusations were made or who ferreted out wrongdoing themselves, and in some cases the disciplinary body was the entire group or its male members. The Society of Friends (the Quakers), begun in seventeenth-century England by George Fox, developed the most distinctive institution, a women's meeting that oversaw the readiness of candidates for marriage, upheld the maintenance of decorous standards of dress, and at times ruled on other moral issues. The delegates to a Quaker women's meeting in Ireland in 1677, for example, investigated whether any young women "live by themselves which may give occasion of liberty and looseness."[15] Because radical groups such as the Quakers were never an official state church, the strictest punishment they could mete out was expulsion from the group, which was generally reserved only for serious offenses such as adultery or marriage out of the group.

Courts, consistories, and congregations are generally viewed as the main institutions of social discipline and the regulation of sexuality in Protestant Europe during this period, but it is important to recognize that less formal institutions also shaped people's attitudes and behavior. Protestants used some of the same means that had been available to the medieval church to spread their message orally, such as sermons and plays. Sometimes these warned against sexual misconduct directly, although some pastors worried that any mention of pre- or extramarital sex would increase desire among their hearers rather than dampen it, so took a more oblique approach.

Protestants also had a tool not available in most of the Middle Ages: the printing press with movable metal type, which was developed in Germany about 1450. Protestant reformers used the printing press to spread their ideas on all issues; the works of major and minor reformers went through many editions so that thousands of copies were available. Well over half of the materials printed in the sixteenth century, and nearly half of those in the seventeenth century, were religious. Indeed, some scholars argue that the Reformation would not have been successful had there not been the printing press.

From the beginning, Protestant materials were not limited to theological discussions for scholars, but included illustrated single-sheet broadsides (similar to posters), small paperback pamphlets, and cheap — sometimes pirated — copies of sermons, lectures, guides, and stories printed in vernacular languages. In many of these materials, Protestant ideas about the evils of celibacy and the importance of marriage and moral conduct were communicated in simple language with colorful examples and visual illustrations. Instead of stories about heroic virgins, there were lascivious nuns who had scores of children and then killed and buried them, and instead of ascetic hermits overcoming the temptations of lust there were monks who had sex with each other and priests who seduced their parishioners. Protestant works also portrayed positive ideals: girls who accepted their parents' choice of a husband, and pious families praying at dinner, with the mother and girls on one side of the table and the father and boys on the other. In the "housefather books," male heads of household were encouraged to read the Bible and other devotional literature out loud to their wives, children, and servants, so that even those who could not read could get religious and moral teachings through printed books. Girls had books written just for them, such as *The Little Flower Wreath of Honor for Christian Girls* or *The Mirror of Virtue for Christian Maidens*, which explicitly encourage proper morality and sexual behavior.

Books and other printed materials might be read at home, but they could also be found in Protestant primary and secondary schools, which served as important agents of instilling moral discipline and confessional conformity. Though education was nowhere universal, slowly an increasingly large share of the population in Protestant Europe attended at least enough school to be able to read. The primary school curriculum was based on the catechism, the small books that taught basic Christian beliefs, and emphasized morality more than intellectual endeavors, especially for girls. In the words of a school ordinance from Luther's Wittenberg in 1533, the aim of girls' education was to "habituate girls to the catechism, to the psalms, to honorable behavior and Christian virtue, and especially to prayer, so that they may grow up to be Christian and praiseworthy matrons and housekeepers."[16] The aim of boys' education was not much different, except for the very few boys who would go on to a secondary and university education (an opportunity not open to girls). Thus from a very young age — at home from their fathers and at school from their teachers — Protestant children and young people were taught the new ideals of marital chastity and sexual morality.

It is of course very difficult to say how well people learned these new ideals, though there is some evidence that they did internalize them. In a few areas, especially among urban Calvinists, church members pressured the consistory to be *more* active than it was, reporting cases of immoral conduct rather than waiting for an elder or visitation to discover them. Specific complaints of neighbors and more general gossip and rumors identifying deviance often preceded official investigations. Some of these cases may have resulted from people using consistories to settle old scores, but they also reflect at least a partial acceptance of what had been taught. This reception was never enough to satisfy religious authorities, however, which is why agents of discipline such as consistories and courts were necessary.

Effects of Protestant measures

Internalization is just one aspect of the impact of Protestant ideas and institutions that is difficult to trace. In some cases such difficulties are the result of too few sources, but in more cases they are the result of too many. The records of many church courts, visitation teams, and consistories are still extant, but because each of these often dealt with only a small geographic area generalizations can be difficult. This becomes even more problematic when we want to go beyond a simple tracing of trends to understanding the possible reasons for these trends, because each particular jurisdiction was enmeshed in specific political, economic, and social circumstances, all of which could have an influence on the regulation of sexuality. The personal circumstances of rulers – their desire for an heir or their own sexual behavior – also played a role, as did the aims of individual judges or reformers who were sometimes obsessed with certain issues, such as sodomy, witchcraft, or illegitimate births. The sheer volume of court records can also mislead us into thinking we have the whole picture, when what we have, of course, is a picture of activities early modern Protestant authorities judged somehow deviant, written in the language and from the perspective of those authorities. Despite these problems, however, there are certain trends we can trace in the Protestant regulation of sexuality.

Clerical marriage

One of the most immediately visible changes brought by the Protestant Reformation was clerical marriage. Some late medieval priests had concubines or short-term sexual relationships with women – despite all the attempts of the church at reform – but this was still very different from having a wife. Almost all of the continental Protestant reformers married, and some, such as Luther, to former nuns.

In England, the situation was somewhat different. Clergy began to marry in the 1530s, but Henry VIII forbade clerical marriage in 1539 and set severe punishments for it, although these were rarely implemented. The ban was lifted under Edward VI, but reaffirmed when Mary reintroduced Catholicism. Elizabeth tolerated but did not favor clerical marriage, and she forbade clerical wives from living at cathedrals and colleges, declaring that "the very rooms and buildings be not answerable for such families of women and young children."[17] She did not recognize the marriages of bishops, and their wives and children were left in a very tenuous position. Bishops and those who hoped to become bishops often hid their marriages. Not until 1604, under James, was clerical marriage finally made fully legal.

Whether openly as on the continent or somewhat clandestinely as in England, clerical marriage was a dramatic change. Male clergy no longer had a special sexual status, but shared that of the lay men around them: husband and father. They were no longer simply "fathers" in a spiritual sense, but actual fathers. The first generation of reformers had generally lived in the all-male environments of the monastery, university, or cathedral chapter, but they now had to create a new ideal of clerical masculinity that included being sexually active and being in charge of a household. This was not simply a matter of ideals, however, but also of practical concerns and day-to-day behavior. The housing and stipends provided for priests had not been designed for a family, and even parishioners who accepted Protestant ideas frequently grumbled about now having to provide more. It was often difficult for people to accept the woman and children living in the pastor's house as his legitimate wife and children, and they jeered at pastors' wives in the street as "priests' whores." In some places people refused to take communion from married clergy, stating to their faces that hands that touched women should never touch the body of Christ. Thus Protestant pastors preached and wrote defenses of their new married state to convince their congregations – and perhaps themselves – that it was respectable and godly.

The wives of pastors and bishops were active in this task as well, although they had no official position in the new Protestant churches. They did this largely by being models of wifely obedience and Christian charity, attempting to make their households into the type of orderly "little commonwealths" that their husbands were urging on their congregations in sermons. After they died, their activities and virtues were described in funeral sermons preached by their husbands or sons, or inscribed in epitaphs on funerary monuments, proclaiming to all who heard or read them their stature as models of piety and charity.

Within a generation or so these efforts by both pastors and their wives were quite successful. Whereas priests' concubines had generally been from a lower social class, by the second generation Protestant pastors had little difficulty finding wives from among the same social class as themselves, a trend that further aided the acceptance of clerical marriage. Sons often succeeded their fathers in clerical positions, just as sons of master craftsmen did, and they married women who were themselves daughters of pastors. By the seventeenth century important preaching positions and professorships of theology were handed down from father to son or father to son-in-law in virtual clerical dynasties.

The new Protestant churches did not leave the task of maintaining orderly households completely up to the clergy and their wives, however. Visitation teams and other officials investigated charges of sexual improprieties or moral laxness among pastoral families, and disciplined those found wanting. Maintaining an orderly household was just as important a mark of being a proper Protestant pastor as teaching and preaching correct doctrine.

Pastors' wives created a new ideal for women, but what about the many women who had followed the old ideal, that of cloistered nun or the women who lived in less formal religious communities? Some, like Katherine von Bora, accepted Protestant teachings with great enthusiasm as a message of liberation from the convent, but others viewed these as a negation of the value of the life they had been living. They thus did all in their power to continue in their chosen path, fighting orders to close or disband convents in the courts or through family pressure. (Fewer male monasteries in areas that became Protestant opposed the Reformation than did convents; monks who remained Catholic when monasteries were closed generally moved to a branch of their order in areas that remained Catholic, an option available to few women.) Some argued they could still be pious Protestants within convent walls, bound not by vows but by choices freely made. The nuns' firmness, combined with other religious and political factors, allowed convents in some areas to survive for centuries as Catholic establishments within Protestant territories, or as Protestant girls' schools and homes for unmarried women. In most places, however, the women were forced out, with very small pensions, and were expected to return to their families. We do not know what happened to them. The Protestant emphasis on marriage made unmarried women (and men) suspect, for they did not belong to the type of household regarded as the cornerstone of a proper, godly society.

Making a marriage

Pastoral households were not the only ones scrutinized for moral failings, as church and state authorities attempted to make their vision of orderly households a reality. Households required a proper foundation, so Protestant officials paid great attention to the wedding ceremony and agreements surrounding the wedding. Catholic marriage liturgies were translated into vernacular languages and modified according to Protestant ideas and sometimes political pressures, though there was also a great deal of continuity. The consent of the spouses remained the core of a valid marriage, but Protestant jurisdictions also added various other requirements. A public ceremony with a priest had been recommended at least since the Fourth Lateran Council in 1215, but many continental Protestant jurisdictions came to require this as part of an emphasis on the public nature of marriage. Particularly in Germany, laws were passed against secret "dark-corner marriages" (*Winckelehen*). Weddings were increasingly held inside the church rather than in front of it, and before the ceremony couples had no right to engage in sexual intercourse, even if they were formally engaged or had held a private ceremony marking their consent.

Parental consent was another key issue. In his revision of the marriage liturgy for the English church in the 1540s, which became the *Book of Common Prayer*, Archbishop Thomas Cranmer added the question: "Who giveth this woman to be married to this man?" before the exchange of vows, requiring the bride to publicly indicate her father's approval. The 1562 and 1563 marriage ordinances of the Palatinate in Germany went further, declaring any marriage of a minor without parental approval as "void, invalid and nonbinding," and condeming the man involved as "a marriage-thief [who] has dishonestly stolen her, contrary to God and His Word"; those who assisted such couples were to be considered kidnappers and "immediately imprisoned and, according to the nature of their offense, punished without mercy by imprisonment, fine, or banishment."[18] Similar measures were passed in other Lutheran states. Even children who were no longer minors were occasionally punished for marrying or entering into an engagement without the approval of their fathers, although courts also very occasionally punished fathers for forcing or attempting to force their children into unwanted marriages.

Some of these cases setting parents against children were quite spectacular, with children – especially daughters – physically locked up by their parents to prevent their marrying unacceptable partners. Such cases have provided evidence in an ongoing debate among historians of the early modern family about the balance between family pressure and personal sentiment in spousal choice. The actual number of cases is very small, however, leading many scholars to conclude that the majority of young people seem to have at least accepted the spouse their parents chose for them, or chosen one themselves who was not objectionable to the family.

On the issue of parental consent, Calvin and his colleagues in Geneva were closer to Catholic practice than Lutheran; engagements made without parental consent were voided, but actual marriages were generally declared valid. In

England, church ordinances passed in 1604 required weddings to take place before noon in the parish of the couple after public statements declaring this was going to happen (termed "banns") had been read from the pulpit for three weeks, and required parental consent unless the couple was over twenty-one. Marriages contracted against these rules were "irregular," but, as in Geneva, they were still valid. Certain London churches were also completely exempt from following the rules, and people who wanted to marry quickly just paid a clergyman at one of these churches, who might also be persuaded to backdate a marriage in order to make children legitimate. Such "Fleet Marriages" – many of these churches were near Fleet Prison – and other uncertainties in English marriage law were sharply criticized by Puritans, and when they came to power during the Civil War they made parental consent obligatory for minors in the 1653 Marriage Act. This law was rendered null when the monarchy was restored in 1660, however, and English marital law remained murky, until Lord Hardwicke's Marriage Act in 1753 made the 1604 rules requirements for all legal marriages. (After 1753, Gretna Green, a small village just across the English border in Scotland, became the favored site for irregular marriages.)

Parents and family were not the only ones with a voice in one's choice of spouse, however, for authorities often forbade people living within their jurisdictions to marry certain types of people, to marry without their permission, and sometimes to marry at all. Many of these prohibitions pre-date the Reformation by centuries, for feudal lords in many parts of Europe controlled the marriages of their serfs – or required serfs to pay a fine if they wanted to choose their own spouse – and cities forbade the marriages of servants and the poor as well as those between citizens and non-citizens. Soldiers were often required to obtain the permission of their commander before marrying, and local women were prohibited from marrying soldiers. Underlying many of these restrictions was a desire to prohibit marriages between those perceived to be unequal, whether that inequality was the result of age, wealth, or social status, and to prevent marriages that might produce children dependent on public welfare. For Protestant authorities, social and economic aims trumped Protestant teachings that all people should be free to marry. Marriages between unequals were also the target of public rituals of disapproval such as *charivaris*, noisy parades often accompanied by throwing rotten food or stones, indicating that this was a matter of popular, as well as official, concern.

With the Reformation, a new form of difference received official and popular attention – religious allegiance. In Germany, for example, rulers were allowed to determine whether their territory would be Protestant or Catholic and were supposed to let those who disagreed leave; according to the terms of the Peace of Westphalia of 1648, however, they were also supposed to allow private worship (*devotio domestica*) by those whose free conscience (*conscientia libera*) led them to follow a different denomination. The right to leave or to hold private services was envisioned as applying to whole families, however. What about families in which the spouses disagreed in matters of religion? In the first generation of the Reformation, this was primarily a matter of conversion, and the magisterial reformers all asserted that converting did not give one the right to leave one's spouse. By the middle of the sixteenth century, however, this was also a matter of marriage *formation*. Should people be allowed to marry across religious lines? Catholics, Lutherans, and Calvinists agreed that the answer was no. Spouses were to be "one in body and spirit" and a mixed marriage would create "one body and two minds" and "cause arguments, quarrels, blasphemous wild conduct, and often half-hearted belief." Authorities ordered sermons to be preached against mixed marriage, warning of the dangers to the soul "seduced by the infamous sweet poison of heretical teaching."[19] Even the body might be endangered, as Catholic blood mixed with Protestant blood.

Authorities in many areas attempted outright prohibition, or required couples to seek approval of the consistory or marital court, which attempted to dissuade them. Not surprisingly, they sometimes made distinctions on the basis of gender. In 1631, for example, the Strasbourg city council, which was Lutheran, considered whether citizens should lose their citizenship if they married Calvinists. It decided that a man would not "because he can probably draw his spouse away from her false religion and bring her on the correct path," though he would have to pay a fine for "bringing an unacceptable person into the city." A woman who married a Calvinist would lose her citizenship, however, "because she would let herself easily be led into error in religion by her husband and be led astray."[20] Such gender-specific rules were not limited to Germany. Reviving decrees that had first been issued as part of the Statutes of Kilkenny in 1366 – designed at that point to keep the Gaelic and Norman populations of Ireland apart – the Irish parliament in 1697 decreed that any Protestant heiress who married a Catholic would lose her property to her Protestant next of kin. Her marriage would be considered treasonous if her husband had not signed the Oath of Succession in support of the English rulers of Ireland.

Despite these prohibitions, however, mixed marriages continued to occur, particularly in areas where Catholics and various types of Protestants lived in close proximity to one another, such as the German territories that were officially bi-confessional, or towns that saw steady immigration. In addition, marital alliances for political reasons among ruling families sometimes led to marriage across religious lines, particularly between Calvinists and Lutherans. In some territories, as many as 20 percent of marriages may have been religiously mixed. Authorities continued to grumble, but they generally agreed to recognize the marriage ceremonies of other denominations. This policy sometimes led people to move until they could find a priest or pastor who would agree to marry them, whatever their own religious convictions were. (This acceptance of marriage across political jurisdictions continues until today, which is why couples in the United States travel to certain places for "quicky" marriages and divorces and why proposals to permit same-sex marriage in any one state are viewed with such interest or alarm in other states.)

Maintaining problem marriages

Once a marriage had taken place, the key aim of religious and political authorities was to keep the couple together. They generally did not intervene in any disputes between spouses unless these created public scandal or repeatedly disturbed the neighbors, and attempted reconciliation first for serious cases. These efforts at reconciliation included horrendous cases of domestic violence, in which one spouse – almost always the wife – accused the other of beatings with sticks or tools, brutal kicking, stabbing, or strangling. The accused spouse was usually simply admonished to behave better, and only on a third or fourth court appearance might stricter punishment be set. Courts generally held that a husband had the right to beat his wife in order to correct her behavior as long as this was not extreme, with a common standard being that he did not draw blood, or the diameter of the stick he used did not exceed that of his thumb. If the wife had left the household she was ordered to return, and there are cases in many jurisdictions where this eventually led to a wife's death at the hands of her husband. The reverse situation, in which a wife killed her husband, was very rare, but the few cases that did exist fascinated people and were often retold many times in illustrated pamphlets and broadsheets.

Wives were more often charged with scolding and verbally abusing their husbands than abusing them physically, with patterns developing like that in a London household in which,

> he has given her . . . one or two blows with the back of his hand upon her cheek by the provocation of the same Margaret [the wife] who upon some fault that this respondent [the husband] has found with her hath most uncharitably and beyond the bounds of modesty called this respondent rogue, rascal, whorehunter, thief.[21]

Verbal abuse was punished with fines and public shaming, with special bridles, iron collars and masks, and ducking stools used with women accused of such behavior. Women who slandered people other than their husbands were also punished in this way, with cases of slander forming a large part of the business of many courts. As in medieval Europe, terms of slander and verbal defamation were highly gender-specific and sexualized; women were almost always called some variant of "whore" and men either something which impugned their own honesty such as "thief" or attacked the sexual honor of their female family members, such as "whoreson" or "cuckold."

Accusations of adultery were taken far more seriously than those of domestic violence or slander, because adultery directly challenged the central link between marriage and procreation as well as impugning male honor. Many legal codes, including the criminal code of the Holy Roman Empire of 1532, called the *Constitutio Criminalis Carolina*, defined adultery as a capital offense, and in a few cases individuals were indeed executed for adultery. In 1508 in Nuremberg, for example, a married woman was burned alive for adultery with several partners, and in 1527 in Zittau a woman was drowned for adultery with sixty-three men. During the early 1560s, though there was no provision for the death penalty in the city ordinances of Geneva, several people were executed for adultery, including two men who were beheaded. (The normal method of execution for female adulterers in Geneva, as elsewhere, was drowning.) In many of these Geneva cases the accused were tortured until they confessed, and in most of them additional charges were involved, such as blasphemy, theft, bigamy, and prostitution. This was also the situation elsewhere, for adulterers were generally punished with fines, prison sentences, corporal punishment or banishment; only when their cases involved multiple partners, public scandal, or incest were they executed. The status of the offender generally determined the punishment, with wealthier individuals fined and told to return to their spouses and poorer ones banished. Punishments also often involved public shaming; offenders were sentenced to sit in the stocks or on the "stool of correction," or to wear a large stone attached to a choker in a procession or around the marketplace.

Social status clearly influenced the investigation and punishment in adultery cases, and gender played a role as well. In contrast to many medieval law codes, sexual relationships between a married man and an unmarried woman were defined as adultery in most sixteenth-century codes, and, as we have seen above, men were actually tried and punished. An adultery law passed in Geneva in 1566 (*after* the executions discussed above) was totally egalitarian in cases of double adultery (in which both parties were married), calling for death for both. On the other hand, adultery by a married man with a single woman did not threaten the family and lineage the way that adultery by a married woman did, for it could not bring the child of another man into a family. The horror with which authorities viewed this prospect is seen in the double standard that many areas established in adultery law. In the 1566

Genevan law, an adulterous married man and his lover were to be punished by twelve days in prison, but an adulterous married woman was to be executed; in the 1650 Adultery Act in England, adultery was made a capital offense for a married woman and her partner, but was only punished by three months' imprisonment for a married man. In Geneva, the punishment set for the lover of a married woman explicitly links considerations of gender and class, for he was to be whipped and banished unless he was a servant, in which case he was also to be executed. Husbands clearly recognized – and shared in – the values of the courts on this issue, for their justifications for severe violence often involve not simply their wife's scolding, but her adulterous or flirtatious behavior.

Childbirth and churching

Good marriages as well as bad ones presented issues for Protestant authorities, and childbirth was one of the most vexing. Continental and English pastors provided advice to midwives, birth attendants, and mothers themselves about acceptable practices and procedures, and visitations investigated whether these were being followed. The Anglican bishop of York, for example, asked in 1571 whether midwives used "any charms or unlawful prayers, or invocation in Latin, or otherwise?"[22] Statues of the Virgin had been removed from English churches by that point, so there was no open sharing of Mary's girdle by laboring women or place for them to make the traditional donations of thanksgiving. This may have gone on in secret, however, and certainly did among those in England, termed *recusants*, who held to Catholic beliefs. Prayers and rituals surrounding childbirth were often the religious practices most resistant to change when the religious allegiance of an area changed.

Protestants rejected the idea that women needed to be purified after giving birth, but Anglicans and some continental Protestants retained the ceremony of churching, terming it instead a service of thanksgiving. In some Lutheran areas, churching was required of all married mothers and forbidden to those who gave birth out of wedlock, creating a mark of the distinction between honorable and dishonorable women. In England, unmarried women who had given birth were only to be churched if they named the father and wore a white sheet signifying their penitence during the service. Churching was violently opposed by English Puritan men in the seventeenth century as a Catholic holdover, but many Puritan women continued to demand it, as did English women well into the twentieth century even if they never attended other church services. We may view churching and similar ceremonies as stemming from clerical hostility toward the female body and childbirth, but there is evidence that early modern women rejected this interpretation and instead regarded churching as a necessary final act of closure to a period of childbirth. A woman attended her churching in the presence of the women who had been with her during the birth, including the midwife, and many of the rituals that were part of churching were of popular, rather than ecclesiastical, origin. Women objected when pastors sought to change the ritual in any way; one report from Abingdon in England in 1668 noted that "women refuse to be churched because they have not their right place, and midwives are excluded . . . from their women, who always used to sit together."[23]

Divorce

In almost all Protestant areas, the ultimate solution for cases of domestic discord or other serious marital problems was divorce. Following the ideas of their reformers, Swiss, German, Scottish, Scandinavian and French Protestant marital courts allowed divorce for adultery and impotence, and sometimes for contracting a contagious disease, malicious desertion, conviction for a capital crime, or deadly assault. Some of them allowed both parties to marry again, and some only the innocent. A difference in religious beliefs alone never justified divorce, but when it was accompanied by a spouse's desertion or refusal to move with the other spouse, divorces were occasionally granted. In 1531 in Zurich for example, a man whose wife had left him and their seven children to join a radical group (telling him "she wished to be obedient to God, and not to the earthly authorities") was granted a divorce, as was an Italian nobleman who became Protestant and migrated to Geneva but whose wife refused to follow him.[24]

This dramatic change in marital law had less than dramatic results, however, at least judging by sheer numbers. In contrast to today, when divorce is a large part of all civil legal procedures, Protestant marriage courts heard very few divorce cases. The cathedral court of Stavanger (Norway), for example, which had jurisdiction over a huge area, granted only eighteen divorces during the period between 1571 and 1596, and the city of Geneva only 3 between 1559 and 1569. In many jurisdictions the annual divorce rate hovered around 0.02 per 1,000 population and even cities that were hotbeds of divorce by early modern standards, such as Basel, had a divorce rate of only 0.57 per 1,000 for the period 1525–92, about 1/8 that of the United States in 2000. (The 2000 US divorce rate was 4.1 per 1,000.)

These tiny numbers resulted from a variety of factors. Marriage was not only the cornerstone of society in theory, but also in economic and social reality, and the consequences of divorce could be disastrous. Most spouses, along with most authorities, thus saw it only as a desperate last resort, once all avenues at reconciliation had been exhausted. Even then petitions for divorce might not be granted; in relatively liberal Basel during the period between 1550 and 1592, for example, about half of the cases for divorce heard by the marriage court were denied. The most acceptable grounds for divorce – adultery or desertion – involved the criminalization of one of the spouses, who would be liable for other penalties and who might not be able to marry again. In many jurisdictions the person bringing the suit also had to prove total innocence, not only in terms of his or her own sexual conduct, but also in terms of collusion with the guilty spouse; charging adultery to escape an unwanted marriage – a common practice in the United States before the introduction of no-fault divorce laws – was, in the eyes of authorities, to be prevented at all costs. Judges were also on the lookout for collusion in divorce cases based on impotence or desertion, and almost always called for a waiting period during which further attempts at sexual intercourse (in the case of impotence) or at contacting the spouse (in the case of desertion) were mandatory.

The situation in England and Ireland was different from that in other Protestant countries, for the Anglican and Anglo-Irish Churches rejected divorce and continued to assert the indissolubility of marriage. They did allow legal separations (separations *a mensa et thoro* – from bed and board) as the medieval church had, but these were not true divorces as neither of the spouses could remarry; even separations were allowed only for adultery and life-threatening cruelty. The Anglican rejection of divorce led England to be one of the first areas of Europe to develop a totally secular divorce process; beginning in 1670, divorces for adultery were granted by Act of Parliament, a procedure that remained the only avenue for divorce in England until 1857. These Acts were very rare – there were only 16 during the period 1670–1749 – and almost all granted to men; of the 325 total acts during the period 1670–1857, only 4 went to women.

Secular divorce proceedings were not limited to England, however, but began about the same time in Lutheran Sweden, where they could be granted by royal dispensation. Church courts in Sweden allowed divorce for adultery and desertion, but the king also began to grant a few divorces for ill-treatment, drunkenness, and severe incompatibility. The number of these was extremely limited, but it marks the first time that grounds other than those mentioned in the Bible were actually used as a justification for divorce, rather than simply discussed as a possibility. Gradually this idea spread to other Protestant areas, such as Prussia and areas under Prussian domination such as Neuchâtel in Switzerland, where first rulers and then consistories began granting a few divorces for cruelty, insanity, banishment and (in a handful of cases) incompatibility. This liberalization of divorce was always on a case-by-case basis and in many areas it preceded any change in marital law, which still gave only adultery and desertion as allowable grounds. It was part of a gradual secularization of the control of marriage, but it was also clearly, though regretfully, accepted by many church officials as well. The Protestant assertion that the best life was one of spousal companionship and marital chastity slowly brought with it in some jurisdictions a recognition that if these were impossible, the only thing to do was to end that marriage and try again.

Though possible for Protestants, divorce remained difficult and expensive, and many people used other less formal avenues of ending unwanted marriages. They simply moved apart, though this was prohibited by church and state authorities, or one deserted the other, which was particularly common among the poor. In certain parts of Europe popular rituals developed to undo a marriage in the minds of the community, especially if there had not been a formal church wedding to begin with. In parts of England, Wales, and America, for example, couples jumped over a broom to indicate they were married, and then backwards over the broom if they discovered within a year they could not live together. Occasionally English-speaking areas also saw wife sales, in which a wife was led with a rope around her neck by her husband to a market or fair, and then auctioned off to the highest bidder, who had sometimes been decided upon in advance and was occasionally her lover in an adulterous relationship. The government tried to stop the practice, but the number of known instances exceeded the number of divorces granted by Parliament, and probably many more went unrecorded. Though such popular rituals of divorce were nowhere accepted by Protestant authorities, Catholic observers occasionally used them to argue against any liberalization of divorce, as one French commentator noted: "Such is the result of schismatic and heretical doctrines of marriage, and this is proved by the fact that in Catholic Ireland, which is ruled by the same government, and under the same civil law as Great Britain, such revolting sales have never been witnessed."[25]

Fornication, illegitimacy, and infanticide

While divorces and wife sales were colorful and scandalous – and thus often the subject of popular pamphlets, ballads, and later novels such as *The Mayor of Casterbridge* – the vast majority of cases involving sexual conduct heard by Protestant courts were for premarital intercourse, usually termed fornication. This emphasis was in part the result of differences between popular and official understandings of the marriage process; while church and state authorities regarded a marriage as complete only after the church ceremony, many people, especially in rural areas, viewed a formal engagement or the signing of a marriage contract as the point at which sexual intercourse was allowable. Thus many of the cases of fornication were actually between individuals who intended to marry or who were in fact married by the time the case came to court. Historians of England have found that between one-fifth and one-half of brides were pregnant upon marriage in the sixteenth and seventeenth centuries, and up to one-half in the eighteenth. This was also the case in Norway, where almost half of first children were born within eight months of marriage, but it was not true in Scotland, where sex was not regarded as a normal part of courting.

If the pregnancy was evident before the formal wedding and both parties affirmed that there had been an agreement, a public church wedding was arranged, though the bride did not wear the usual wedding crown and the pair were instructed not to hold a wedding feast. (Instructions to which they often paid no attention.) They were both generally subject to punishment as well, which might include fines, public shaming rituals, and imprisonment. If the man disputed the woman's claim to an agreement, she or her father could take him to court to force him to marry her, though her chances of winning the case were slim in many jurisdictions.

Cases of fornication might also lead to rape charges, although these were quite rare. To win a rape charge the woman had to prove that she had screamed and made attempts to fight off the attacker, come to the authorities quickly after the incident, and was of spotless reputation. In the minds of some judges, pregnancy disproved rape, as one early modern theory of how conception occurred posited that women also released "seed" upon orgasm; pregnancy indicated the woman had enjoyed the intercourse and thus it wasn't rape. This notion was not accepted everywhere, however, and a more serious hindrance to bringing rape charges was the severity of sentence if it was proved. Rape was a capital crime, but this was viewed by many communities as too harsh a sentence; men were instead charged with lesser crimes and punished with fines or brief imprisonments.

Many instances of fornication did not involve either rape or a promise of marriage, and for these the treatment and punishment varied widely. In theory both men and women were to be treated equally, but in fact single men found guilty of fornication were let off with a light fine or simply an oath vowing not to engage in such behavior again. Single women were imprisoned, punished corporally, and sometimes banished, even when no pregnancy resulted, although some reformers advocated milder treatment. (Fornication cases in which no pregnancy was involved were only a small share of the cases, for they had to rely on eye-witnesses and the confessions of the accused to be prosecuted; of the 1,951 fornication cases recorded in the Scottish county of Sterlingshire for the period between 1637 and 1747, for example, only 26 women were not pregnant.)

When pregnancy was involved the matter was much more serious. An unmarried woman suspected of being pregnant out of wedlock was watched, questioned, and sometimes physically examined; those who worked in the same household were questioned about whether she had been menstruating. During the birth, midwives or officials were sent to force her to reveal the identity of the father; in England, midwives were instructed to refuse to assist her until she named the father. In the Swiss city of Neuchâtel, officials warned women about lying, for to do so "would be an unforgivable sin instead of simply fornication"; women's words on these occasions were generally trusted, for the only way a man could deny a paternity charge was for both him and the woman to undergo torture, a procedure that did happen occasionally.[26] In other areas as well, unmarried men often confessed when accused of fathering children out of wedlock, even though this might make them liable for child support. Sometimes, however, the woman refused to name a father, or admitted to having sexual relations with several men, or was known to be promiscuous; in these cases, and in those where the father had left the area, the woman was the only one charged with fornication. (The sexual history of the putative father was never mentioned in court, though that of the mother always was.) By the eighteenth century the balance in fornication accusations in many jurisdictions was between four and ten women for every one man, making fornication a female crime.

The consequences of having an illegitimate child varied widely across Protestant Europe, and were often related more to economic structures and changes than to religious ideology. Areas in which there was a labor shortage were relatively tolerant, including places such as Scotland and Prussia where one might have expected harsh punishment; unmarried mothers had to do a humiliating public penance, but then they were regarded as purged of their sin and could gain employment. In rural Norway, mothers frequently married men other than the father of their child shortly after the birth.

For many women, however, the economic and personal consequences of a pregnancy out of wedlock were severe. This was particularly the case for pregnancies in which the father was the woman's married employer or was related by blood or marriage to her, for this was adultery or incest rather than simple fornication and could bring great shame on the household. Women in such situations were urged to lie about the father's identity or were simply fired; they received no support from the wife of the father, whose honor and reputation were tightly bound to her husband's. Even when the man was accused of rape, his wife would stoutly defend him, asserting, as one village woman did that "he always acted honorably during the 23 years that they have been married, so this person [the pregnant maid] must have seduced him into doing this."[27] A pregnant woman fired by her employer was often in a desperate situation, as many authorities prohibited people from hiring or taking in unmarried pregnant women, and charged them with aiding in a sexual offense if they did.

In situations such as these, women attempted to deny the pregnancy as long as possible and occasionally attempted abortion. They tied their waists very tightly, carried heavy objects, slammed their stomach into walls, or took herbal mixtures that they made themselves or bought from someone with a reputation for knowledge about such things. Recipes for what we would term abortificients were readily available in popular medical guides, cookbooks, and herbals, generally labeled as medicine that would bring on a late menstrual flow, or "provoke the monthlies." Both doctors and everyday people regarded regular menstruation as essential to maintaining a woman's health, so anything that stopped her periods was dangerous. Pregnancy was only one possible reason, and a woman could not be absolutely sure she was pregnant until she quickened – that is, felt the child move within her. As we saw in Chapter 1, this was the point at which the child was regarded as gaining a soul to become fully alive; a woman taking medicine to start her period before quickening was generally not regarded as attempting an abortion.

Penalties for attempting or performing an abortion after the child had quickened grew increasingly harsh during the early modern period in both Protestant and Catholic areas. The *Carolina* made aborting a "living" child a capital offense in 1532, prescribing death by decapitation for men and by drowning for women. (Thus the same methods of execution specified for adulterers in Geneva.) Midwives were ordered, "when they come upon a young girl or someone else who is pregnant outside of marriage, they should speak to them of their own accord and warn them with threats of punishment not to harm the fetus in any way or take any bad advice, as such foolish people are very likely to do."[28] Abortion was very difficult to detect, however, and most accusations of abortion emerged in trials for infanticide, in which a mother's attempts to end her pregnancy before the birth became evidence of her intent. Contraception was even harder to detect, and though Protestants all opposed it, there were almost no cases in which it was an issue; it was also never a major theme in Protestant attacks on extra-marital sexuality.

Infanticide had always been the method of last resort for desperate women, but during the Middle Ages courts heard very few cases of infanticide as they recognized it was very difficult to tell if a child had been born dead, had died of natural causes, or had been killed. Though there were no improvements in medical procedures or understanding, this reticence about infanticide changed during the sixteenth century, and more women were executed for infanticide in early modern Europe than any other crime except witchcraft. In some areas it was much more dangerous to be accused of infanticide than witchcraft; in Geneva, for example, 25 women out of 31 charged with infanticide during the period 1595–1712 were executed, as compared with 19 out of 122 for witchcraft.

With justifications that spoke of a rising tide of infanticide, early modern governments, both Protestant and Catholic, began to require all unmarried women who discovered they were pregnant to make an official declaration of their pregnancy; if they did not and the baby subsequently died before baptism, they could be charged with infanticide even if there was no evidence that they actually did anything to cause the death. This was made law in France in 1556, in England in 1624, in Scotland in 1690, and in various German states throughout the seventeenth century. In some jurisdictions, midwives were ordered to help enforce these laws by checking the breasts of women who denied giving birth to see if they had milk, and at times even checking the breasts of all unmarried women in a parish for signs of childbirth; male heads of household were required to report any unmarried female employee they thought might be pregnant. Sometimes this surveillance, or at least suggestions for surveillance, bordered on the pornographic; a German physician suggested, for example, that all unmarried women between the ages of 14 and 48 should be viewed monthly at a public bath to see if their bodies showed any signs of pregnancy.

In some parts of Europe, executions for infanticide or presumed infanticide decreased in the late seventeenth century, though the laws remained on the books. Whether this represented a decrease in the number of infanticides or only a change in enforcement is difficult to say, although there were more orphanages and foundling homes available for infants than there had been earlier. The death rate at such places was extremely high, however, so that placing a child in them did not increase his or her life expectancy by much.

Immodest behavior

Such examinations of the bodies of unmarried women indicate how far early modern governments were willing to go in their attempts not only to stop infanticide, but also to control the sexual activities of those who did not gain the rights to such activities through marriage. Suspicion of unmarried women also took the form of laws forbidding them to live in inns or on their own, and sometimes even to live with their own mothers if their fathers were not alive. In the words of the Strasbourg city council in 1665, allowing unmarried women to live outside of a male-headed household "causes nothing but shame, immodesty, wantonness and immorality."[29] The city council of Wismar in Germany ordered all unmarried women who were not domestic servants to leave town in 1572, noting that these women "pretended to sew in order to have a free life," but really "carried out great lewdness," and in the eighteenth century the city of Neuchâtel banished women for walking around the streets at night.[30] Even domestic servants were not freed from such suspicions, for increasing numbers of moralists and pamphleteers in the sixteenth and seventeenth centuries described maids as whores who were out to seduce the head of household or one of his sons, though court records reveal that the reverse was much more often the case.

Unmarried men were also the targets of preachers and moralists, but this was more often for flamboyant clothing, drinking, and rowdy behavior than for sexual activities. This might be seen as evidence of a continuation of the traditional double standard, but it may also have been the result of men policing their own behavior. Craft guilds often expelled journeymen found guilty of fornication, a punishment the journeymen themselves supported. Indeed, independent journeymen's guilds sometimes became more moralistic than craft guilds or clerical officials. While in the fifteenth century they had organized gang rapes of prostitutes and put great emphasis on sexual prowess, by the last half of the sixteenth they barred members known to frequent prostitutes or associate with women of questionable reputation. Any contact with women, whether in the streets, the shop, or even a marital bed, was disparaged, with journeymen refusing to work next to either a woman or a married colleague. These trends were reinforced by misogynist ideas that rivalled those of medieval monks, but journeymen's hostility to all contacts with women is somewhat surprising given the importance of sexual activity in most notions of ideal lay masculinity. Their rejection of sex may have partly resulted from journeymen's attempts to distinguish themselves from the guild masters who employed them; for masters, a true man was a sexually active head of household with a wife and children. Thus by not associating with women, journeymen asserted their independence from their elders, although this also may have contributed to their propensity for drinking and fighting.

Church and state authorities were not willing to let guilds be the only guarantors of male sexual behavior, however. (Nor were most unmarried men members of journeymen's guilds.) Along with punishing those found guilty of fornication, they also attempted to restrict occasions that they increasingly viewed as sources of sexual temptation, such as parish festivals, spinning bees, and dances. Pastors harangued against male clothing styles in which the penis was contained in a separate codpiece, often brightly colored, stuffed to make it more prominent, and worn with a shortened doublet so that everyone could see it; municipal sumptuary laws that regulated the clothing of urban residents sometimes specifically prohibited codpieces. Dancing was attacked in great detail in laws and sermons, such as that of the Protestant preacher Melchior Ambach:

> To the music of sweet strings and unchaste songs people practise easygoing, whorish gestures, touch married women and virgins

with unchaste hands, kiss one another with whorish embraces; and the bodily parts, which nature has hidden and covered in shame, are uncovered by lechery; and under the cloak of diversion and entertainment, shame and vice are covered.[31]

The most thoroughgoing attempts at restriction of activities judged immoral were in Calvinist cities such as Geneva and Nîmes, where along with dancing the consistories condemned low-cut necklines, cosmetics, certain hairstyles, codpieces, comic plays, games of cards and dice, masquerades, and carnival (Mardi Gras) parties. In Nîmes, dancing proved the hardest to eradicate, with over 1,000 people (out of a population of about 20,000) hauled before the consistory in about 50 years for participating in what one elder called "the devil's pimp."[32]

Prostitution

Along with metaphorical pimps such as dancing, Protestant authorities also combated real pimps and prostitutes. During the period from 1520 to 1590, almost all cities in Germany, first Protestant and then Catholic, closed their municipal brothels, sometimes quietly and sometimes with great fanfare and proclamations against "whoredom" (*Hurerei*) and "procuring" (*Kuppelei*). In England, the Bankside brothels, the only legal and protected brothels in the country, were closed by royal statute in 1546. Until recently, scholars linked this wave of closings to fears about syphilis, which first entered Europe in 1493. Intensive study of city records has shown, however, that leaders very rarely mentioned syphilis as a cause; no one discussed brothel closings at all until several decades after the 1490s, although people realized very quickly that syphilis was spread most easily by sexual contact and associated syphilis with sin.

Moral concerns were more influential than worries about disease in the increasing restrictions on brothels. Selling sex was couched in moral rather than economic language, as simply one type of "whoredom," a term that also included fornication, adultery, and any other sex outside of marriage. The boundaries between prostitution and fornication were not sharp, in the minds of authorities, who charged people with pimping if they arranged any sexual encounter outside of marriage, even if no money was explicitly involved. The figure of the female pimp – the procuress – was portrayed extremely negatively in sermons, popular plays, and ballads, and the word "whore" was used metaphorically to describe one's religious opponents. Luther, for example, regularly called Rome a "whore" and English anti-Catholic writers were even more vituperative, terming the Catholic Church "a foul, filthy, old withered harlot . . . the great Strumpet of all Strumpets, the Mother of Whoredom."[33] Religious and civic leaders increasingly regarded women who sold sex as worse than other criminals, for they seduced other citizens from the life of moral order that authorities regarded as essential to a godly city. Because many women combined occasional prostitution with other types of wage labor such as laundering or selling at the public market, this concern with "whores" contributed to the suspicion of all unmarried women noted above.

Closing the official brothels did not end the exchange of sex for money, of course, but simply reshaped it: smaller, illegal brothels were established; women moved to areas right outside city walls; police and other authorities were bribed to overlook it. In the late seventeenth and early eighteenth centuries large cities such as Amsterdam organized police forces, which monitored taverns and streets, arresting women suspected of selling sex. In English cities, especially London, the Societies for the Reformation of Manners

Figure 2.1
In this scene from the Book of Revelation, the Whore of Babylon rides the seven-headed beast while kings, nobles, merchants, and peasants all honor her. This woodcut was produced in the workshop of Lucas Cranach, an artist who was one of Luther's early followers, as an illustration for Luther's 1522 translation of the New Testament into German. The artist links sexuality, the end of the world, and the papacy by depicting the Whore of Babylon in a papal tiara carrying a chalice.

led the charge, bringing women to court and closing brothels and bawdy houses. Women accused of prostitution were often so poor that punishment by fine was impossible, so they were imprisoned, punished corporally and then banished; by the seventeenth century in England this banishment occasionally included deportation to the colonies. Repeat offenders were sometimes executed, especially if they were also involved in other sorts of crime or had previously been banished and had broken their oath not to return to an area. The increasingly harsh criminal penalties did not keep women from prostitution, however, and the religious wars brought about by the Reformation may have actually led to an increase in the number of women – and occasionally men – who made their living at least in part by selling sex after war forced them to migrate or curtailed other types of employment.

Sodomy

Whoredom was often linked rhetorically with sodomy in Protestant preaching and polemical pamphlets; both were sexual sins that were signs of disorder and depravity, but sodomy was also something more. Protestant writers and jurists accepted the medieval notion that heresy and sodomy were connected, and that both were sins against God; one German jurist commented that "such a monster (*unmensch*) is called a heretic, and generally punished as a heretic, by fire."[34] Now it was Catholics, however, not Templars or Albigensians, who were more likely to be portrayed as sodomites, and particularly the high clergy of the papal court in Rome or members of certain religious orders who lived in enclosed monasteries. German Protestants mixed anti-Italian sentiment in these charges as well; as one anonymous pamphleteer noted, "the sodomitical shrine in Rome" had conspired to "bring the vices of sodomy to Germany."[35] This charge was often repeated, and "Italian marriage" became a standard term for same-sex relations or other types of illicit carnal behavior in Protestant polemic, with Luther noting that even the words for such acts came from across the Alps: "by the grace of God there is no mother tongue in Germany that knows anything about such wickedness."[36]

Protestant writings about the Turks – by which they meant all Muslims – also accused them of sodomy, and authors built on each other's descriptions to imagine ever more shameful acts, particularly in the concealed enclosure of the sultan's court in Istanbul. The Ottoman Empire, wrote Luther, was an "open and glorious Sodom" where "illicit sexual practices have no bounds." Long and vivid discussions of Turkish sexual depravities were often part of stories about Christians captured by Turkish forces, which both titillated and alarmed European readers. Other authors used coded language, simply referring to "Turkish vices" or "dumb sins," leaving their readers or hearers free to imagine what was going on. ("Dumb" here means unspoken rather than stupid, reflecting the notion that these were sins "that cannot be named.") Associating Muslims with sexual deviance was not new in the sixteenth century, but such descriptions reached a wider and more frightened audience in this era when the Ottoman Empire was larger and more powerful than any European state. Protestant authors also lumped their opponents together in terms of false teaching and vice. "Because both the Papacy and the Turk are so blind and senseless," wrote Luther, "they both commit dumb sins without shame, as an honorable, praiseworthy thing."[37]

Protestant authorities could do nothing about the sodomy they imagined was rampant in Rome or Istanbul except use such accusations to defame their opponents, but they could attempt to control it in their own territories. Sodomy became a capital crime in both England and the Holy Roman Empire during the 1530s, although the two areas defined it slightly differently; in the Empire it included relations between two men, two women, or any person and an animal, while in England relations between two women were not mentioned. Theoretical definitions did not always matter in reality, however, for both church and state authorities sometimes acted without any specific statutes. The Scots Parliament, for example, refused a request from the leaders of the Scottish church to outlaw the vices described in the book of Leviticus in the Old Testament, but courts executed people for sodomy and bestiality anyway, with an eighteenth-century Scottish jurist noting that the authority of Leviticus was sufficient and actual laws were not necessary. (Along with adultery in Geneva, this is a good example of law following practice rather than shaping it.)

Despite the harsh polemic, however, the number of actual sodomy cases in the sixteenth and seventeenth centuries was very small, with many jurisdictions never seeing a single case in either ecclesiastical or secular courts. Calvinist areas were more likely than Lutheran or Anglican ones to prosecute individuals for same-sex relations, although the level of prosecution varied widely. In Geneva there were sixty-two prosecutions for sodomy and thirty executions during the period between 1555 and 1678, while in the Calvinist city of Emden in Germany same-sex cases made up less than 1 percent of all of the cases of sexual misconduct that came before the consistory during the period 1558–1745. The Puritans who ruled England during the period 1640–60 were much more worried about blasphemy and illegitimacy than sodomy, and there were very few cases, most of which also involved other crimes such as heresy or assault.

This lack of concern about sodomy in comparison with other types of sexual misconduct resulted in part because same-sex relations did not lead to a child who might require public support, and in part because most male same-sex relations seem to have occurred between a superior and inferior, such as an older man and a younger, or a master and servant. The dominant individual was generally married and had sex with his wife, so he did not fit the stereotype of the sodomite created in Protestant polemics: he was not Italian or Turkish, and did not live behind the walls of a monastery or palace, so in most people's minds he could not be a "sodomite." Because authorities feared that simply mentioning sodomy or other "dumb sins" would lead to such dreadful acts, they also often hesitated to bring accusations to court.

In the late seventeenth century, in a few large cities such as London, Paris, and Amsterdam, alongside age-based same-sex relations homosexual subcultures began to develop with special styles of dress, behavior, slang terms, and meeting places. These networks brought together men of different social classes and backgrounds, and did not necessarily involve a dominant and subordinate partner. Some men began to dress and act effeminately, at least in private, with wigs and even fancier clothing than that worn by most well-to-do men, and distinctive gestures. They met in special houses for sexual relations and socializing. In England such men were called "mollies," a word used originally for prostitutes, and the areas of town where mollies gathered were also frequented by female prostitutes and their customers. By the late eighteenth century, these effeminate men began to describe themselves as having a "condition" or "way of being" that was different from other men, as having what we might term a "homosexual identity."

Authorities occasionally responded brutally when they discovered same-sex networks and subcultures, although the timing of these crackdowns – what historians have termed "moral panics" – has not been fully explained. During the 1730s, upon (in the words of a Dutch newspaper), "the most extraordinary and accidental discovery of a tangle of ungodliness," authorities in the Dutch Republic carried out a campaign that involved interrogations with torture and secret denunciations.[38] Perhaps as many as a hundred boys and men were executed, and others punished by long imprisonment; waves of persecutions continued throughout the eighteenth century, though the number of executions declined. In London the various Societies for the Reformation of Manners organized raids on molly-houses, some of which led to trials and executions. Gradually the link between sodomy and heresy grew weaker in the minds of many authorities, however, and by the middle of the eighteenth century punishments were much more likely to be imprisonment or banishment than burning or hanging.

Women were not immune from sodomy accusations and trials on the continent, although there were only a handful in all of Europe during the early modern period. In part this was because, in the minds of most male authorities, true sexual intercourse always involved penetration, so that female–female sex was seen as a kind of masturbation. (And though Protestants opposed masturbation, they worried very little about it during this period; the great concern with masturbation began in the late eighteenth century.) The cases that did come to trial generally involved women who wore men's clothing, used a dildo or other device to effect penetration, or married other women. The horror with which they were regarded sprang more from the fact that they had usurped a man's social role than that they had been attracted to another woman. In all of these cases, the woman who had remained in women's clothing received a milder punishment. Female–female desire was increasingly portrayed in poetry, drama, pornography, medical literature and the visual arts, sometimes coded as passionate friendship and sometimes as suspicious sexual deviance; the women's quarters of the sultan's palace in Istanbul was one site of such imagined vice. Women themselves did express powerful same-sex emotions in letters and poetry, but there is no evidence of the female equivalent of a molly-house.

Trials for same-sex acts and the development of male homosexual subcultures were urban phenomena in early modern Europe. Trials or even accusations in rural areas were very rare throughout this whole period, in part because people were unwilling to believe that people they knew engaged in behavior portrayed as so monstrous it could not be described. What accusations of sodomy there were in rural areas were more likely to involve animals than persons of the same sex. In Sweden, for example, during the period between 1635 and 1754, 1,500 people (1,486 males and 14 females) were charged with bestiality and only 8 with homosexuality (all males). Of those accused of bestiality, at least 500 people were executed, together with the animals involved; bestiality accounted for about one-third of all capital punishment in Sweden, far more than witchcraft. These figures are extremely high compared to the rest of Europe, where bestiality trials usually numbered less than one per decade in most jurisdictions, and the reasons for the Swedish situation are complex. There was clearly no popular condoning of the practice, for most cases were brought to court by watchful neighbors, who later willingly turned in any animals that had been implicated rather than "feel abomination to have such an animal in her house." Both learned and popular opinion linked bestiality with the devil; as one maid who caught a herdsboy behind a cow stated, "God help you, you have let the devil betray you."[39]

Witchcraft

Other than in Sweden, the devil in Protestant Europe led far more people to witchcraft than to bestiality. Exact numbers are impossible to obtain, but scholars estimate that during the sixteenth and seventeenth centuries somewhere between 100,000 and 200,000 people were officially tried for witchcraft and between 40,000 and 60,000 were executed. Both Protestant and Catholic authorities tried and executed witches, and secular courts were far more deadly than religious ones; the Inquisition, as we will see in Chapter 3, was remarkably mild in comparison to courts in central Europe.

Nearly all pre-modern societies believe in witchcraft and make some attempts to control witches, who are understood to be people who have contact with supernatural powers and use them for evil purposes. Only in early modern central and northern Europe and the English colony in Massachusetts, however, did these beliefs lead to wide-scale hunts and mass executions. Not surprisingly, this early modern upsurge in witch trials — often called the "Witch Craze" or the "Great Witch Hunt" — has been the subject of a huge number of studies over the last forty years. These studies have explored the economic, social, political, legal, theological, and intellectual aspects of witchcraft, and have applied the various theoretical perspectives outlined in the Introduction to their analyses.

Sexual issues emerge in many different ways in witch beliefs, accusations, and trials. In terms of intellectual underpinnings, during the Late Middle Ages, Christian philosophers and theologians developed a new idea about the most important characteristics of a witch. Until that period in Europe, as in most cultures throughout the world, a witch was a person who used magical forces to do evil deeds (*maleficia*). One was a witch, therefore, because of what one *did*, causing injuries or harm to animals and people. This notion of witchcraft continued in Europe, but to it was added a demonological component. Educated Christian thinkers in the Late Middle Ages began to view the essence of witchcraft as making a pact with the devil, a pact that required the witch to do the devil's bidding. Witches were no longer simply people who used magical power to get what they wanted, but people used by the devil to do what *he* wanted. (The devil is always described and portrayed visually as male.) This demonological or Satanic idea of witchcraft was fleshed out, and witches were thought to engage in wild sexual orgies with the devil, fly through the night to meetings called sabbats that parodied the Mass, and steal communion wafers and unbaptized babies to use in their rituals. Some demonological theorists also claimed that witches were organized in an international conspiracy to overthrow Christianity.

Trials involving this new notion of witchcraft as diabolical heresy began in Switzerland and southern Germany in the late fifteenth century, became less numerous in the early decades of the Reformation when Protestants and Catholics were busy fighting each other, and then picked up again about 1560, spreading to much of western Europe and to European colonies in the Americas.

While the trials were secret, executions were not, and the list of charges was read out for all to hear.

Though the gender balance varied widely in different parts of Europe, between 75 and 85 percent of those tried and executed were women. Ideas about women, and the roles women actually played in society, were thus important factors shaping the witch hunts. Most people viewed women as physically, mentally, and morally weaker than men, and so more likely to give in to any kind of offer by the devil, including better food or nicer clothing. Whereas a man could fight or take someone to court, a woman could only scold, curse, or cast spells. Women were associated with nature, disorder, and the body, all of which were linked with the demonic. Women also had more contact with areas of life in which bad things happened unexpectedly, such as preparing food or caring for the ill, aged, new mothers, children, and animals.

Some demonologists expressed virulent misogyny, and particularly emphasized women's powerful sexual desire, which could be satisfied only by a demonic lover. The classic expression of these ideas is the *Malleus Maleficarum The Hammer of* [Female] *Witches*), published in 1486 and traditionally attributed to two German Dominican monks, Heinrich Krämer (ca. 1430–1505 – also known by his Latinized name Institoris) and Jacob Sprenger (ca. 1436–95). In 1484, Pope Innocent VIII (pontificate 1484–92) authorized Krämer and Sprenger to hunt witches in several areas of southern Germany. Krämer oversaw the trial and execution of several groups – all of them women – but local authorities objected to his use of torture and his extreme views on the power of witches, and banished him. While in exile, he wrote a justification of his ideas and methods, the *Malleus Maleficarum*; the treatise also gave Sprenger as an author, but recent research has determined that his name was simply added because he was more prominent and respected than Krämer, and that Krämer was its sole author. A long, rambling, and difficult work, the *Malleus* draws on the writings of many earlier authors as it lays out Krämer's theories about the nature and danger of witchcraft, and provides advice about how to identify and prosecute witches. It repeats standard ideas about women's weakness, and is obsessed with the sexual connection between witches and the devil: "All witchcraft comes from carnal lust, which in women is insatiable . . . Wherefore for the sake of fulfilling their lusts they [women] consort even with devils."[40] In the *Malleus*, the essence of witchcraft was an abjuration of faith by women, and an abjuration directly connected to sex with demons; the women's unbridled lust led them to seek sexual intercourse with the devil, through which they gained power over men, particularly over men's power of procreation. The *Malleus* shaped ideas about witchcraft held by learned scholars and officials, particularly in the heartland of the witch craze in central Europe.

Details of satanic sex were explored in other works on demonology as well, and these then shaped interrogations and trials. The devil and his demons were impotent, so they changed first into female demons (*succubi*) and drew as much semen as possible out of men, either by seducing them with a voluptuous appearance or extracting the semen when the men were asleep or drunk. (Same-sex relations with the devil appear only rarely in demonology.) This could be drastically debilitating to the man, both because of its diabolical nature, and because all sexual intercourse was widely thought to draw brain tissue down the spine and out the penis, making any intercourse a threat to a man's reason and health. (Brain tissue, bone marrow, and semen were often regarded as essentially the same substance, and men were advised to limit their sexual relations if they wished to live a long life.) Once they had what they wanted, demons or the witches they were with might also cast spells to make the men impotent or make their penis disappear.

The demons then changed into male demons (*incubi*) and had sex with female witches, who were attracted to them out of lust; widows and unmarried older women were particularly likely candidates, because women's sexual drive was thought to increase with age. Sex with the devil was not satisfying, however, for his penis was cold and hard, and so witches also had sex with other demons, their animal companions (called "familiars" and more likely a dog than a black cat), and with each other. These orgiastic sexual relations left their mark on a witch's body, which was either an extra nipple for the animal familiar to suckle or a place that did not feel pain. Thus many trial processes included a search for extra nipples (which often involved shaving off all body hair) or "witch-pricking" with needles to find insensitive parts. These investigations were generally carried out by a group of male officials – judges, notaries who recorded the witch's answers, the executioner who did the actual pricking or other types of torture – with the witch at least partially naked, so that it is difficult not to view them as at least partly motivated by sexual sadism.

Authors of demonological works included highly learned theologians, jurists, philosophers, and scientists who also discussed witchcraft in their other writings. Earlier historians viewed their concerns with witches as embarrassing remnants of older beliefs or as marginal to their main concerns. Surely such intelligent men could not really have accepted the idea that thousands of people made pacts and had sex with the devil, through which they gained powers to harm their neighbors? More recently, however, intellectual historians have explored demonology as an intellectual system that made sense to those who accepted it. Such studies have been part of the "linguistic turn" in history, in which greater attention is paid to discourse expressed in words and images. Stuart Clark, for example, analyzes ways in which notions of witchcraft held by

European intellectuals fitted rationally with their ideas about science, history, religion, and politics. He argues that witchcraft was an *idea*, not simply a matter of belief, and that it was inseparable from ideas about social order, proper hierarchies, nature's normal processes, and the consequences of sin. Demonologists included lurid discussions of what went on at witches' sabbats not to sensationalize their works, but because "thinking with demons" helped them to consider other intellectual problems involving the natural world, the political order, and God's purpose in the world.

Walter Stevens provides a very different interpretation of the connection between sex and witchcraft, though one also based on studying the discourse of demonology. He argues that the dramatic upsurge in accusations of witchcraft and development of demonological theory resulted not from certainty about the reality of witchcraft, but from growing skepticism. In the Late Middle Ages, Stevens asserts, highly learned churchmen, lawyers, and officials increasingly doubted the reality of the supernatural order, divine as well as demonic. This "crisis of belief" led them to search desperately for proof of the physical existence of demons, for which sexual interactions between human and demonic bodies were the best verification. Although they arrive at the opposite conclusion about whether learned authors thought demons and witches were real, both Clark and Stevens agree that demonology was a central part of Christian theology and political theory during this period.

While intellectual historians have focused on learned demonology, other scholars have examined actual trials. Most witch trials began with a single accusation in a village or town. Individuals accused someone they knew of using magic to spoil food, make children ill, kill animals, raise a hailstorm, or do other types of harm. Once a charge was made, judges began to question other neighbors and acquaintances, building up a list of suspicious incidents that might have taken place over decades. One of the reasons that those accused of witchcraft were often older was that it took years to build up a reputation as a witch. At this point, the suspect was brought in for questioning by legal authorities, using the type of inquisitorial procedure developed in the thirteenth century, in which all proceedings were in secret and the judge had wide discretionary powers. Judges and inquisitors sought the exact details of a witch's demonic contacts, including sexual ones. Suspects were generally stripped and shaved in a search for a "witch's mark," or "pricked" to find a spot insensitive to pain, and then tortured.

Social historians have pointed out that tensions within families, households, and neighborhoods often played a role in these accusations. Robin Briggs, for example, notes that hostilities between husbands and wives, or between stepmothers and step-children, or between family members at a wedding, could become potent forces in witch accusations. In the intimate circle of the family, love and loyalty were often accompanied by hatred and hostility, and complicated family relationships – step-children, half-siblings, childless families, orphans – created even more possibilities for resentment and allegations. Accusations that a stepmother or a woman not invited to a baptism or wedding was causing a child to sicken and die were not simply part of fairy tales, but also of actual trials.

Learned demonology – with its *incubi* and *succubi*, sabbats, night-flying, and animal familiars – gradually infiltrated popular notions of witchcraft (including our own with its black cats and broomsticks) in many parts of Europe. Trials still began with an accusation of *maleficia*, but many of these also had a sexual component. (Neither demonology nor sexual relations with the devil were important aspects of witch trials in Scandinavia, England, or eastern Europe, however.) Witches were sometimes accused of stealing penises or causing them to be non-functional, drying up a woman's menstrual flow, or lessening fertility in women or animals; the witches themselves were described as barren, hard, dry, unable to menstruate, weep, lactate, or feel either emotional or physical pain. The witch was the inversion of a "good woman," and set a negative standard for women; she was portrayed as argumentative, willful, independent, aggressive, and sexual, rather than chaste, pious, silent, obedient, and married. To those prosecuting her, the witch did not fulfill her expected social and sexual role as a wife; the sixteenth-century scientist and physician Theophrastus Paracelsus describes witches as "turning away from men, fleeing men, hiding, wanting to be alone, not attracting men, not looking men in the eye, lying alone, refusing men."[41] As the indictment of Margaret Lister in Scotland in 1662 put it, she was "a witch, a charmer, and a libber."[42] The last term carried the same connotation and negative assessment of "liberated woman" that it does today.

Were women accused of witchcraft really like this? The first person accused in many trials, especially in the German heartland of the witch craze, often closely fit the Halloween and Hollywood stereotype of a witch: female, old, poor, unmarried or widowed, and in some way peculiar looking or acting. She may indeed have aggressively cursed her neighbors, and might even have provided them with "magical" services such as finding lost objects, attracting desirable suitors, or harming enemies. Even without torture, women some-times confessed, and perhaps after decades of providing magical services, they were as convinced as their neighbors of their own powers. They also often argued, however, that they *had* indeed been good women, until Satan led them astray; thus they were his victims, not his accomplices, and had usually been enticed with food, not sex. When they did describe demonic sexual encounters, they emphasized violence, framing these as rape in hopes of winning judicial sympathy.

The witch was also seen as the inversion of the good mother, for anxieties about motherhood emerge as often as sexual antagonism in witch trials. Witches were charged with actions that destroyed, rather than sustained, infants and children, such as drying up a woman's milk or poisoning children with food. As one English witch confessed, "she touch[ed] the said John Patchett's wife in her bed and the child in the grace-wife's [midwife's] arms. And then she sent her said spirits to bewitch them to death, which they did."[43] Women who took care of the mother and infant immediately after birth were often victims of witch accusations, accused by mothers whose infants had sickened or died under their care. Women brought charges against other women in other situations as well, for accusations frequently arose in situations that were largely confined to women, such as food preparation and preservation or the care of young children. A woman also gained economic and social security by conforming to the standard of the good wife and mother and by confronting women who deviated from it.

Every aspect of sexuality could thus be affected by witchcraft: desire, potency, coition, fertility, reproduction, and family survival from one generation to the next. Witch trials therefore involved a powerful mix of emotions as well as ideas, which Lyndal Roper has used to explore the psychic world of both the accuser and accused. Roper draws on ideas from modern psychoanalysts, including the Austrian-born Melanie Klein, to examine the deep psychic structures that underlay these emotions. She uses the word "fantasy" to describe the story that people told to themselves to express and relieve this powerful emotional dynamic, but does not imply with this that people were consciously making something up. "Fantasy" is instead exactly what Stuart Clark describes as "thinking with demons," using the idea of witches to explain and cope with the world around them.

Fantasies of witchcraft could sometimes grip whole towns and provinces, what historians have called a "witch panic." Panics generally grew out of individual trials; people who had been implicated by the initial accused were brought in for questioning, and the circle grew into a much larger hunt. Panics were most common in the part of Europe that saw the most witch accusations in general – the Holy Roman Empire, Switzerland, and parts of France. Most of this area consisted of very small governmental units, which were jealous of each other and after the Reformation were divided by religion. The rulers of these small territories often felt more threatened than did the monarchs of western Europe, and they saw persecuting witches as a way to demonstrate their piety and concern for order. In areas where diabolism never became an important part of the witch stereotype, such as Scandinavia, the northern Netherlands, or England, mass trials were very rare and the rate of execution was much lower than in places where demonic connections were emphasized.

Panics often occurred after some type of climatic disaster, such as an unusually cold and wet summer, and they came in waves. In large-scale panics a wider variety of suspects were taken in – wealthier people, children, a greater proportion of men. Mass panics tended to end when it became clear to legal authorities, or to the community itself, that the people being questioned or executed were not what they understood witches to be, or that the scope of accusations was beyond belief. Some from their community might be in league with Satan, they thought, but not this type of person and not as many as this.

Similar skepticism led to the gradual end of witch hunts in Europe. Even in the sixteenth century a few individuals questioned whether witches could ever do harm, make a pact with the devil, or engage in the wild activities attributed to them. Doubts about whether secret denunciations were valid or torture would ever yield a truthful confession gradually spread among the same type of religious and legal authorities who had so vigorously persecuted witches. Prosecutions for witchcraft became less common and were gradually outlawed. The last official execution for witchcraft in England was in 1682, though the last one in the Holy Roman Empire was not until 1775.

The timing of the most extreme phase of the witch craze – from 1560 to 1660 – suggests some link with the Reformation, and historians have pointed out that extirpating witches was regarded by all sides in the religious controversy as proof of their religious zeal. A godly society that could not include fornicators, adulterers, or sodomites could certainly not include witches. Religious differences do not explain very much about witchcraft patterns, however: Calvinist Geneva had an extremely low execution rate (21 percent) while the nearby Calvinist area of Vaud had the highest in Europe (90 percent); the Catholic prince-bishops of Germany sometimes oversaw the executions of hundreds of people in less than a decade, while there is no clear evidence the Roman Inquisition ever executed any witches. The Protestant ideal of the nurturing wife and mother certainly provided a standard against which deviant female behavior could be judged and found wanting, as women charged with either infanticide or witchcraft (or both) discovered to their peril. That ideal, however, and the corresponding ideal for masculine behavior of the responsible household head who has sex only with his wife and never with maids, boys, or demons, was one that – as we shall see in the next chapter – came to be accepted by Catholics as well.

* * *

Witchcraft cases provide the most extreme – and deadly – example of the coming together of popular traditions, learned ideas, and new mechanisms for control, but in many ways all regulation of sexuality in Protestant Europe was dependent on these three factors operating together. The Protestant message about the centrality of marriage to the social order fit with urban and village values that preceded the Reformation, and Protestant authorities depended on the cooperation of city residents and villagers to report infractions. (Indeed, in an era before professional police forces, there was no other way.) Thus courts and consistories reinforced older forms of local and communal decision making along with the aims of the larger state. Protestant authorities did intervene in people's sexual lives more than their pre-Reformation counterparts had, but for many people appropriate marriages and stable families were their aims as well. In contrast to contemporary family courts, where most cases involving marriage are brought by people seeking to end theirs, the majority of marriage cases in most early modern Protestant courts were brought by people – almost always women – seeking to form a marriage. This was not simply a result of their religious values, of course, but of the social and economic benefits of marriage; plaintiffs found support for their case in the sermons and writings of the reformers, however. Those reformers' own marriages – even those that were not good models of family order – provided every village and city with visible examples about what was different in Protestant teachings about sex.

Obviously the aims of authorities and of those they governed did not always correspond. (If they had, this would be a very short book.) Practices that reformers opposed but that did not upset marriage – such as sexual relations between engaged persons – continued, despite all efforts to eradicate them. Brothels were closed, but prostitution continued. Sodomy was demonized, but persecution was sporadic. Efforts to control sin discriminated by class and gender. Kings and high nobles were open about their mistresses and other sexual exploits, and those mistresses – often members of the upper classes themselves – were not arrested, but instead became wealthy and powerful, and their children given property and noble titles. Men's heterosexual activities outside of marriage were condemned, but only women's were regularly punished. Some individuals did internalize the moral norms communicated to them, but others paid little attention to them, or acted on their sexual desires despite them. This internal conflict between Christian teachings and sexual proclivities has left only a few traces in early modern Protestant Europe, however, in contrast to today, when newspapers and television programs are filled with prominent religious leaders apologizing for sexual lapses.

This chapter has often referred to "church and state authorities" in one breath because, despite frequent disputes over jurisdiction, the treatment of sexual issues did not differ markedly in secular and ecclesiastical courts.

Although some sexual activities merited only religious sanctions such as temporary or permanent exclusion from communion, in general territorial and national ordinances adopted stringent church prohibitions into secular law during the sixteenth and seventeenth centuries, in the "criminalization of sin." In the eighteenth century – in England as early as 1660 – ecclesiastical courts lost their jurisdiction over some sexual matters to secular courts, which increasingly concentrated on sexual conduct that had economic consequences, such as the bearing of illegitimate children. As this happened, some sins began to be decriminalized; in parts of Prussia, for example, pregnancy out of wedlock was decriminalized in 1765 with the argument that this might lessen infanticide. Such changes were not simply the result of changes in jurisdiction, however, for by this point church courts had also begun to stop prosecution of fornication, though the laws against it had not changed.

This cooperation and agreement between church and state authorities in Protestant Europe may come as no surprise because the Protestant churches throughout Europe were to a large degree state churches, with their officials regarded as state employees and often responsible for political actions like announcing new laws from the pulpit. (Calvinist churches in some parts of Europe and radical groups such as Mennonites and Quakers were the exceptions.) The following chapter will allow us to see whether this was also the case where church and state were at least in theory independent from one another.

Selected further reading

A solid survey of developments across Europe during this period is Katherine Crawford, *European Sexualities, 1400–1800* (Cambridge: Cambridge University Press, 2007). Several recent essay collections bring together the work of historians, art historians, and scholars of literature on topics related to the discussion in this chapter: Robert Purks Maccubbin, ed., *'Tis Nature's Fault: Unauthorized Sexuality during the Enlightenment* (Cambridge: Cambridge University Press, 1987); James Grantham Turner, ed., *Sexuality and Gender in Early Modern Europe: Institutions, Texts, Images* (Cambridge: Cambridge University Press, 1993); Richard Burt and John Michael Archer, eds, *Enclosure Acts: Sexuality, Property, and Culture in Early Modern England* (Ithaca, N.Y.: Cornell University Press, 1994).

The reformers' ideas about sexuality are usually presented in the context of their ideas about women and the family or human nature and sin. On Luther, see Merry E. Wiesner, "Luther and Women: The Death of Two Marys," (123–37) and Daphne Hampson, "Luther on the Self: A Feminist Critique," (215–24), both in Ann Loades, ed., *Feminist Theology: A Reader*

(London: SPCK, 1990); Stephen B. Boyd, "Masculinity and Male Dominance: Martin Luther on the Punishment of Adam," in Stephen B. Boyd, W. Merle Longwood, and Mark W. Muesse, eds, *Redeeming Men: Religion and Masculinities* (Louisville, Ky.: Westminster John Knox, 1996), 19–32; Scott Hendrix, "Luther on Marriage," *Lutheran Quarterly* 14(3) (2000): 335–50; Mickey L. Mattox, "Luther on Eve, Women and the Church," *Lutheran Quarterly* 17(4) (2003): 456–74. For articles that focus particularly on Luther's ideas about sex, see Thomas A. Fudge, "Incest and Lust in Luther's Marriage Theology and Morality in Reformation Polemics," *Sixteenth Century Journal* 34 (2003): 321–28 and Merry E. Wiesner-Hanks, "Lustful Luther: Male Libido in Luther's *Lectures on Genesis,*" in *Sexuality and Culture in Medieval and Renaissance Europe,* edited by Philip M. Soergel (New York: AMS Press, 2005), 123–48. *Luther on Women: A Sourcebook*, ed. and trans. Susan C. Karant-Nunn and Merry E. Wiesner-Hanks (Cambridge: Cambridge University Press, 2003) contains translations and analysis of Luther's main writings on women, the family, and sexuality.

Susan Karant-Nunn, "*Kinder, Küche, Kirche:* Social Ideology in the Sermons of Johannes Mathesius," in Susan Karant-Nunn and Andrew Fix, eds, *Germania Illustrata: Essays Presented to Gerald Strauss* (Kirksville, Mo.: Sixteenth Century Journal Publishers, 1991), 121–40 discusses the ideas of a typical early Lutheran pastor. Steven Ozment, *When Fathers Ruled: Family Life in Reformation Europe* (Cambridge, Mass.: Harvard University Press, 1983) discusses the ideas of a number of Protestant thinkers, as does Scott Hendrix, "Masculinity and Patriarchy in Reformation Germany," *Journal of the History of Ideas* 56 (1995): 177–93. See also the essays in Scott Hendrix and Susan C. Karant-Nunn, eds, *Masculinity in the Reformation Era* (Kirksville, Mo.: Truman State University Press, 2008).

The ideas of John Calvin about women have been the focus of a number of good studies, including Jane Dempsey Douglass, *Women, Freedom and Calvin* (Philadelphia: Westminster John Knox, 1985) and John Lee Thompson, *John Calvin and the Daughters of Sarah: Women in Regular and Exceptional Roles in the Exegesis of Calvin, His Predecessors and His Contemporaries* (Geneva: Droz, 1992). As yet there is no similar study of Calvin's ideas about sexuality. For an analysis of the thought of other reformers, see: Amy Nelson Burnett, "Church Discipline and Moral Reformation in the Thought of Martin Bucer," *Sixteenth Century Journal* 22 (1991): 439–56; H.J. Selderhuis, *Marriage and Divorce in the Thought of Martin Bucer*, trans. John Vriend and Lyle D. Bierma (Kirksville, Mo.: Sixteenth Century Journal Publishers, 1998).

For the ideas of English reformers, see Kathleen M. Davies, "The Sacred Condition of Equality – How Original were Puritan Doctrines of Marriage?" *Social History,* 2 (1977): 563–80; John K. Yost, "Changing Attitudes towards

Married Life in Civic and Christian Humanists," *American Society for Reformation Research, Occasional Papers*, 1 (1977), 151–66; Edmund Leites, *The Puritan Conscience and Modern Sexuality* (New Haven, Conn.: Yale University Press, 1986); Margo Todd, *Christian Humanism and the Puritan Social Order* (Cambridge: Cambridge University Press, 1987); Belden C. Lane, "Two Schools of Desire: Nature and Marriage in Seventeenth-century Puritanism," *Church History* 69(2) (June 2000): 372–402.

For the ideas of the radicals, see Joyce Irwin, ed., *Womanhood in Radical Protestantism* (New York: E. Mellen, 1979); Wes Harrison, "The Role of Women in Anabaptist Thought and Practice: The Hutterite Experience of the Sixteenth and Seventeenth Centuries," *Sixteenth Century Journal* 23 (1992): 49–70; Craig D. Atwood, "Sleeping in the Arms of Christ: Sanctifying Sexuality in the Eighteenth-Century Moravian Church," *Journal of the History of Sexuality* 8 (1997): 25–47; Stephen B. Boyd, "Theological Roots of Gender Reconciliation in Sixteenth Century Anabaptism: A Prolegomenon," *Journal of Mennonite Studies* 17 (1999): 34–51; Kimberly D. Schmidt, Diane Zimmerman Umble, and Steven D. Reschly, eds, *Strangers at Home: Amish and Mennonite Women in History* (Baltimore: Johns Hopkins University Press, 2002); Paul Peucker, "'Inspired by Flames of Love': Homosexuality, Mysticism, and Moravian Brothers Around 1750," *Journal of the History of Sexuality* 15(1) (2006): 30–64; Sylvia Monica Brown, ed., *Women, Gender, and Radical Religion in Early Modern Europe* (Leiden: Brill, 2007); Sigrun Haude, "Gender Roles and Perspectives among Anabaptist and Spiritualist Groups," in John D. Roth and James M. Strayer, eds, *A Companion to Anabaptism and Spiritualism* (Leiden: Brill, 2007); Snyder and Hecht, *Profiles of Anabaptist Women* (note 24); Lyndal Roper, "Sexual Utopianism in the German Reformation," in her *Oedipus and the Devil* (note 31 for Chapter 2 in "Notes").

Changes in legal codes have been discussed in two books by R.H. Helmholz, *Roman Law in Reformation England* (Cambridge: Cambridge University Press, 1990) and *Canon Law in Protestant Lands* (Berlin: Duncker and Humboldt, 1992). For the actual operation of Protestant church courts in England, see Ralph Houlbrooke, *Church Courts and the People During the English Reformation, 1520–1570* (Oxford: Oxford University Press, 1979); G.R. Quaife, *Wanton Wenches and Wayward Wives: Peasants and Illicit Sex in Early Seventeenth Century England* (New Brunswick: Rutgers University Press, 1979); John Addy, *Sin and Society in the Seventeenth Century* (London: Routledge, 1989); R.B. Outhwaite, *The Rise and Fall of the English Ecclesiastical Courts, 1500–1860* (Cambridge: Cambridge University Press, 2007). Paul Hair, ed., *Before the Bawdy Court: Selections from Church Court and Other Records Relating to the Correction of Moral Offences in England, Scotland, and New England, 1300–1800* (London: Elek, 1972) provides extracts from court documents, and Ian McCormick, ed., *Secret Sexualities: A Sourcebook of 17th and 18th Century Writing* (London: Routledge,

1997) includes pamphlets about trials, though not actual trial documents themselves. Marjorie Keniston McIntosh, *Controlling Misbehavior in England 1370–1600* (Cambridge: Cambridge University Press, 1998), David Turner, *Fashioning Adultery: Gender, Sex, and Civility in England, 1660–1740* (New York: Cambridge University Press, 2002), and Laura Gowing, *Common Bodies: Women, Touch and Power in Seventeenth-century England* (New Haven, Conn.: Yale University Press, 2003) use the records of church courts and other institutions as well as other types of sources to study the way bodies and behavior were constructed and controlled.

For studies in English of the process of social disciplining in German-speaking areas, see: Lorna Jane Abray, *The People's Reformation: Magistrates, Clergy, and Commons in Strasbourg, 1500–1598* (Ithaca, N.Y.: Cornell University Press, 1985); Thomas Robisheaux, *Rural Society and the Search for Order in Early Modern Germany* (Cambridge: Cambridge University Press, 1989); Scott Dixon, *The Reformation and Rural Society: The Parishes of Brandenburg-Ansbach-Kulmbach, 1528–1603* (Cambridge: Cambridge University Press, 1996); Amy Nelson Burnett, "Basel's Rural Pastors as Mediators of Confessional and Social Discipline," *Central European History* 33(1) (2000): 67–85. A number of essay collections include discussion of social disciplining in various parts of continental Europe: R.W. Scribner, *Popular Culture and Popular Movements in Reformation Germany* (London: The Hambledon Press, 1987); R. Po-Chia Hsia, ed., *The German People and the Reformation* (Ithaca, N.Y.: Cornell University Press, 1988); Karin Maag, ed., *The Reformation in Eastern and Central Europe* (New York: Scolar Press, 1997); Ulinka Rublack, ed., *Gender in Early Modern German History* (Cambridge: Cambridge University Press, 2002); John M. Headley, Hans Joachim Hillerbrand, and Anthony J. Papalas, eds, *Confessionalization in Europe, 1555–1700: Essays in Honor and Memory of Bodo Nischan* (Aldershot: Ashgate, 2004); Bridget Heal and Ole Peter Grell, eds, *The Impact of the Reformation: Princes, Clergy and People* (Aldershot: Ashgate, 2008).

The impact of Calvin's ideas about marriage and morals in Geneva has been investigated in: Jeffrey R. Watt, "Women and the Consistory in Calvin's Geneva," *Sixteenth Century Journal* 24 (1993): 429–39; Robert M. Kingdon, *Adultery and Divorce in Calvin's Geneva* (Cambridge, Mass.: Harvard University Press, 1995); John Witte Jr. and Robert M. Kingdon, *Sex, Marriage, and Family Life in John Calvin's Geneva: Courtship, Engagement and Marriage* (Grand Rapids, Mich.: W.B. Eerdmans Pub. Co., 2005); John Witte, "Honor Thy Father and Thy Mother? Child Marriage and Parental Consent in Calvin's Geneva," *The Journal of Religion* 86(4) (October 2006): 580–605. For the practice of Calvinism elsewhere in Europe, see: Heinz Schilling, *Civic Calvinism in Northwestern Germany and the Netherlands* (Kirksville, Mo.: Truman State University Press, 1991); Michael F. Graham, *The Uses of Reform: "Godly Discipline" and Popular Behavior in Scotland and Beyond 1560–1610* (Leiden: Brill, 1996); Ben Kaplan, *Calvinists and Libertines: Confession and Community in Utrecht, 1578–1620* (Oxford: Oxford University Press, 1995); Raymond A. Mentzer Jr., "Morals and Moral Regulation in Protestant France," *The Journal of Interdisciplinary History* 31(2) (Summer 2000): 1–20; Benjamin B. Roberts and Leendert F. Groenendijk, "'Wearing out a pair of fool's shoes': Sexual Advice for Youth in Holland's Golden Age," *Journal of the History of Sexuality* 13(2) (April 2004): 139–56; Philip Benedict, *Christ's Churches Purely Reformed: A Social History of Calvinism* (New Haven, Conn.: Yale University Press, 2004); Greaves, *God's Other Children* (note 15); Mentzer, *Sin and the Calvinists* (note 32).

The Societies for the Reformation of Manners have been best studied in England. See: Faramerz Dabhiowala, "Sex, Social Relations, and the Law in Seventeenth and Eighteenth-Century London," in Michael J. Braddock and John Walter, eds, *Negotiating Power in Early Modern Society* (Cambridge: Cambridge University Press, 2001), 85–101; Jennine Hurl-Eamon, "Policing Male Heterosexuality: The Reformation of Manners Societies' Campaigns against the Brothels in Westminster, 1690–1720," *Journal of Social History* 37 (2004): 1017–35.

Three books that directly address issues of sexuality and the state are: Rosalind Mitchison and Leah Leneman, *Sexuality and Social Control: Scotland 1660–1780* (London: Basil Blackwell, 1989); Isabel V. Hull, *Sexuality, State, and Civil Society in Germany, 1700–1815* (Ithaca: Cornell University Press, 1996); Tim Hitchcock, *English Sexualities, 1700–1800* (New York: St. Martin's, 1997).

There are several studies that focus specifically on the regulation of marriage, using court cases and a variety of other documents: Thomas Max Safley, *Let No Man Put Asunder: The Control of Marriage in the German Southwest* (Kirksville, Mo.: Sixteenth Century Publishers, 1984); Martin Ingram, *Church Courts, Sex and Marriage in England 1570–1640* (Cambridge: Cambridge University Press, 1987); Lyndal Roper, *The Holy Household: Women and Morals in Reformation Augsburg* (Oxford: Clarendon Press, 1989); Eric Josef Carlson, *Marriage and the English Reformation* (Oxford: Blackwell, 1994); Richard Adair, *Courtship, Illegitimacy and Marriage in Early Modern England* (Manchester: Manchester University Press, 1996); Watt, *Making of Modern Marriage* (note 26); Harrington, *Reordering Marriage* (note 18). On clerical marriage, see Helen L. Parish, *Clerical Marriage and the English Reformation: Precedent Policy and Practice* (Burlington, Vt.: Ashgate, 2000); Gerritdina D. Justitz, "The Abbot and the Concubine: Piety and Politics in Sixteenth-Century Naumburg," *Archiv für Reformationsgeschichte* 92 (2001): 138–64, and Sherlock, "Monuments" (note 17). On the households of married clergy, see Susan C. Karant-Nunn, "The Emergence of the Pastoral Family in the German Reformation: The Parsonage as a Site of Socio-Religious Change," in C. Scott Dixon and Luise Schorn-Schütte, eds, *The Protestant Clergy in Early Modern Europe* (Basingstoke: Palgrave Macmillan, 2003), 79–99.

Changes in engagement, wedding, and churching ceremonies have been explored most fully in: Susan C. Karant-Nunn, *The Reformation of Ritual: An Interpretation of Early Modern Germany* (London: Routledge, 1997) and David Cressy, *Birth, Marriage* (note 23); see also Lyndal Roper, "Going to Church and Street: Weddings in Reformation Augsburg," *Past and Present* 106 (1985): 62–10; Christine Peters, "Gender, Sacrament and Ritual: The Making and Meaning of Marriage in Late Medieval and Early Modern England," *Past & Present* 169 (November 2000): 63–96; Bryan D. Spinks, "Conservation and Innovation in Sixteenth Century Marriage Rites," in *Worship in Medieval and Early Modern Europe: Change and Continuity in Religious Practice*, edited by Karin Maag and John D. Witvliet (Notre Dame, Ind.: University of Notre Dame Press, 2004) 243–80; and several of the essays in Robert Forster and Orest Ranum, eds, *Ritual, Religion and the Sacred: Selections from the Annales* (Baltimore: Johns Hopkins, 1982). For childbirth, see Judith P. Aikin, "Gendered Theologies of Childbirth in Early Modern Germany and the Devotional Handbook for Pregnant Women by Aemilie Juliane, Countess of Schwarzburg-Rudolstadt," *Journal of Women's History* 15(2) (Summer 2003), 40–67; Crowther-Heyck, "Be fruitful" (note 7); Fissell, "Politics of Reproduction" (note 22).

The books noted above on marriage all discuss divorce, and there are also several works that focus on divorce specifically: Phillips, *Putting Asunder* (note 25) and Lawrence Stone, *Road to Divorce: England 1530–1987* (Oxford: Oxford University Press, 1990) are both broad overviews. Stone has also written two books of case studies, *Uncertain Unions: Marriage in England 1660–1753* (New York: Oxford, 1992) and *Broken Lives: Separation and Divorce in England 1660–1857* (New York: Oxford, 1993).

Along with being viewed through the lens of marriage, the control of sexuality has also been explored as part of the history of crime. Studies of crime that focus particularly on issues of gender and sexuality include: Jenny Kermode and Garthine Walker, eds, *Women, Crime and the Courts in Early Modern London* (Chapel Hill: University of North Carolina Press, 1994); Frances E. Dolan, *Dangerous Familiars: Representations of Domestic Crime in England 1550–1700* (Ithaca, N.Y.: Cornell University Press, 1994); Ulinka Rublack, *The Crimes of Women in Early Modern Germany* (Oxford: Oxford University Press, 1999); Garthine Walker, *Crime, Gender and Social Order in Early Modern England* (Cambridge: Cambridge University Press, 2003); Florike Egmond, "Incestuous Relations and their Punishment in the Dutch Republic," *Eighteenth-Century Life* 25(3) (Fall 2001): 20–42; William G. Naphy, *Sex Crimes: From Renaissance to Enlightenment* (Stroud, Glos.: Tempus, 2004). Richard van Dülmen, *Theatre of Horror: Crime and Punishment in Early Modern Germany,* trans. Elisabeth Neu (New York: Polity Press, 1990) provides good statistics.

Peter C. Hoffer and N.E.H. Hull, *Murdering Mothers: Infanticide in England and New England 1558–1803* (New York: New York University Press, 1981); Mark Jackson, *New-Born Child Murder: Women, Illegitimacy and the Courts in Eighteenth-Century England* (Manchester: Manchester University Press, 1996); Laura Gowing, "Secret Births and Infanticide in Seventeenth-Century England," *Past & Present* 156 (August 1997): 87–115; Marilyn Frances, "Monstrous Mothers, Monstrous Societies: Infanticide and the Rule of Law in Restoration and Eighteenth-century England," *Eighteenth-Century Life* 21(2) (May 1997): 133–56; Mark Jackson, ed., *Infanticide: Historical Perspectives on Child Murder and Concealment, 1550–2000* (Burlington, Vt.: Ashgate, 2002) all examine legal, economic, and social factors affecting women charged with killing their infants or small children, while Ulinka Rublack focuses on the role of the community in "The Public Body: Policing Abortion in Early Modern Germany," in Lynn Abrams and Elizabeth Harvey, *Gender Relations in German History: Power, Agency and Experience from the Sixteenth to the Twentieth Century* (Durham, N.C.: Duke University Press, 1997), 57–79.

On sexual violence, see: Garthine Walker, "Rereading Rape and Sexual Violence in Early Modern England," *Gender and History* 10 (1998): 1–25; Elizabeth Foyster, *Marital Violence: An English Family History, 1660–1857* (Cambridge: Cambridge University Press, 2005); Frances E. Dolan, *Marriage and Violence: The Early Modern Legacy* (Philadelphia: University of Pennsylvania Press, 2008).

The fullest study of late medieval and early modern prostitution is that by Beate Schuster mentioned in note 30, which has, unfortunately, not been translated. See also: Lyndal Roper, "Discipline and Respectability: Prostitution and the Reformation in Augsburg," *History Workshop* 19 (Spring 1985): 3–28; Randolph Trumbach, "Sex, Gender, and Sexual Identity in Modern Culture: Male Sodomy and Female Prostitution in Enlightenment London," *Journal of the History of Sexuality* 2(2) (1991): 186–203; Sophie Carter, *Purchasing Power: Representing Prostitution in Eighteenth-century English Popular Print Culture* (Burlington, Vt.: Ashgate, 2004). Peter Spierenberg includes discussion of prostitutes in his *The Prison Experience: Disciplinary Institutions and their Inmates in Early Modern Europe* (New Brunswick, N.J.: Rutgers University Press, 1991). On the use of images of "whoredom" for religious opponents, see especially Frances Dolan, *Whores of Babylon: Catholicism, Gender and Seventeenth-Century Print Culture* (South Bend, Ind.: Notre Dame University Press, 2005).

The first major study of same-sex relations in the early modern period was Alan Bray, *Homosexuality in Renaissance England* (London: Gay Men's Press, 1982; revised edition New York: Columbia University Press, 1995), which still remains extremely useful, as does E. William Monter, "Sodomy and Heresy in Early Modern Switzerland," *Journal of Homosexuality* 6 (1980/81): 41–53. Since then there have been a number of important collections and monographs: Kent Gerard and Gert Hekma, eds, *The Pursuit of Sodomy: Male Homosexuality in Renaissance and Enlightenment Europe* (New York: Harrington Park Press, 1989); Jonathan Goldberg, *Queering the Renaissance* (Durham, N.C.: University of North Carolina Press, 1994); Thomas Betteridge, ed., *Sodomy in Early Modern Europe* (New York: Manchester University Press, 2002); Katherine O'Donnell and Michael O'Rourke, eds, *Love, Sex, Intimacy, and Friendship between Men, 1550–1800* (New York: Palgrave Macmillan, 2003); Katherine O'Donnell and Michael O'Rourke, *Queer Masculinities, 1550–1800* (London: Palgrave, 2006). Richard Davenport-Hines, *Sex, Death and Punishment: Attitudes to Sex and Sexuality in Britain since the Renaissance* (London: Collins, 1990) looks at both homosexuality and venereal disease. On the role of sodomy in Protestant discourse, see: Christopher Elwood, "A Singular Example of the Wrath of God: The Use of Sodom in Sixteenth-Century Exegesis," *Harvard Theological Review* 98(1) (January 2005): 67–93; Jacqueline Pearson, "'One Lot in Sodom': Masculinity and the Gendered Body in Early Modern Narratives of Converted Turks," *Literature and Theology* 21(1) (March 2007): 29–48; Puff (note 35), Falkner (note 37).

Most of the studies in the previous paragraph focus exclusively or primarily on men. Same-sex relations between women have been investigated in: Emma Donoghue, *Passions Between Women: British Lesbian Culture 1668–1801* (London: Scarlet Press, 1993); Randolph Trumbach, "London's Sapphists: From Three Sexes to Four Genders in the Making of Modern Culture," in Gilbert Herdt, ed., *Third Sex, Third Gender: Beyond Sexual Dimorphism in Culture and History* (New York: Zone Books, 1994), 111–36; Valerie Traub, *The Renaissance of Lesbianism in Early Modern England* (Cambridge: Cambridge University Press, 2002).

Early modern witchcraft has a huge literature. The best place to start on any topic is the four-volume *Encyclopedia of Witchcraft: The Western Tradition,* edited by Richard Golden (New York: ABC-Clio, 2006). The most up-to-date general survey is Brian P. Levack, *The Witch-Hunt in Early Modern Europe,* 3rd edn (London: Longman, 2006). For a recent overview of new scholarship, see: Thomas A. Fudge, "Traditions and Trajectories in the Historiography of European Witch Hunting," *History Compass* 4(3) (2006): 488–527. For an overview of witchcraft studies relating to women, see the chapter on witchcraft in my *Women and Gender in Early Modern Europe,* 3rd edn (Cambridge: Cambridge University Press, 2008). Good collections of original sources include Alan C. Kors and Edward Peters, eds, *Witchcraft in Europe 400–1700: A Documentary History,* 2nd edn (Philadelphia: University of Pennsylvania Press, 2001); Brian Levack, *The Witchcraft Sourcebook* (New York: Routledge, 2003).

The works of historians mentioned by name in the text are: Stuart Clark, *Thinking with Demons: The Idea of Witchcraft in Early Modern Europe* (Oxford: Oxford University Press, 1997); Walter Stevens, *Demon Lovers: Witchcraft, Sex, and the Crisis of Belief* (Chicago: University of Chicago Press, 2002); Robin Briggs, *Witches and Neighbors: The Social and Cultural Context of European Witchcraft* (New York: HarperCollins, 1996); Lyndal Roper, *Witchcraze: Terror and Fantasy in Baroque Germany* (New Haven, Conn.: Yale University Press, 2004).

Dyan Elliott, *Fallen Bodies: Pollution, Sexuality, and Demonology in the Middle Ages* (Philadelphia: University of Pennsylvania Press, 1999) provides a thorough examination of ideas linking witches and sex before the Reformation. The full *Malleus Maleficarum* has now been translated into English: Christopher S. Mackay, *Hammer of Witches* (Cambridge: Cambridge University Press, 2009). Hans Peter Broedel, *Malleus Maleficarum and the Construction of Witchcraft: Theology and Popular Belief* (New York: Manchester University Press, 2003) is the first book-length study in English of the most influential witchcraft treatise. Two studies that address the issue of motherhood and witchcraft are Lyndal Roper, "Witchcraft and Fantasy in Early Modern Germany," in her *Oedipus and the Devil* (note 30) and Deborah Willis, *Malevolent Nurture: Witch-Hunting and Maternal Power in Early Modern England* (Ithaca, N.Y.: Cornell University Press, 1995). Moira Smith, "The Flying Phallus and the Laughing Inquisitor: Penis Theft in the Malleus Maleficarum," *Journal of Folklore Research* 39(1) (January/April 2002): 85–117 and Edward Bever, "Witchcraft, Female Aggression, and Power in the Early Modern Community," *Journal of Social History* 35(4) (2002): 955–88 both look at sexual issues. Two studies that link witchcraft with male control of female sexuality are Marianne Hester, *Lewd Women and Wicked Witches* (London: Routledge, 1992) and Anne Llewellyn Barstow, *Witchcraze: A New History of the European Witchhunts* (New York: Pandora, 1994). Diane Purkiss, *The Witch in History: Early Modern and Twentieth-Century Representations* (London: Routledge, 1996) provides a thorough and often witty analysis of contemporary representations of witchcraft and the recent academic study of witchcraft.

CATHOLIC AND ORTHODOX EUROPE

THE PROTESTANT REFORMATION divided western Christianity, and was responsible for significant changes in areas that remained Catholic as well. Many historians see the developments within the Catholic Church after the Protestant Reformation as two inter-related movements, one a drive for internal reform linked to earlier reform efforts, and the other a Counter-Reformation that opposed Protestants intellectually, politically, militarily, and institutionally. Reform measures that had been suggested since the late Middle Ages – such as doing away with the buying and selling of church offices (termed simony), requiring bishops to live in their dioceses, forbidding clergy to hold multiple offices (termed pluralism), ending worldliness and immorality at the papal court, improving clerical education, changing the church's tax collection and legal procedures – were gradually adopted during the sixteenth century. Reform-minded bishops instituted changes in their dioceses, and beginning with Pope Paul III (pontificate 1534–49), the papal court became the center of the reform movement rather than its chief opponent. Paul III and his successors supported the establishment of new religious orders that preached to the common people, the opening of seminaries for the training of priests, the end of simony, and stricter control of clerical life.

Reforming popes also supported measures designed to combat the spread of Protestant teaching. Paul III reorganized the Inquisition or Holy Office, put its direction in the hands of a committee of cardinals in Rome, and gave it the power to investigate those suspected of holding heretical opinions or committing acts deemed theologically unacceptable. His successor Paul IV (pontificate 1555–59) promulgated an Index of Prohibited Books, which forbade the printing, distribution, and reading of books and authors judged heretical.

(The Index was formally abolished in 1966.) Both of these popes patronized what would become the most important of the new religious orders, the Society of Jesus or Jesuits founded by St. Ignatius Loyola. Jesuits were soon active in establishing schools and colleges throughout Europe and converting areas that had become Protestant back to Catholicism; they also ministered to Catholics in Protestant areas such as England and Ireland, and traveled far beyond Europe as missionaries in Asia and the Americas. In 1545 Paul III convened the Council of Trent, an ecumenical council that met with several breaks over the next eighteen years to define Catholic dogma and reform abuses. In terms of dogma, Trent reasserted traditional Catholic beliefs in response to Protestant challenges: good works as well as faith were necessary for salvation; tradition along with Scripture contained essential Christian teachings; seven sacraments aided salvation and could usually be administered only by a priest; the Virgin Mary and the saints were to be venerated. The Council of Trent also issued a large number of disciplinary decrees, though these were not accepted in all Catholic areas of Europe the way Tridentine dogmatic decrees were. (Regulations from the Council of Trent are termed "Tridentine" from the Latin name for the city of Trent, Tridentum.)

Popes were not the only officials intent on both reforming the Catholic Church and countering Protestantism. In many parts of Europe, other church officials such as bishops, abbots, or abbesses carried out reform movements to raise standards of education and conduct in the institutions under their jurisdiction, and individuals such as Saint Teresa of Avila (1515–82) founded new institutions that followed stricter standards. As they had in the Middle Ages, secular rulers also saw themselves as religious reformers and defenders of the faith, supporting seminaries, promoting higher standards of clerical morality, suppressing heretical opinions, and fighting Protestants. The most dramatic example of secular rulers taking the lead was in Spain, where in 1478 the rulers Ferdinand and Isabella established independent Inquisitions under their control rather than the papacy's, initially designed to investigate the sincerity of Jewish conversions to Christianity. The Inquisition in Spain later investigated a huge range of individuals and activities (including Teresa of Avila for suspected heretical opinions), always answering to the rulers of Spain. In the 1520s Charles V established an Inquisition in the Netherlands, and in the 1530s the rulers of Portugal received papal approval to establish a separate Inquisition there as well. Though the kings of France never established an Inquisition, they, and not the papacy, determined the level of toleration accorded Protestants within their territory. In 1598 Henry IV (ruled 1589–1610) gave French Protestants (termed Huguenots) political and religious rights in a decree termed the Edict of Nantes, and in 1685 Louis XIV (ruled 1643–1715) revoked the Edict of Nantes and declared France a Catholic country.

In some parts of eastern Europe as well, secular rulers also controlled many aspects of church life. With the Turkish overthrow of Constantinople in 1453, many Orthodox Christians lived under Muslim rule, so that the patriarch had greater control over their religious and civil lives than he had had when the Christian emperors were still in power. The limits of Christian independence were set by the Turkish rulers, however, and in other parts of eastern Europe secular rulers had even more authority. The Russian patriarchate was moved from Kiev to Moscow, and in 1589 came under direct control of the tsar. This level of control was not enough for Tsar Peter the Great, who in 1721 abolished the patriarchate and established a synod which he controlled as the ultimate voice of authority in the Russian Orthodox Church. Eastern Orthodoxy did not see a dramatic split in the sixteenth century the way the Western Church did, but it was affected by movements of moral and institutional reform.

Whether the impetus came from the papacy or other church and secular officials, regulating the sexual lives of both clergy and lay people was a key part of Catholic (and to a lesser degree, Orthodox) reform moves that began in the sixteenth century. Both clergy and laity had to be taught correct doctrine on matters of sexual and marital conduct, so that sexual issues became a central part of Catholic confessionalization as well as Protestant. Education and training alone were not sufficient to encourage godly behavior, however, and Catholics along with Protestants used church and secular courts and other institutions in a process of social disciplining. The valorization of one form of sexual relations – those between properly married couples – and the criminalization of all others became a tool in Catholic state building. So, too, did the celebration of virginity, accomplished through increasingly ardent devotions to the Virgin Mary and higher symbolic value accorded to the virginal purity of nuns, the latter guarded through stricter enforcement of enclosure for convents.

As noted in Chapter 2, reformers of all religious denominations aimed to create a moral and pious society, with patterns in the regulation of sexuality differing less across Europe than one might have expected. Nevertheless, Catholic and Orthodox ideas, institutions, and procedures did differ from those of Protestants, as well as from each other. This chapter will explore the regulation of sexuality in Catholic Europe – Spain, Portugal, Italy, France, Poland, parts of Ireland, Germany, and Austria – and in Orthodox eastern Europe. The boundaries of Catholic, Protestant, and Orthodox Europe were not stable during the early modern period, as Catholics and Protestants in western Europe fought wars of religion for over a century and Christians in eastern Europe fought the Turks. There was wide variety within Catholicism and Orthodoxy as well, with the situation, for example, in Spain differing greatly from that in small Catholic principalities in Germany. This fluidity and diversity make generalizations difficult today, and it also made early modern religious and secular authorities uneasy and fearful; they responded by attempting to enforce greater uniformity in the handling of sexual issues as well as matters concerning doctrine and ritual.

Catholic ideas

In the same way that the Catholic Reformation as a whole was both a continuation of earlier reform moves and a battle against Protestantism, Catholic ideas about sexuality both linked with pre-Reformation notions and developed in certain ways because of Protestant ideas. As we saw in Chapter 2, Luther and most other Protestant thinkers affirmed Augustine's link between original

Figure 3.1
The Glorification of the Virgin Saints, attributed to the Jesuit artist Giovan Battista Fiammeri, and hung in 1600 in San Vitale in Rome, the first permanent Jesuit novitiate for the Roman Province. San Vitale was endowed and founded by Isabella della Rovere, a wealthy Italian noblewoman, and the painting reflects her interest in virginity. Here the crowned Virgin Mary is surrounded by other virgin saints as light streams from the sky and cherubs hover above her, suggesting that she will soon be taken up into heaven. Photo: ICCD, Rome 20262.

sin and sexual desire, and regarded sexual desire as so powerful that only a very few individuals could ever live a truly chaste life. They thus recommended marriage for almost everyone, clergy and lay alike, writing voluminously in praise of appropriate marriages and in condemnation of all other forms of sexual activity.

This Protestant championing of marriage and family life was not completely new, however. As noted in Chapter 1, civic leaders and guilds in the late Middle Ages favored stable family units and supported the suppression of any sexual activity that disrupted public order. At the same time, Christian humanists went beyond a critique of the practice of clerical celibacy to question the entire theory behind it; the most prominent of these, Desiderius Erasmus (1464–1536), praised marital life in his treatise *The Institution of Christian Matrimony*. Two theologians at the University of Paris, Martin Le Maistre (1432–81) and John Major (1470–1550), suggested that marital sex for pleasure was no more sinful than, in Major's words, "to eat a handsome apple for the pleasure of it."[1]

Catholic doubts about the value of celibacy continued to the very end of the Council of Trent. Many representatives to the Council reported that most priests in their areas had concubines, and that Protestant accusations of hypocrisy on the issue of clerical chastity were certainly warranted. The delegate representing the staunchly Catholic Duke Albrecht V of Bavaria called for an end to mandatory clerical celibacy, commenting that:

> Many other men who are aware of the current state of affairs in Germany . . . believe that chaste marriage would be preferable to sullied celibacy. They further warn that most able and knowledge-able men in the population would rather have wives without ecclesiastical benefices than benefices without wives.[2]

Delegates sent by Emperors Charles V and Ferdinand I also argued that priests should be allowed to marry, and the issue was debated at Trent in committee for years.

Only in the very last session, with the personal intervention of Pope Pius IV, did the council affirm the policy of mandatory clerical celibacy. Perhaps because this was a matter of such dispute, the language of the Tridentine decree was extreme in its condemnation:

> How shameful a thing, and how unworthy it is of the name of clerics who have devoted themselves to the service of God, to live in the filth of impurity, and unclean bondage, the thing itself doth testify, in the common scandal of all the faithful, and the extreme disgrace entailed on the clerical order.[3]

The decree included a series of increasingly harsh punishments: first the cleric was to be admonished to give up his "concubine, or any other woman of whom any suspicion can exist"; if this did not work, he was to lose a third of his income; if that was not enough, lose his full income; and if even that was not enough, be deprived of his position forever; if he renewed a relationship with "scandalous women of this sort" he was to "be smitten with the sword of excommunication." No other Tridentine decree delineates so many levels of punishment, an indication that the delegates realized this would be a difficult battle.

The sexual lives of religious women were also of great concern to the delegates at Trent, in part because accounts of lustful nuns were a staple of Protestant criticism, both learned and popular. Trent's solution was a new emphasis on Pope Boniface VIII's policy of strict enclosure for all female religious houses, so that women were sharply cut off from the temptations of the world:

> The holy council . . . enjoins on all bishops, by the judgment of God to which it appeals, and under pain of eternal damnation . . . that the enclosure of nuns be carefully restored, wheresoever it has been violated, and that it be preserved, wheresoever it has not been violated . . . for no nun, after her profession, shall it be lawful to go out of her convent, even for a brief period, under any pretext whatever . . . And it shall not be lawful for any one, of whatsoever birth, or condition, sex, or age, to enter within the enclosure of a nunnery, without the permission of the bishop.[4]

The punishments set out were strikingly different than those for priests with concubines; rather than a series of gradual measures, violators immediately risked excommunication. In addition, "the aid of the Secular arm" was to be sought both to keep women in and keep others out; those "Christian princes" and "civil magistrates" who refused to help in this risked excommunication themselves. Thus priestly sex was a matter for church authorities alone (a policy that continued for centuries), while the violation of enclosure was a matter for secular authorities as well. The physical virginity of nuns was not to be a source of independent power for the women, however, for convents were to be closely supervised by male officials.

The Council of Trent thus reaffirmed clerical celibacy, and it also confirmed that marriage was indeed a sacrament and that virginity and celibacy were superior to marriage. It did make changes in other areas of marital doctrine, however, after another discussion that went on for years. The new rules were finally codified in 1563 in the decree *Tametsi*, which affirmed that the basis of marriage was still the free exchange of vows by spouses, but stipulated that to be valid this exchange had to take place before witnesses, including the priest of the parish where the parties had originally agreed to wed; priests were ordered to keep records of all marriages in their parishes. Trent transformed marriage from a union with a series of steps into one in which only one ritual mattered: the priest's verification of the couple's public affirmation of consent. Secret marriages were not binding, and though parental consent was not explicitly required, it became much more difficult for individuals to contract a marriage without the knowledge of their families. *Tametsi* contained a number of other provisions, including ones banning concubinage for lay men as well as priests and adjusting the rules regarding consanguinity and affinity in the choice of marital partners. The Council debated many options in terms of divorce, but finally decreed that adultery, desertion, or religious conversion did not create grounds for divorce and that separation from bed and board with no right of remarriage was the only option for spouses who no longer wished to live together. *Tametsi* made no mention of annulment, but Catholic canon law continued to allow annulment in a very few cases, such as total impotence.

Geminianus Monacensis, a popular seventeenth-century preacher in Munich, brought together Catholic doctrine succinctly in his sermon on marriage. In describing the paintings of a cherub surrounded by lilies and two palm trees that decorated Solomon's temple in Jerusalem, he commented:

> Enlightened by God, Solomon wanted to prefigure with his temple's adornments in what way the Holy Christian Catholic Church was going to be adorned with three kinds of estates: the first being the ecclesiastical epitomized through the Angel Cherub . . . The lilies [next] are an image of the virginal [estate] and the chaste estate of the widow . . . The third adornment of God's church is the holy estate of matrimony represented by the palm trees; it appears as if God created this plant for this very end as to be a mirror for the spouses . . . these plants have such love for one another they cannot bear fruit without each other . . . as soon as they get close to one another . . . their roots . . . intertwine to such a degree that no human being can dissolve them . . . In between these images of marriage Solomon places the Cherub in order to explain: Who is it that must unite these two loving plants? The Angel, that is the Priest: after this kind of union has taken place the two plants can never be divorced again.[5]

Thus the top of the hierarchy is a celibate priesthood, which solemnizes marriage and makes it a sacrament; in the middle are women who have eschewed a sexual life, either virgins or widows; at the bottom are married persons who "can never be divorced" living in a "holy estate."

Catholicism was fortunate in having a single figure who could be venerated both for virginity and matrimony, the Virgin Mary. As we saw in Chapter 1, Marian devotion was strong in the later Middle Ages, and it became even stronger in Catholic areas after the Reformation. Many of the most prominent Catholic reformers were especially devoted to the Virgin, and new buildings, organizations, and ceremonies were added to traditional forms. Jesuits and secular rulers who were attempting to re-Catholicize areas where Protestant ideas had spread emphasized aspects of Mary that were unacceptable to Protestants, particularly her role as intercessor. They dedicated chapels and churches explicitly to "Mary's help" and praised her as the protector of Catholic causes after military victories against Protestants and Turks. New confraternities and sodalities founded in her honor often stressed her sinlessness by declaring that they were particularly devoted to the Virgin of the Immaculate Conception, and portrayed her as the *Immaculata* without a child. Paintings showed her in a crown being carried to heaven by angels, depicting her "bodily assumption" into heaven, an idea that had been widely accepted for centuries but was increasingly questioned by Protestants. (The Assumption of Mary – the teaching that she was transported in body and soul to heaven after her life on earth was finished – became official Catholic dogma in 1950.)

Mary was not only a spotless virgin, of course, but also a wife, and the veneration of her earthly husband Joseph also underwent a transformation with the Catholic Reformation. In sermons and paintings, Joseph changed from a weak old man hovering at the edge of the story to a strong man in the prime of life on whom Mary could depend. The events of Mary and Joseph's marital life, particularly their betrothal and the dream in which Joseph learned the facts of her pregnancy, became very popular as subjects of paintings, plays, and sermons. In Spain three special feast days were set in honor of the betrothal, and the Inquisition regulated how this event was to be depicted and described. Inquisitors attempted, without success, to suppress a very popular story about how Joseph in the company of other young men first met Mary; all the young men were carrying staffs, but only Joseph's staff burst into white flowers when he saw her. The sexual imagery of this story (reinforced by Joseph's being shown with a flowering staff even in non-betrothal scenes) and Joseph's growing role as the patron saint of marriage – prayed to by couples who were having difficulty conceiving or who were reconciling after an adulterous relationship – captures Catholic ambiguity about male sexuality. Joseph carried a flowering staff and offered Mary husbandly protection, but official opinion declared that their marriage was unconsummated; the patron saint of marriage was thus a virile man who remained a virgin all his life. Like Mary, Joseph was an adaptable figure who could have many meanings.

Though some parts of Catholic Europe were slow in adopting them, once they were adopted the decree *Tametsi* and other Tridentine decrees regarding marriage and sexuality formed the basis for Catholic marriage law to a great degree until today. They were codified in the Roman Catechism of 1566, designed to present Tridentine theology in simple language to the faithful, and inspired commentaries and elaborations; the most influential of these was *The Holy Sacrament of Matrimony*, by the Spanish Jesuit Tomás Sánchez (1550–1610). In this work, Sánchez treats marital sexuality in great detail, taking a position in agreement with Le Maistre and Major (and Luther) that sexual enjoyment in marriage was at most only a minor sin. He clinically discusses the levels of sin involved in fondling, fantasies, fellatio, and foreplay, and ultimately judges them to be minor sins or perhaps even sinless as long as they were a prelude to "natural" intercourse, with the man on top and no barriers to conception. Masturbation was still a mortal sin, according to Sánchez, and even spontaneous orgasm should be discouraged if possible through prayers and pious thoughts, but between spouses almost anything that could "show and foster mutual love" was acceptable.[6] Along with several other Catholic theologians such as the Dominicans Peter de Ledesma (d. 1616) and Domingo de Soto (1495–1560), Sánchez asserted that either spouse could refuse intercourse if he or she thought the family was too poor or the educational opportunities for existing children might be harmed by the birth of another. Even more startlingly, Sánchez proposed that in a sexual relationship outside of marriage (already a mortal sin, of course), *coitus interruptus* might be preferable to completed intercourse because having an illegitimate child only made the situation worse.

This move away from viewing procreation as the only justification for sexual intercourse was opposed by more rigorist theologians, including Pope Sixtus V (pontificate 1585–90). Sixtus was an extremely severe moralist who made adultery a capital crime in Rome and declared in the papal bull *Effraenatam* of 1588 that all abortion and contraception were homicide. Those found guilty of administering or taking contraceptives or abortificants were to be excommunicated, an excommunication that could be lifted only by the pope himself. Sixtus's stance was too extreme even for most of the rigorists, however, and his successor Gregory XIV ordered a return to earlier policy, in which excommunication was the punishment only for abortion after the fetus had been "ensouled," a point set at forty days after conception for males and eighty for females. (In 1869 the papacy reverted to Sixtus's opinion and determined that ensoulment occurred at conception, which remains official Catholic teaching.) Sixtus V also forbade all men without testicles or the ability to produce semen to marry (a policy that remained in force until 1977), which had particular effect on the castrated male singers who were becoming increasingly popular in Italy during this time. (Castrati often sang female parts in secular and sacred performances in Spain and Italy from the sixteenth through the nineteenth centuries, a practice encouraged by bans on women singing in church and on public stages.)

Sixtus was not alone in his more rigorist stances, but was joined by zealous bishops. Many of these tried to restrict "occasions to sin," defining these as broadly as any Calvinist: dances, taverns, card games, and weddings. In his effort to promote what he termed a "Christian lifestyle," Carlo Borromeo (1538–84), the moralistic archbishop of Milan, instructed confessors to forbid people who had attended dances on Sundays or holidays to marry for two years, ordered women to wear veils in church, and divided the nave of Milan's main church into men's and women's sections with a wooden screen. He even forbade certain types of clothing, which might "give off suggestions of indecent love . . . with various colors or otherwise."[7] The reforming bishop of the Italian city of Verona was concerned about gatherings in the evenings where women spun and men gathered to socialize, and in 1576 ordered men to "leave the women to spin . . . and do some other activity at home, never leaving in the evening without having first knelt with their families saying three Our Fathers and three Ave Marias . . . praying to that giver of all good, that he keep sin far from the house."[8] A 1680 ordinance from Troyes in France reflected similar worries: "We prohibit men and boys on pain of excommunication . . . to meet with women and girls in the places where they gather at night to spin and work."[9]

While some of Pope Sixtus's measures were very short lived, and many of Borromeo's provoked vigorous opposition or non-compliance, a more rigorist position gradually gained greater acceptance, with theologians like Sánchez and Soto accused of "laxism" and their works placed on the Papal Index. In the seventeenth century the attack on "laxism" became associated in France and some parts of the Low Countries and Germany with a movement called Jansenism, named after a Dutch Catholic theologian, Cornelius Jansen (1585–1683). Jansenism called for personal holiness and moral reform and was attractive to many lay people and nuns as well as male clergy. Jansenists took a harsh, neo-Augustinian view of all sexuality, including marital; the Jansenist theologian Louis Habert (d. 1718), for example, declared that the flood of the Old Testament was brought about by lust in the marriage bed.

Jansenists were particularly concerned that "lax" ideas about sexual relationships were not simply discussed in learned theological treatises, but were communicated to ordinary Christians in confession. The Council of Trent had reiterated the requirement that all believers confess their sins at least once a year after minutely examining their own conscience and actions. Thus the onus of recognizing sexual sins shifted from the priest to the penitent, and priests were even advised *not* to ask too-detailed questions about sexual acts but to rely on penitents' self-reflection. Jesuit confessors in particular developed a new style of moral theology often termed "casuistry" or "moral probabilism," in which the intentions and desires of the individual were weighed in any assessment of the level of guilt. As the moral theologian Jean Benedicti (1573–1662) wrote regarding masturbation: "If a person commits this sin while fantasizing about a married woman, as well as masturbation he is guilty of adultery; if he desires a virgin, indecent assault; if he fantasizes about a relative, incest; a nun, it is sacrilege; if he fantasizes about another male, then it is sodomy."[10]

This concentration on subjective feelings in confession was part of what many scholars see as a gradual transformation of European culture from one in which shame acted as the most effective control of people's actions to one in which guilt was the more important motivator. To the Jansenists, however, most confessors were not making people feel guilty enough, but were instead excusing their actions and thoughts by noting the mitigating factors and moral complexity of many situations. Because such casuistry was particularly associated with Jesuit confessors, the battle in France is often described as one between Jansenists and Jesuits. Many Jansenists in France also opposed the power of the papacy, and Jansenism was condemned several times in the seventeenth century and officially suppressed by papal bulls in the early eighteenth century. Despite these measures, its influence continued among many Catholic clergy.

Among the bulk of the clergy, however, attitudes toward sexual issues moderated in the eighteenth century, or at least moderated in terms of calls for the investigation and punishment of sexual sins. The most influential Catholic writer on moral issues from this period, St. Alphonsus Liguori (1697–1787), clearly advised confessors not to treat too harshly those who were unaware their practices were sinful or to concentrate too much on sins they had little hope of eradicating, such as lustful thoughts or fornication. In his opinion, explaining the sinfulness of acts that people would not give up simply transformed unwitting sins into mortal ones.

Institutions

Had Liguori lived two hundred years earlier, such statements would have led to a trial rather than a canonization process. Not only could committing fornication get one hauled up before a church court, but even saying that fornication was not a mortal sin could as well. The system of church courts that had been set up in the Middle Ages continued after the Reformation in

Catholic areas, but the level of their activities increased right after Trent as they attempted to enforce the new decrees. One of the aims of the Council of Trent was to increase the power of bishops, and the ability of other sorts of church officials such as archdeacons or papal legates to hear cases was curtailed. Episcopal decisions could be appealed to Rome, however, and after Trent the papacy attempted to centralize and standardize procedure, requiring local court decisions to fit with those of the central papal courts such as the Rota. Judges in the Rota often published collections of Rotal decisions and their justifications, and these became standard reference works for church lawyers throughout Europe.

Episcopal courts were thus more active after Trent than they had been before, but many of them concentrated more on doctrinal uniformity than on matters of morality. One reason for this shift in emphasis was Tridentine directives that ordered bishops to pay more attention to extirpating heresy than policing morality. The visitations that bishops were to conduct every two years, sending officials around the diocese to investigate clergy and laity, were also to concentrate primarily on doctrinal issues. As in Protestant areas, these visitations were sometimes a joint venture of state and church, with both ecclesiastical and secular officials asking questions about religious beliefs and practices. The sanctions for heresy also blended church and state; in many areas one could not only be excommunicated for unrepentant heresy, but banished and sometimes executed as well.

Another reason that bishops' courts were less active in policing marriage and morality than they had been earlier was the shift in jurisdiction over these issues to secular courts in many parts of Catholic Europe. The French monarchy, for example, refused to register the disciplinary decrees of the Council of Trent, and ruled on many issues involving marriage, which were then handled by royal courts. Any case in which a priest was involved in a "public scandal" – increasingly defined as any sexual relationship – also came before a royal court. In 1667 Louis XIV created the office of lieutenant general of police, charged with investigating and punishing religious, moral, and sexual offenses. Cities also took over control of certain types of marriage and sexual cases. In 1537, Venice established the Executors against Blasphemy, a panel of nobles that heard cases of blasphemy, gambling, and sexual misdeeds including prostitution, adultery, rape, and fornication. Venice did accept the decrees of Trent, but in 1577, the Venetian council explicitly put this body of lay men in charge of enforcing the Tridentine rules about marriage formation. Another secular court in Venice also began to hear cases of women whose husbands mistreated them, sometimes decreeing separations without any church authorization. In 1623, breach of promise cases in Florence were moved to a secular city court. Municipal courts in France also heard cases of separation, usually brought by women seeking to leave a violent or spendthrift husband.

Along with secular courts, new forms of ecclesiastical courts also took over control of certain types of sexual issues from bishop's courts. The most infamous of these was the Inquisition in its various forms – Spanish, Roman, Netherlandish, Portuguese. Just as with bishops' courts, the primary focus of the Inquisition was investigating heresy, which in different parts of Europe meant different things. In Spain and Portugal the Inquisition initially focused on converted Jews and Muslims, and later on those suspected of magical and superstitious practices. In Italy and the Netherlands it primarily investigated suspected Protestants and freethinkers, and after the 1580s – when religious heterodoxy had been almost completely eradicated – those accused of magical practices. In all of these places, however, certain actions involving sexuality also came under its jurisdiction, though its jurisdiction was sometimes contested by secular courts or bishops' courts, and in some places such as Naples it operated through the bishops' courts. In Spain, for example, of roughly 44,000 cases heard by the Inquisition during the period 1540–1700, 2,645 or 5.9 percent were for bigamy, 1,131 or 2.5 percent for solicitation of sexual favors by priests within the confessional, and thousands more for carrying out love magic or making statements which differed from the church's teachings on sexuality. In the Kingdom of Aragon about 15 percent of the Inquisition's activity in this period involved sexual matters, with similar figures for the Roman Inquisition.

In sharp contrast to Liguori's later position, the Iberian Inquisitions regarded unfamiliarity with Church doctrines as something to be corrected rather than indulged. For example, committing fornication was a sin, but saying that sexual relations between two unmarried people was not a sin was much worse, even if done in ignorance. Such persons were to be punished, "for in this way they will be relieved of their ignorance, and the punishment will have its terrifying effect on others."[11] Such ignorance was also to be combated by an annual reading of the Edict of Faith from every pulpit, in which approved Catholic positions on a range of matters were explained in simple language, and people were encouraged to report to the Inquisition any neighbor or acquaintance whose statements or actions were in contrast to these. In addition to accusations that originated from private witnesses, the Inquisition also conducted regular visitations and established a system of commissioners and unpaid lay agents, called *familiares*, who were to report suspects and also assist in bringing them in for investigation. In some cities there came to be as many as one *familiar* for every fifty people, though there were far fewer in the rural areas.

According to many of its historians, the Inquisition thus created a climate of suspicion in some parts of its jurisdictions; the social stigma of being investigated had such a strong "terrifying effect" that severe punishments were not necessary. In contrast to its modern reputation, executions based on trials before the Inquisition were rare; of the 44,000 cases in the Spanish Inquisition noted above, only 826, or 1.8 percent resulted in an execution, though in an additional 1.7 percent a sentence of execution was set, but the accused had fled and so he or she was burned in effigy. Both the execution rate and the number of investigations as a whole also decreased beginning in the late seventeenth century, as the result of a clear decline in inquisitorial zeal and activities, and a possible decline in prohibited activities after decades of repression. Studies of the Roman Inquisition based on local records have also found decreasing fervor and a moderation in punishment in the eighteenth century similar to that of the Spanish Inquisition. (The records of the Roman Inquisition and Papal Index were just opened to scholars in 1997, so that future research will be able to give a more detailed picture of their activities.) Inquisitors had to be reminded that they were supposed to report cases to their superiors, and *autos-da-fé* became rare occurrences.

Like Protestantism, Catholicism did not rely solely on courts and visitations to communicate its ideas about proper sexual behavior and concepts. Though the sermon was not the center of the Catholic mass the way it was of the Protestant service, the Council of Trent emphasized the importance of preaching for both communication and control. The frequency of sermons increased in many areas, and by 1600 printed collections of Catholic sermons on moral as well as theological topics were widely available in Latin and the vernaculars. Trent authorized the preparation of the Roman Catechism of 1566, which explained basic doctrine on all issues. Its discussion of the purposes of marriage added nothing new, but it did give a slightly more positive interpretation than many medieval commentators had by ranking companionship and mutual help as more important than procreation and the avoidance of fornication. Catholic officials supported the publication of other devotional books and pictures and the presentation of plays that also communicated Catholic doctrine and stressed both heroic deeds of chastity and pious family life. While some materials were promoted, others were banned; the Index censored books that it judged "lascivious and obscene" as well as those it judged heretical, ordered books to be confiscated and offending passages to be blacked out, or prevented publication of them altogether.

Many Catholic areas lagged behind Protestant ones in the establishment of primary and secondary schools, but they had other types of institutions for communicating moral values that were unavailable to Protestants. As noted above, confession was one avenue, and during the seventeenth century confession became more routine and frequent for many Catholics. Both the Jesuits and reforming bishops saw confession as a "fortress of Christian virtue."

Bishops in some dioceses began to require confessors to fill out pre-printed certificates of confession to make sure that everyone had fulfilled at least their yearly obligation, usually done during the Lenten season preceding Easter. Those who had not, or who were denied absolution by the priest because he felt they were not penitent enough for grave sins or continued to commit them despite promises of better behavior, could not take mass at Easter, which was an obligation for all Catholics. Thus though the contents of confession were private, whether one had properly confessed or not was a matter of public knowledge. Wooden confessionals, in which a priest sat on one side of a screen and the penitent kneeled or sat on the other, were introduced in many churches, beginning in Italy. They were to be set in a place where other people could not hear what was being said, but fully open to public view, making confession actually *less* private than it had been when priests heard confessions in secluded corners of a church.

For the more severe bishops, confession was a matter of imposing clerical authority and requiring dramatic changes in behavior from a sinful populace. Others recommended a less rigorous approach. Printed Spanish manuals of confession, sold to lay people as well priests as guides for devotion and proper behavior, advised priests to engage in dialogue with their penitents, not simply lecture them, and to accommodate to their needs somewhat. Confessors operating under stringent bishops also called for exemptions, compromise, and leniency, arguing that setting extreme penance or barring people from church services only led them to avoid confessing or attending church, a much more dangerous spiritual consequence.

New kinds of religious confraternities, congregations, and sodalities devoted to Mary or to other aspects of Catholic devotion such as the rosary developed in many parts of Europe. In these organizations, lay men and women – under the direction of clergy – devoted themselves to piety, prayer, and good works. Especially in northern Europe, these congregations and confraternities, which sometimes included hundreds of people, encouraged their members to uphold high standards of moral purity in their own lives. "Because the brotherhood was founded above all for the purpose of rooting out sins and vices," went the rules of one confraternity devoted to the rosary in the small German town of Görwihl, "public evils . . . should, with the help of the secular authority, be avoided and punished."[12] In the urban Marian confraternities limited to men, members pledged that they would keep their bodies chaste in Mary's honor, and not even visit the house of their betrothed between engagement and marriage.

While lay people learned pious moral values in confession and confraternities, priests learned them in the new seminaries that were established after the Council of Trent. Trent ordered each bishop to establish a seminary in his diocese, and although this level was never attained, slowly a seminary education became more common for priests, even those in areas such as Ireland that did not have their own seminaries. Seminaries promoted the virtues of celibacy to candidates for the priesthood, and turned away some who were clearly unable to maintain a celibate life. Particularly those schools and seminaries run by Jesuits promoted a new ideal of clerical masculinity that combined sexual continence with learnedness, social activism, physical freedom, and "care of souls." Seminary-trained priests could perform basic pastoral duties such as preaching, administering the sacraments, and teaching catechism better than their predecessors, thus enabling Catholic doctrine to reach a wider audience. They came to view themselves more clearly as part of an ecclesiastical hierarchy and thus superior to their flocks, rather than as loyal primarily to the local community.

Jesuit schools were the best in Europe in the late sixteenth and seventeenth centuries, but in the eighteenth century they declined. The Jesuit Order itself came under increasing attack as rulers resented their wealth and autonomy, members of other orders charged they were watering down Christianity in areas outside of Europe to gain converts, and political leaders accused them of diplomatic intrigue. Rulers of many countries in Europe suppressed the Jesuits in the middle of the eighteenth century, and in 1773 successfully pressured Pope Clement XIV to disband the order. Pope Pius VII lifted the ban in 1814, but it would take a long time for clerical education to recover.

Effects of the Catholic Reformation

As in Protestant areas, generalizing about the effects of new or reinvigorated ideas and institutions in Catholic areas is difficult. We might expect more uniformity in Catholicism than in Protestantism, and expect that uniformity to increase during this period as conformity to approved practice was such an important issue for the Council of Trent, but in actuality variations continued. Conflicts between "rigorists" and "laxists," bishops' courts and inquisitors, and church and secular authorities created national and local differences in the way sexuality was regulated and the impact of these measures. Attempts to control sexuality also varied over time within a single area with the personality and concerns of individual bishops. Some led intensive campaigns against specific activities that at least in the short run gained wide support, what historians have termed "moral panics." Other bishops were far more relaxed, however. Tridentine rules and other measures of social discipline were much easier to enforce in cities and towns than in more isolated rural areas, where older notions and practices continued and reform efforts often had little or no impact. Enforcement of regulations and discipline was particularly difficult in areas where

Catholics lived under Protestant governments, such as Ireland or England, for such institutions as bishops' courts, and even bishops themselves, were illegal.

Because of these variations, historians often focus on a single geographic area, studying in depth a city or region that offers rich sources about marital relations, sexual conduct, policing efforts and other matters. Occasionally records such as trial documents or episcopal visitations are so extensive that patterns may best be discerned by computer-assisted indexing; cases for which trial summaries (termed *relaciones de causas*) survive for the Spanish Inquisition, for example, number about 100,000, and are currently being indexed by a team of scholars. (The numbers cited above about sexual cases come from their initial indexing of about 44,000 cases.) Thus both qualitative and quantitative research are contributing to our understanding of sexual practices and their control in post-Reformation European Catholicism.

Clerical concubinage and solicitation

Assessing the success of reform efforts to promote chastity and sexual propriety among the male clergy depends to some degree on where one looks and how long a time frame one takes. Simply ending clerical concubinage was a very slow process in some areas, where more than two-thirds of the clergy lived with women at the time of the Council of Trent. Reforming bishops often met with defiance or duplicity, particularly from priests or cathedral canons– the clergy who oversaw a cathedral – who thought that the rules of celibacy might apply to monks and nuns, but not to them. The establishment of seminaries that stressed celibacy to priestly candidates was slow – all of Spain had only twenty-six seminaries by 1700 and even Paris did not have a seminary until 1696. As late as 1652, the bishop of Autun in France reported:

> Concubinage here is extremely common and priests have no fear
> of maintaining in their quarters immodest women and the children
> they have with them. They nourish and raise these children, train
> them to serve at the altar, marry them, dower them all as if they
> were legitimate. Parishioners are so accustomed to these practices
> that when interrogated about the morals and deportment of the
> clerics who keep these immodest women, they respond that these
> clerics live justly . . . and so they see no evil, being so used to
> seeing their priests live with women that they assume it is
> acceptable.[13]

This lay tolerance of clerical concubinage continued into the nineteenth century in some parts of Europe, particularly in rural parts of southern Europe;

complaints against clerical sex occurred only when the priest was promiscuous or negligent in the support of his children, or the relationship was adulterous.

In other rural areas, however, lay toleration of clerical concubinage declined. People came to view the celibate clergy as a symbol of their identity as Catholics, an identity that was strengthened by what they were hearing from reforming preachers and also their own devotional activities. In some cases lay people took the lead in forcing higher standards of behavior among the clergy. In Burgundy in the 1560s, for example, lay courts grew frustrated at the leniency of church courts and began to try sexually active clergy; in the early seventeenth century lay courts even sentenced some priests and their lovers to death. By the late seventeenth century they usually ordered banishment or galley service rather than execution, but still took seriously any priest whose behavior made him unworthy of being a mediator between God and his parishioners or who used his office to gain sexual favors. Such secular jurisdiction over the sexual lives of clergy was highly unusual, however, for in most parts of Europe only the women involved with clergy came before secular courts, while the priests continued to appear before bishops' courts or the Inquisition; this generally resulted in a great disparity in their punishments, with the priest simply fined and then sometimes moved to a different parish, and the woman forced to endure public humiliation on the pillory and then exiled.

As with nuns in places that closed convents as a result of Protestant teachings, we generally do not know what happened to priests' concubines and children. Most of these women were of lower social status, and their words never made it into official documents. There are occasional glimpses that they did not go meekly, however. Priests' concubines in the German diocese of Münster, for example, had earlier been proud enough of their status to want it indicated on their tombstones. When ordered to leave the priest she had long cared for, one asked church officials for financial compensation for the "pains, damage of my honour and health of my body," as well as the costs of raising her children.[14] The response of the Münster church officials is not known, but in general the church offered no support for these women.

The process was much slower than reformers envisioned, but gradually clerical concubinage declined in most of Catholic Europe. In the diocese of Würzburg in Germany, for example, 45 percent of the rural clergy had or were suspected of having concubines at the time of the Council of Trent, but by 1616–31, after a series of reforming bishops, only 4 percent of the clergy lived with concubines. Punitive measures by courts and bishops were accompanied by a strong positive message about the value of priestly celibacy in the seminaries, and in each generation there were fewer priests who attempted to live in permanent relationships with women.

Concubinage was only one type of clerical sexual transgression. Another was seduction, solicitation, or rape that occurred during confession, a matter that became a staple of first Protestant and then Enlightenment polemic against Catholic priests. Because confession was a sacrament and viewed as one of the key elements of post-Tridentine Catholic practice, the papacy regarded this as a serious issue and gave the various Inquisitions jurisdiction over solicitation during confession. People were ordered to report any solicitation and denied absolution if they did not, though the requirement of two independent witnesses often meant that cases were only reported years after they happened. The accused priest was imprisoned, given a defense attorney, questioned, and urged to confess; if the Inquisition decided there was enough evidence to convict, he was usually deprived of the right to hear confession, exiled from his parish, and often secluded in a monastery. Opportunities for solicitation were many, as confession often occurred with priest and penitent simply sitting together somewhere in the church; the divided confessional box was first introduced in the 1560s in Italy, but was not introduced in many parishes until the eighteenth century, and even then the divider was often torn or missing.

Solicitation by priests had certainly occurred in the pre-Reformation church, but some aspects of post-Tridentine Catholic practice encouraged it. People were urged to confess frequently, and there is some evidence that they did confess more often, particularly if they belonged to one of the new religious organizations such as the confraternities dedicated to the Virgin Mary. As noted above, confession was to entail a detailed examination of one's conscience and a minute accounting of sins; confessors sometimes defended themselves by saying they needed to use sexually suggestive language to get a penitent to understand her or his sins. Women who were religiously scrupulous, whether nuns or lay women, were especially likely to confess often, and to develop an intense and intimate emotional relationship with their confessor. By the seventeenth century, church authorities recognized that not all confessors could handle this, and sometimes excluded nuns and women under forty from a priest's first license to hear confessions; only after a second examination and trial period could he hear confessions from all parishioners.

The special situation of Catholics who lived in Protestant states provoked further concerns. In Ireland, convents had been dissolved and solemn vows officially prohibited by English laws. Some nuns fled to the continent, but most could not afford this, and some sought shelter in priests' households in areas where Protestant control was ineffective. The officials gathered at the Synod of Dublin saw this as a dangerous "occasion to sin," however, and ruled in 1614, "we decree that priests shall not have in their houses any women – even more those who have made a vow of virginity or chastity, or any others, since they might be a cause of scandal: and they are not to undertake the care of such women, even as a spiritual ministry, without further authorization."[15] They did grant such authorizations, recognizing that nuns often had nowhere else to go, but sought to oversee such households more closely.

English Catholics were another special case, for here women sheltered priests rather than priests sheltering women. During the late sixteenth and early seventeenth centuries, everyone in England was required to be a member of the Protestant Church of England and attend church, or risk fines and imprisonment. According to common law, however, married women controlled no property, and imprisoning a woman would disrupt family life. Thus though officials fined and imprisoned Catholic men for recusancy (refusing to attend church), they were generally unwilling to apply the law to women. English Catholicism thus increasingly centered on households, where women sometimes hid Jesuits and other priests, who were liable to execution if they were caught. Protestant critics of recusancy often focused on the relationship between women and priests, portraying it as both spiritual and sexual seduction. "The Emissaries of Rome" wrote one, "steal away the hearts of the weaker sort; and secretly do they creep into houses, leading captive simple women laden with sins, and led away with diverse lusts."[16] Adulterous priests were no doubt much more common in the imaginations of Protestant polemicists than in reality, but suspicious officials sometimes searched couples' bedrooms for priests, intruding into the most private part of the household. Protestants also worried about the influence Catholic wives would have on their husbands, and Catholic mothers would have on their children. Throughout the early seventeenth century Parliament regularly debated bills that would remove children from recusant families. Catholic wives and mothers during this period included a succession of queens from Catholic countries – the French Henrietta Maria, wife to Charles I, the Portuguese Catherine of Braganza, wife to Charles II, and the Italian Mary of Modena, wife to James II – who were often accused in highly sexualized language of tempting their husbands to return to or be stronger in the Catholic faith.

Convents

While education and supervision were the main tools of the post-Tridentine church in its efforts to enforce chastity on male clerics, strict enclosure and greater control by male clergy were its main tools for female religious. Despite calls for the enclosure of women's communities since the twelfth century, in the sixteenth century many convents allowed women out to visit their families or permitted family members and friends to visit or even attend services, plays, and musical performances within the convent. Women behind convent walls shaped family dynamics in terms of marriage and inheritance and thus influenced political life. Elite women expected that their lives within a convent would not be very different from that outside, particularly because women with little religious vocation were often placed in convents by their families if the family could not find an appropriate marriage partner or raise the dowry necessary for a good marriage. Although the Council of Trent called for each nun to affirm her voluntary consent, in some places forced vocations increased in scope in the late sixteenth century. In Venice, for example, nearly 60 percent of all upper-class women entered convents in the period from 1580 to 1620, sent there by their families to avoid the loss of prestige that marriage to a man lower down the social scale would bring. Reforming bishops in many cities occasionally tried to limit convent entrance to those women who had a true vocation as a nun, but prominent families fought such measures and the bishops resigned themselves to emphasizing spiritual direction and physical control. Convent residents also included wives whose husbands were maneuvering to get their marriages annulled and daughters whose parents regarded them as difficult to control.

Women who had been forced into convents fought increasing enclosure, as did many who had entered willingly, for they viewed the convents' relative independence and interactions with the outside community as guaranteed by long traditions. Resistance also came from new types of religious communities founded by women in the sixteenth century. These groups wanted to devote themselves to education, care of the sick, and assistance to the poor out in the world, just as the Jesuits and other new orders for men did, not be separated from the world behind convent walls.

Along with women religious who sought to maintain their activities in the world, there were also a number of lay women, especially in Spain, the Spanish colonies, and Italy, who felt a strong sense of religious vocation, sometimes enhanced by mystical visions. Such "holy women" (*beatas* in Spanish) or "living saints" were often revered by people in their neighborhood and beyond; they resolved local conflicts and were sought for advice on personal, political, and religious matters. They sometimes gained power over political leaders all the way up to the king, who in turn used the approval of such women as an endorsement of their policies and an enhancement of their prestige. Others were not so sure about the source of the women's visions and ecstatic trances, however, and they were sometimes investigated by the Inquisition or other church courts and charged with fraud and falsifying miracles. Church courts were concerned about the modesty and chastity of such women as well as the validity of the miracles attributed to them. Diego Pérez de Valdivia, a professor at the University of Barcelona, complained that some holy women had "much freedom and little modesty" and were easily tempted by "the devil, the world, and their own flesh."[17] Valdivia advised that the women put themselves under the close direction of their confessors, though other authors warned about the dangers of this and advised priests to "apply [themselves] more to the treatment of men, where there is less danger and greater advantage."[18] The best solution, in the minds of most authorities, would be for such women to enter convents; they might still develop an emotional or sexual relationship with their confessors, but other dangers to their chastity would be avoided.

Reforming officials used a variety of means to counter resistance to or circumvention of enclosure. Bishops carried out investigations, found (or claimed to find) various irregularities, and deposed abbesses or other leaders who opposed the increasing restrictions. Groups that advocated nuns be allowed to teach or care for the sick outside of the convent were ridiculed and charged with disobedience and immorality. In the words of a papal bull of 1631 suppressing one of these groups, although such actions were undertaken "under the pretext of promoting salvation of souls," they were actually "least suitable to their sex, its mental weakness as well as womanly modesty [and] in particular to the honor of virgins."[19] Warnings about the power of female sexuality were combined with extravagant praise of female virginity; especially in Italy, new chapels and churches were dedicated to the virgin martyrs of early Christianity as well as the Virgin Mary, and cults in their honor developed in many cities. Ceremonies in which novices took their vows as nuns reinforced their status as "brides of Christ," with the women wearing the same symbols of virginity, such as wreaths on their heads, that other brides did. These measures were not simply a matter of men imposing control on unwilling women, however. Some nuns and abbesses themselves – most famously Teresa of Avila – reformed convents and imposed stricter standards of poverty, enclosure, and spiritual practice. In the early seventeenth century, the convent of Port-Royal in Paris became the spiritual center of Jansenism, the moral reform movement that emphasized personal holiness. Enclosed convents were clearly prisons for many women, but for others they offered opportunities for leadership and a fulfilling life.

Stricter enclosure gradually became the reality for most convents, but this did not have the impact on women that the prohibition of concubinage did for priests, for neither before nor after the Reformation were many nuns involved in permanent sexual relationships the way priests were. Enclosure did affect the stories that were told about sex in convents by their opponents, both Protestant and Catholic. In the sixteenth century the most lurid of these told of babies born, killed, and buried in the convent after wild encounters when nuns met their lovers in the convent or outside of it, while in the eighteenth they reflected the enclosed setting and instead told of lesbian sadism or exotic rituals of exorcism conducted over swooning nuns by lascivious confessors.

Marriage among the laity

Tridentine rules about clerical concubinage and the enclosure of nuns were often resisted or ignored for decades or even centuries, and so was the Tridentine definition of what made a marriage. Local betrothal and wedding practices that stood in sharp contrast to the Council of Trent's call for publicity and piety were often maintained in opposition to the wishes of local clergy and sometimes with their participation. In parts of Italy and France, for example, people were very worried that envious or malicious neighbors might try to cast a spell on the marriage, so did not want to celebrate their weddings publicly. Despite prohibitions, they went to neighboring villages for the blessing or began sexual relations immediately after the marriage contract was signed (before a priestly blessing) so that magical or demonic forces would not intervene and cause impotence or marital strife. In parts of Europe where Catholics lived under Protestant governments, such as Ireland and England, Catholic marriages, particularly those of prominent people, often had to be conducted secretly in the sixteenth and seventeenth centuries. Once some level of toleration was accorded Catholics, marrying parties still had to pay a fee to a Church of England or Ireland minister before a priest could marry them, and it was difficult to observe Tridentine rules.

Catholic reformers encouraged solemnity in the marriage ceremony, suggesting that the ritual blessing of the marriage bed, when it was continued at all, be the occasion of a solemn sermon about marital chastity rather than that of a noisy and ribald celebration of fertility. Wedding feasts and dances (which continued despite all efforts of reformers) were moved away from the church and churchyard, however, in an effort to free the sacrament of marriage from profanation by worldly concerns. Traditional marital rituals changed slightly to incorporate post-Tridentine emphases, such as that on Mary; in parts of Germany, for example, Mary's image was carried in a procession to the home of newlyweds, then placed on the marital bed before the priestly blessing.

Both church and state officials also attempted to restrict or prohibit popular rituals of social control such as *charivaris* or *asouades* (forcing someone, usually a man, to ride a donkey or pole if he was viewed as hen-pecked or if there were frequent marital disputes), or the setting up of maypoles with phallic symbols outside the houses of marriageable girls. These rituals were generally carried out by the young men in a village, and prohibitions were largely ineffective, for the men in power in most villages had taken part in them when they were young and so tolerated them. They usually culminated in the victims' buying off the young men with drinks and food, but sometimes they escalated into more serious violence. Seminary-trained priests preached and spoke against such rituals, but they then became the targets of youth gangs themselves, who "in response to my prayers and warnings . . . told me to address their behinds, and . . . accompanied their words with gestures of the hand."[20]

Reformers' efforts to draw a sharp line between married and not-married were also difficult to enforce. Trent explicitly prohibited lay concubinage as well as clerical, declaring it a "grievous sin" for a man to live with a woman not his wife, punishable by excommunication for him and banishment for her. In this, the council banned a sexual arrangement that was fairly common in many parts of Spain, Portugal, and Italy, particularly among wealthier men and poorer women. Concubinage might involve immediate monetary payments, but more commonly involved food, clothing, and housing, and then money for a dowry for the woman when the relationship ended. Reforming bishops attempted to provoke opposition to concubinage by instructing priests to preach that concubinage was no different than fornication or adultery, and a danger to the whole community. As with so many other aspects of sexual conduct, elite men were largely unaffected by the new rules, however, but continued to have long-term sexual relationships with women; they supported and arranged the marriages of the children of those relationships, and even legitimated them if this worked to their advantage. The church set out official categories of legitimacy based on the status of the parents, but people manipulated these to control the social and legal standing of their offspring.

Because of their connection with elite men, the women involved in concubinage were less liable to censure or punishment than were other women who had sex outside of marriage. Their honor was generally regarded as "restored" through a subsequent marriage – often arranged by her lover – and the dowry allowed her to attract a higher-status husband than she would have otherwise. Such relationships were certainly exploitative, but court records indicate that the young women clearly regarded their sexuality as a resource and made decisions about how best to invest it.

Court records and visitation reports have also indicated that among lower-class people as well as elites sexual norms were much slower to change than reformers hoped. Well into the seventeenth century in many parts of Europe the signing of a marriage contract or verbal agreement between families was the point at which villagers expected sexual relations to begin; as one horrified reformer noted of the Basque peasants of northern Spain, "They marry their wives on a trial basis . . . and do not receive any nuptial blessing until they have lived with them a long time, have probed their habits and have learnt by results about the fertility of their soil."[21] Peasant women in this area were little stigmatized by bearing children out of wedlock, nor were their children, who were publicly baptized with godparents in attendance, received inheritances, and made marriage contracts. Research in other parts of Spain has also found that women who had become pregnant outside of marriage regularly and openly brought cases of defloration to court, requesting monetary recompense for what they termed "seduction by promise of marriage." For them, and their families, honor could be lost through sexual activity, but then regained, or mostly regained, through money and through redefining the woman as a victim. Spanish intellectuals tied female honor closely to chastity, but for average people it was a more malleable category.

The Iberian peninsula appears to have maintained a more malleable idea of marriage as well. Informal domestic partnerships sealed by some sort of vague promise continued to be regarded as marriages by many couples and their neighbors, despite Tridentine rules against such clandestine marriages. The Spanish crown ordered all couples who married clandestinely to be exiled and their property confiscated, but hesitated to actually carry out such punishments. In 1645, the Portuguese King Joao IV went even further, declaring that long-term domestic partnerships were valid marriages "according to the customs and laws of Portugal."[22]

The situation in France was quite different, both in terms of sex outside of wedlock and clandestine marriage. In most parts of France, the rural illegitimacy rate in the seventeenth century was around 1 percent, the lowest in Europe. How much this was the result of Catholic Reformation preaching or the actions of church courts and how much the result of existing traditions that discouraged post-betrothal or out-of-wedlock intercourse is difficult to say, however. Children born out of wedlock in France were often not recorded in baptismal records, a mark of their social exclusion.

French secular laws provided much stronger sanctions against clandestine marriage than did church laws elsewhere. (Research on Italian cities suggests that the near-universal exchange of dowries made marriage a public matter and gave parents stronger control over their children's marriages even before the sixteenth century, thus playing the role of the secular law in France.) Because the French Royal Council refused to acknowledge the decisions of Trent as the laws of the kingdom, royal and not church legislation became the basis of matrimonial law. To a large decree the edicts of the French kings agreed with *Tametsi*, but they made parental consent almost always obligatory, and provided severe penalties, including in theory capital punishment, for minors who married against their parents' wishes or in secret. (Minors were defined as men under thirty and women under twenty-five.) French ordinances defined all marriages without parental consent as *rapt* (abduction), even if they had involved no violence (such cases were termed *rapt de seduction*). Though in actuality they were not executed, young people who defied their parents were sometimes imprisoned by what were termed *lettres de cachet*, documents which families obtained from royal officials authorizing the imprisonment without trial of a family member who was seen as a source of dishonor. *Lettres de cachet* were also used against young people who refused to go into convents or monasteries when their families wished them to, or against individuals whose behavior was regarded as in some way scandalous, such as wives whose husbands suspected them of adultery or men from prominent families who engaged in same-sex activities; this practice was often abused, and individuals imprisoned for years if their families refused to agree to their release.

Throughout Catholic Europe – even in France – court cases concerning clandestine marriage were usually brought by one of the parties, not by church or state officials. Generally this was a pregnant woman, who stated that there had been an informal marriage or at least a clear promise of marriage, and requested that the court force the man to honor his promise, or at least order financial support for the child. Courts regularly awarded the woman at least some money, but they varied in how willing they were to force a marriage, as this directly violated the doctrine of consent. There is evidence from some parts of Catholic Europe that the amounts and frequency of monetary compensation declined in the sixteenth century, as did the total number of cases. Authorities at the time may have chosen to view this decline as a mark of the success of campaigns against extramarital sex, though it may also have resulted from women's recognition that the court was not going to be very sympathetic to their plights, so they did not bother to take their cases to court.

Problem marriages

The Council of Trent and subsequent canon law affirmed that marriage was indissoluble, but church and secular courts heard a variety of cases in which one or both spouses sought to end a marriage. One way was to seek an annulment, a statement saying that a proper marriage had never existed in the first place, which could give a spouse the right to marry someone else. To gain an annulment, a spouse had to convince the court that one of the rules for a valid marriage had been broken: there had not been free consent, or the spouses were too closely related, or one spouse was impotent, so that the marriage had not been consummated. (Today the Catholic Church in the United States grants annulments on many other grounds, including emotional immaturity at the time of the marriage.) Those seeking to prove lack of consent had to show that the pressure brought by their family or their spouse involved serious "fear or force"; not simply coercion, but intimidation so strong that it was impossible to resist. Neighbors were called in and asked whether they had heard the unwilling spouse screaming or seen her or him being beaten. Not surprisingly, successful cases were rare.

Requests for annulment based on impotence – whether "natural" or caused by castration – were more likely to be successful than those based on other grounds. This was not a secret, and as a result in many areas nonconsummation became the most common grounds for those seeking annulment, although canon law required that spouses try for at least three years. The vast majority of these were brought against men, who in France and Spain then had to prove to the court that they could get and maintain an erection. Spanish church courts employed surgeons, who "used baths of warm water, rubbing, and other acts" to provoke an erection, and made public pronouncements asking for witnesses who could testify for or against.[23] If a husband accused of impotence fled the area, the courts put up notices of the charge on local churches, thus shaming him into responding. Court decisions that a man *was* impotent were also publicized, for this made him ineligible to marry again. Such public notices were much like those issued for sex offenders today, and in many ways impotent men were "sex offenders" – they did not fulfill a basic requirement for masculinity, physical virility. As might be expected, men tried everything they could to avoid the stigma of impotence, and many cases dragged on for years. The many fewer cases of female impotence – defined as the inability to receive semen – also involved physical tests using fingers and instruments conducted by physicians, surgeons, and midwives. As with men, women found to be impotent were not to marry again, and probably most went into convents. Canon law required that impotence be permanent to be a valid grounds for an annulment, but, as in all types of sexual cases, courts found ways around this. They occasionally declared that spouses were only impotent with each other – because of a misfit in the genitals – and allowed both to marry again.

Annulment cases provide fascinating evidence about ideas regarding the body and about social and gender norms, but they were quite rare. Much more common were cases asking for "separation from bed and board," usually sought by the wife for violence, adultery, or both. Some of these came to the courts independently, and some as counter-suits when men brought cases to court asking that wives who had left them be forced to return. Canon law allowed husbands to practice "mild and moderate correction" on wives who disobeyed, and neighbors often approved of husbands' physical coercion, especially if the wife was perceived as shrewish or quarrelsome. "I heard Madonna Benedetta insulting her husband from the balcony by calling him a swine, a wimp, and a cuckold," reported one neighbor to the church court in Venice in 1636 after Benedetta sued for separation, "and he gave her some slaps. And the people in the street below were saying 'Blessed are those hands', meaning that he had done well to beat her."[24] The court ordered Benedetta to reconcile with her husband and to return to him. Women thus had to prove that the violence was extreme, long-lasting, and even life-threatening, and called on doctors, midwives, and neighbors to verify their testimony that they were indeed women whose marriages had failed, termed *malmaritate* in Italian sources. "Once he battered her so severely that she almost lost consciousness and he hit her so hard she lost a tooth," reported a neighbor in one case, "several times my husband yelled at him that he should not treat his wife in this way."[25] Moderate correction was acceptable, but not deadly force, for this went against the ideals of proper masculine rationality and self-control. Women often charged their husbands with deviating from other masculine ideals as well: they drank up the family's income instead of providing for their children, gambled instead of worked, and endangered their wives' honor by calling them "whores" or even forcing them into prostitution.

The primary aim of both secular and church courts in Catholic areas was to keep couples together, and they often tried various types of mediation rather than come to an actual verdict. Thus in many jurisdictions in the vast majority of separation cases suits were withdrawn, decisions were delayed, and out of court settlements were arranged. The circumstances were so terrible that courts did order a separation in a few cases, allowing *malmaritate* to live apart from their husbands with family, friends, and sometimes in one of the asylums for women that were founded in the sixteenth century in many Catholic cities. Somewhat ironically, these same asylums might house "disobedient" wives put there unwillingly by their husbands.

Along with bad marriages, church courts also heard cases of bigamy, particularly in areas in which there was a great deal of mobility, such as the port cities of Spain and Portugal or the border area between Spain and France. Most bigamists were young, male, and mobile, and were liable for punishment in secular courts, episcopal courts, and/or the courts of the Inquisition. (The Inquisition claimed jurisdiction over bigamy because it was an offense against the sacrament of marriage, although its jurisdiction was often disputed by other types of courts.) Though bigamists were only rarely executed, male bigamists were generally sentenced to row five years in the king's galleys, which was often the functional equivalent of a death sentence, while female bigamists were whipped and exiled.

As noted in Chapter 2, marriages between Protestants and Catholics were not unusual, especially in areas where denominations lived close to one another. Religious authorities agreed to recognize the marriages of other religions, but the possibility of divorce among Protestants created a problem for Catholic authorities. Should a person who had legitimately divorced while a Protestant but then converted be allowed to marry someone else in a Catholic ceremony? Generally this was decided on a case-by-case basis and depended on the situation and the status of the parties involved.

In southern Europe, "mixed" marriages or other types of sexual relationships involved non-Christians or converts as well as different types of Christians. Around 1500, Muslims and Jews were ordered to leave the various states of the Iberian peninsula or convert to Christianity. All three of these religions had long discouraged marriage outside of the faith, and after the expulsion of the Muslims and Jews such marriages were no longer officially possible. There were still Muslims and Jews in Iberia, but they could not acknowledge this openly in a public ceremony such as a wedding. Christian authorities allowed marriages between Christians and converts, and occasionally even promoted these; in 1548, for example, as part of an edict designed to force Muslim converts to assimilate to Christian culture, the archbishop of Seville ordered converted Muslims to marry their children to Old Christians. (Old Christians were those whose ancestors were not known to have been Jewish or Muslim.) At the same time, however, purity of blood laws that favored "purely" Old Christian families worked against intermarriage. In general, Christians, Muslim converts, and Jewish converts all tended to marry within their communities, to people with whom they already had some lineage ties.

Blasphemy and insults

Throughout Catholic Europe, the various Inquisitions shared jurisdiction over sexual behavior with other courts, but the Inquisition had exclusive jurisdiction over sexual talk. Particularly worrisome were people who said that sex outside of marriage was not a sin or was only a venial sin, as this implied disrespect for the sacrament of marriage. The actual rate of prosecution for such statements varied widely and changed over time; in some areas they were ignored, in others, such as Toledo, they made up as much as one-third of the Inquisition's cases during brief campaigns of repression. Both men and women discussed sex outside of marriage in casual conversation later reported to the Inquisition, or their ideas emerged in trials involving actual sexual relationships. "Witnesses said that she said that she had been a concubine for a year and a half, and that it was in the service of God, and at present she was married, and that was in the service of the devil," read one case, in which the accused was sentenced to "hear mass wearing the tunic of the penitent and stay away from trivial things, and she was reprimanded and exiled from this city for one year."[26] "Better a happy concubinage than a miserable wife" went a Spanish proverb, often repeated to exasperated Inquisitors.[27] The church's teachings about fornication became part of the Edict of Faith read regularly to parishioners, and slowly the idea was communicated to villagers, as the following deposition makes clear:

The witness declared that he believed he had been summoned to testify about a certain statement that García Ruiz had made which seemed to him to run counter to what the parish priest had said in a sermon fifteen or twenty days ago. In effect, he had declared that their Honors the Inquisitors of Toledo had ordered all the parish priests in the district of Santa Olalla to admonish their parishioners in such a way that no one could pretend ignorance that having relations with a woman other than one's own legitimate wife was a mortal sin, and that to maintain the opposite view was heresy. Now on Friday the 14th of May, when García Ruiz and Diego Gómez were shearing their sheep at the witness's house, they spoke with his son, Juan Hernández Duque the younger. García Ruiz said, "Do you know that I had sex with a woman that I met on the road?" And then she said, "Sweetie, would you give me something to eat?" And García Ruiz promised her some eggs and fish and gave her a coin because he had made love with her. And he stated that, for a man, it was not a sin to make love to a woman even if she was a prostitute. Then his friends Diego Gómez and Sancho de Rojas the elder who were there, admonished him and told him to shut up because this was heresy. And the other continued to insist that if one paid it was not a sin. Everyone there stared at him and continued to reproach him, saying: "Shut up: it was a great sin, didn't you hear the priest?" Diego Gómez said: "May the devil take you. With the wife you have why are you looking for another woman?" And García Ruiz replied, saying, "Leave me in peace, I had a good time with her!" Then he said to this witness's son, "Don't look so sad, sell one of your father's sheep and find another like her." At this time the said Juan Hernández Duque the younger replied: "Go to the devil, you and your filth."[28]

Along with trying people for statements about fornication, the Inquisitions also tried people for "heretical blasphemy" which often had to do with sex. Sometimes this occurred when people found certain Christian doctrines hard to believe. Women, in particular, were charged with claiming marriage was more holy than celibacy, and María de Cardenas, a shepherd's daughter in central Spain, appeared before the Inquisition in 1568 because she asserted that "God did it to Our Lady like her father [did] it to her mother" and "persisted in believing that God had known Our Lady carnally."[29] Men's statements were generally more direct: "Christ the cuckolded faggot" or "Virgin Mary the whore." Even clergy were not immune from such comments, terming their fellow clerics "God's vaginas," or making sexual insults about other men's wives. Inquisition records from southern Italy and Sicily are especially full of such cases, with one priest charged with singing insults of a man's wife through a window, calling her a "pock-marked whore, public and practiced" who sold her "fig, fig" (a hand gesture symbolizing a woman's genitals) for "a penny a pound."[30] Punishments for insulting private persons were generally fines, but obscenities that mentioned religious figures or Inquisition officials might be punished with years of galley service.

Whoredom, prisons, and moral panics

Though we have no way of knowing whether the priest's insult was warranted in the case just cited, it does capture the fact that in Catholic Europe as well as Protestant, "whore" was a category with unclear boundaries. A woman who sold sex was a whore, but so was one whose sexual life was simply irregular by community standards. Particularly in villages where there were no official brothels, women charged with "whoredom" might be occasional sellers of sex, but they might also be servants, widows, or women whose husbands had deserted them who were living in a non-marital arrangement with a man. As noted above, if the village accepted such a couple, the arrangement could go on for years, but if the villagers did not approve, they could use charges of sexual deviance to drive the couple away. Single women who lived on their own were also subject to charges of whoredom or simply "bad living." "His Honor has discovered information against some single women of this parish whose way of living is so bad and who are bad examples," recorded one episcopal visitation report in Spain in 1571. The women were ordered "from here forward to live honestly and chastely, under the penalty of one silver mark."[31]

Such fluid borders became increasingly unacceptable to Catholic reformers intent on drawing sharp lines between honor and dishonor. In some areas, they, like Protestants, closed all licensed brothels and attempted to eradicate prostitution by imprisonment and banishing the women involved. Their more common response, however, was to defend legal brothels as a way to maintain the virtue of "honorable" women, and to require women who sold sex to register and live in particular houses or quarters of the city. In 1570, for example, King Philip II of Spain reaffirmed that brothels were legal, and that brothel-keepers were not to abuse the women in them or forbid them to leave if they wanted to repent. Fifty years later (in 1623) Philip IV reversed this, and ordered all brothels closed in Spain; the royal edict had less of an effect than did the general decline of the Spanish economy during this period, however, for many municipal brothels were apparently already in ruins, and women who sold sex were dispersed all over the towns.

In general, major Italian cities such as Florence and Venice were the most tolerant, favoring regulation over suppression and often viewing prostitutes as significant sources of municipal income. From 1559 until the mid-eighteenth century in Florence, for example, all women registered as prostitutes were required to contribute an annual tax based on their income, which went to support a convent for those women who wished to give up prostitution; payment of extra taxes would allow a woman to live where she wished in the city and wear whatever type of clothes she chose.

The official contempt of "whoredom" was not always internalized by women themselves. In Rome – where the number of men who could not marry was extremely high – prostitutes often offered their customers music and poetry along with sexual services, and worked independently, living with other women or with their mothers or children; they often described their occupation in terms of the quality of their clients instead of simply monetary terms. Their neighbors did not shun them, but socialized with them and defended them against verbal and physical attacks.

Reformers had a more lasting impact on prostitution through institutions they opened rather than closed. During the sixteenth and seventeenth centuries, reforming bishops, leaders of religious orders, and groups of well-to-do women in many southern European cities established houses for repentant prostitutes and other "fallen women" whose honor was questionable. They were an attractive charity for those interested in moral reform, and were sometimes also supported by taxes on registered prostitutes and courtesans. Such houses, often dedicated to Mary Magdalene, also began to admit women who were regarded as in danger of becoming prostitutes, generally poor women with no male relatives, girls who had been raped, or women whose husbands had threatened them or left them destitute. Their mission was to "shelter the modesty of girls from the lewdness of men," and their ordinances stated explicitly that the women admitted had to be pretty or at least acceptable looking, for ugly women did not have to worry about their honor.[32]

In such asylums, the women did not take vows and could leave to marry, but otherwise they were much like convents, with the women following a daily regimen of work and prayer. Some of them stressed penitence and moral reform while others were more purely punitive, closer to prisons than convents. The latter were seen as particularly appropriate for women who refused to change their ways; who, in the words of the reforming nun Madre Magdalena de San Gerónimo, "insult the honesty and virtue of the good ones with their corruption and evil" and as "wild beasts who leave their caves to look for prey" spread "family dishonor and scandal among all the people." Madre Magdalena recommended the establishment of a special women's prison to King Philip III of Spain in 1608, "where in particular the rebellious incorrigible ones will be punished."[33]

This mixture of punishment and penitence may be seen very clearly in the Parisian women's prison of the Salpêtrière. In 1658, Louis XIV ordered the imprisonment there of all women found guilty of prostitution, fornication, or adultery, with release only coming once the priests and sisters in charge determined the inmate was truly penitent and had changed her ways. Imprisoning women for sexual crimes marks the first time that prison was used as a punishment in Europe rather than simply as a place to hold people until their trial or before deportation. Such prisons later became the model for similar institutions for men and young people – often specifically called "reformatories" – in which the inmate's level of repentance determined to a great degree the length of incarceration. (This, of course, is still true for prisons and "reform schools" today.) Once men and boys as well as women and girls were locked up, however, sexual crimes were no longer the basis of the majority of incarcerations the way they were in the earliest women's prisons.

Along with refuges for former prostitutes, city and church officials tried to use foundling homes as a way to combat prostitution and other sex out of wedlock. They forbade unwed mothers to raise their own children, and required them instead to leave them in foundling homes (*ospizi*). If women could not afford the fees required, they were forced to give birth in jail and then work in a foundling home as a wetnurse for their own and other infants; despite attempts to feed and care for them, the vast majority of children in such homes died.

Imprisonment and other punishments of women for actions judged sinful often increased sharply when a new official took over in a district or a city was in a crisis of some sort, both of which could create "moral panics" around specific issues. The issue was used as a symbol of disorder, and its control tied in with the general well-being. During the Thirty Years' War, for example, the rulers of Bavaria became convinced that the main cause of food shortages and other economic woes was "the evil of profligacy [sex outside of marriage] and nonmarital impregnations, which has highly incensed the almighty God." A special commission was set up to punish offenders, particularly the "many single women with pregnant bodies running around."[34] Midwives were ordered to report all births out of wedlock, and conviction for profligacy brought public shaming as well as fines and imprisonment. In France, royal worries about the spread of Calvinism were accompanied by panic about a rising tide of infanticide. In 1556 the French crown declared that a woman "be held and reputed to have murdered her child and, in reparation, be punished by death and the last agony" if the child died subsequent to birth and the mother had "hidden, covered and concealed both her pregnancy and her childbearing, without having declared one or the other."[35] While the bubonic plague raged in Milan in 1576, Archbishop Carlo Borromeo and his officials became obsessed with mothers who accidentally smothered their infants in their beds when they nursed them. They declared that this was sinful negligence and ordered women to stop taking their infants into bed with them or risk excommunication. Instead, women stopped coming to confession, or "when recounting this sin to their confessors laughed about it, as if it were a joke," which only incensed the diocesan officials more.[36]

Sometimes moral panics subsided when the crisis passed or the official was replaced by another, but they often left a lasting legacy. As we saw in Chapter 2, other governments in Europe (including Bavaria) followed the French example and passed statutes requiring a declaration of pregnancy by all unmarried women, and increased their penalties of women suspected of infanticide. Convictions of unmarried women for sex outside of marriage did not end in Munich once the Thirty Years' War was over, but continued. The plague passed in Milan, but officials expanded their rules prohibiting sleeping with infants, and ordered priests to read them regularly from parish pulpits. Only when this led to so many excommunicates that the system could not handle them did later archbishops decide to offer a periodic amnesty.

Sodomy

Most moral panics centered on women's bodies, but a few focused on men. In 1625, for example, the Inquisition in Valencia learned that a local Christian teenager was acting as a pimp for a number of his friends, who engaged in sexual activity as the passive partners for Muslim slaves from well-to-do households. (Slaves in the Iberian peninsula often worked for pay for someone other than their owner, and were allowed to keep a small portion of their wages.) Inquisitors were shocked at these "sodomites who display such harmful shamelessness and licentiousness" between "slaves and Christians," for the Muslim slaves' sexual domination of the Christian young men inverted the proper hierarchy. This was a sign of "dissoluteness," that is, of both immorality and a breakdown in social order.[37] All of the slaves, nine in all, were executed by burning at a public *auto-da-fé*, as was the Christian teenager who had arranged the sex; the other adolescents received long sentences of galley service.

This trial was only one of many held by the Inquisition in the kingdom of Aragon, for there were 1,000 trials for male–male sodomy and bestiality during the period between 1570 and 1630, in which about 150 men died (roughly as many as were executed for heresy in Aragon during this period).

Many of those executed for homosexual sodomy were Italians or slaves from Africa and Asia, a situation exacerbated by the reputation both groups had among the Spanish for being particularly likely to engage in this "nefarious sin." Others were from all-male environments such as monasteries or the military, and, as in the 1625 case, almost all of the cases involved an older and younger man or a man and an adolescent. Those charged with sodomy were sometimes tortured to reveal other names, so that accusations often occurred in waves. The executions were generally carried out at public *autos-da-fé*, where bigamists and other individuals regarded as disturbing God's natural order were also either executed or displayed for public ridicule. Bestiality cases often involved young men from rural areas who occasionally denounced themselves when their consciences became too burdened; a disproportionate number of these were farm workers from France, which both resulted from and supported Spanish stereotypes about French sexual habits. The severity of the Aragonese Inquisition in sodomy cases ended early, however; no one was executed in Aragon after 1633, about a century before executions for sodomy ended in both Castile and northern Europe.

Along with charges of male homosexual sodomy and bestiality, the Inquisition in Aragon also heard a handful of cases of heterosexual and female homosexual sodomy. In the mid-sixteenth century the Inquisition ruled that sex between women was not sodomy unless they used an artificial phallus (a ruling they later forgot in one case), but that heterosexual anal intercourse, even between husband and wife, was. Cases were rare and usually emerged when a wife who was angry at her husband denounced him or a confessor urged a woman to bring the accusation; if the husband could prove malice on the wife's part, the case was dropped, though there are a few instances of executions or lesser punishments for heterosexual sodomy, including one in which the charge was brought by a group of neighbors. Courts elsewhere in Catholic Europe similarly heard very few cases of sodomy involving women, whatever the gender (or species) of their sexual partners; female sodomy was not unimaginable to most religious authorities, it was simply rare. (Trial records indicate that people in some areas *did* regard female sodomy as unimaginable, and even had difficulties understanding male sodomy; two young peasants in Hungary, for example, accused their employer of witchcraft when he stroked their penises, explaining that he must have wanted their sperm for magical purposes because why else would a man do this?)

Like so many other sexual crimes, jurisdiction over sodomy was often shared or disputed. In the Iberian peninsula, the Inquisition had jurisdiction over all sodomy in Aragon after 1524 (though in some areas local authorities fought this) and over homosexual sodomy in Portugal; in Castile, secular courts heard all sodomy trials after 1509. Though Sicily was part of the Crown of

Aragon, the Inquisition was denied jurisdiction over sodomy there unless the case involved its own officials or *familiares*.

All of these areas had somewhat distinctive patterns of prosecution. The Portuguese Inquisition, for example, compiled two large books with over 4,400 names of all those accused of or confessing to homosexual sodomy during the period 1587–1794; of these about 400 were actually put on trial and about 30 appear to have been executed. Secular courts in Castile were less thorough in record-keeping, but more harsh in punishment. Sodomy was punished by burning adult offenders alive, with juvenile offenders – who were not liable for execution – quickly passed through the fire so that, as officials commented, they could get a foretaste of what was to come if they did not change their ways. In contrast to prostitution, imprisonment was rarely set as a punishment for sodomy in Catholic Europe until the mid-eighteenth century, though men accused of sodomy might spend months or years in prison awaiting trial. (And in Seville in Spain they were isolated from other prisoners in a special royal jail.)

Throughout Catholic Europe, the social standing of the accused could shape the punishment, even in sodomy trials. Though some clergy were executed and sent to the galleys, most were generally treated more mildly than lay men, and the wealthy more leniently than the poor. The toleration of male homosexuality at the highest levels has been studied most for the French court, because it included the royal family; King Henry III (ruled 1574–89) wore women's clothing to balls and parties and surrounded himself with male favorites, his so-called *mignons*, while Philippe d'Orléans, the brother of Louis XIV, also regularly cross-dressed and had homosexual affairs. The goings-on at court were avidly reported in scurrilous pamphlets and broadsides, with religious reformers in France worried that this "aristocratic vice" would spread to other classes. By the early eighteenth century in Paris, police began to track "sodomites" using spies and informers, including clergy to spy on other clergy. In some cases, the police continued to use religious language in sodomy cases, and occasionally sent those they rounded up to confession, in the hopes that this would induce guilt and repentance. Men found guilty of sodomy were forced to sign a document repenting their acts if they wished to avoid or get out of prison; one of these confessions in a police report from 1738 notes, "He [the accused] admitted the above facts, saying that he is a miserable sinner, whom God would not want to ruin, that he had permitted it [the arrest] to happen to him so that he would repent and do penance."[38] In other cases, however, the police spoke less about sin and more about the containment of a sodomitical subculture. They actually prosecuted men for sodomy only very rarely, and used banishment or army service, not execution, as punishment.

Witchcraft and magic

The chronological pattern of prosecution for sodomy and other sexual crimes in Catholic Europe – an upsurge in the 1560s after Trent, and then a decline to the eighteenth century, punctuated by brief moral panics and group arrests – was very similar to the pattern of prosecution for witchcraft. The geographical pattern of witch trials was very different, however, for only certain parts of Catholic Europe felt the full force of the witch craze as it was described in Chapter 2. These were the Duchy of Lorraine in eastern France along with the Rhineland and territories ruled by prince-bishops in Germany, all of which saw mass panics and the execution of hundreds or thousands of people. By contrast, Ireland saw almost no witch trials, and the only mass panic in Spain was in Navarre in 1610, when the area came briefly under the influence of the French demonologist Pierre de Lancre. Other than this, the Inquisition in Spain executed only a handful of witches, the Portuguese Inquisition only one, and the Roman Inquisition none, though in each of these areas there were hundreds of cases.

The development of diabolism and the links between witchcraft and sexuality traced in the previous chapter for Protestants were very similar to those of the parts of Catholic Europe that saw mass trials, and the most eminent demonologists of the late sixteenth century were Catholic, including the French jurist Jean Bodin and the Flemish Jesuit Martin Del Rio. Thus the aspect of Catholic treatment of witchcraft that was most distinctive was the leniency of the Inquisition. Inquisitors firmly believed in the power of the devil and were no less misogynist than other judges, but they doubted very much whether the people accused of doing evil deeds (*maleficia*) had actually made a pact with the devil which gave them special powers. They viewed them not as diabolical devil-worshippers, but as superstitious and ignorant peasants who should be educated rather than executed. Their main crime was not heresy, but rather undermining the church's monopoly on supernatural remedies by claiming they had special powers. Thus Inquisitors set witchcraft within the context of false magical and spiritual claims, rather than within the context of heresy and apostasy.

Other types of magical and spiritual claims investigated by the Inquisition often had a sexual component. Women who asserted God had given them special powers – to survive through eating nothing but the Communion host, to see visions – occasionally described the angels who appeared to them as attractive young men. In their assessment that such women were "false saints," Inquisition officials agreed with this description, but noted that these were either "demons [who] appeared to her in the form of a handsome young man" or completely faked.[39] Throughout Catholic Europe, women who claimed to be possessed by demons often described this possession in sexual and bodily terms, and the exorcisms which were the Catholic Church's main weapons against possession might involve touching the woman or anointing her with oil as she lay on her bed with her hair and clothes in disarray.

Some claims to magical powers were not only sexual in origin, but also in purported effects. Included among the many cases of illicit magic that came before the Inquisition there were always a good share involving love charms, incantations, and concoctions. Many of these blended Christian and non-Christian rituals and objects: prayers to the Virgin were combined with magical incantations, knots thought to cause impotence were tied in strings at mass, holy water mixed with semen or menstrual blood was sprinkled or poured on doorsills and clothing, scraps of paper with charms written on them were placed under the altar cloth at mass. At times local priests were not unknowing parties in such magic, but actively involved. They said masses over magical objects, or baptized magnets with a person's name, complete with godparents and holy oil. (Magnets baptized with a name were thought to have the power to draw that person to the holder of the magnet.) They also conducted rituals designed specifically to lift love charms, for people who thought they had been the victims of such a charm often turned first to their priest to lift its spell; only after this did not work did they bring the matter to the attention of the court, a step they were loath to take as this required admitting they believed the love charm had worked.

Official Inquisitorial opinion about love charms was somewhat self-contradictory. Charms were outlawed both because the women who sold them cheated their customers by selling something that was ineffective, and because they subverted free will and coerced people to sin by being *too* effective. Despite the ambiguity in official reasoning, love magic was uniformly condemned, with punishments ranging from scoldings to whipping and exile. The making of love charms was often a specialized practice of networks of women on the margins of society, who traveled around peddling their wares in the same way that itinerant medical practitioners pulled teeth and treated cataracts. Their continued success in finding hopeful customers, most of them women, demonstrates the importance most women in Catholic Europe attached to a permanent relationship with a man. If one's dowry and family connections could not win one a husband, then a charm that made the object of one's affections impotent with any other woman was an option, whatever the Inquisition or other religious authorities might say.

Orthodoxy

Many aspects of Catholic teachings about sex and the treatment of sexual issues found parallels in the Orthodox churches of eastern Europe, although there were also major differences. The most prominent of these was the presence of married clergy. Married men had always been allowed to be priests in the eastern churches, and by the sixteenth century some Orthodox churches, including that of Russia, required priests to be married.

Beginning in the fifteenth century, the Ottoman Turks ruled a large part of southeastern Europe and many Orthodox Christians lived under Muslim rule. The official religion in the Ottoman Empire was Islam, but Orthodoxy was tolerated, and the patriarch in Constantinople – now renamed Istanbul – was given civil and religious authority over all Christians under Ottoman rule. Christians were understood to belong to a semi-autonomous community called the *millet*, which followed Orthodox law in terms of marriage, divorce, and other matters. As in Spain, intermarriage between Christians and Muslims who continued to practice different religions was not acceptable, but in some areas, such as Cyprus, women who had been Orthodox converted to Islam in order to marry Muslim men. In a few cases Orthodox women who were already married divorced their husbands and married Muslim men, though to do this they had to swear in a Muslim court that they had converted of their own volition and that their husbands had refused conversion. Because no Christian courts were in operation, Orthodox and Catholic Christians in Cyprus used the Muslim courts to settle other issues regarding marriage as well.

The patriarchs in Istanbul periodically attempted to impose uniformity in worship and the Greek liturgy across the entire Ottoman Empire, provoking great resentment from Serbian, Rumanian, Bulgarian, and other churches that had long used their own languages and ceremonies. In practice, national and even local churches were often quite independent. Communities sometimes chose their own priest from among the married men of the village; he went off for a few months to a monastery to learn the services, and then returned to take up both his family and clerical duties. Monasteries and convents – of which there were many in the Ottoman Empire – devoted themselves to prayer, and often owned icons understood to be miracle-working, so were places of pilgrimage as well as residences. This religious diversity was further enhanced by the fact that as the Ottoman Empire expanded, it also came to have jurisdiction over Catholics and Uniates (groups that swore allegiance to the Pope, but used their own language and rituals and accepted married clergy). War between the Ottomans and the Catholic Hapsburgs in southeastern Europe throughout the early modern period meant political boundaries shifted frequently and various groups were forced to migrate to areas they hoped would be more hospitable. Thus the ability of Catholic or Uniate authorities to regulate sexual activity or other behavior was probably more limited than in more stable states, although historians have not yet investigated this aspect of the complicated religious situation in southeastern Europe.

While many Orthodox Christians lived under Ottoman rule, others lived in Christian states, of which the largest was the principality of Muscovy, with its capital at Moscow, which also served as the center of the Russian Church. The head of the Russian church, called the metropolitan, was initially appointed by the patriarch at Constantinople, but with the fall of Constantinople to the Turks in 1453 metropolitans became largely independent. The Turkish conquest left Moscow as the only major city in the east to be ruled by a Christian prince, which many Russians interpreted as the will of God. Hundreds of monasteries and convents were established in the fifteenth through the seventeenth centuries, which came to be major landholders, especially in the vast Russian North. In 1551 the Russian church issued a law code known as the *Stoglav* ("Hundred Chapters") that called for uniformity in rituals and practices, and gave church courts jurisdiction over ecclesiastical matters and over marriage. In 1589 Muscovite political and religious authorities pressured church leaders throughout the east to declare the metropolitan of Moscow a patriarch, which gave him a status equal to the pope in Rome and the Greek Orthodox patriarch in Istanbul. During periods when the tsars were weak, the patriarch had significant power, but never as much as the pope.

For Orthodox Christians under Muslim rule as well as those in Christian states, the most important means of communicating church ideas about sexuality was confession. As in the post-Tridentine Catholic Church, confession was required and people appear to have followed this requirement. Penances were imposed for a range of acts related to sex, including those that were not under the control of the penitent, such as nocturnal emissions and miscarriages. Thus the strong emphasis on the intentions of the penitent found in post-Tridentine Catholicism was not a major part of Orthodox confession, which still concentrated primarily on correct sexual conduct rather than subjective motives and feelings, although confessors were advised to set at least some penance for lustful thoughts. Penances and punishments ranged up to excommunication, which excluded one from church rituals and was reinforced by social ostracism from the community.

Because of the centrality of confession, priests sometimes gave short sermons as part of the ritual, which often included discussion of moral issues. Metropolitan Daniil (in office 1522–39), for example, warned about prostitutes and effeminate young men who paid too much attention to their appearance. He noted that marriage and the monastery were both appropriate paths to salvation, but that the monastery was harder; married life with all things in moderation was his recommendation for most people. Marriage was also the main theme of a popular handbook on behavior, *Domostroi*, written in the 1560s, which stressed the importance of sexual purity especially for women and obedience to the wishes of one's parents for both sexes. Children who disobeyed their parents and wives who disobeyed their husbands were to be disciplined with physical force, according to *Domostroi*, but, as did similar western European guides, the suggestion was made that this not be excessive.

Studies of illicit sexuality based on records of large numbers of actual cases like those of the Inquisition in Aragon have not yet been undertaken for eastern Europe, but evidence from laws and prescriptive literature indicates that, as expected, fornication and prostitution were prohibited, though the penances and punishments set were dependent on the social status of the people involved. Sodomy was construed quite widely to include masturbation and heterosexual intercourse other than in the approved position, as well as bestiality and same-sex relations. As noted in Chapter 1, male homosexual relations were not regarded as that much worse than illicit heterosexual relations, particularly if they did not involve anal penetration. Actions that upset the proper gender order, such as a man shaving off his beard so that he looked more like a woman, were regarded as more serious violations of church law. This also applied to female same-sex relations, which were generally considered a form of masturbation unless one of the women sat on top of the other as a man was expected to. Occasionally, however, female homosexual activity was linked with pagan rituals that had survived the Christianization of Russia; women who engaged in same-sex relations were called "God-insulting grannies" and charged with praying to evil spirits.[40] Witchcraft was also linked with paganism, but not with sexuality. There were no large-scale witch hunts in Russia nor a strong demonic concept of witchcraft. Most of the people prosecuted for witchcraft were men who were seen as socially deviant; they were often vagrants who were new in an area, charged with sorcery or harming people and animals through folk magic.

Rituals of pre-Christian origin became a focus of reformers in the Russian Orthodox Church. They complained, for example, of wild and bawdy cele-brations that undercut the solemnity of weddings and religious holidays:

> From Christmas to Epiphany they have games in their houses and men and women assemble for the evil games . . . and they perform these games of the devil's imagining with evil images, blaspheming God's mercy and his Mother's holidays. They make wooden figures like horses and bulls and decorate them with linen cloth and hang bells on the horse; and on themselves they put hairy animal masks and clothes to fit and in back they put tails, looking like devils, and on their faces they carry the shameful members [penises] and bleat devilish things like goats and reveal their shameful members.[41]

Disastrous Russian military losses in the early seventeenth century led both church and government leaders to leaders to wonder whether God had abandoned Russia in the same way he had earlier abandoned the Greeks. Tsar Aleksei (ruled 1645–76) and some church officials increasingly thought that this had happened because the Russian church had strayed from "true" Christian practice in its rituals, which were the center of Russian church life. Under the leadership of bishop Nikon (1605–81), whom Aleksei promoted to patriarch in 1652, the church outlawed rituals that seemed to contain non-Christian elements or promote carnivalesque celebrations. It instituted modest reforms in church liturgy, prayers, and rituals to make these more like those of the Greek Orthodox Church, and excommunicated those who did not accept them.

The reforms were opposed by those who wanted to stay with traditional practices, later termed Old Believers, and by local church officials who opposed Nikon's centralizing measures. Some groups of Old Believers opened new religious communities and held services that followed the old rituals, while others were convinced that the changes were the work of the Antichrist and that the Apocalypse was at hand, so in 1688 they did not plow their fields and lay in white shrouds in coffins. They saw little purpose in marriage and procreation, although they moderated this position when it became apparent that the end of the world was more distant than they had originally calculated. Because they cast the tsar and the government as the "spirit of the Antichrist," and refused to serve in the army, obey central directives, or pay taxes, Old Believers were subjected to persecution, often in the form of military campaigns. Some Old Believers chose the route of martyrdom, usually by self-immolation, while others fled to the fringes of the enormous Russian Empire or even abroad.

Old Believers opposed all changes, and traditional customs such as scandalous songs and indecent games were difficult to stop, but gradually reforming officials were able to exercise some control over marriage and introduce a few modifications. By the end of the seventeenth century, even peasants included the obligatory church ceremony as part of their wedding celebrations. Officials collected wedding fees from the couple in return for a document authorizing the marriage. Before issuing permission, the priest was to make sure that the couple was not too closely related by blood or godparentage, and that both spouses were of legal age. (The minimum age for marriage was fifteen for boys and twelve for girls, though this was later raised to fifteen.) Priests were instructed to record all weddings, along with baptisms and deaths, in parish books of records, and to report these to higher church authorities, to whom they were supposed to send the collected fees.

Parental consent was required for first marriages in much of Orthodox Europe; as a Serbian law put it, "If a maiden refuses to marry the young man to whom her parents promised her, she shall be considered shameless and dishonorable among her friends and before the people."[42] At the end of the seventeenth century, revised versions of the church marriage ceremony introduced an innovation: the bride and groom themselves stated their consent to the marriage. Divorce was allowed, for desertion, incompatibility, drunkenness, and violence as well as adultery, though it was frowned on. Remarriage after divorce, or even after the death of a spouse, was also unwelcome. Those who remarried were required to pay a higher marriage fee and perform various acts of penance. Third and fourth marriages were even worse, in the minds of some church officials, who termed them "a swine's life" and often attempted to prohibit them outright. People knew about these restrictions, and sometimes tried to hide their earlier marriages when seeking authorization to marry, or to argue that their circumstances were desperate. "Disorder prevails in my house," reported a peasant asking to marry a fourth wife, "for there is no one to light the stove and cook, no one to sew or wash clothes, no one to feed anyone."[43]

Russian church and secular law strongly protected the honor of women of all classes, ordering that men who dishonored them, either by actions or by insulting them verbally, be required to pay a fine, with the fine going either to the woman or her male relatives. In the sixteenth and seventeenth centuries it became customary in Russia to further protect the honor of elite women, especially marriageable daughters, by secluding them in the *terem*, separate women's quarters. Although women in the *terem* could carry out economic activities and invite guests, they rarely appeared in public.

The modest adoption of new practices advocated by Patriarch Nikon paled in comparison with those demanded several decades later by Alexsei's son, Peter I (ruled 1682–1725), who became known as Peter the Great. In his church reform of 1721, Peter abolished the office of patriarch (which had been vacant since 1700) and instead established a committee, the Holy Synod, as the church's ruling body. This effectively made it into a department of the secular government. Peter was intent on modernizing and westernizing Russia, in order to make it a larger and more powerful state. To this end he engaged in nearly constant warfare, and so favored anything that would increase the Russian population. Peter was convinced that unhappy marriages produced fewer children; in 1722 he added his voice to that of the Orthodox Church forbidding forced marriages at all social levels. Landlords were not to force their serfs to marry against their wishes – a common practice despite church opposition – for, in the words of the eighteenth-century scholar Mikhail Lomonosov, "where there is no love, there is no hope of fruitfulness either."[44] Peter required that elite women abandon the *terem,* and appear at public social gatherings, mingling with men. He required that men and women of the elite dress in western style, ordering men to shave their beards in defiance of Orthodox tradition, and women to don the corseted gowns and adopt the bare-headed coiffures of the West.

In the new political and social milieu, young men and women found greater authorization to choose their own spouses, without being pressured to yield to parental will. The opportunities for romantic liaisons outside of marriage increased, and the stigma attached to them declined. To take care of the children from such liaisons, the state established foundling homes, and encouraged desperate mothers to bring their newborns there, instead of abandoning their babies or practicing infanticide, which was criminalized. Male homosexual activity was also criminalized, based on Western models.

Popular rituals that stressed female purity, such as showing the bride's bloody sheets or nightgown after the wedding night, were prohibited, and women who bore children out of wedlock were not to be forced to marry the father of their child, though they were allowed to. (As in western Europe, children conceived or even born out of wedlock in rural areas generally brought little dishonor if their parents subsequently married.) Peter regarded marriages between social equals as preferable, and so required spouses to be of the same social class. Religious differences, on the other hand, were not an issue; over the objections of the church, he allowed marriages between spouses of different Christian denominations, demanding only that the children be baptized into the Orthodox faith. With the endorsement of the church hierarchy, Peter required parish priests to keep records of births, baptisms, marriages, and deaths. These records allowed the state to determine men's status for taxation and military service, and also allowed the Church to try to prevent bigamous or incestuous marriages. Because Peter saw no purpose in wasting human resources on monastic life, he forbade physically capable men and women of childbearing years from taking vows.

Although the church and state of Peter's era issued many new regulations, it proved difficult to alter ingrained attitudes and behavior. Most people did follow church rules when marrying, but church leaders complained that they were otherwise ignorant of Christian teachings. Nobles successfully pressured Peter's successors to undo some of his laws concerning the financial provisions of marriage. Among peasants especially, young people could not exercise free choice of spouses. Rules concerning entrance into monasteries were relaxed, and displaced middle-aged women in particular sought this alternative. Western concepts of romantic love and western forms of socializing gradually spread, however, despite the objections of conservatives, who bemoaned what they saw as a lack of morals.

* * *

The attitude toward sexuality that is often loosely termed "Puritan" was clearly shared by religious reformers of all confessions in early modern Europe.

Catholic and Orthodox leaders were just as suspicious of sexual pleasure as many Protestants, and just as intent to reform or repress sexual activities that they viewed as improper in a godly community. The actual effects of their reform efforts came much more slowly than they had anticipated – just as they did for Protestants – and were accepted most readily when they fit with local traditions or when the priests or other officials who implemented them responded to local ideas. Though the exact timing differed slightly, all of Europe saw increasing clerical and bureaucratic control of marriage and sexual discipline during the sixteenth and seventeenth centuries, accompanied by activities and institution designed to help – or force – clergy and laity to internalize stricter moral standards. Church and state authorities throughout all of Europe despaired over people's inability or unwillingness to live up to the standards they wished to impose, however, and by the mid-eighteenth century, or even earlier, they decided that draconian punishments for most moral and sexual crimes were ineffective or inappropriate.

Church and state attempts at reform and repression did not end at the borders of Europe, for this period also saw, of course, the first wave of European overseas exploration and colonization. Christian missionaries and institutions accompanied all of the colonial powers, and the control of the sexuality of both indigenous people and colonists was an essential part of colonial religious and political policy. The following three chapters will thus examine developments outside of Europe, where the local traditions and ideas were far more diverse than any reformer complaining about Basque trial marriages or Russian blasphemous costumes could have imagined.

Selected further reading

Many of the works mentioned in the suggested readings of previous chapters also include material that discusses post-Reformation Catholicism and Orthodoxy. For an overview of Catholicism in this period, see R. Po-Chia Hsia, *The World of Catholic Renewal, 1540–1770* (Cambridge: Cambridge University Press, 1998). For a recent theoretical discussion, see the "Focal point: Confessionalization and Social Discipline in France, Italy, and Spain," with articles by James R. Farr, Wietse de Boer, and Allyson Poska, in *Archiv für Reformationsgeschichte* (hereafter *ARG*) 94 (2003), 276–319.

There are a number of broad collections that include articles on the issues discussed in this chapter. For France see: Philippe Aries and André Bejin, eds, *Western Sexuality: Practice and Precept in Past and Present Times* (London: Blackwell, 1985); Jean-Louis Flandrin, *Sex in the Western World: The Development of Attitudes and Behavior*, trans. Sue Collins (Chur, Switzerland: Harwood, 1991); Suzanne Desan and Jeffrey Merrick, eds, *Family, Gender, and Law in*

Early Modern France (University Park: Penn State University Press, 2009). For Italy see: Edward Muir and Guido Ruggiero, eds, *Sex and Gender in Historical Perspective: Selections from* Quaderni Storici (Baltimore, Md.: Johns Hopkins, 1990); Marilyn Migiel and Juliana Schiesari, eds, *Refiguring Women: Perspectives on Gender and the Italian Renaissance* (Ithaca, N.Y.: Cornell University Press, 1991); Samuel K. Cohn Jr., *Women in the Streets: Essays on Sex and Power in Renaissance Italy* (Baltimore, Md.: Johns Hopkins, 1996). For Spain see: Magdalena S. Sanchez and Alain Saint-Saëns, eds, *Spanish Women in the Golden Age: Images and Realities* (Westport, Conn.: Greenwood Press, 1996); Alain Saint-Saëns, ed., *Religion, Body, and Gender in Early Modern Spain* (San Francisco: Edwin Mellen Press, 1991) and *Sex and Love in Golden Age Spain* (New Orleans: University Press of the South, 1996); Eukene Lacarra Lanz, ed., *Marriage and Sexuality in Medieval and Early Modern Iberia* (New York: Routledge, 2002); Cruz and Perry, *Culture and Control* (note 33). For Ireland, see MacCurtain and O'Dowd, *Women* (note 15 for Chapter 3 in "Notes"). The special issue "Marriage in Early Modern Europe" of the *Sixteenth Century Journal* (34(2), Summer 2003) includes articles on several countries.

Ute Ranke-Heinemann, *Eunuchs for the Kingdom of Heaven: Women, Sexuality and the Catholic Church,* trans. Peer Heinegg (New York: Doubleday, 1990) provides an extremely critical analysis of Catholic ideas. For the opinions of the most influential Christian humanist on marriage and women, see Erika Rummel, ed., *Erasmus on Women* (Toronto: University of Toronto Press, 1996) and Reinier Leushuis, "The Mimesis of Marriage: Dialogue and Intimacy in Erasmus's Matrimonial Writings," *Renaissance Quarterly* 57(4) (2004): 1278–307.

Many books assess the impact of the Council of Trent and other measures of Catholic reform in various parts of Europe. For Germany, see W. David Myers, *"Poor, Sinning Folk": Confession and Conscience in Counter-Reformation Germany* (Ithaca, N.Y.: Cornell University Press, 1996); Marc Forster, *The Counter-Reformation in the Villages: Religion and Reform in the Bishopric of Speyer, 1560–1720* (Ithaca, N.Y.: Cornell, 1992); Strasser, *State of Virginity* (note 5); Forster, *Catholic Revival* (note 12). For France, see: Louis Châtellier, *The Religion of the Poor: The Rural Missions in Europe and the Formation of Modern Catholicism, c. 1500–1800,* trans. Brian Pearce (Cambridge: Cambridge University Press, 1997). For Spain, see: Henry Kamen, *The Phoenix and the Flame: Catalonia and the Counter-Reformation* (New Haven: Yale University Press, 1992); Allyson Poska, *Regulating the People: The Catholic Reformation in Seventeenth-Century Spain* (Leiden: E.J. Brill, 1998); Nalle, *God in La Mancha* (note 29). For Italy, see: de Boer, *Conquest of the Soul* (note 7); Gentilcore, *From Bishop to Witch* (note 30).

The way confraternities and other new religious groups shaped post-Tridentine piety has been examined in: Maureen Flynn, *Sacred Charity:*

Confraternities and Social Welfare in Spain, 1400–1700 (Ithaca, N.Y.: Cornell University Press, 1989); Elizabeth Rapley, *The Dévotes: Women and Church in Seventeenth-Century France* (Montreal: McGill/Queen's University Press, 1990); Nicolas Terpstra, *Lay Confraternities and Civic Religion in Renaissance Bologna* (Cambridge: Cambridge University Press, 1995); John Patrick Donnelly and Michael W. Maher, eds, *Confraternities and Catholic Reform in Italy, France, and Spain* (Kirksville, Mo.: Truman State University Press, 1999); Barbara B. Diefendorf, *From Penitence to Charity: Pious Women and the Catholic Reformation in Paris* (New York: Oxford University Press, 2004); Châtellier, *Europe of the Devout* (note 32). On Marian veneration, see Bridget Heal, *The Cult of the Virgin Mary in Early Modern Germany: Protestant and Catholic Piety, 1500–1648* (Cambridge: Cambridge University Press, 2007).

The Inquisition's role in the regulation of sexuality has been studied in many works by William Monter, such as: "Women and the Italian Inquisitions," in Mary Beth Rose, ed., *Women in the Middle Ages and the Renaissance: Literary and Historical Perspectives* (Syracuse: Syracuse University Press, 1986), 73–89; *Ritual, Myth, and Magic in Early Modern Europe* (Athens, Ohio: Ohio University Press, 1983); *Frontiers of Heresy: The Spanish Inquisition from the Basque Lands to Sicily* (Cambridge: Cambridge University Press, 1990). Other relevant studies of the Inquisition include: Henry Kamen, *Inquisition and Society in Spain in the Sixteenth and Seventeenth Centuries* (London: Weidenfeld and Nicolson, 1985); Stephen Haliczer, *Inquisition and Society in the Kingdom of Valencia, 1478–1834* (Berkeley: University of California Press, 1990); André Fernandez, "The Repression of Sexual Behavior by the Aragonese Inquisition between 1560 and 1700," *Journal of the History of Sexuality* 7 (1997): 469–501; Haliczer, ed., *Inquisition and Society* (note 28); Henningsen and Tedeschi, *Inquisition* (note 11).

Clerical concubinage has been the focus of study in Gerritdina D. Justitz, "The Abbot and the Concubine: Piety and Politics in Sixteenth Century Naumburg," *ARG* 92 (2001), 138–64; Laqua, "Concubinage and the Church" (note 14).

Silvia Evangelisti, *Nuns: A History of Convent Life* (Oxford: Oxford University Press, 2008) provides an excellent introduction to convents in the period 1450–1700. Elizabeth Makowski, *Canon Law and Cloistered Women: Periculoso and Its Commentators 1298–1545* (Washington, DC: The Catholic University of America Press, 1997) and Ruth P. Liebowitz "Virgins in the Service of Christ: The Dispute over an Active Apostolate for Women during the Counter-Reformation," in *Women of Spirit: Female Leadership in the Jewish and Christian Traditions* (New York: Simon and Schuster, 1979), 131–52 analyze theological arguments related to the cloistering of women. Studies that focus on actual developments in women's convents include: Jutta Gisela Sperling, *Convents and the Body Politic in Renaissance Venice* (Chicago: University of Chicago Press,

2000); Mary Laven, "Sex and Celibacy in Early Modern Venice," *Historical Journal* 44(4) (2001): 865–88; P. Renée Baernstein, *A Convent Tale: A Century of Sisterhood in Spanish Milan* (New York: Routledge, 2002); K.J.P. Lowe, *Nuns' Chronicles and Convent Culture in Renaissance and Counter-Reformation Italy* (New York: Cambridge University Press, 2003); Silvia Evangelisti, "'We do not have it, and we do not want it': Women, Power, and Convent Reform in Florence," *SCJ* 34 (2003), 677–700; Mary Laven, *Virgins of Venice: Broken Vows and Cloistered Lives in the Renaissance Convent* (New York: Penguin, 2004); Elizabeth Lehfeldt, *Women and Religion in Golden-Age Spain: The Permeable Cloister* (Burlington, Vt.: Ashgate, 2006); Cordula van Wyhe, ed., *Female Monasticism in Early Modern Europe* (Burlington, Vt.: Ashgate, 2008).

Relationships between confessors and penitents have been explored in: Rudolph M. Bell, "Telling Her Sins: Male Confessors and Female Penitents in Catholic Reformation Italy," in Lynda L. Coon, *et al.,* eds, *That Gentle Strength: Historical Perspectives on Women in Christianity* (Charlottesville, Va.: University of Virginia Press, 1990), 118–33; Patrick J. O'Banion, "'A Priest Who Appears Good': Manuals of Confession and the Construction of Clerical Identity in Early Modern Spain," *Dutch Review of Church History* 85 (2005): 333–48; Stephen Haliczar, *Between Exaltation and Infamy: Female Mystics in the Golden Age of Spain* (New York: Oxford University Press, 2002); Colleen M. Seguin, "Ambiguous Liaisons: Catholic Women's Relationships with their Confessors in Early Modern England," *ARG* 95 (2004): 156–85; Jodi Bilinkoff, *Related Lives: Confessors and their Female Penitents* (Ithaca, N.Y.: Cornell University Press, 2005); Haliczer, *Sexuality in the Confessional* (note 17); Bilinkoff, "Confessors" (note 18).

Richard Kagan, *Lucrecia's Dreams: Politics and Prophecy in Sixteenth Century Spain* (Berkeley: University of California Press, 1990), Fulvio Tomizza, *Heavenly Supper: The Story of Maria Janis*, trans. Anne Jacobsen Schutte (Chicago: University of Chicago Press, 1993), and Anne Jacobson Schutte, *Aspiring Saints: Pretense of Holiness, Inquisition, and Gender in the Republic of Venice, 1618–1750* (Baltimore: Johns Hopkins University Press, 2001) analyze women accused of being false saints.

Studies of changes in marriage practices include: P.J. Corish, "Catholic Marriage under the Penal Code," in A. Cosgrove, ed., *Marriage in Ireland* (Dublin: College Press, 1985), 56–74; Guido Ruggiero, "Marriage, Love, Sex, and Renaissance Civic Morality," in James Grantham Turner, *Sexuality and Gender in Early Modern Europe: Institutions, Texts, Images* (Cambridge: Cambridge University Press, 1993), 10–30; Julie Hardwick, "Seeking Separations: Gender, Marriages, and Household Economies in Early Modern France," *French Historical Studies* 21(1) (Winter 1998): 157–80; James R. Farr, "The Pure and Disciplined Body: Hierarchy, Morality, and Symbolism in France During the Catholic

Reformation," *Journal of Interdisciplinary History* 21 (1991): 391–414; Joanne Marie Ferraro, *Marriage Wars in Late Renaissance Venice* (Oxford: Oxford University Press, 2001); Eisenach, *Husbands, Wives* (note 8); Sperling, "Marriage" (note 22); Hacke, *Women, Sex* (note 24).

The records of Spanish church and secular courts have provided insights into ideas about sexuality held by ordinary people, as well as the actual impact of Catholic institutions. See: Mary Elizabeth Perry, *Gender and Disorder in Early Modern Seville* (Princeton, N.J.: Princeton University Press, 1990); Renato Barahona, *Sex Crimes, Honour, and the Law in Early Modern Spain: Vizcaya, 1528–1735* (Toronto: University of Toronto Press, 2003); Abigail Dyer, "Seduction by Promise of Marriage: Law, Sex, and Culture in Seventeenth-Century Spain," *The Sixteenth Century Journal* 34(2) (2003), 439–56; Allyson M. Poska, "Elusive Virtue: Rethinking the Role of Female Chastity in Early Modern Spain," *Journal of Early Modern History* 8(1) (2004): 135–46; Lisa Vollendorf, *The Lives of Women: A New History of Inquisitional Spain* (Nashville, Tenn.: Vanderbilt University Press, 2005); Edward Behrend-Martínez, "Female Sexual Potency in a Spanish Church Court, 1673–1735," *Law & History Review* 24(2) (2006): 297–330 and *Unfit for Marriage* (note 23); Grace E. Coollidge, "'A Vile and Abject Woman': Noble Mistresses, Legal Power, and the Family in Early Modern Spain," *Journal of Family History* 32(3) (2007): 195–214; Scott K. Taylor, *Honor and Violence in Golden-Age Spain* (New Haven, Conn.: Yale University Press, 2008); Poska, *Women and Authority* (note 27). On Christian/Muslim intermarriage and sexual relations, see: Mark D. Meyerson, *The Muslims of Valencia in the Age of Ferdinand and Isabel: Between Coexistence and Crusade* (Berkeley: University of California Press, 1991) and Mary Elizabeth Perry, *The Handless Maiden: Moriscos and the Politics of Religion in Early Modern Spain* (Princeton, N.J.: Princeton University Press, 2005).

Popular rituals and their control have been examined in: Edward Muir, *Ritual in Early Modern Europe* (Cambridge: Cambridge University Press, 1998); Natalie Zemon Davis, "The Reasons of Misrule," in her *Society and Culture in Early Modern France* (Stanford, Calif.: Stanford University Press, 1975), 97–123; Christiane Klapisch-Zuber, "The 'Mattinata' in Medieval Italy," in her *Women, Family, and Ritual in Renaissance Italy,* trans. Lydia Cochrane (Chicago: University of Chicago Press, 1982), 261–82; Peter Burke, *Popular Culture in Early Modern Europe* (London: T. Smith, 1978).

Robert Forster and Orest Ranum, eds, *Ritual, Religion and the Sacred: Selections from the Annales* (Baltimore, Md.: Johns Hopkins University Press, 1982) contains several articles on wedding rituals in Catholic areas. Sharon T. Strocchia, "When the Bishop Married the Abbess: Masculinity and Power in Florentine Episcopal Rites, 1300–1600," *Gender & History* 19(2) (August 2007): 346–68 is a fascinating look at a ritual in which new Florentine bishops celebrated a symbolic marriage, complete with fictive sexual consummation; sixteenth-century bishops refused to perform it, as it violated their new notions of clerical masculinity and episcopal power.

The especially strong alliance in France between families and state authorities in the control of marriage and other aspects of behavior has been investigated in James R. Farr, *Authority and Sexuality in Early Modern Burgundy* (New York: Oxford University Press, 1995) and Sarah Hanley, "Engendering the State: Family Formation and State Building in Early Modern France," *French Historical Studies* 16 (1989): 4–27.

Questions relating to illegitimacy, infanticide, and abandonment are discussed in: Peter Laslett, Karla Oosterveen, and Richard M. Smith, eds, *Bastardy and its Comparative History* (Cambridge, Mass.: Harvard University Press, 1980); René Leboutte, "Offense against Family Order: Infanticide in Belgium from the Fifteenth through the Early Twentieth Centuries," *Journal of the History of Sexuality* 2 (1991): 159–85; David I. Kertzer, *Sacrificed for Honor: Italian Infant Abandonment and the Politics of Reproductive Control* (Boston: Beacon, 1993); Jeremy Hayhoe, "Illegitimacy, Inter-Generational Conflict and Legal Practice in Eighteenth-Century Northern Burgundy," *Journal of Social History* 38(3) (2005): 673–84; Joanne M. Ferraro, *Nefarious Crimes, Contested Justice: Illicit Sex and Infanticide in the Republic of Venice, 1557–1789* (Baltimore, Md.: Johns Hopkins University Press, 2008).

Asylums for repentant prostitutes and other women have been studied in: Philip F. Riley, "Michel Foucault, Lust, Women, and Sin in Louis XIV's Paris," *Church History* 59 (1990): 35–50; Sherrill Cohen, *The Evolution of Women's Asylums Since 1500: From Refuges for Ex-Prostitutes to Shelters for Battered Women* (Oxford: Oxford University Press, 1992); Lucia Ferrante, "Honor Regained: Women in the Casa del Soccorso di San Paolo in Sixteenth-Century Bologna," in Muir and Ruggiero, *Sex and Gender,* 46–72; John Henderson and Richard Wall, eds, *Poor Women and Children in the European Past* (London: Routledge, 1994); Monica Chojnacka, "Women, Charity and Community in Early Modern Venice: The Casa Delle Zitelle," *Renaissance Quarterly* 51(1) (1998): 68–91; Nicholas Terpstra, "Mothers, Sisters, and Daughters: Girls and Conservatory Guardianship in Late Renaissance Florence," *Renaissance Studies* 17(2) (2003): 201–29. Other studies of prostitutes in Catholic Europe include: Elizabeth S. Cohen, "No Longer Virgins: Self-Representation by Young Women in Late Renaissance Rome," in Marilyn Migiel and Juliana Schiesari, eds, *Gender and the Italian Renaissance* (Ithaca, N.Y.: Cornell University Press, 1991), 169–91; Elizabeth S. Cohen, "Seen and Known: Prostitutes in the Cityscape of Late-Sixteenth-Century Rome," *Renaissance Studies* 12(3) (1998): 392–409; Diane Yvonne Ghirardo, "The Topography of Prostitution in Renaissance Ferrara," *Journal of the Society of Architectural Historians* 60(4) (2001): 402–31; Stefano

D'Amico, "Shameful Mother: Poverty and Prostitution in Seventeenth-Century Milan," *Journal of Family History* 30(1) (2005): 109–20; Tessa Storey, *Carnal Commerce in Counter-Reformation Rome* (Cambridge: Cambridge University Press, 2008).

Many of the works on same-sex relations listed in the suggested readings of Chapter 2 also discuss Catholic Europe; see also Judith C. Brown, *Immodest Acts: The Life of a Lesbian Nun in Renaissance Italy* (Oxford: Oxford University Press, 1986); Jeffrey Merrick, "Sodomitical Scandals and Subcultures in the 1720s," *Men and Masculinities* 1(4) (1999) and "Chaussons in the Streets: Sodomy in Seventeenth-Century Paris," *Journal of the History of Sexuality* 15(2) (May 2006): 167–203; Katherine B. Crawford, "Love, Sodomy, and Scandal: Controlling the Sexual Reputation of Henry III," *Journal of the History of Sexuality* 12(4) (October 2003): 513–42. Hurteau, "Catholic Moral Discourse" (note 10); Berco, *Sexual Hierarchies* (note 37). A fine source collection is: Jeffrey Merrick and Bryant Ragan, eds, *Homosexuality in Early Modern France: A Documentary Collection* (New York: Oxford University Press, 2001).

Similarly, many of the works on witchcraft listed in Chapter 2 also discuss Catholic Europe. Local studies of witchcraft in Catholic areas include Ruth Martin, *Witchcraft in Venice, 1550–1650* (Oxford: Blackwell, 1989) and Jonathan B. Durrant, *Witchcraft, Gender, and Society in Early Modern Germany* (Leiden: Brill, 2007).

For love magic, see: María Helena Sánchez Ortega, "Sorcery and Eroticism as Love Magic," in Mary Elizabeth Perry and Anne J. Cruz, *Cultural Encounters: The Impact of the Inquisition in Spain and the New World* (Berkeley: University of California Press, 1991), 58–92; Guido Ruggiero, *Binding Passions: Tales of Magic, Marriage, and Power at the End of the Renaissance* (New York: Oxford University Press, 1993); Mary O'Neil, "Magical Healing, Love Magic, and the Inquisition in Late Sixteenth Century Modena," in Haliczer, *Inquisition and Society* (note 28), 88–114. On possession, see: Anita M. Walker and Edmund H. Dickerman, "A Notorious Woman: Possession, Witchcraft and Sexuality in Seventeenth-Century Provence," *Historical Reflections* 27(1) (2001): 1–26 and Moshe Sluhovsky, "The Devil in the Convent," *American Historical Review* 107(5) (2002): 1378–411.

For Orthodoxy, in addition to the studies mentioned in the notes and in the bibliography following Chapter 1 see several articles by Nancy Shields Kollman: "The Seclusion of Muscovite Women," *Russian History* 10 (1983): 170–87; "Women's Honor in Early Modern Russia," in Barbara Evans Clements, *et al.*, eds, *Russia's Women: Accommodation, Resistance, Transformation* (Berkeley: University of California Press, 1991), 60–73 and "The Extremes of Patriarchy: Spousal Abuse and Murder in Early Modern Russia," *Russian History* = *Histoire Russe* 25(1) (1998): 133–40. See also several articles by

Daniel H. Kaiser: "'He Said, She Said': Rape and Gender Discourse in Early Modern Russia," *Kritika: Explorations in Russian & Eurasian History* 3(2) (2002): 197–216; "'Whose Wife Will She be at the Resurrection?' Marriage and Remarriage in Early Modern Russia," *Slavic Review* 62(2) (Summer 2003): 302–23; "Church Control Over Marriage in Seventeenth-Century Russia," *The Russian Review* 65(4) (October 2006): 567–85. On Russian witchcraft, see: Russell Zguta, "Witchcraft Trials in Seventeenth-century Russia," *American Historical Review* 82 (1977): 1187–207; Valerie A. Kivelson, "Male Witches and Gendered Categories in Seventeenth-Century Russia," *Comparative Studies in Society & History* 45(3) (2003): 606–31. Additional articles on Russia include Georg Michels, "Muscovite Elite Women and Old Belief," *Harvard Ukrainian Studies* 19 (1995): 428–50; Debra Coulter, "The Muscovite Widowed Clergy and the Russian Church Reforms of 1666–67," *The Slavonic and East European Review* 80(3) (July 2002): 459–78. The articles in Valerie A. Kivelson and Robert H. Greene, eds, *Orthodox Russia: Belief and Practice under the Tsars* (University Park, Pa.: Penn State University Press, 2003) include several that discuss the issues in this chapter. For the situation in Cyprus, see Ronald C. Jennings, *Christians and Muslims in Ottoman Cyprus and the Mediterranean World, 1571–1640* (New York: New York University Press, 1993).

LATIN AMERICA

A T THE SAME TIME THAT Catholics and Protestants in western Europe were combating one another from the pulpit, on paper, and on the battlefield, and Christian religious authorities of all denominations were attempting to impose stricter moral standards on those under their authority, some European countries were engaging in overseas explorations and colonization. The first European colonies outside of Europe were those of the Portuguese in the Atlantic islands, Brazil, west Africa, and Asia, and the Spanish in the Americas and the Philippines. In all of these areas, colonial forces included Catholic missionaries and religious authorities who worked both to convert indigenous people and to establish church structures for immigrants. Two years after Columbus's first voyage, in fact, the pope divided the world between Spain and Portugal in the Treaty of Tordesillas, and later granted special privileges – the *Patronato* – to the Spanish and Portuguese crowns to control almost all aspects of religious life in the colonies.

Catholic missionaries, primarily members of religious orders such as the Franciscans, Dominicans, and later the Jesuits, also traveled to areas outside of European control such as China and Japan in conversion efforts, and in 1622 the papacy established a special group to supervise missionaries worldwide, the *Congregatio de Propaganda Fide*. Beginning in the seventeenth century, Protestant clergy accompanied Dutch and English merchants and settlers as they established trading centers and colonies in Asia, South Africa, and North America, although the main Protestant missionary effort did not begin until the early nineteenth century.

Along with explaining the theological and spiritual concepts central to Christianity, missionaries also attempted to persuade – or force – possible converts to adopt Christian sexual morality; in many areas, after baptism, following Christian patterns in terms of a person's marriage rituals and sexual demeanor became a more important mark of conversion than understanding the Trinity or transubstantiation. As they did in Europe, Catholic religious authorities began to oversee marriages, hear cases of fornication, adultery, bigamy, and love magic in church courts, and to attempt to shape sexual life through confession. They worked with colonial political authorities in areas under European control, and in some areas, such as the missions of the Americas, they actually *were* the political authorities.

Catholic clergy largely shared the dominant ideas about proper sexual morality we traced in the last chapter – that all sexual intercourse was to be limited to monogamous marriage, that marriage was indissoluble, that virginity and celibacy were superior to marriage and required of the clergy, that masturbation, sodomy, contraception, and abortion were mortal sins, that all sexual sins were to be confessed to a priest. Though some of these ideas were already present in the cultures they encountered, many of them were perhaps even more strange than Christian theological concepts. In addition, indigenous peoples quickly noted that Christian conquerors and colonists – sometimes including the clergy themselves – did not practice what they preached, but raped local women, made bigamous marriages, or engaged in numerous sexual relationships. As the Maya of Central America wrote in the books of Chilam Balaam, their histories, "When the Spanish arrived, they brought shameful things . . . Whoremongering came with them . . . With them came the selling of the women and the unclean things."[1] Thus even those who converted often rejected certain aspects of Christian sexual morality while selectively adopting and then modifying others in a process of creolization, in the same way that they selectively adopted and modified Christian spiritual notions. In some places, missionaries and other clergy also adapted their teachings to fit better with existing sexual mores or with those developing in the colonial context.

Before examining the Christian regulation of sexuality outside of Europe in the early modern period, then, we must know something about sexual mores and marital patterns before contact with Europeans. Thus this chapter and the two chapters that follow each begin with a brief examination of indigenous sexual ideas and norms before going on to discuss changes that accompanied the introduction and institutionalization of Christianity. It is important to keep in mind that the areas under examination are vast and have widely varying patterns. The historical record is often thin and involves layers of interpretation, with most written records coming from Europeans or from indigenous authors who learned to read and write from European clergy, so were seeing and describing their original cultures through eyes that were already acculturated to Christian and European ways. We also tend to know more about cultures, such as the Aztecs in central Mexico or the Incas in the Andes, that were politically dominant at the point of first European contact. Because encounters with these cultures shaped the way the colonial church developed and responded to groups with which it later came into contact, however, their ideas were the most influential.

Ideas and patterns before the arrival of the Europeans

Historical and archaeological research makes clear that there was wide variety in indigenous sexual mores throughout the Americas. Some scholars suggest that the more highly organized and stratified societies, such as the Aztecs and Incas, were more strict than those that did not have strong centralized political control. Information about jungle and tribal societies in the early modern period is very limited, and in some cases is largely based on anthropological research conducted within the last century. How much one can project these findings back to earlier centuries is hotly contested, with some scholars arguing that existing patterns continued completely or largely unchanged for centuries, and others that assuming this overlooks how changeable and dynamic "tradition" can actually be.

Generalizing is thus fraught with perils, but there do appear to be a few traditions that most cultures shared: They had some sort of marriage ceremony, with marital partners generally chosen by the family or community rather than the individuals themselves. The marriage was sometimes preceded by a period of trial marriage in which the potential husband lived and worked in his father-in-law's house; sexual relations might begin during this period. If a marriage did not work out, the partners were often free to leave the marriage and marry elsewhere. Certain close relatives appear to have been prohibited as marital partners, although in some cultures a man was expected to marry his brother's widow – a practice similar to the Jewish tradition of levirate marriage – and in others endogamous marriage within the larger kin group was the norm. Marriage was often monogamous, although more powerful men in some groups had more than one wife and rulers sometimes had a great many wives. Marriage among the powerful might be used as a means of cementing alliances, with women given to men to gain their favor or their allegiance, and outsiders incorporated into a kin group through marriage or other sexual ceremonies. In many places kinship groups were linked to specific holy places, gods, or religious figures.

For women, pre-marital sexual relations were regarded as much less serious than extra-marital ones, which could be punished very severely; for men, sexual relations before or outside of marriage were generally not punished unless they upset community norms or family alliances. Some cultures linked control of the body with order and control in society and the cosmos, with excessive sexual energy or activity in both women and men viewed as harmful; no sex was also deemed harmful, however, so the sexual ideal was moderation, not virginity. In a few cultures, all sexual activity was seen as disruptive so that sexual intercourse occurred outside houses or other buildings, but in many areas symbolic or actual sexual acts were part of ceremonies honoring the gods.

Many scholars emphasize that notions of gender among the indigenous peoples of the Americas were marked by a sense of parallelism, with men and women having complementary roles in economic life and male and female gods complementary roles in the creation and continuation of the cosmos. Among some groups gender was a fluid category, at least ceremonially, as rulers adopted male and female dress and roles in rituals honoring the gods, and the gods themselves changed and combined genders. This gender fluidity incorporated individuals who combined the tasks, behavior, and clothing of men and women. Most of these individuals were morphologically male, and the Europeans who first encountered them regarded them as sodomites and called them "berdaches," from an Arabic word for male prostitute. Now the more accepted term is "two-spirit people," a phrase that captures the idea that such individuals both combined and transcended the categories "men" and "women," and so were thought of as a third gender.

Other scholars warn about over-emphasizing gender egalitarianism; they note that though both women and men appear to have had positions as religious leaders, women were generally not the primary religious leaders, and women who were still in child-bearing years were specifically excluded from some religious ceremonies. Women may have inherited land, but they were not independent rulers. Two-spirit people were tolerated, but only rarely had important advisory or military roles.

This debate about gender is connected to a debate about sexuality. Some scholars argue that because certain cultures valued femininity, they did not disparage men or boys who dressed as women or took the female role (i.e., passive and penetrated) in actual or ritualized same-sex relations. Others argue that such transvestism and sex was always forced, and that it represented a symbolic reenactment of conquest by a superior (male) over an inferior (female), with the passive partner mocked and vilified. Still others assert that European and indigenous concepts of same-sex relations were so different that it is difficult to determine both what was actually going on and what value was being ascribed to the activity. Sexual relations between a two-spirit person and a man may have not been understood as "same-sex," because two-spirit people were actually thought of as a third group rather than as effeminate males.

Whatever their position in the debates about gender and sexuality, scholars agree that it easier to find information about certain indigenous cultures than others. Those of central Mexico and the Andes have left the most sources, and so have been most extensively studied. About a century before Spanish conquest in 1521, central Mexico was conquered by the Mexica, who formed the Aztec state; the Mexica were one of the Nahua peoples, who shared a language – Nahuatl – and many cultural traits with other groups in central Mexico. Many of the earliest missionaries in Mesoamerica learned Nahuatl in order to be more effective at conversion, producing a Nahuatl catechism as early as 1539. They were interested in Nahua traditions, and recorded conversations with Nahua elders that described Nahua laws and practices. Missionaries were particularly excited when they found what appeared to be parallels between Nahua values and Christian ones. For example, Nahua devotional practices included periods of sexual abstinence, sexual transgressions led people to participate in rituals of confession, and infants were given a ritual bathing to free them from pollution associated with the parents' sexual activity. Adultery (defined as sex with a married woman), abortion, and incest were at least in theory harshly punished, as was homosexual activity (though there is some debate about this among contemporary historians). Marriages were marked by a ceremony tying the cloaks of a man and a woman together, and a distinction was made in terms of inheritance between children born in and out of wedlock. Couples living together without being married could be harshly punished, and young women were advised to be modest in their demeanor. Particularly in the period of the Aztec Empire, patriarchal restrictions on Nahua women grew, and wives were instructed to obey their husbands; in the words of a *huehuetlatolli* (a discourse by Nahua elders), "when he [your husband] asks you something [or] entrusts something to you [or] when he tells you to do something, you are to obey him properly."[2]

The missionaries' desires to find similarities between Christianity and Nahua beliefs and their unfamiliarity with Nahua culture caused them to misinterpret certain things, however. Nahua culture saw the basic conflict in the cosmos as order vs. disorder rather than good vs. evil, but regarded the proper life as a balance between these two rather than a life of order alone. Thus the Nahua sexual ideal was moderation, not abstinence. There was no notion of consequences in an afterlife or a soul distinct from the body, so nothing that directly equated with Christian ideas of guilt or sin; sex made one physically, not morally, impure. Some Aztec religious rituals also linked human sexuality and fertility with agricultural fertility in ways that the missionaries found shocking, including (most famously) human sacrifice and ritual cannibalism, and young male priests processing with erect penises or dressed in the flayed skin of a woman. Most Nahua peoples and other residents of Mexico such as the Maya did not carry out ceremonies of large-scale human sacrifice, which were part of the Aztec state cult of the sun; many of the Aztecs' sacrificial victims actually came from other groups, who because of this allied themselves with the Spanish against the Aztecs. Mayas did share some basic notions of sexuality with the Nahuas, such as a concern for balance and moderation and a condemnation of sexual excess.

The political situation in the Andes was similar to that of central Mexico, in that the Inca Empire – whose ruler was also called the Inca – conquered a large territory shortly before the Spanish came. Though human sacrifice was very rare, the Inca also had a cult of the sun, and a large number of other gods and revered ancestors. Certain young women were chosen as *acclas* (women dedicated to the sun), and either remained virgin-priestesses in special buildings or married the Inca or one of his favorites. The Incas demanded such women from all the peoples they conquered, and sent a special official, the *ochacamayo* ("he who chastizes") to order any man killed who had sexual relations with a woman chosen to be an accla. Like Aztec, Inca cosmology was based on a notion of equilibrium and balance, including balance between masculine and feminine, though things associated with men – order, height, structure, light – were also viewed as superior to those associated with women, and defeated warriors were paraded through the streets of Cuzco in women's dress. This plus the tribute of acclas linked the Incas with masculinity and all other groups with femininity. In addition to the Inca state cults, individuals, families, and groups also venerated *huacas*, ancestors or gods that had often been transformed into sacred objects or places. Some devotional practices involving *huacas* had sexual aspects; girls occasionally married a *huaca*, or married men and women abstained from sexual relations during certain ceremonies. According to Catholic authorities, married persons were more likely to have *huacas* or other sacred objects than unmarried persons were, indicating that perhaps people received them as part of Andean marriage ceremonies.

In Inca society everyone except the acclas was expected to marry, and marriages, apart from those of the Inca and his favorites, were monogamous. Fertility and procreation were viewed as extremely important, with a girl's first menstruation marked by a special ceremony giving her her adult name and clothing. The coming-of-age ceremony for a boy also included his being given his adult name and a loincloth, and having his ears pierced for large ear spools, so that he shed blood the way a girl did at menstruation. The emphasis on procreation and on the complementarity of men and women may have been part of the reason why Incas appear to have ordered death for homosexual activity, though some historians argue that this may be a later addition by Christian authors. In contrast to central Mexico, missionaries in the Andes rarely took the time to learn Quechua, the native language, and works describing Inca practices by both Europeans and indigenous peoples are all in Latin or Spanish; Incas did keep records on *quipus*, groups of knotted strings, but deciphering these was the work of trained officials and knowledge of how to do this has been lost.

Smaller and less centralized Indian groups have left much less information, so that what we know comes from generally hostile Spanish reports or much later records. These indicate wide varieties in sexual and religious patterns. The Caribs of the Caribbean and northern South America, for example, appear to have gained most of their marital partners through raiding other tribes, a practice that was also found elsewhere. In contrast to the state religions of the Incas and Aztecs, indigenous groups elsewhere, including Florida and what later became the American Southwest, had largely animistic religions in which natural objects such as animals and plants were viewed as guardian spirits, and there was no organized priesthood.

Colonial institutions

The arrival of Europeans and Africans in the Americas brought dramatic change. Initial Hispano-Indian contact began between 1492 and 1519 in the Caribbean; in 1519, Hernando Cortés led an expeditionary force to Mexico, and two years later defeated the Aztec Empire; in 1532, Francisco Pizarro led a force that took over the Inca Empire. From these bases, Spanish officials and colonists established various types of economic and administrative units that sought to extract the natural and agricultural wealth of the New World and provide resources for Spanish power. They thus attempted to organize the indigenous population into tribute-paying units or groups for labor, which worked in some areas, but did not in many others because of resistance combined with dramatic depopulation brought on by disease.

Soon after conquest, the Spanish began to bring slaves from Africa to work on plantations and in mines, and slightly later the Portuguese in Brazil and other European powers in the Caribbean did as well. There were also some licenses for "white slaves" (*esclavos blancos*) given to Mexican residents in 1530s and 1540s, who were probably Arabs, Berbers, or Jews from Morocco, and were most likely women imported for household service or prostitution. (At least one *morisca* woman accompanied Pizarro's army on its initial conquest of the Incas.) Beginning in the 1560s, Spanish ships that became known as the "Manila galleons" began regular trade between the Philippines and Mexico. Along with Asian products, they also brought Asian people, primarily sailors, slaves, and servants from a variety of countries, but known collectively as *chinos*. Tens of thousands of *chinos*, most of whom were male, stayed in

Mexico over the centuries of regular galleon trade, working in a variety of trades, and by the seventeenth century there were also a few Asian women in Latin America, generally slaves or household servants.

The Spanish Crown initially envisioned ruling a separate Realm of Spaniards and Realm of Indians, but the population groups did not stay separate, for the vast majority of Europeans, Africans, and Asians who went to Mexico, Peru, Brazil, and the Caribbean were men. They immediately began sexual relations with indigenous women, and soon there were sexual relationships across many lines. It was thus clear from the beginning to Spanish – and to a lesser extent Portuguese – authorities that the regulation of sexuality would be a key part of colonization. Within less than a decade after Columbus's initial voyage, church and state were already setting policies regarding intermarriage and other aspects of sexual life, and establishing institutions that would enforce these policies.

Through the papacy's granting of the *Patronato*, the Spanish and Portuguese Crowns officially controlled almost all aspects of religious life, but as in Europe, church and state generally worked together to control marriage and sex; the Crown set policies and appointed church officials, who then exercised control of marriage and sexual life largely free of royal interference. To the 1760s or 1770s the church had complete legal control over marital issues in all parts of Latin America. Within the framework set by royal decree, institutions like those which operated in Europe – church courts, the Inquisition, confession – shaped sexual life, as did new institutions, such as the mission, which were created specifically for the colonial situation. In addition to enforcing Christian sexual norms among Europeans, many of these institutions were also working to convert Native Americans, Africans, and persons of mixed race to Christianity. A rejection of Christian teachings (often termed "idolatry" by clergy) was closely linked with sexual practices that deviated from Christian norms, in the same way that heresy and "deviant" sexuality had been linked in medieval Europe. In the Latin American setting, however, these issues were also linked with race and with the acculturation of indigenous people and Africans to European Christianity.

Racial hierarchies

The institutions established by the church for the control of sexuality both shaped and were shaped by formalized systems of hierarchy that developed in the Spanish and Portuguese colonies. As sexual relations produced children that did not fit into the existing categories of Indian and Spaniard, the response of colonial authorities was to create an ever more complex system of categories, called *castas,* for persons of mixed ancestry. About one-quarter of the population of Latin America was of mixed ancestry by the end of the eighteenth century, and in urban areas the number was much higher. The Catholic Church and Spanish and Portuguese officials defined as many as forty different categories and combinations that were in theory based on place of birth, assumed geographic origin, and status of one's father and mother, with a specific name for each one: "mestizo," "mulatto," "caboclo," "lobo," and so on. New laws passed after 1763 in the French Caribbean colonies set out a similar system, with various categories based on the supposed origin of one's ancestors.

The casta system built on earlier Iberian notions of "purity of blood," in which descendants of Muslim and Jewish converts to Christianity were viewed as tainted, because their religious allegiance was carried in their blood. In the same way, American natives' loyalty to their traditional beliefs was often described by Spanish colonial writers as the result of a "bad seed that has grown deep roots and has turned itself into blood and flesh [in the Indians] . . . a vice that comes in the blood and is suckled as milk . . . [through which] the customs of parents and ancestors are converted into nature and transmitted through inheritance to their children."[3] In the Latin American colonies, people of indigenous and African ancestry both had lower rank than did Europeans, with blood that was viewed as less pure. Native ancestry could more easily be "whitened" than could African, however. Particularly in the first century after the conquest, the status of one's father was more important than that of one's mother, and Indian and mestiza women who married European men were easily absorbed into the population viewed as "Spanish." In the late sixteenth century the Mexican Inquisition ruled, in fact, that those with only one-quarter native ancestry would be considered "Spanish" in terms of eligibility for office. "Black blood" remained a permanent impurity, however, linked with the slavery that was increasingly limited to Africans and their descendants. The Asian origins of many residents of New Spain were often forgotten, and the category "chino" came to be viewed as a type of mixture of African and native, one of the many categories that carried the irredeemable stain.

The various castas and the relationships among them were clearly delineated in treatises and by the eighteenth century in paintings that showed scenes of parents of different castas and the children such parents produced: *India + Spaniard = Mestizo; India + Negro = Lobo; Chamiza + Cambuza = Chino* and so on. Some of these castas had fanciful names, or ones derived from animals, such as *coyote* or *lobo* (wolf). Determining the proper casta in which to place actual people was not as easy as setting these out in theory, however, for the treatises and paintings were attempts to impose order on a confused and fluid system, not a description of reality. In practice, the category in which one was placed was to a large extent determined by how one looked, with lighter-skinned mixed-ancestry persons often accorded a higher rank than darker, even if they were siblings. Many historians have thus termed the social structure that developed in colonial Spanish and Portuguese America, including the Caribbean (and later in the French Caribbean) a "pigmentocracy" based largely on skin color, but also facial features and hair texture. Contemporaries always claimed that color was linked to honor, virtue, and family, however, so that one's social status – termed *calidad* – involved a moral as well as physical judgement, but in reality as intermarriage increased, people passed quite easily from one casta to another.

The precarious balance of moral, physical, and class judgements used in determining status also frequently shifted over time. Since one's ability to marry or inherit, enter a convent or the priesthood, or attend university relied on official determination of ancestral purity, individuals not only passed as members of a higher group, but also sought to officially "whiten" their social status in order to obtain privileges in society. In many areas families of property and status bought licenses to be considered descendants of Europeans, regardless of their particular ethnic appearance and ancestry. In frontier areas of Spanish America, or during times of political and social transitions, family members classified their children as "Spanish" or "Castellano (Castilian)" on baptismal records, often in open defiance of the presiding priest's observations about the actual appearance of the child. In addition, individuals might define themselves, or be defined, as belonging to different categories at different points in their life, in what scholars have called a "racial drift" toward whiteness. Thus the hierarchy became increasingly confused and arbitrary over generations. By forbidding Indian, African, and mixed-race men to become priests, the church bolstered the system; by occasionally granting licenses that made mixed-race men "white" and allowed them to attend seminaries, it also affirmed how subjective it was.

Crown policies

The Spanish and Portuguese Crowns hoped to recreate family and sexual relationships as they had been at home, but as the colonial situation changed, the ways they attempted to do this also changed. There were also competing schools of thought in Iberia and among Iberian officials in the New World about how to handle relations, sexual and otherwise, between population groups, and policy never followed a clear line. Because of hostility toward Jews and Muslims in Spain, sexual intercourse between Christians and non-Christians was officially prohibited, which meant that the earliest conquistadores often claimed they baptized Indian women before they had sexual relations with them. The secretary on Fernando De Soto's expedition across Florida, for example, commented that soldiers who wanted women "to make use of them and for their lewdness and lust . . . baptized them more for their carnal intercourse than to instruct them in the faith."[4] The earliest royal instructions (in 1501, 1504, and 1514) encouraged marriage between European men and Indian women in the Caribbean, with governors instructed to "make sure that some Christian men marry some Indian women and Christian women marry Indian men, so that they will communicate with and teach each other."[5] Records indicate that in some areas a significant number of Spanish men had native wives, although the more common pattern was one of concubinage or casual relationships. (There were almost no Spanish women in the colonies at this time, so although the royal order is gender-neutral, marriage between a Spanish woman and an Indian man was not a realistic possibility.) The Spanish Crown officially prohibited the enslavement of Indians (unless they were judged to be cannibals), although it is clear that enslavement continued, sometimes specifically for sexual purposes.

Policies on marriage had to address the issue of Africans as well as Europeans and Indians. There were Africans on the expeditions of both Cortés and Pizarro, and slaves began to be imported from Africa in substantial numbers in the early sixteenth century. The Crown officially promoted marriage for slaves among themselves, and prohibited masters from selling spouses too far apart so that conjugal relations could be maintained; because of such restrictions owners prevented or did not encourage slave marriage. Africans worked in mines and plantations as these were established, but also in towns as artisans and servants, and in some cities by the end of the sixteenth century people of African descent outnumbered those from any other single racial group. Many of these gradually bought or otherwise obtained their freedom; in Mexico by the end of the seventeenth century the majority of blacks and mulattoes were free.

In Mexico, the Spanish Crown initially hoped to keep the various populations apart, but the shortage of Spanish and African women made this impossible, and some policies of the crown actually promoted intermarriage; men granted *encomiendas,* the rights to collect tribute and labor from the natives, were ordered to marry or forfeit their grant, and in the early decades after conquest the racial origins of the wife did not matter. By the mid-sixteenth century things had changed. There was more immigration of Spanish women – perhaps as much as 30 percent by the 1570s – and racial origins became a consideration in inheritance and the ability to attend school or enter a convent. There were no explicit laws against intermarriage, but racial prejudice worked just as effectively, especially at the upper reaches of society. Eventually Crown policies followed elite opinion, and maintaining social distinctions – including those of class as well as race – was declared more important than maintaining women's honor in many cases of seduction:

If the maiden seduced under promise of marriage is inferior in
status, so that she would cause greater dishonor to his lineage if
he married her than the one that would fall on her by remaining
seduced, he must not marry her . . . for the latter is an offense
of an individual and does no harm to the Republic [i.e., New Spain],
while the former is an offense of such gravity that it will denigrate
an entire family, dishonor a person of pre-eminence, defame and
stain an entire noble lineage, and destroy a thing which gives
splendor and honor to the Republic.[6]

The Crown actively promoted the immigration of married European women,
ordering all men who had been married when they immigrated to send for
their wives or it would send them back to Spain. In Mexico, the bishop was
in charge of enforcing these policies, and he sometimes ordered searches for
single men, and then arrested and deported them; only those who were too
old or were physically impaired (a condition determined by the bishop) were
exempt from the marital requirement. In general, however, these laws were
very difficult to enforce, and the wife could also certify in writing that the
husband's presence in the New World was necessary to support her, so there
were ways to get around them. Such laws did eventually lead to more
immigration by women, especially as married women often brought their
unmarried daughters, nieces, and servants. The Spanish Crown officially
opposed unmarried women going to the Indies by themselves, however, and
there was never any organized movement of immigration by unmarried women
as there would be later in Quebec, Louisiana, and Virginia.

Though the Portuguese Crown did at times limit government positions to
white men married to white women, and sponsored the immigration of white
married couples, it never passed laws requiring husbands to cohabit with their
wives, and there appear to have been an even smaller proportion of European
women in Brazil than in the Spanish New World. Most relationships between
European men and Indian women in Brazil did not result in formal marriages,
although both the Crown and church recognized forms of common law
marriages as legally binding. In the eighteenth century policy changed rapidly:
In 1726 the Crown decreed that only white women were acceptable marriage
partners for white men; in 1755, under the influence of the reforming Prime
Minister the Marques de Pombal, it ordered that those men who married
Indians be preferred for government offices and positions; after Pombal fell
from power in 1777, it reversed itself again.

Whatever the Crown policies of the moment were, in reality most sexual
relations between races were outside marriage, and by the late sixteenth century
about half of the mixed-race and free black population in urban areas of Latin

America was born out of wedlock. Royal policies toward these children vacillated as much as those regarding mixed marriages did. In 1591, for example, the Spanish Crown authorized the Viceroy of Mexico to legitimate mixed-blood children born out of wedlock, then in 1625 it reversed itself and barred the legitimation of such children. Children born of unions between slave men and free Indian women remained legally free, however, which is one reason such relationships were attractive to male slaves and often opposed by their owners.

Church courts

The Spanish military conquest of what became Latin America was remarkably swift, and the church was nearly as swift in establishing ecclesiastical structures modeled on those of Europe. The first bishopric west of the Atlantic was set up in 1511 (Santo Domingo in the Caribbean), and by the mid-sixteenth century there were bishops throughout the Caribbean and Mexico and in Venezuela, Peru, Argentina, and Brazil. Along with overseeing missionary work, the establishment of parishes, and the construction of churches, bishops were officially appointed as inquisitors; they ran church courts and appointed various officials to hear cases, including those of sexual misconduct. Initially these courts had jurisdiction over natives as well as Europeans and Africans, and the first case involving an Indian was in 1522 for concubinage.

The level of activity by church courts varied with the personality of the bishop. During the mid-sixteenth century, there were several vigorous campaigns to wipe out native beliefs along with indigenous sexual practices such as concubinage and bigamy, including a campaign by the first bishop of Mexico, Juan de Zumárraga, who had been active fighting witches in the Basque country of northern Spain before coming to the New World. Zumárraga concentrated primarily on prominent individuals who had been converted and then relapsed rather than on ordinary people, but the harshness of his judgements toward these people led to his being removed from office of inquisitor, though he remained bishop. Subsequent campaigns against indigenous beliefs and practices, such as those carried out against the Mixtecs (in 1544–47 by Francisco Tello de Sandoval) and the Yucatan Maya (in 1559–62 by Fray Diego de Landa), were broader and even more stringent. Similar attacks on "idolatry" were undertaken in the Andes in the seventeenth century, again under the leadership of crusading bishops such as Pedro de Villagómez. In all of these episcopal investigations and visitations, clerics asked people to speak out about their own or other's "sinful" activities, with charges of idolatry and immorality closely linked.

Jurisdiction over serious matters of faith was taken from the bishops in 1571, when independent branches of the Spanish Inquisition were established by King Philip II in Mexico City and Lima; Mexico's first major *auto-da-fé* was held in 1574, attended by a huge crowd, with many sentences read out. (The Portuguese Crown never established an independent Inquisition in Brazil, although visiting officials from the Portuguese Inquisition did carry out investigations, and those found guilty were deported to Lisbon for trial and punishment.) These branches were given more restricted powers over sexual matters than those in parts of Spain, for they were to hear only bigamy cases and those involving clergy; all other sexual irregularities were to be tried by episcopal church courts, and the Mexican Inquisition was specifically warned by Rome in 1580 that it was not allowed to try incest or sodomy.

A more substantial restriction of powers was Phillip II's removal of Indians from the authority of the Holy Office in 1571, with the justification that their conversion was too recent so that they were not "gente de razón" (rational people) and could not be held fully responsible for any deviations from the faith. However, another institution, called by various names – the Indian Inquisition, the Office of the Provisor of Natives, the Tribunal of the Faith of the Indians – did have jurisdiction over them. Staffed by ecclesiastical judges under the authority of the bishops, it lasted until 1820. It held *autos-da-fé* for bigamy and concubinage, as well as idolatry, superstition, sorcery; its most common punishments were whipping and public humiliation. Though in theory the Indian Inquisition was separate from the Inquisition proper, in practice the same individuals often acted as judges in both, so that differences in jurisdiction were not clear.

By the eighteenth century, church courts were no longer linking immorality to idolatry, but to activities similar to those in Europe, such as dancing, drinking, and festivals. Mexican priests sound much like their Calvinist counterparts, warning about the dangers of dance: "You women, dancers of the devil, scandalous persons, you are the damnation of so many souls. Oh! What horror! . . . You provocative women, dancers of the devil, scandal, nets of the devil, basilisks of the streets and windows, you kill with your stirrings . . ."[7] As in Protestant Neuchâtel, public dances were prohibited in parts of Mexico for a brief time.

Clergy and their assistants

Along with church courts, both regular clergy (members of religious orders such as the Dominicans and the Franciscans) and secular clergy (parish priests) were important agents of church control of sexuality. In general, regulars had the role of converting and disciplining indigenous people, seculars of enforcing orthodoxy and correct behavior among Spanish and mixed-race people. In most of Latin America and the Caribbean, church officials and other clergy generally paid little attention to converting enslaved Africans. Though royal decrees ordered slave owners to let their slaves hear mass and provide religious services for them, these were only sporadically enforced. Parish priests made little systematic effort to convert slaves, and masters often thought Christianization lowered slaves' value because it made them more rebellious. In some areas, however, members of religious orders did work to convert Africans, promoting confession in the "language of Angola" and using music and incense to attract converts. As more and more people of African ancestry gained their freedom and intermarried with other groups, they came under the supervision of parish priests.

The most distinctive type of religious unit in Latin America was the mission, in which the Indians were settled by members of religious orders into compact villages (termed *reducciónes* or *congregaciónes*) for conversion, taxpaying, assimilation, and in some areas, protection from slave-raiding. Converts to Christianity in missions were wards of the Spanish Crown, and missionaries had great control over all aspects of their lives, including hearing both civil and criminal cases. They also acted as agents of punishment, whipping and jailing mission residents, or forcing them to sit in stocks. The first Spanish missions were in the sixteenth century in Mexico and Florida, and by the seventeenth century missions existed from what is now northern California to Argentina, in some areas serving as the only real evidence of Spanish power. In some places mission priests vigorously enforced royal aims, but in others they conflicted with secular political authorities such as governors and military commanders. The most famous example of this was the Jesuit mission with the Guaraní Indians in Paraguay, where the missionaries fought Spanish demands for tribute. Mission priests, who were regular clergy, also came into conflict with secular clergy over the treatment of Indians under their jurisdiction or over issues involving Indian/white relations.

Both regular and secular clergy tended to be concentrated in certain areas; for example, by 1560, there were 800 regular clergy in Mexico, but many fewer elsewhere in New Spain, such as Honduras. The shortage of clergy could have been solved by ordaining Indian or *mestizo* converts, but the earliest Latin American church councils (in 1555 and 1565) declared all Indian men and those of mixed blood unfit for the priesthood, and in some areas mission priests refused even to teach their converts Spanish. Lack of interest in virginity was one of the reasons given for excluding Indians from the priesthood; Bishop Zumárraga of Mexico commented in 1540 that elite Indian young men were very skilled at learning Latin, but "the best students among the Indians are more inclined to marriage than to continence."[8] These absolute prohibitions were relaxed somewhat for *mestizos* later in the century, and *mestizos* could be granted dispensations to enter the priesthood or a religious order if their father was prominent enough, but in actuality there were very few *mestizo* or Indian priests until late in the eighteenth century.

Prejudice against *mestizo* or Indian clergy did not apply to assistants, however, and from the earliest decades after conquest, European clergy were assisted by lay Indian or *mestizo fiscales* who did much of the parish work. The *fiscales* (they sometimes had a different title) kept church records, supervised building projects and Sunday services, punished those found guilty of moral lapses, taught catechism classes, examined candidates for marriage and communion, buried, and baptized; though most of these officials were male, in some places female officials made sure women went to church and administered disciplinary whippings to married women, whose honor would have been violated by being whipped by a priest. (Priests did administer whippings to women themselves from time to time, occasioning complaints to their superiors from mission residents.) Women also occasionally served as translators for missionaries when they confessed women, providing models of good Christian behavior as they served as go-betweens; as one Jesuit in Brazil remarked about his translator, "I believe she is the best confessor I have because she is so virtuous."[9]

In places where the number of European clergy was particularly small or where they were uninvolved with their Indian parishioners, Indian officials even conducted their own masses and confessions, bringing in elements of traditional forms of worship. The *fiscales* were central to church control of sexuality, as they often brought cases of alleged adultery, consanguinity, and bigamy to the attention of the local priest, who rarely began an investigation on his own, and carried out the questioning of those who wished to marry. In addition, the Indian "governors" of towns and villages often acted with church authorities, so that courts in cities sent Indians found guilty of sexual crimes back to their home villages for punishment, especially if the crime was something like adultery that was also regarded as illicit in indigenous society.

Race also shaped the possibilities for religious women. The first New World convent was founded in Mexico City in 1540, and the first convent in South America was founded in Cuzco, Peru in 1558. Convents mirrored the society around them: professed nuns (who took final vows) were wealthier and of European background, lay sisters were poorer and of mixed race, servants and slaves were still poorer, and of indigenous or African background. Particularly in larger cities, convents were increasingly popular solutions for housing unmarried women. One-fifth of the female population of Lima, Peru in the seventeenth century, for example, lived in convents, though most of these were servants, slaves, and lay sisters, not professed nuns. Some of these were young women who were boarders, sent to convents until they married, but many stayed their whole lives. In some cities, indigenous Christians established small, unenclosed communities for indigenous women, where they lived simply, prayed, and performed religious observances. Such *beaterios*, as they were called, emphasized that they provided a life of "decency" for girls and women who might otherwise have nowhere to go. The first cloistered convent for Indian nuns, Corpus Christi in Mexico City, opened only in 1728, overcoming Jesuit objections that Indian women would never be able to fulfill a vow of chastity; the women admitted had to be full blooded, and have their virtue attested by the nuns or chaplains of convents in which they had previously worked as lay sisters or servants.

Religious confraternities similarly reflected racial hierarchies. European, Indian, and African Christians formed confraternities for men and women, almost always racially separate; in some cities of New Spain, Asian *chinos* had their own confraternities as well, as did specific sorts of mixed-race groups, such as *pardos* and *morenos*. The confraternities had various purposes: Some sponsored religious festivities, or carried out public penance such as flagellation in honor of certain saints or sacraments. Others provided charity for the poor, or arranged hospital care and funerals for their members, thus serving as a sort of fictive family. Members of these confraternities were ejected for immoral or "scandalous" behavior, so they served as an additional policing agent. Confraternities also shaped marital arrangements, as they frequently gave dowries to poor girls and women who wished to marry if they judged them "honorable" and the potential husband acceptable. The activities and aims of confraternities were shaped by the cultural values of their members along with Christian teachings, so that African, European, Indian, and Asian confraternities played somewhat different social and religious roles, though they all served as agents of acculturation for new immigrants.

Indoctrination methods

External agents such as courts could only go so far in keeping people's behavior in line with Christian teachings; most missionaries and church authorities regarded the development of internal agents, such as notions of guilt and sin, as much more effective in the long run. Thus as in Europe, they used a variety of means to communicate church teachings about marriage and morality. In central Mexico, missionaries preached sermons in Nahuatl, opened schools to teach local boys, and sponsored plays with songs and dances loosely translated from Spanish plays by missionaries or Nahua scholars. In a play written in the 1530s, for example, the Franciscan friar Andres de Olmos presented the fate of Lucía, a Nahua woman who did not get married in a Christian ceremony. As she is pushed toward demons and hell, she wails "How unfortunate I am! I am a sinner. I have merited suffering in the place of the dead . . . Ah! Ah! If only I had gotten married!" To which Satan replies, "Get moving, O wicked one! Not until now do you remember that you should have gotten married? How is it that you did not remember it while you were still living on earth? But now you will make restitution for all your wickedness. Run along! Get moving!" In Olmes's stage directions, wind instruments and gunpowder explosions accompany Lucía's being dragged off the stage.[10]

The Virgin Mary had been the patron saint of the reconquest of Spain from the Muslims, and missionaries promoted her veneration in the New World as well. They hired local artists to paint and sculpt images of Mary designed to be admired and venerated. "I made a very fine and beautiful image," wrote a missionary in Peru, "upon which many pearls and precious emeralds were stuck, and to such a winning effect that the entire city turned up to see . . . I painted her a little dark . . . and they loved her a lot because she was of their color."[11] Sermons, catechisms, plays, prayers, and hymns describing the events of Mary's life were written and presented in local languages by missionaries and native converts. These emphasized her role as a nurturing mother, but also as an eternal virgin, whose own conception had been "immaculate," free from the normal sin accompanying sex. University students, confraternities, and even artisans' guilds often took special vows to defend the doctrine of the Immaculate Conception, highlighting Mary's sexless and sinless nature. Among indigenous people in many areas, Mary took on aspects of pre-conquest goddesses. Among the Maya of the Yucatán, for example, she came to incorporate aspects of the fire goddess and the moon goddess; like the moon goddess, Mary "the Queen, the Virgin, the miraculous one descended . . . [on a] cord from heaven" to help humans who sought her assistance.[12] The powers of this hybrid deity, Virgin Mary Moon Goddess, also derived from her status as a "virgin," though this term had a different meaning for indigenous people than it did for Spanish Catholics, for it symbolized her connection with cosmic female forces rather than her status as a non-sexual being.

Devotion to various aspects of Mary was powerful among many groups throughout Spanish America, and was further enhanced in Mexico when in the mid-seventeenth century, published texts in Spanish and Nahuatl told of the appearance of the Virgin Mary in 1531 to Juan Diego Cuauhtlatoatzin, an indigenous farmer and Christian convert, on a hill near Tenochtitlan (now within Mexico City). Speaking in Nahuatl, the apparition told Juan Diego that a church should be built at this site. Shortly afterward a church dedicated to the Virgin of Guadalupe was begun, named after a royal monastery in Spain where various miracles associated with the Virgin Mary had been reported, including some involving Christian victories over Muslim forces. The Mexican

Virgin of Guadalupe soon far outstripped her Spanish counterpart in significance; preachers and teachers interpreted her appearance as a sign of the Virgin's special protection of indigenous people and *mestizos*, and pilgrims from all over Mexico began to make the trek to her shrine. The Virgin of Guadalupe was made patron of New Spain in 1746 and her banner was carried by soldiers in the Mexican War of Independence in 1810. (In the twentieth century, many scholars, including some members of the Mexican clergy, came to doubt whether the apparition had ever happened or Juan Diego himself had even existed. The Catholic Church has addressed these doubts resoundingly, declaring Guadalupe the patron of the whole American hemisphere in 1999 and raising Juan Diego to a saint in 2002; he is the first fully indigenous American to be canonized. Many Mexicans have interpreted this canonization, like the Virgin of Guadalupe herself, as a symbol of the place of their heritage within the Catholic Church, while others view Juan Diego and Guadalupe as symbols of the destruction of indigenous culture. Intense controversies have emerged in recent years over the ways various artists have portrayed Guadalupe in their work, many of which involve her relationship with sexuality and female power.)

Missionaries also used St. Joseph to communicate Christian notions of marriage and family life. Joseph became the patron saint of the conversion of Mexico, the Viceroyalty of Peru, and in 1672 of the entire Spanish Empire, celebrated as a symbol of perfect masculinity who as a husband, (foster) father, and good provider was a model of Spanish colonial authority.

Informal teaching, especially about Christian norms of marriage, occurred at the screening process before marriage (*diligencia matrimonial*), when every couple had to come before a priest and say that they were free to marry and that they consented to the marriage; often this occurred before witnesses, who would both verify the couple's statements and hear the priest's message. Couples were instructed about the proper hierarchy in marriage, with the word for the woman's expected submission to her husband, *reducción*, the same as that describing native subordination in the missions.

Formal teaching was more limited than early colonial church authorities had hoped; though Bishop Zumárraga urged that Indian girls be taught the virtues of monogamous marriage as well as housekeeping, very few schools for Indians were actually established, and those few were almost all for elite boys. Mission priests often singled out a small group of boys for more intensive teaching, pulled them from their kin group, and gave them a new name. Such boys often later became clerical assistants and were more vigorous than the European friars in their condemnation of indigenous religious and cultural practices. Most Indian or mixed-race children did not receive this kind of indoctrination, however, and their training in church doctrine was limited to occasional catechism classes.

The sacrament of confession and penance provided a more wide-spread opportunity for teaching Christian ideas than schools. Penitential guides for priests prepared by missionaries took special interest in sex, with specific questions in Latin, Spanish, and Indian languages about sodomy, anal intercourse, bestiality, abortion, contraception, adultery, fornication, and marriage among kin. Confessionals and dictionaries written for missionaries working among the Maya of the Yucatan, for example, use the word *keban* – which meant "a sad or miserable thing" – to describe many traditional sexual and marital practices, declaring them all sin.[13] The 1631 penitential of Juan de Pérez Bocanegra, a bilingual priest working in the Andes, listed 236 questions to be asked in regard to sex, many of which were designed to teach converts that traditional practices such as marriage of relatives or trial marriage were now to be considered sinful. Confessors also asked about thoughts, "the filthy pleasure within your heart," a concept new to many Indian groups for whom fault could only arise from something one had actually done and not simply fantasized or contemplated.[14] This interest in both sexual practices and desires continued throughout the colonial period, for a confessional guide from the eighteenth century in Chumash for the Indians of the Santa Barbara area by Fray Juan Cortés instructs priests to ask parishioners whether they had wished to do or had done "bad things for pleasure with a woman, with women, with a man, with men."[15]

Many historians regard confession and penance as ultimately more successful than the Indian Inquisition in shaping the conduct of Christian converts, for the Inquisition concentrated only on spectacular cases while confession was expected of all converts. After the Council of Trent, annual confession was also expected of European, African, and *mestizo* Christians, and though such frequency was rarely achieved, confession was sometimes powerful enough to convince adulterers or bigamists to denounce themselves.

Effects

If generalization about the effects of sexual regulations is difficult for Catholicism in Europe, it is even more so in Latin America. Some areas were totally untouched by church authority throughout the early modern period, and indigenous groups continued their original practices. In other areas there were a few isolated missions where converts were taught Christian notions, surrounded by vast territories whose inhabitants were hostile to Christianity and to colonial political power, which they correctly viewed as linked. In these missions and among the Indian and *mestizo* population elsewhere, the understanding of Christianity that developed was often one that blended indigenous ideas and Christian teachings in a process of cultural negotiation and creolization. In areas of Latin America with African populations, this blending also included African elements. (Africans in the Americas also created new religions, such as *Vodun* in Saint Domingue and *Santería* in Cuba. Although in the colonial period many of their adherents – most of them slaves – were baptized and buried in Catholic ceremonies, these were (and are) religions distinct from Christianity.)

In the same way that Christian parishes and other ecclesiastical units (termed *doctrinas*) were based on existing indigenous governmental units, and Christian devotional practices such as the Day of the Dead grew in importance if they paralleled existing ceremonies, Christian sexual mores were more readily accepted if they fit with indigenous notions. The colonial setting itself also affected the handling of sexual issues among all population groups; though authorities tried to recreate Iberian society, many patterns were distinct to Latin America.

Marriage

Iberian authorities, both clerical and secular, claimed to be imposing a Christian model of marriage and Iberian notions of sexual honor on their colonial holdings. In reality, not only did the sexual relationships that developed never live up to the ideal, but authorities themselves aided in making distinctions – such as those between married and unmarried, legitimate and illegitimate, honorable and dishonorable – much less clear than they were in the abstract. Thus it is not as easy as it is in Europe to divide heterosexual relations between lay persons into licit and illicit; marriage, concubinage, fornication, and even prostitution were a spectrum of possibilities, not necessarily mutually exclusive categories.

Marriage was still the ideal, however. The earliest colonization occurred decades before the Council of Trent defined Catholic marriage doctrine explicitly, but during the first decades clergy sought to introduce the central aspects of Christian marriage customs, viewing this as a key part of Christianizing the indigenous population. As we have seen, many of these were not very different from existing customs, and Catholic wedding rituals were often simply added to existing rituals. On certain issues there was more divergence, and thus more avoidance and resistance. One of these was polygyny. Observing polygyny among the Tupinamba of Brazil, the French missionary Claude d'Abbeville pondered whether "those married in the native fashion, with many wives," be denied baptism, but decided that they should be baptised anyway.[16] At the Jesuit mission to the Guaraní, polygyny led to a verbal and then armed battle between the local shaman Miguel Artiguaye and the Jesuit Antonio Ruiz de Montoya. "You are no priests sent from God to aid our misery," Artiguaye shouted at the Jesuits, "you are devils from hell, sent by their ruler for our destruction. What teaching have you brought us? What peace and happiness? Our ancestors lived in liberty. They enjoyed all the women they wanted, without hindrance from anyone. Thus they lived and spent their lives in happiness, and you want to destroy their traditions and impose on us this heavy burden of being bound to a single wife."[17] Montoya reports that he convinced Artiguaye to give up his resistance, but in many other places Indian men, particularly nobles, were unwilling to give up the privilege of multiple wives, and either simply refused to alter their household, or chose their favorite as their wife and kept their additional wives on as servants. Because of the Catholic prohibition of divorce, people often had a Catholic service for their first marriage and then traditional ceremonies for any subsequent ones. Thus monogamy remained an ideal, but serial and occasionally simultaneous polygamy continued in practice.

Another issue was marriage among kin, a common practice among many groups. Catholic rules on consanguinity in marriage partners were often avoided or bent by not revealing family relationships, or were overcome by obtaining a priestly dispensation; in 1537 Pope Paul III officially ruled that consanguinity prohibitions in indigenous marriages would be much more lenient than the normal rules. Colonial authorities in some areas forcibly relocated native peoples, combining kin groups as they did; this worked to end endogamous marriage patterns more effectively than did church regulations alone. Rules about consent were also bent as families and clans continued to exert influence on spousal choices. Because procreation was viewed as vital to marriage, "trial marriages" continued for centuries after conquest in some areas and actual marriage was delayed until the woman became pregnant. This disturbed some clergy, such as the Jesuit José de Acosta, who misunderstood the practice and used it to disparage Indian morals in general: "However great and almost divine is the honor which all other peoples pay to virginity, these beasts consider it to be all the more despicable and ignominious."[18]

There was occasional overt resistance to Catholic marriage doctrine; Indians abandoned missions when priests tried to enforce policies against the marriage of cousins, and some native priests and curers supported a continuation of concubinage and bigamy as symbols of resistance. In the late 1520s to 1530s, some Nahua leaders argued that the religion of the friars opposed all earthly happiness, and the marriage and moral standards they preached was only meant for Indians, because the Spanish did not follow these ideals themselves. In 1680, the Pueblo Indians revolted against Spanish Franciscan missionaries, with the missionaries' attempts to enforce monogamous marriage one of the grounds for the revolt.

Not every avoidance of Christian marriage can be seen as a sign of resistance, however, as many times this may have been done more out of a desire to avoid clerical marriage fees or simple negligence. In widely dispersed communities clergy were simply unable to enforce Christian marriage practices, and traditional practices, including polygamy, continued for decades. Many missionaries clearly regarded success on this issue as extremely important, however, and occasionally reported miracles that assisted their efforts, such as that in the memorial of Fray Alonso de Benavides, a Franciscan missionary in New Mexico:

> These Indians were well taught in church doctrine. And in the year just past of 1627, Our Lord confirmed His Holy Word with a miracle among them. As it happened, it was difficult for them to stop having so many women, as it was their custom before they were baptized. Each day, the friar preached to them the holy sacrament of matrimony, and the person who contradicted him most strongly was an old Indian sorceress. Under the pretext of going to the countryside for firewood, she took along four good Christian women, and married at that, all conforming to the good order of Our Holy Mother Church. And coming and going in their wood gathering, she was trying to persuade them not to continue with the kind of marriage our padre was teaching, saying how much better off a person was practicing her old heathenism.
>
> These good Christians resisted this kind of talk. They were getting close to the pueblo again, and the sorceress was carrying on with her sermon. The sky was clear and serene, but a bolt from the blue struck that infernal instrument of the devil right in the middle of those good Christian women who had been resisting her evil creed. They were spared from the bolt, and quite confirmed in the truth of the holy sacrament of matrimony. The entire pueblo ran to the spot. Seeing the results of the thunderclap from heaven, everyone who had been secretly living in sin got married and began to believe mightily in everything the padre taught them. He, of course, made this episode the subject of a sermon.[19]

Emphasis on monogamous marriage in the missions was accompanied by an emphasis on the nuclear family, which upset existing kinship patterns and hierarchies of gender and age. Christian doctrine on the centrality of a hierarchical spousal relationship as the core of the family was reinforced by colonial legal practice that affirmed the authority of husbands over wives and fathers over children, and kept all records according to nuclear families rather than according to existing indigenous household structures. Indigenous paternal authority had a limit in the missions, however, for everyone – including adult men – was under the authority of the friars, who often carried out ceremonies designed to humiliate adult men at the same time as they took away their traditional powers in hunting and choosing the clan's marital partners.

Among white elites, concerns about honor, color, and bloodlines combined with increasing dowry size and families' desires to hold on to property and privileges to create a pattern of intermarriage within the extended family oddly similar to that among many native groups. Because of church prohibitions of consanguinity, distant cousins were the favored spouses, with older women in the family often in charge of keeping track of who could marry whom; if a likely spouse was too closely related, the family could also apply for a dispensation of the church's consanguinity rules. For high-status white women, the group of suitable spouses was often very small, and many were sent into convents instead of making what the family regarded as a disadvantageous marriage. This trend was most dramatic in Portuguese colonies such as Bahia, where in the seventeenth century only 14 percent of the daughters of leading families married, while 77 percent went into convents. By the eighteenth century the pattern of cousin-intermarriage had spread to *mestizo* elites as well, as had the practice of giving a significant dowry upon marriage.

Thus for Indian and white families, marriage remained a family matter, which at times conflicted with the Catholic doctrine of the centrality of spousal consent. Sometimes the church enforced its requirement of consent, prohibiting, for example, the custom whereby Indians married only with the permission of their native leaders, and occasionally annuling a marriage if one of the spouses could prove he or she had been tricked or forced into it. At other times it turned a blind eye to forced marriages, especially if these involved the servants, slaves, or sometimes daughters of prominent men. Both Indian and white families generally used tactics other than force to convince children to marry in the family's best interests, instead using persuasion and coercion (which was allowed by the church), making marital arrangements when children were young, or (for whites) secluding girls so that they met no other men. Girls whose parents had died were thought to be especially at risk of seduction or making bad marital choices, and they were often secluded in convents or other houses of refuge.

For the growing number of mixed-race individuals, actual marital practices were widely varied, and changed throughout the period. At the very beginning of the colonial era, the Spanish tried to work through native elites (termed *caciques*); intermarriage between Spanish men and the daughters of *caciques* was both encouraged and practiced. The acceptance of intermarriage changed during the middle decades of the sixteenth century, when racial origins became a consideration in inheritance and the ability to attend school or enter a convent, and when more Spanish women had immigrated. Sexual relations between European men and native or *mestizo* women continued, but these were more likely to be concubinage or prostitution, either instead of or along with marriage to a European wife. Like the households of wealthier Indians, those of wealthier Spaniards and Spanish-background men born in Latin America (termed "creoles") tended to include a hierarchy of women and children; one official wife and her children, who were regarded as legitimate, and several other women, slave and free, whose children were not regarded as legitimate and so were legally disadvantaged. In some frontier areas where the number of European women was very small, Spanish and Portuguese men could have essentially polygamous households with five or six Indian or African concubines; they would then choose the most intelligent male offspring to legitimize, and might make his mother the official wife.

Africans also had diverse marital patterns. Both the Spanish and Portuguese crowns wanted slaves to marry, hoping this would make them less likely to run away, and pushed for their marrying other blacks. In Brazil and the Caribbean, slaves did marry other slaves in Catholic ceremonies, yet the sex ratio among slaves (three men for every one woman) meant that this was not an option for most people, and it required the owner's permission in any case. Thus the more normal arrangement for both male and female slaves was informal unions, either with other slaves or across racial categories, for men with Indian women and for women with whites or mixed-race men. Crown policies discouraged marriages between whites and Africans, though they took no notice of non-marital unions involving women who were not white. Almost all European men in the Caribbean had sexual relations with slaves or free mixed-race women, and half of all slave children in Brazil were baptized with an unknown father, often a white or mixed-race man. Children born to a slave mother were also slaves, though they might later be freed by their fathers; those with slave fathers born to Indian women were generally free. Individual clerics sometimes objected to the sexual activities of white men, but such protestations did not affect church policy. Slaves were occasionally successful in gaining annulments of forced marriages in church courts, but usually only if these were especially scandalous.

Individuals occasionally used church courts to try to enforce marriages as well as break them up. By the late sixteenth century, enslaved Africans in Mexico appealed to church courts if their owners tried to keep them from marrying or separated their families. Conversion to Christianity did not bring freedom from slavery, but it did bring the right to marry, which Africans and their descendants recognized. The Spanish Crown as well as the church supported their marriages, and such suits were often successful. Women of all races also brought cases in which they charged that a man had made a promise of marriage (termed a *palabra de casamiento*) before the two began sexual relations, but was now refusing to marry. At least in Mexico, to about 1690, church and state authorities generally cooperated in enforcing the marriage, giving the man the choice of marriage or deportation to the Philippines to work on building royal fortresses there. After that point, punishment for seduction declined to a three-year prison sentence or financial compensation for the woman, and by the eighteenth century the church decided such suits were no longer its business at all, but a private legal matter between the woman and her seducer. Suits in which couples alleged their families were trying to block a marriage were also less likely to be heard by the eighteenth century; in earlier centuries, church courts had even broken their own rules in regard to marriage and performed secret marriages to get around family pressure, justifying this as the best way to preserve the woman's honor and prevent the sins of fornication or concubinage.

Heterosexual relations outside of marriage

Although some slaves used church courts to validate their marriages, many slaves, persons of mixed race, and poor people of all types did not marry at all. The number of births out of wedlock in Latin America remained startlingly high by comparison with most of Europe (although Spain did have the highest rate of out-of-wedlock births in Europe). During the period from 1640–1700 in Central Mexico, one-third of the births to Spanish or creole women were out of wedlock, along with two-thirds of those of mixed-race individuals. These relationships were not always short-term, however, for a very large number of what the church termed "irregular unions" or "concubinage" involved planning and commitment and lasted for years; such unions were recognized and sanctioned by the community, and those involved expected to uphold standards of fidelity.

Church leaders were certain of who was to blame for concubinage: women. The bishops gathered at the Second Council of Lima in 1567 commented, "Many women had abandoned their own husbands and joined themselves to others. In order to live licentiously and shamelessly they had chosen themselves a man, whom they call either a spouse, or a brother, or blood relative, but never lover or male concubine."[20] Judging by the frequency with which attacks on sexual misconduct were repeated, the bishops' criticism had little effect; two hundred years later the bishop of Peru, Mariano Martí, continued to blame women, charging that their dancing, drinking, riding horses with men, and wearing capes in a provocative manner seduced men into sin. At times church leaders resigned themselves to recognizing what was actually happening, occasionally sponsoring group weddings to regularize a number of informal unions at one time, complete with legitimization of the existing children.

Both Spanish and Portuguese law also made distinctions among varieties of illegitimacy. In Spanish America, the degree of illegitimacy depended on the relationship between one's parents – children born of long-term irregular unions ranked the highest ("natural" children), those of prostitutes in the middle, and those of adulterous unions or unions with clergy on the bottom ("illegitimate" or "sacrilegious" children). Portuguese law in Brazil also made a distinction between natural children (those born to people who *could* have been married but were not) and spurious children (those born to people who could not have married, such as priest's children or those born in adulterous relationships). Natural children were equal to legitimate children in matters of inheritance except among the nobility, while spurious children could not inherit. Pregnant women of high social standing could also give birth privately, with their family then adopting the child as an "orphan"; the church colluded in this by not giving the mother's name on the birth certificate, in the same way it agreed to decree mixed-race men white so that they could be priests. A subsequent marriage – even on the deathbed – usually also legitimated the children, so that the boundaries of sexual honor were not as sharp in reality as they were in theory.

Irregular unions were favored by many people for a number of reasons. In a society intensely concerned with racial and class status, they allowed relationships between people for whom marriage was socially unacceptable. (Though in the mid-eighteenth century the Marquis of Pombal tried to promote intermarriage, at least in Brazil, this reform was short-lived. By the late eighteenth century, marriages between "persons of different quality" were legally prohibited by secular law as well as social custom, though the church officially continued to favor the marriage of unequals over concubinage.) Concubinage was socially useful for a number of other reasons as well. Spouses were often separated for long periods of time, and women in particular might spend years not knowing whether their husband was alive or dead. To avoid charges of bigamy, they thus chose an irregular union.

For some people, the possibility or actuality of bigamy was preferable to concubinage. As in Spain, the Inquisition had jurisdiction over bigamy in Latin America because it violated the sanctity of a sacrament; records from bishops' courts and the Inquisition reveal a great deal about bigamous unions involving white, black, or mixed-race individuals. Bigamists had clearly internalized Christian notions of the importance of marriage, sometimes stating this explicitly; a Spanish woman named Inés Hernández stated to Mexican inquisitors in 1525 (after she had married again without knowing if her first spouse was dead), that it was "better to live [as a bigamist] in one sin than as a single woman in many."[21] Though men sometimes entered bigamous marriages in order to snatch more than one dowry, in more cases bigamy was caused by people accepting the ideal of married life taught them by their priests. They thus left marriages that did not live up to this ideal, that were instead a *mala vida* (bad life), which for women usually involved abuse, overwork, and lack of financial support, and for men wifely insubordination and fighting.

As in Spain, the punishments for bigamy could be harsh: for women, whipping, public abjuration, and three to five years' confinement, and for men, 100–200 lashes, parading through the streets with a crier shouting their crime, and five to seven years' galley service. Both women and men were held in cells while the investigation was carried out, which could take months. Though no bigamists were executed directly, many died during their period of punishment, and if they returned it was back to the original spouse. In contrast to Indian caciques, no Spanish bigamist defended bigamy in theory, though they did try to justify their actions by pointing to the evils of their first marriage. As with concubinage, it is clear that, despite church doctrines, bigamy was often socially accepted as a way to get around marital difficulties; many known bigamists lived peacefully for years and were only investigated when a local dispute led their neighbors to denounce them.

Divorce

If desertion (and perhaps subsequent bigamy) was not an option, there were other ways to get out of an unacceptable marriage. Though official church doctrine did not allow divorce, colonial church officials in many areas were willing to grant annulments (which were usually termed divorces) at a rate that worried some church officials. The Second Council of Lima blamed the same group it had blamed for concubinage, women:

> Many persons, especially women, for extremely shallow reasons and with the intention of regaining their freedom, fulfilling their lust, and avoiding the burdens of marriage, are too quick to initiate divorce proceedings . . . We order that from now on nobody, but the bishop himself, may be allowed to hear divorce cases. The bishop may do so only for absolutely certain, rational, and manifest causes.[22]

Later reports indicate rulings such as these were ineffective in limiting the number of annulments, especially for the wealthy, which were granted for lack of consent, consanguinity, previous agreements to marry someone else, total or "partial" impotence (defined as the inability to have sexual relations with one's spouse, though one could with others), or the lack of proper procedure during the wedding. Annulments were also granted if one could prove one's spouse had been deceptive or in error about his or her social or racial status.

If one could not gain an annulment for any of these reasons, church courts were sometimes willing to grant a separation from bed and board (also often termed a divorce) though these did not allow remarriage. Petitions for separation were almost always brought by women, and generally involved abuse or desertion. While the case was being investigated – which might take months – the woman was locked up in the home of a respected man or a convent in a process termed *deposito*, being deposited. The damage to one's honor resulting from such treatment no doubt gave women pause about proceeding with separation cases, and the difficulties of getting out of an unhappy marriage may have made concubinage a more attractive option.

Brothels and recogimientos

Both church and state authorities despaired that the lines separating honorable and dishonorable sexual conduct, especially among women, were not as sharp as they should be, and attempted to rigidify them. One way of doing this was to separate women who sold sex clearly from other women, in the same way that European cities had. This began very early in the Spanish colonies; in 1527, for example, the Crown issued licenses to one man in Puerto Rico and another in Santo Domingo to open "a house for public women . . . in a suitable place, because there is a need for it in order to avoid (worse) harm."[23] Many of the residents in such houses were women of mixed race, as were those who were brought along largely for their sexual services on expeditions of conquest, euphemistically labeled "ladies of games" or "women of love" in the records. Some of these women came of their own accord and, at least in the early period before social categories hardened, later married men from the Spanish force. The Crown occasionally worried about the type of Spanish women who were immigrating when it received reports that they were running brothels as well as working in them. It attempted – with little success – to examine their background. In the 1530s, because of such worries, the crown outlawed immigration by single women on their own, but illegal immigration continued.

Church authorities largely followed the Crown (and St. Augustine) and accepted prostitution as a necessary evil; it was generally not criminalized in Latin America until the nineteenth century. As in Catholic Europe, however, authorities also attempted to encourage women to change their ways by opening asylums for repentant prostitutes and other – in the words of the Count of Lemos, the viceroy of Peru who established such a house – "women accustomed to living licentiously [who] have decided to reform and act in a modest and penitent manner."[24] These houses – termed *recogimientos* – subsequently came to be used as places where men sent their wives when they traveled or if they suspected them of adultery, preferring informal seclusion to the scandal of a public accusation. In larger cities such as Lima or Mexico City, they might also take in orphan girls, women seeking separation from their husbands, or women who simply wanted a secluded life without the vows of a convent. The number of willing penitents or other inmates was often not equal to the capacity of such houses, however, so by the late seventeenth century they were also used as prisons where women accused of scandalous behavior were held against their will, or as places for women waiting to hear church court decisions about their petitions for separation. The various types of inmates were supposed to be housed separately, but being sent to such a place marked one as a woman whose honor was in question, whatever one's ostensible reason for going, and they thus served to blur the very border between honor and dishonor they were established to enforce.

In most of Latin America such asylums did not exist, and women found guilty of serious moral offenses were deposited in the households of prominent white male heads-of-households or priests, ordered to obey them and work as their servants. (Men found guilty of moral offenses might be banished, but were generally only required to confess and promise to change their ways; they were never deposited as servants in this way.) Although in theory being held *en deposito* was supposed to be a safeguard and corrective, giving a woman a "Christian education" so that "her eyes might be opened to her blind passion," it might actually put the women in greater danger; in several cases from Mexico, priests who were housing women were charged with rape.[25]

Clerical sexuality

Raping women whom they were supposed to educate and care for was clearly unacceptable sexual behavior on the part of clergy. In many instances the tolerance of theoretically illicit sexual behavior accorded to lay people was extended to clergy, however, and they lived quietly with women for years, provoking little comment. Complaints emerged only if the cleric's behavior was publicly scandalous, or if there were other objections to him as well. Often these emerged as the final straw in a long list of complaints, and may have been used by communities who wanted to get rid of a priest because they knew these would be effective with the Holy Office. For example, in 1631 eleven Maya women complained that their friar was violent and forced them to spin for his profit; they urged authorities, "do not let the maidens be instructed at the church anymore, because nothing good comes from it, for he [the friar] fornicates with them."[26] The most common sexual complaints against priests were solicitation in the confessional, having children with their housekeepers, and public lewdness, though none of these was especially frequent. Of the 1,474 cases in records of Lima Inquisition during the period 1569–1820, for example, only 109 were for clerical solicitation. Punishments for clerical solicitation ranged up to ten years' exile and loss of the license to hear confessions. Such sentences were given only for notorious repeat offenders, however, despite the fact that the Supreme Council of the Inquisition in Madrid gave specific instructions to the Inquisition in Mexico to punish priests found guilty of sexual crimes more severely. Women were often hesitant to bring charges, knowing the reluctance of the church to punish priests and the general skepticism about women's testimony, and, as in Europe, came to church courts only when ordered to do so by a subsequent confessor.

Along with being tried for sexual conduct, clergy were occasionally tried for unorthodox sexual ideas, mostly for saying that concubinage was acceptable or that fornication was not a sin. The most spectacular of these cases was that of the Dominican Francisco de la Cruz, who was burned by the Inquisition in Lima in 1578. De la Cruz had adopted ideas found among the Andean people, combining these with visions to predict the establishment of a millenarian kingdom somewhere in America where the clergy would marry and laymen live in polygamy.

Charges of sexual misconduct involving nuns or other female religious were rare, despite the fact that in some areas large numbers of women lived in convents. In Peru, the Tridentine rules on enclosure made little impact, and bishops constantly complained about the number of servants employed by nuns and the number of visitors in convents at all hours. These complaints were often expressed in language about the unseemliness of convent life, but the main problem appeared to be luxury rather than lust. This – to male eyes surprising – lack of sexual misconduct also included Indian women who lived in convents or convent-like situations. Antonio Pérez, a priest commenting on the foundation of Corpus Christi convent for Indian women in Mexico City, noted that Indian women were already living like nuns without actual vows, and that this "increases my confusion . . . seeing young girls who have no obligation to fulfill the greatest perfection, living with such total perfection."[27]

Pérez would no doubt have been even more startled by the stringent spiritual practices of the mystic Rose of Lima (1586–1617). Rose was the daughter of a Spanish soldier and at least partly indigenous mother who began engaging in intense pious practices and severe bodily penance as a child. She persuaded her parents to allow her to live as a recluse, and had regular visions, often

Figure 4.1
Illustration from *El Primer Nueva Corónica y Buen Gobierno* [The First New Chronicle and
Good Government] (1615), a history of the Inca Empire and the Spanish conquest of
the Andes written and illustrated by Filipe Guaman Poma y Ayala, an indigenous
Peruvian Christian noble. The text reads, "The judge, the priest and the lieutenant go
wandering about and looking at the shameful parts of women." Guaman Poma
addressed his huge text with its hundreds of line drawings to King Philip III of Spain,
pointing out the injustices of the colonial regime and suggesting that a "good
government" would blend Inca practices and Christian teachings. The king never
received the book. Rape was a common part of conquest, although complaints about
clergy seducing or raping women could be brought to bishop's courts.

while praying and meditating. Rose joined the Dominican order, gathered
around her a group of spiritually devout women, including married women
who gave up sexual relations with their husbands. At her early death in 1617
Rose was viewed by many as a living saint, but eight years later religious
authorities cracked down on her followers, calling them deluded and demonic.
In similar cases in Europe such charges often included imputations of aberrant
sexual behavior, but these did not emerge in the attack on Rose's followers.
Criticism of her followers did not dent Rose's great public following, however,
and in 1671 she was made a saint, the first person born in the Western
hemisphere to be canonized.

Same-sex relations

As noted earlier, the issue of same-sex relations in pre-colonial Latin America is complicated, and currently quite contentious. Many European travelers, clergy, and officials accused certain Indian groups of sodomy, but these charges were very often part of a standard list of practices, also including cannibalism, incest, anal intercourse, and polygamy, designed to show the inferiority or barbarity of that group. (Cannibalism was an essential part of this stereotype, as the Spanish crown had banned the enslavement of Indians except for those who were cannibals.) This complex of charges was often used to separate "good" Indians – those who were less resistant to Spanish domination – from "bad" Indians – those who resisted colonial moves – and also to separate "advanced" Indians, such as the Aztec and Inca Empires, from "backward" ones; bad and backward Indians always engaged in cannibalism and sodomy. These charges were also used by Indians themselves to describe other tribes who were their enemies, either because they knew it would be effective with the Spanish or because they also viewed sodomy and cannibalism as signs of inferiority. Among the Maya, Aztec and Inca, defeated enemies were regarded as feminized and forced to wear women's clothing, with ceremonies of defeat that may have included being penetrated by their conquerors. This link between sexual domination and military prowess or political leadership may have provided one context in which homosexual relations among men were acceptable, as long as one took the active "male" role and not the passive "female" one. It also led to the Spanish conquest being understood in sexualized terms, for the Inca and the Maya conceived of Spanish swords as penises and saw themselves as having suffered symbolic sexual violation.

How much – or whether – this symbolic sexual violation extended to actual practice, how often Indians engaged in same-sex relations in other contexts, and how they evaluated these relations when they did, has been hotly debated since the sixteenth century. In his multi-volume *General History of the Indies* (1535), the Spanish historian Gonzalo Fernández de Oviedo charged natives with a range of aberrant sexual practices, including male homosexual sodomy and cross-dressing; his work was widely read, and (not surprisingly) similar charges emerge from many other authors. His charges were vigorously refuted by the Dominican bishop Bartolomé de las Casas (1484–1566), who denied that any Indians engaged in same-sex relations, and went on to write extensive – and also very influential – defenses of Indian culture and attacks on Spanish actions. He pointed out that the Aztecs and the Incas both punished male same-sex relations severely and that they saw such punishment as one of many indications of their advanced level of culture.

As with most issues regarding sexuality, all sources about same-sex relations or cross-dressing are from Europeans or indigenous authors who were at least partly acculturated and Christianized, so that it is impossible to escape the influence of Christian attitudes. This has led a few historians to argue that all reports of laws against same-sex relations among the Incas and Aztecs were the post-conquest inventions of European or Indian writers, designed to make these more advanced empires look more like Christians, and that same-sex relations and/or cross-dressing were acceptable in certain contexts. Cross-dressed shamans gained power and prestige because of their connections with realms understood to be both masculine and feminine.

Whatever the prevalence or acceptability of homosexual relations before European conquest, there is no disagreement about the opinions of church and state authorities during and after conquest. During his march across Panama in 1513, the conquistador Vasco de Balboa was reported to have massacred the brother and forty followers of the *cacique* Quarega who were dressed like women. Missionaries throughout Latin America preached that God had sent the Spanish to conquer the Indians because they had engaged in sodomitical behavior, and, as noted above, confessionals advised priests to ask their parishioners about sodomitical behavior, both homosexual and heterosexual. Pérez Bocanegra's extensive penitential includes questions for men asking whether they had touched or been touched by male friends, and for women asking whether they had "sinned with another woman, like yourself?" Bocanegra apparently could not imagine that such behavior in women could be motivated by same-sex desire, because he then instructs priests to ask the women who they had been thinking about: "When you were engaged in this abominable sin, were you thinking about married men? unmarried men? the priest? the friars? your male kinfolk? those kin of your husband?"[28] Special prayers for the delivery from sodomy were printed in Mexico City in the early eighteenth century.

The effects of prohibition and confession on actual same-sex practices are more difficult to trace in Latin America than in Iberia, because the Inquisition did not have jurisdiction over these and records are scattered among different church courts; none of these courts maintained the type of records the Aragonese Inquisition did, or kept a list of sodomy accusations like that of the Portuguese Inquisition. There were occasional waves of persecution and mass trials, such as one in 1658 in which 123 men in the Mexican city of Puebla de los Angeles were accused and fourteen executed. This multi-ethnic group included some who cross-dressed and, as one contemporary reported, "called each other by names that fallen women use in this city," suggesting that there was some type of urban homosexual subculture in this fairly large city.[29] Mass trials such as this were rare, however; most cases involved only a few individuals, and punishments were not severe, especially in the case of priests or members of the elite.

Sodomy was in theory punishable by death to the mid-eighteenth century, though, as in Spain, actual executions ended during the seventeenth century. It is clear from scattered reports that prosecutions were much rarer than the practice; for example, anal intercourse, both heterosexual and homosexual, was the most commonly confessed sin to visiting Portuguese Inquisitors at Pernambuco in Brazil during their visitation of 1594–95, but this did not lead to any upsurge in trials. Such confessions may be used as evidence for both sides of the debate about homosexuality before the conquest: those who argue that it was widespread note the continued frequency, those who argue that it was unacceptable before Christianization note that it was easy to make people view it as a sin. What is clear from these records – and sometimes stated explicitly by confessants – is that even in cases of sodomy, people distinguished between a "vida práctica" which people actually lived and religious and legal standards set so high that people could not follow them.

Magic and witchcraft

The distinction between theoretical standards and actual practice was also clear in matters involving witchcraft and magic. European demonologists such as Pierre de Lancre linked witchcraft in the Old and New Worlds by asserting that the reason for the rise in witchcraft in Europe was the coming of Christian missionaries to the New World, which had forced Satan and his demons to return to Europe. They regarded both New World and Old World witches as guided by Satan in the same way, an idea that slowly spread to missionaries active in the New World, who began to define pre-conquest religious practices as demonic. Thus it was important to destroy all religious objects, which missionaries saw as physical signs of satanic deceit, as well as anything that might have a link to idolatry, such as texts in native languages. Fr. Diego de Landa's campaign against idolatry among the Maya is generally regarded as having destroyed 90 percent of the existing Maya texts; intentional and unintentional destruction has left only three pre-conquest Maya texts intact.

Campaigns against witchcraft and idolatry continued the longest in the Andes, which was more resistant to Christianization than Mexico, with prac-titioners of indigenous religions, female and male, accused of both magic (hechicería) and the more serious demonic witchcraft (brujería). These campaigns picked up in the seventeenth century, as some Andean residents combated Spanish policies by returning to earlier beliefs and practices. As they smashed objects regarded as holy in indigenous traditions, Christian clergy in Peru also handed out pictures of saints, hoping to encourage veneration of individuals who exemplified Christian virtues, particularly those whose relics were housed in Lima.

As in Europe, the demonic was frequently linked to sexuality. A group of Indians in Mexico was charged with worshiping the devil as God, and being "taken up into the air by a devil while copulating carnally"; their leader was accused of having a picture showing her and other Indians "coupled with each other."[30] The Florentine Codex – a huge collection of descriptions and depictions of Mexican life produced under the supervision of missionaries – presents a procuress attempting to lure a woman into prostitution with a horned and hoofed devil standing right behind her; in the words that accompany the picture, the procuress is described as "truly the eyes, the ears, the messenger of the devil."[31] A later Jesuit report that women's ritual dances were "demonically inspired lascivious and drunken spectacles" designed to promote "indolence, incest, and idolatry."[32] In the Andes, witchcraft charges might result from too little sex as well as too much; women who chose to abstain from sexual relations in order to serve as leaders in resurgent native belief systems were often charged with witchcraft along with paganism and idolatry.

Same-sex relations and gender-crossing were also seen as the result of contact with the devil. After being captured by the Mapuche of southern Chile in 1629, the son of a Spanish conquistador watched a healing ritual in which a male shaman wore a skirt "used by women" and kept his hair "long and loose." "Those that take on the role of women," he commented, "are called *weye*, which in our language means nefarious ones and more precisely *putos* [the slang word both for prostitute and passive males in same-sex relations] . . . They become this because they have a pact with the devil."[33]

Despite campaigns against idolatry, however, Spaniards often approached Indians for the very magical (and perhaps demonic) powers the church judged so dangerous. Indians, Africans, and persons of mixed race, especially women, were widely regarded as having special skills in finding lost objects, healing illnesses, and performing love magic designed to attract, repel, or hold a lover or spouse. Love magic was used by clients – usually women – of all social classes. For example, of five African women tried for magic during Zumárraga's campaign, two were slaves, accused of buying aphrodisiacs to better please their masters sexually so that they would get better treatment. At the other end of the social scale was an upper-class Spanish woman in Colombia, accused in 1551 of paying a mixed-race woman named Juana Garcia for magical assistance in aborting a child conceived out of wedlock. The bishop and the governor decided to hush up the case by exiling Garcia rather than opening an official church investigation, probably to hide the identity of her client, whose name is not mentioned in the records. As in this instance, magic often brought women of different social groups and ethnicities together as they shared remedies. Not surprisingly, the treatment accorded such women by the Inquisition and other authorities was determined by their social group. In the 1680s in Guatemala, for example, rumors spread about the magical powers of a mulata woman who had provided potions and incantations to kill several husbands and bewitch officials; scores of people denounced her to the Inquisition, and she ultimately died while imprisoned. One of her clients, the Spanish widow of an official, was able to escape punishment by confessing that though "in the grip of the devil and pulled by animal instincts, I consulted these persons to use love magic spells and avenge my jealousies, I never denied any mystery of Our Lady of the Holy Roman Catholic Church."[34] Her social status, assertion that she had remained a good Christian, and use of stereotypes of female weakness combined to allow her to avoid punishment, despite persistent rumors that she had, in fact, caused her husband's death by feeding him a powder bought from the accused mulata.

Many spells and cures mixed elements from many cultures: a woman who wished to keep her spouse loyal might sew a love bundle made of a hummingbird into her clothing (an Indian remedy), feed him soup made from water in which she had washed her body mixed with the dust from an altar (a European remedy), and seek a spirit medium (an African remedy). Potions designed to attract men or end domestic violence often mixed hair, menstrual blood, sweat, or saliva into hot chocolate, and women were advised to drink this in church during mass to make it especially strong. Rituals and invocations mixed approved and unacceptable practices, as women called on the saints or the Virgin Mary, but also the stars, for help.

Most of those involved in cases of sexual magic that made it into the records tell quite desperate stories, of husbands who beat or abandoned them, of poverty out of which marriage was the only hope, of rape or seduction that left them pregnant. Cases sometimes emerged when men came to church authorities charging that women were performing love magic on them, but more often when the women themselves confessed, seemingly voluntarily, to the Inquisition, thus turning to the church to resolve their ambivalent feelings about love magic. A few men also show up in church records voluntarily confessing their use of love magic, though their feelings of guilt at doing so may have been influenced by the fact that their efforts were unsuccessful; offering their soul while "inflamed with desire for a woman" had not allowed them to "lull women to [their] carnal desires."[35]

Because most cases of sexual magic involved were women, many of whom were socially marginal, church courts and the Inquisition generally did not take such actions terribly seriously, but trivialized them and denied that the women accused of practicing magic had any powers. If making a demonic pact was part of their love magic, the women were taken more seriously during the sixteenth and seventeenth centuries; in 1691 authorities in Guatemala even built a special women's jail to house such "women who live evil lives." By the eighteenth century parish priests discounted even cases in which women called on the devil, however, no longer sending them on to the Inquisition but simply scolding the women for deluding themselves.

*   *   *

The process of Christianization in Latin America used to be described as a "spiritual conquest," in which indigenous beliefs and practices were largely wiped out through a combination of force and persuasion, transforming most of the countries of Latin America into Catholic countries on a European model. The spread of Catholic Christianity is now viewed very differently, not simply as conquest and resistance, but as a process of cultural negotiation and creolization, during which Christian ideas and practices were accepted but also transformed. This transformation involved indigenous people, Europeans, Africans, Asians, and people of mixed race; Latin American Christianity became part of a new shared culture, though a culture with many local differences.

The church's regulation of sexual practices was part of that shared culture and of its local distinctions. Theories about proper marital relationships and sexual deportment were shared across wide areas, but they played out differently in areas where indigenous traditions varied and differently in cities than they did in the missions or the countryside. They also played out differently over time, as much of Latin America developed into a multi-racial society. The Catholic Church in Latin America was an important player in the link between sexuality and race, as it was in other parts of the world where European traders and colonists journeyed. Here it was joined by Protestant churches as well, and it is in Africa and Asia that we can find an even more complex and varied situation developing.

Selected further reading

Good places to start for many of the issues discussed in this chapter are Susan Migden Socolow, *The Women of Colonial Latin America* (New York: Cambridge University Press, 2000), Cecelia F. Klein, ed., *Gender in Pre-Hispanic America: A Symposium at Dumbarton Oaks, 12 and 13 October 1996* (Washington, DC: Dumbarton Oaks Research Library and Collection, 2001), and Karen Vieira Powers, *Women in the Crucible of Conquest: The Gendered Genesis of Spanish American Society, 1500–1600* (Albuquerque: University of New Mexico, 2005). For a study that focuses on men and masculinity, see Federico Garza Carvajal, *Vir: Conceptions of Manliness in Andalucia and Mexico, 1561–1699* (Amsterdam: Amsterdamse Historische Reeks, 2000). Older works include Ann Pescatello, *Power and Pawn: The Female in Iberian Families, Societies, and Cultures* (Westport, Conn.: Greenwood, 1976) and the collections of articles edited by Asuncion Lavrin, *Latin American Women: Historical Perspectives* (Westport, Conn.: Greenwood, 1978) and *Sexuality and Marriage in Colonial Latin America* (Lincoln: University of Nebraska Press, 1989). For a broad chronological sweep, see Susan Kellogg, *Weaving the Past: A History of Latin America's Indigenous Women from the Prehispanic Period to the Present* (New York: Oxford University Press, 2005). The many books of Charles R. Boxer provide useful general information: *Race Relations in the Portuguese Colonial Empire 1415–1825* (Oxford: Clarendon Press, 1963); *The Church Militant and Iberian Expansion, 1440–1770* (Baltimore, Md.: Johns Hopkins, 1978); *Mary and Misogyny* (note 18 of Chapter 4 in "Notes").

An excellent overview of gender in pre-contact Mesoamerica is Rosemary A. Joyce, *Gender and Power in Prehispanic Mesoamerica* (Austin: University of Texas, 2001); an insightful discussion of the relationship among gender, sexuality, and religion is Sylvia Marcos, *Taken from the Lips: Gender and Eros in Mesoamerican Religions* (Amsterdam: Brill Academic, 2006). For the Maya, see Traci Ardren, ed., *Ancient Maya Women* (Walnut Creek, Calif.: AltaMira, 2002); Lowell S. Gustafson and Amelia M. Trevelyan, eds, *Ancient Maya Gender Identity and Relations* (Westport, Conn.: Bergin & Garvey, 2002); Jennifer Dornan, "Blood from the Moon: Gender Ideology and the Rise of Ancient Maya Social Complexity," *Gender & History* 16(2) (August 2004): 459–75. On the Inca, see: Constance Classen, *Inca Cosmology and the Human Body* (Salt Lake City: University of Utah Press, 1993); Peter Gose, "The State as a Chosen Woman: Brideservice and the Feeding of Tributaries in the Inka Empire," *American Anthropologist* 102(1) (2000): 84–97.

Gender relations in the Aztec Empire are hotly debated; for a review of the debate, see Louise M. Burkhart, "Mexica Women on the Home Front: Housework and Religion in Aztec Mexico," and Stephanie Wood and Robert Haskett, "Concluding Remarks" in Schroeder *et al., Indian Women* (note 2), 25–54 and 313–30. (This book also has an extremely useful 30-page bibliography.) For other discussions of gender among Nahua peoples, see Cecelia Klein, "Fighting with Femininity: Gender and War in Aztec Mexico," *Estudios de Cultura Náhuatl* 24 (1994): 219–53; Susan Schroeder, "The First American Valentine: Nahua Courtship and Other Aspects of Family Structuring in Mesoamerica," *Journal of Family History* 23(4) (October 1998): 341–54; Camilla Townsend, "'What in the World have You done to Me, My Lover?' Sex, Servitude, and Politics among the Pre-Conquest Nahuas as seen in the 'Cantares Mexicanos'," *The Americas* 62(3) (January 2006): 349–89; Robert

McCaa, "The Nahua 'Calli' of Ancient Mexico: Household, Family, and Gender," *Continuity & Change* 18(1) (2003): 23–48.

Most studies of pre-Hispanic and early colonial cultures published in the last several decades stress the ways in which post-conquest culture blended European and indigenous elements in many areas of life, among them marital patterns and other aspects of sexuality. For the Maya, see: Nancy M. Farriss, *Maya Society Under Spanish Rule: The Collective Enterprise of Survival* (Princeton, N.J.: Princeton University Press, 1984); Inga Clendinnen, *Ambivalent Conquests: Maya and Spaniard in Yucatan* (Cambridge: Cambridge University Press, 1987); Matthew Restall, *The Maya World: Yucatec Culture and Society, 1550–1850* (Stanford, Calif.: Stanford University Press, 1997); John D. Early, *The Maya and Catholicism: An Encounter of World Views* (Gainesville: University Press of Florida, 2006).

On the Aztecs, see: S.L. Cline, *Colonial Culhuacan, 1580–1600: A Social History of an Aztec Town* (Albuquerque: University of New Mexico, 1986); Inga Clendinnen, *Aztecs: An Interpretation* (Cambridge: Cambridge University Press, 1991); Louise M. Burkhart, *The Slippery Earth: Nahua-Christian Moral Dialogue in Sixteenth Century Mexico* (Tucson: University of Arizona Press, 1989); James Lockhart, *The Nahuas After the Conquest: A Social and Cultural History of the Indians of Central Mexico, Sixteenth through Eighteenth Centuries* (Stanford, Calif.: Stanford University Press, 1992); Susan Kellogg, *Law and the Transformation of Aztec Culture 1500–1700* (Norman: University of Oklahoma Press, 1995); Rebecca Horn, *Postconquest Coyoacan: Nahua–Spanish Relations in Central Mexico, 1519–1650* (Stanford, Calif.: Stanford University Press, 1997); Davíd Carrasco, "Uttered from the Heart: Guilty Rhetoric among the Aztecs," *History of Religions* 39(1) (1999): 1–31; Susan Schroeder, "Jesuits, Nahuas, and the Good Death Society in Mexico City, 1710–67," *Hispanic American Historical Review* 80(1) (2000): 43–76; Serge Gruzinski, *The Mestizo Mind: The Intellectual Dynamics of Colonization and Globalization*, trans. Deke Dusinberre (New York: Routledge, 2002); Viviana Díaz Balsera, *The Pyramid Under the Cross: Franciscan Discourses of Evangelization and the Nahua Christian Subject in Sixteenth-Century Mexico* (Tucson: University of Arizona Press, 2005); Martin Austin Nesvig, ed., *Local Religion in Colonial Mexico* (Albuquerque: University of New Mexico Press, 2006).

For work on Mesoamerica that focuses specifically on issues of sexuality, see: S.L. Cline, "The Spiritual Conquest Reexamined: Baptism and Christian Marriage in Early Sixteenth-century Mexico," *Hispanic American Historical Review* 73 (1993): 453–80; Sonya Lipsett-Rivera, "The Intersection of Rape and Marriage in Late-Colonial and Early-National Mexico," *Colonial Latin American Historical Review* 6 (1997): 559–90; Matthew Restall and Pete Sigal, "'May They Not Be Fornicators Equal to those Priests': Post-colonial Yucatec Maya

Sexual Attitudes," and Kimberly Gauderman, "Father Fiction: The Construction of Gender in England, Spain, and the Andes," in Lisa Sousa, ed., *Indigenous Writing in the Spanish Indies, Special Issue of UCLA Historical Journal* 12 (1997): 91–121, 122–51; Pete Sigal, *From Moon Goddesses to Virgins: The Colonization of Yucatecan Maya Sexual Desire* (Austin: University of Texas Press, 2000); Zeb Tortorici, "Masturbation, Salvation, and Desire: Connecting Sexuality and Religiosity in Colonial Mexico," *Journal of the History of Sexuality* 16(3) (September 2007): 355–72. "Sexual Encounters/Sexual Collisions: Alternative Sexualities in Colonial Mesoamerica," special issue of *Ethnohistory* 54(1) (Winter 2007): 3–194 has a number of articles.

On devotion to the Virgin Mary in Mesoamerica, see: Louise M. Burkhart, *Before Guadalupe: The Virgin Mary in Early Colonial Nahuatl Literature* (Albany, N.Y.: Institute for Mesoamerican Studies, University at Albany, 2001); David A. Brading, *Mexican Phoenix: Our Lady of Guadalupe: Image and Tradition* (Cambridge: Cambridge University Press, 2001). On St. Joseph, see: Charlene Villaseñor Black, *Creating the Cult of St. Joseph: Art and Gender in the Spanish Empire* (Princeton, N.J.: Princeton University Press, 2006). The best recent study of Rose of Lima and her followers is Frank Graziano, *Wounds of Love: The Mystical Marriage of Saint Rose of Lima* (New York: Oxford University Press, 2004). On other saints, see Greer and Bilinkoff, *Colonial Saints* (note 11).

On religious encounters in the Andean regions, see: Karen Spalding, *Huarochirí: An Andean Society under Inca and Spanish Rule* (Stanford, Calif.: Stanford University Press, 1984); Regina Harrison, *"True" Confessions: Quechua and Spanish Cultural Encounters in the Viceroyalty of Peru,* Latin American Studies Series 5 (College Park: University of Maryland Press, 1992); Steve J. Stern, *Peru's Indian Peoples and the Challenge of Spanish Conquest: Huamanga to 1640,* 2nd edn (Madison: University of Wisconsin Press, 1993); Ward Stavig, "Living in Offense of Our Lord: Indigenous Sexual Values and Marital Life in the Colonial Crucible," *Hispanic American Historical Review* 75 (1995): 597–622; Sabine MacCormack, *Religion in the Andes: Vision and Imagination in Early Colonial Peru* (Princeton, N.J.: Princeton University Press, 1991); Irene Silverblatt, *Moon, Sun and Witches: Gender Ideologies and Class in Inca and Colonial Peru* (Princeton, N.J.: Princeton University Press, 1987) and "Andean Witches and Virgins: Seventeenth-Century Nativism and Subversive Gender Ideologies," in Margo Hendricks and Patricia Parker, eds, *Women, "Race," and Writing in the Early Modern Period* (London: Routledge, 1994), 259–86 and "Family Values in Seventeenth-Century Peru," in Elizabeth Boone and Tom Cummins, eds, *Native Traditions in the Postconquest World* (Washington, DC: Dumbarton Oaks, 1998), 63–89; Verena Stolcke, "Invaded Women: Gender, Race, and Class in the Formation of Colonial Society," in Hendrichs and Parker, *Women, Race, and Writing,* 272–86; Karen Vieira Powers, "Andeans and Spaniards in the Contact Zone: A Gendered Collision," *The American Indian Quarterly* 24(4) (Fall 2000): 511–36; David Cahill, "The Virgin and the Inca: An Incaic Procession in the City of Cuzco in 1692," *Ethnohistory* 49(3) (Summer 2002): 611–49; Bacigalupo, "Struggle" (note 33) and *Shamans of the Foye Tree: Gender, Power, and Healing among the Chilean Mapuche* (Austin: University of Texas Press, 2007).

For the experience in Spanish Florida and the American Southeast, see David Hurst Thomas, ed., *Columbian Consequences, Vol. 2: Archeological and History Perspectives on the Spanish Borderlands East* (Washington, DC: Smithsonian Institution Press, 1990); Charles Hudson and Carmen Chaves Tesser, eds, *The Forgotten Centuries: Indians and Europeans in the American South, 1521–1704* (Athens: University of Georgia Press, 1994); Jerald T. Milanich, *Florida Indians and the Invasion from Europe* (Gainesville: University Press of Florida, 1995); James Axtell, *The Indians' New South: Cultural Change in the Colonial Southeast* (Baton Rouge: Louisiana State University Press, 1997); Robert C. Galgano, *Feast of Souls: Indians and Spaniards in the Seventeenth-Century Missions of Florida and New Mexico* (Albuquerque: University of New Mexico Press, 2005).

For northern New Spain, see Evelyn Hu-DeHart, *Missionaries, Miners, and Indians: Spanish Contact with the Yaqui Nation of Northwestern New Spain 1533–1820* (Tucson: University of Arizona Press, 1981); James Brooks, *Captives and Cousins: Slavery, Kinship, and Community in the Southwest Borderlands* (Chapel Hill: University of North Carolina Press, 2002); Susan Deeds, *Defiance and Deference in New Spain: Indians under Colonial Rule in Nueva Vizcaya* (Austin: University of Texas Press, 2003); and Gutiérrez, *When Jesus Came* (note 6). Studies of California missions focus on a slightly later period: James A. Sandos, *Converting California: Indians and Franciscans in the Missions* (New Haven, Conn.: Yale University Press, 2004); Miroslava Chávez-García, *Negotiating Conquest: Gender and Power in California, 1770s to 1880s* (Tucson: University of Arizona Press, 2004); Steven W. Hackel, *Children of Coyote, Missionaries of St. Francis: Indian–Spanish Relations in Colonial California, 1769–1850* (Chapel Hill: University of North Carolina Press, 2005).

General works on the experience of Africans in Latin America that touch on issues of the regulation of sexuality include: Frederick P. Bowser, *The African Slave in Colonial Peru, 1524–1650* (Stanford, Calif.: Stanford University Press, 1974); Colin A. Palmer, *Slaves of the White God: Blacks in Mexico, 1570–1650* (Cambridge, Mass.: Harvard University Press, 1976); Della M. Flusche and Eugene H. Korth, *Forgotten Females: Women of African and Indian Descent in Colonial Chile, 1535–1800* (Detroit: Blaine Ethridge, 1983); John Thornton, *Africa and Africans in the Making of the Atlantic World, 1400–1680* (Cambridge: Cambridge University Press, 1992); Kathleen J. Higgins, *"Licentious Liberty" in a Brazilian Gold-Mining Region: Slavery, Gender and Social Control in*

Eighteenth-Century Sabara, Minas Gerais (University Park: Penn State University Press, 1999); Matthew Restall and Jane Landers, eds, "The African Experience in Early Spanish America," special issue of *Americas*, 52(2) (2000). Two studies of Africans' creation and use of Christian institutions are Herman L. Bennett, *Africans in Colonial Mexico: Absolutism, Christianity, and Afro-Creole Consciousness, 1570–1640* (Bloomington: Indiana University Press, 2003) and Nicole von Germeten, *Black Blood Brothers: Confraternities and Social Mobility for Afro-Mexicans* (Gainesville: University Press of Florida, 2006).

For discussions of racial mixing, see Magnus Mörner, *Race Mixture in the History of Latin America* (Boston: Little, Brown, 1967); Stuart B. Schwartz, "Colonial Identities and the 'Sociedad De Castas'," *Colonial Latin American Review* 4(1) (1995): 185–201; Elizabeth Anne Kuznesof, "Ethnic and Gender Influences on 'Spanish' Creole Society in Colonial Spanish America," *Colonial Latin American Review* 4(1) (1995): 153–76 and "More Conversation on Race, Class and Gender," *Colonial Latin American Review* 5(1) (1996): 129–33; Muriel Nazzari, "Concubinage in Colonial Brazil: The Inequalities of Race, Class, and Gender," *Journal of Family History* 21 (April 1996): 107–24; Thomas Ward, "Expanding Ethnicity in Sixteenth-Century Anahuac: Ideologies of Ethnicity and Gender in the Nation-Building Process," *MLN* 116(2) (March 2001): 419–52; Maria Elena Martinez, "The Black Blood of New Spain: Limpieza de Sangre, Racial Violence, and Gendered Power in Early Colonial Mexico," *The William and Mary Quarterly* 61(3) (July 2004): 479–520. Studies of the casta paintings include Ilona Katzew, ed., *New World Orders: Casta Painting and Colonial Latin America* (New York: American Society Art Gallery, 1996); Susan Kellogg, "Depicting 'Mestizaje:' Gendered Images of Ethnorace in Colonial Mexican Texts," *Journal of Women's History* 12(3) (2000): 69–92; Magal M. Carrera, *Imagining Identity in New Spain: Race, Lineage, and the Colonial Body in Portraiture and Casta Paintings* (Austin: University of Texas Press, 2003). The fullest analysis of Asians in colonial Mexico is Edward R. Slack Jr., "The *Chinos* of New Spain: A Corrective Lens for a Distorted Image," *Journal of World History* 20 (March 2009): 35–68. On racial ideologies in the French Caribbean, see Doris Lorraine Garraway, *The Libertine Colony: Creolization in the Early French Caribbean* (Durham: Duke University Press, 2005).

Some of the most influential descriptions of indigenous practices by acculturated Indians or European clergy who had learned native languages are available in translation: *The Incas: The Royal Commentaries of the Inca Garcilaso de la Vega 1539–1616*, trans. Maria Jolas (New York: Orion Press, 1961); Fr. Bernardino de Sahagún, *Florentine Codex; General History of the Things of New Spain,* 12 vols, ed. and trans. Arthur J.O. Anderson and Charles E. Dibble (Sante Fe and Salt Lake City: School of American Research and University of Utah Press, 1950–82). Rebecca Overmyer-Velázquez, "Christian

Morality in New Spain: The Nahua Woman in the Franciscan Imaginary," in Tony Ballantyne and Antoinette Burton, eds, *Bodies in Contact: Rethinking Colonial Encounters in World History* (Durham, N.C.: Duke University Press, 2005), 67–83 analyzes the representation of women in Sahagún's work.

There are many works that investigate various attempts to extirpate native religious practices, and include information on attempts to end polygamy and concubinage and to alter gender hierarchies. These include: J. Jorge Klor de Alva, "Colonizing Souls: The Failure of the Indian Inquisition and the Rise of Penitential Discipline," and Roberto Moreno de los Arcos, "New Spain's Inquisition for Indians from the Sixteenth to the Nineteenth Century," both in Anne J. Cruz and Mary Elizabeth Perry, *Colonial Encounters: The Impact of the Inquisition in Spain on the New World* (Berkeley: University of California Press, 1991), 3–22, 23–36; Amos Megged, *Exporting the Catholic Reformation: Local Religion in Early Colonial Mexico* (Leiden: Brill, 1996); Kenneth Mills, *Idolatry and Its Enemies: Colonial Andean Religion and Extirpation* (Princeton, N.J.: Princeton University Press, 1997) and "The Limits of Religious Coercion in Mid-Colonial Peru," *Past and Present* 145 (1994): 84–121; Celia L. Cussen, "The Search for Idols and Saints in Colonial Peru: Linking Extirpation and Beatification," *The Hispanic American Historical Review* 85(3) (August 2005): 417–48. Some of the works of those intent on ending native religion have been translated, and in these we can get a glimpse of at least what Christian writers understood native practices to be. These include: Pablo Joseph de Arriaga, *The Extirpation of Idolatry in Peru*, ed. and trans. L. Clark Keating (Lexington: University of Kentucky, 1968); Hernando Ruiz de Alarcón, *Treatise on the Heathen Superstitions That Today Live Among the Indians Native to This New Spain,* ed. and trans. J. Richard Andrews and Ross Hassig (Norman: University of Oklahoma Press, 1984); Montoya, *Spiritual Conquest* (note 17).

Studies of the activities of church courts and the Inquisition in Latin America include: Richard Greenleaf, *Zumárraga and the Mexican Inquisition, 1536–1543* (Washington: Academy of American Franciscan History, 1961) and *The Mexican Inquisition of the Sixteenth Century* (Albuquerque: University of New Mexico Press, 1969); Nicholas Griffiths, *The Cross and the Serpent: Religious Repression and Resurgence in Colonial Peru* (Norman: University of Oklahoma Press, 1996); Irene Marsha Silverblatt, *Modern Inquisitions: Peru and the Colonial Origins of the Civilized World* (Durham, N.C.: Duke University Press, 2004). In *All Can be Saved: Religious Tolerance and Salvation in the Iberian Atlantic World* (New Haven: Yale University Press, 2008), Stuart B. Schwartz examines the opposite of repression – that is, attitudes of religious toleration found among common people in Spain, Portugal, and the New World.

On convents, see: Asunción Lavrin, "Indian Brides of Christ: Creating New Spaces for Indigenous Women in New Spain," *Mexican Studies* 15(2)

(1999): 225–60; Kathryn Burns, *Colonial Habits: Convents and the Spiritual Economy of Cuzco, Peru* (Durham, N.C.:, Duke University Press, 1999); Nora E. Jaffary, *Gender, Race, and Religion in the Colonization of the Americas* (Burlington, Vt.: Ashgate, 2007); Stephanie Kirk, *Convent Life in Colonial Mexico: A Tale of Two Communities* (Gainesville: University Press of Florida, 2007). For studies of the institutions that housed "problem" women, see: Lee M. Penyak, "Safe Harbors and Compulsory Custody: Casas De Deposito in Mexico, 1750–1865," *The Hispanic American Historical Review* 79(1) (February 1999): 83–99; Nancy E. van Deusen, *Between the Sacred and the Worldly: The Institutional and Cultural Practice of Recogimiento in Colonial Lima* (Stanford, Calif.: Stanford University Press, 2001).

The history of missions was for many years generally researched and written by members of the religious order that had established the mission, and so is sometimes more hagiography than history. Studies that break from this pattern and also contain information on sexuality include: David Bock, *Mission Culture on the Upper Amazon: Native Tradition, Jesuit Enterprise and Secular Policy in Moxos, 1660–1880* (Lincoln: University of Nebraska Press, 1994); Erick Langer and Robert H. Jackson, eds, *The New Latin American Mission History* (Lincoln: University of Nebraska, 1995); Christopher Vecsey, *On the Padres' Trail* (South Bend, Ind.: Notre Dame University Press, 1996). William B. Taylor's monumental study, *Magistrates of the Sacred: Priests and Parishioners in Eighteenth Century Mexico* (Stanford, Calif.: Stanford University Press, 1996), includes material on church regulation of sexual matters both on and off the missions.

For articles that look specifically at women's activities in response to colonialism and the spread of Christianity, see Inga Clendinnen, "Yucatec Maya Women and the Spanish Conquest: Role and Ritual in Historical Reconstruction," *Journal of Social History* 15 (1982): 427–42; Frank Salomon, "Indian Women of Early Colonial Quito as Seen through their Testaments," *The Americas* 44(3) (January 1988): 325–41; van Deusen, "Defining the Sacred" (note 24); Tudela, "Fashioning," (note 27); and the special issue of *Ethnohistory,* "Women, Power, and Resistance in Colonial Mesoamerica," 42(4) (1995), edited by Kevin Gosner and Deborah E. Kanter.

For works which focus primarily on European-background people, see Patricia Seed, *To Love, Honor and Obey in Colonial Mexico: Conflicts Over Marriage Choice, 1574–1821* (Stanford, Calif.: Stanford University Press, 1988); Ann Twinam, *Public Lives, Private Secrets: Gender, Honor, Sexuality, and Illegitimacy in Colonial Spanish America* (Stanford, Calif.: Stanford University Press, 1999); María Emma Mannarelli, *Private Passions and Public Sins: Men and Women in Seventeenth-century Lima*, translated by Sidney Evans and Meredith Dodge (Albuquerque: University of New Mexico Press, 2007); Boyer, *Lives of the Bigamists* (note 21); Martin, *Daughters of the Conquistadores* (note 20). R. Douglas

Cope, *The Limits of Racial Domination: Plebian Society in Colonial Mexico City, 1660–1720* (Madison: University of Wisconsin, 1994), Lyman L. Johnson and Sonya Lipsett-Rivera, eds, *The Faces of Honor: Sex, Shame and Violence in Colonial Latin America* (Albuquerque: University of New Mexico Press, 1998), and Martin, *Governance and Society* (note 25) include information on sexual behavior and marital patterns for a range of urban groups.

In terms of same-sex relations, a good place to begin is Martin Nesvig, "The Complicated Terrain of Latin American Homosexuality," *The Hispanic American Historical Review* 81(3/4) (August/November 2001): 689–729. The subject is not only "complicated," but also controversial. In *Sex and Conquest: Gendered Violence, Political Order, and the European Conquest of the Americas* (Ithaca, N.Y.: Cornell University Press, 1995) and later articles, such as "Making the American Berdache: Choice Or Constraint?" *Journal of Social History* 35(3) (Spring 2002): 613–36, Richard C. Trexler asserts that indigenous peoples linked male same-sex practices to conquest, and always viewed the passive partner as a feminized man and thus negatively. Ramón Gutiérrez, "Warfare, Homosexuality, and Gender Status Among American Indian Men in the Southwest," in Thomas A. Foster, ed., *Long before Stonewall: Histories of Same-Sex Sexuality in Early America,* (New York: New York University Press, 2007), 19–31, also emphasizes violence and humiliation. By contrast, Walter L. Williams, *The Spirit and the Flesh: Sexual Diversity in American Indian Culture* (Boston: Beacon Press, 1986) and Will Roscoe, *Changing Ones: Third and Fourth Genders in Native North America* (London: Macmillan Press, 1998) present very positive evaluations of the role of two-spirit people among Native American groups, and Michael J. Horswell, *Decolonizing the Sodomite: Queer Tropes of Sexuality in Colonial Andean Culture* (Austin: University of Texas Press, 2005) argues that ritual same-sex practices were important to Andean peoples, and that the passive partner – who he sees as a third gender – was valued. Sigal, *Infamous Desire* (note 29) contains articles by both Trexler and Horswell, as well as others. On the Maya, see further a series of articles by Pete Sigal, "The Politicization of Pederasty among the Colonial Yucatecan Maya," *Journal of the History of Sexuality* 8 (1997): 1–24; "Gender, Male Homosexuality, and Power in Colonial Yucatan," *Latin American Perspectives* 29(2) (2002): 24–40; "The 'Cuiloni,' the 'Patlache,' and the Abominable Sin: Homosexualities in Early Colonial Nahua Society," *Hispanic American Historical Review* 85(4) (2005): 555–93. A recent analysis centering on the post-Conquest period is Federico Garza Carvajal, *Butterflies Will Burn: Prosecuting Sodomites in Early Modern Spain and Mexico* (Austin: University of Texas Press, 2003). Though it deals with a later period and so pays less attention to religion, Rudi Bleys, *The Geography of Perversion: Male-to-Male Sexual Behavior outside the West and the Ethnographic Imagination, 1750–1918* (New York: New York University Press, 1995) reviews reports about homosexuality among non-Westerners from a range of sources and includes translations as well as original language quotations. One of the few studies of female same-sex relations is Stephanie Kirk, "Illicit Passions: Mala Amistad in the Eighteenth Century Mexican Convent," *Latin American Literary Review* 33(6)6 (July/December 2005): 5–30.

On magic and witchcraft, see Ruth Behar, "Sex and Sin, Witchcraft and the Devil in Late Colonial Mexico," *American Ethnologist* 14 (Feb. 1987): 34–54; Carole A. Myscofski, "The Magic of Brazil: Practice and Prohibition in the Early Colonial Period, 1590–1620," *History of Religions* 40(2) (2000): 153–76; Laura de Mello e Souza, *The Devil and the Land of the Holy Cross: Witchcraft, Slavery, and Popular Religion in Colonial Brazil*, translated by Diane Grosklaus Whitty (Austin: University of Texas Press: 2003); Laura Lewis, *Hall of Mirrors: Power, Witchcraft, and Caste in Colonial Mexico* (Durham, N.C.: Duke University Press, 2003); Lisa Sousa, "The Devil and Deviance in Native Criminal Narratives from Early Mexico," *The Americas* (West Bethesda, Md.) 59(2) (October 2002): 161–79; Susan M. Deeds, "Subverting the Social Order: Gender, Power, and Magic in Nueva Vizcaya," in *Choice, Persuasion, and Coercion: Social Control on Spain's North American Frontiers*, edited by Jesus F. de la Teja and Frank Ross (Albuquerque: University of New Mexico Press, 2005); Joan Cameron Bristol, "From Curing to Witchcraft: Afro-Mexicans and the Mediation of Authority," *Journal of Colonialism & Colonial History* 7(1) (2006); Rachel Sarah O'Toole, "Danger in the Convent: Colonial Demons, Idolatrous 'Indias,' and Bewitching 'Negras' in Santa Clara (Trujillo Del Peru)," *Journal of Colonialism & Colonial History* 7(1) (2006); Few, *Women Who Live Evil Lives* (note 34). Both Silverblatt (*Moon, Sun, and Witches* and "Andean Witches and Virgins") and Griffiths *(The Cross and the Serpent)* discuss the campaigns against magic in Peru, though they come to different conclusions; Silverblatt views these as serious campaigns directly primarily against women who were practitioners of native religion, while Griffiths asserts that the Spanish did not single women out, and were attempting to trivialize all native religious practitioners by saying they simply claimed to do magic to defraud people.

Chapter 5

AFRICA AND ASIA

T HE DEVELOPMENT AND OPERATION of Christian institutions for the regulation of sexuality in Africa and Asia parallels that of Latin America in many ways. In all of these areas, small numbers of European clergy attempted to oversee the actions of Europeans, while others, primarily members of Catholic religious orders, worked at converting indigenous peoples. Existing beliefs and practices blended with Christian ones in a process of syncretism that some clergy opposed and others participated in or supported. The religious orders sometimes established missions or otherwise tried to centralize communities of converts, in which they had secular as well as religious authority. Religious personnel urged the establishment of schools, though the actual number of schools was much smaller than they hoped, and most religious instruction was oral and informal. Church courts were established to oversee doctrinal conformity and sexual morals, but their level of activity and enforcement was highly erratic.

However, there are significant contrasts between Latin America, on the one hand, and Africa and Asia, on the other. In Latin America, most pre-colonial religious traditions were localized and based largely on oral transmission; in Asia and Africa, Christians confronted both local religions and other text-based and widespread religions, such as Hinduism, Buddhism, and Islam, which had complex and highly developed structures for regulating sexuality. Islam in particular was winning converts at the same time that Christianity was, and people often had to work hard to negotiate the hostilities between these two faiths. These hostilities could split families as some family members joined one faith and others another, or force families and villages to switch religions quickly when the faith of government leaders or the overseeing authority changed.

In addition to other text-based religions, in a few places there were also indigenous variants of Christianity that long pre-dated European voyages. When the Portuguese reached the southwest coast of India in 1498, for example, they met a well-organized Christian community with perhaps 100,000 people that used Syriac as their liturgical language. Christianity here dated back at least to the fifth century, and probably earlier, for there were strong oral traditions that Christianity was brought to this area by the apostle Thomas shortly after the death of Christ. (For that reason, this group is generally termed the "St. Thomas Christians.") When European missionaries reached Ethiopia, they also discovered a Christian community with ancient roots and a long history of independent rule.

In Latin America, the establishment and operation of Christian institutions for the regulation of sexuality before 1750 was – with a few exceptions like the brief period of Dutch rule in Brazil or British, Dutch, and Danish colonies in the Caribbean – a completely Catholic undertaking, while in Asia and Africa Protestants and indigenous Christians were also involved. In some of these areas, Protestants moved in after Catholics had already begun conversions and established institutions, so that Protestants confronted Catholic ideas and practices, indigenous non-Christian traditions, indigenous Christian traditions, and mixtures of all of these. Thus the patterns of sexual regulation that developed were highly varied.

In Latin America, the Spanish and the Portuguese were intent on establishing colonies based on agriculture or extractive industries, with a significant European population, at least in urban areas. In many parts of Africa and Asia, the colonial powers before 1750 were largely interested in the profits of maritime trade and had no intentions of setting up large land-based colonies or transplanting large numbers of Europeans. They were consequently much less interested in the conversion of the indigenous population than was the Spanish Crown in Latin America, for conversion did nothing to further their national objectives. (As we will see, the Spanish colony in the Philippines was an exception to this, and intentionally followed the Latin American model.)

In Latin America, the establishment of Christian institutions and European-based political institutions occurred at roughly the same time. This was also true in some parts of Africa and Asia, but in many areas, such as China and Japan, Christian missions operated within political structures that were modified only slightly, if at all, by European influence. In other areas, such as the Dutch colonies of South Africa, Ceylon (now Sri Lanka), Formosa (now Taiwan), the Moluccas, and much of Indonesia, the ruling political body was a private company – the United East Indies Company (Verenigde Oost-Indische Compagnie in Dutch, and generally abbreviated VOC) – rather than the Dutch state.

As these differences suggest, the influence of Christian ideas and institutions was much more geographically limited in Africa and Asia before 1750 than it was in Latin America. Except in places with indigenous Christian churches such as southwest India or Ethiopia, and in the Kingdom of Kongo in central Africa, Christians were generally found in a few pockets surrounding European trading centers, with isolated missionaries operating in between. For the vast majority of the populations of Africa and Asia, Christianity – along with other aspects of European culture – made no difference at all. Until the second wave of European colonialism that began in the nineteenth century, most people had not heard of Christianity, and in large areas – Africa and Asia away from the coasts, most of Australia and the Pacific islands – no one had seen a European. Nevertheless, just as Spanish contacts with the Aztec and Inca states shaped subsequent encounters with other Latin American groups, in Africa and Asia early encounters were extremely influential. Reports by early European missionaries, merchants, and explorers were avidly read by missionaries and colonial officials of the nineteenth century, and so influenced later religious, political, and social developments. Many historians are currently evaluating the complex relationships among race, gender, sexuality, and empire in the nineteenth century, yet the roots of these relationships go back to the first European voyages of exploration.

Ideas and patterns before the arrival of European Christianity

It is very difficult to summarize sexual ideas and practices across such a vast geographic area; over the last century anthropologists, historians, and religious scholars have taken great pains to point out how such things as marital patterns, kinship structures, religious beliefs and practices, and sexual norms differ among groups that are often geographically quite close to one another and similar in terms of political or technological development, to say nothing of the populations of regions as disparate as were those of Africa and Asia before 1450. The following will thus necessarily be a very general overview.

In most cultures of Africa south of the Sahara, some men had more than one wife, with families living in house-compounds in which each wife had her own house, cattle, fields, and property. Marriage was an agreement between families and involved a transfer of wealth, often in the form of animals. Family elders thus had a large say in the choice of spouses, though this was mitigated in some areas by religious groups that provided support for young people's own marital choices. Among the Anlo of what is now Ghana, for example, young women joined the Nyigbla and later Yewe religious orders as a way to defy their parents and also maintain rights to property after marriage. In areas where there were larger states, rulers used marriage to cement political and military alliances; as a result they might have a very large number of wives and concubines. Even in stateless areas, men demonstrated their wealth and power by the size of their households. Most women married young and lived in polygynous households, while men married later in life and some had no opportunity to marry at all. Children born outside of marriage were not stigmatized: as Giovanni Cavazzi, a seventeenth-century missionary to Angola, commented, "The importance of being a legitimate child, so appreciated in Europe and in other parts, still seems to be completely unknown to many Ethiopes [by which he meant Africans]. They give as much equal consideration to the illegitimate child as they do the legitimate."[1] Because much of Africa had too little population for the land available, fertility was a constant concern in religious and magical rituals, and barrenness or impotence was ascribed, as it was in Europe, to witchcraft, with barren women particularly suspect.

African religious beliefs and practices were highly varied, but underlying many of them was a conception of the universe as divided between a visible world of the living and an unseen world of spirits, the gods, and the dead. The unseen world regularly intervened in the visible world, for good and ill, and communicated through messages and revelations sent to spiritually adept individuals or to ordinary people through dreams and portents. Conversely, the actions of dead ancestors, spirits, and gods could be shaped by living people. Spiritual healers and diviners could intervene through complex rituals designed to assure the health and prosperity of an individual, family, or community, and objects understood to have special power could give additional protection. Both men and women acted as priests and healers, and in some places, such as Central Africa, diviners included cross-dressing men similar to those found in the Americas who performed burial ceremonies and provided advice. Spirits and ancestors were often represented by masks and statues in rituals and sacrifices held in their honor.

In Ethiopian Christianity, only men were priests, although, as in Orthodoxy, married men could be accepted into the priesthood. Priests could not marry after ordination, however, and monks were expected to be celibate and ascetic; it was these monks, rather than priests, who provided the intellectual and political leadership in the Ethiopian church.

In northern Africa, the Near East, and parts of Asia, sexual norms and patterns were shaped primarily by Islam, though with some adaptations to local practices. Intermarriage played an important role in the growth of Islam. Arabic traders often married local women to gain access to economic and political power through kin connections; such households then blended Islamic and indigenous marital practices, religious rituals, and norms of behavior for men and women. These blends were also shaped by social class, with elite households generally following Islamic norms more closely than those of more ordinary people.

Women seem to have been quite active in the spread of Islam during Muhammad's lifetime (570–632), but shortly thereafter the seclusion and veiling of women became part of official Muslim law – the shari'a – which is regarded as having divine authority. Marriage in the shari'a was viewed as a reciprocal relationship in which the husband provides support in exchange for the wife's obedience. Seclusion and veiling were marks of class status as well as religious or cultural norms, and appear to have begun among the upper classes, although they were gradually adopted even by quite poor families whenever possible. The seclusion of women was possible in large part because of the expansion of slavery, for slave women – who came from outside Islam and were unveiled – could carry out many basic female tasks such as getting water or marketing. Slave women also served as concubines – the Qur'anic limitation of four wives at any one time did not apply to concubines – and their children were regarded as fully legitimate and free. Marriages were often arranged by family members or marriage brokers, and in some parts of the Islamic world marriages within the extended family were favored in order to promote the consolidation of family property.

The Qur'an recommends marriage for everyone, and women generally married at quite a young age; men often married later when they had established themselves. Because Islam regarded sexuality within marriage or other approved relationships as a positive good, contraception was acceptable and, judging by discussions in medical and legal texts, a fairly common practice. In contrast to Christianity, sexual relations in Islam did not have to be justified by reproduction, though having children, and particularly having sons, was seen as essential to a good life. This lesser emphasis on procreation may have played a role in Islam's toleration of same-sex relations between men; although officially forbidden by Muslim law, they were not punished with any great severity, and in the period of the Abbasid caliphate (750–1258) homoerotic literature praising beautiful young men was a popular genre among some urban circles. Heterosexual relations outside of marriage, especially adultery with a married woman, were punished much more severely for men than were homosexual relations. Same-sex relations between women in the Muslim world have left few literary or legal records, and so are very difficult to study.

Religious beliefs and practices in South Asia were – and are – extremely diverse, with many gods, goddesses, saints, and demons; rich textual, oral, and visual traditions; and religious specialists (priests, monks, holy men and women) of many types. The Muslims and later the Europeans who attempted to understand these religious practices from their own perspectives called them "Hindu," a word that is now used universally to describe the indigenous religions of South Asia. In Hinduism, individuals are understood to be connected to and thus obligated to the deities, and to their ancestors, descendants, and larger kin group. Life moves through various stages, each of which has particular duties and attitudes attached to it, known collectively as *dharma*. Any single life is part of a cycle of successive rebirths, which could be better or worse depending on how one has fulfilled one's duties in previous lives. Society is properly organized in a set of hierarchical social relations, which became formalized in the caste system. Because of the obligation toward the family, all men and women were expected to marry, and having children was viewed as a religious duty. Anything that interfered with procreation, including exclusively same-sex attachments, was viewed negatively. Ascetic practices such as fasting and abstaining from sex were worthy, but such renunciation of worldly things was to be done later in life, once one had already had a family.

Hindu families often attempted to marry their daughters off at a very young age – the recommended age by the year 1000 was between eight and ten – to insure that they were already married before they became sexually mature. People who represented a rupture in the goal of family continuity, such as widows or women who could not bear children, were viewed as unlucky, so they were not welcome at festivities or rituals. They often had a dismal life, though by doing their duty they could always work and hope for a better life in their next birth. For some widows, this understanding of duty included immolation on their husbands' funeral pyres, a practice termed *sati*.

In the Hindu tradition, male sexuality was often celebrated; one of the most important male gods, Siva, was often worshipped in the form of a symbolic phallus, the *lingam*. Female sexuality was regarded more ambiguously, as both creative and destructive; this duality can be seen in the nature of Hindu goddesses, who range from beneficent life-givers such as Devi or Ganga to faithful spouses such as Parvati or Radha to fierce destroyers such as Kali or Durga. In Tantric Hinduism, one of the many variant traditions, adherents emphasized the sexual androgyny of the Supreme Being and incorporated sexual activities as part of their rituals. In northern India, this divine androgyny was replicated in the human world by religious ascetics termed *hijra*, impotent or castrated men who nonetheless are believed to have the power to grant fertility.

During the tenth century, Islam began to spread into parts of India, and Islamic ideas mixed with those of Hinduism to encourage the veiling and seclusion of women – termed purdah – although the strictness and exact rules of this practice varied according to social status and region. In southwest India, the St. Thomas Christians combined Christian with Hindu practices, following many of the same birth, puberty, marriage, and death rituals as their Hindu neighbors. Though they had a loose affiliation with patriarchs in

Persia, each church was largely independent, led by married hereditary archdeacons rather than celibate priests.

Buddhism began in India, and its traditions regarding marriage and the family rested on those of Hinduism. Buddhism taught that life on this earth is suffering, which comes from human desires for wealth, power, sex, and other things. The only way to lessen suffering is to end desire and search for enlightenment (*nirvana*), and the best way to do this is to reject worldly concerns as a solitary ascetic or member of a monastic community. Renouncing the world in favor of the life of a monk or nun made one spiritually superior, so an important way for most people to show their piety was to provide support for monastic communities. In theory, the Buddhist path to enlighten- ment was (and is) open to all, but in reality, Buddhism developed in world permeated with caste and gender distinctions, many of which were carried over into Buddhism. Some Buddhist texts, for example, deemed women incapable of achieving enlightenment unless they first became men. As Buddhism spread from northern India into China, Korea, Ceylon, and Southeast Asia, it split into many different variants, but none of these were completely comfortable with women who renounced family life. The ideal woman in Buddhism – both historically and in sacred texts – was more often a married woman with children who supported a community of monks or who assisted men in their spiritual progress rather than a nun.

In the thirteenth century, Islam began to spread into some parts of Southeast Asia, bringing with it greater expectations for female seclusion. Other parts of Southeast Asia, Australia, and the Pacific islands did not experience the introduction of any text-based religion, however, but remained animist, with local cults of various spirits and deities. Women often served as the religious personnel or spirit mediums in these local religions. Both women and men also took part in rituals of ancestor worship, generally at home altars rather than at specialized temples; deceased ancestors assisted and watched over everyone, in particular warning against possible dangers. These rituals brought together all members of the extended family and were ways to demonstrate one's loyalty to the family and a sense of debt and obligation for having been given life. This sense of moral debt to one's parents and family, termed *òn* in Vietnamese and *hiya* in Tagalog, the language of part of the Philippines, was as powerful as the notion of original sin in Christianity, but it was not linked to sexuality other than obliquely through having been born.

The concepts of debt and obligation were important not only in family life in Southeast Asia, but also in the larger political and economic realm. People were often enmeshed in a complex system of dependency, sometimes placing themselves or family members into slavery to another in return for support – what is often termed "debt-slavery" – or otherwise promising loyalty or service. One also gave gifts in order to have others in one's debt; gift-giving was an important way to make alliances, pacify possible enemies, and create links and networks of obligations among strangers. Often these gifts included women, for exchanging women was considered the best way to transform strangers into relatives. These unions were often accompanied by a marriage ceremony and the expectation of spousal fidelity, but they were also understood to be temporary. If the spouses disagreed with one another or the man returned to his home country, the marriage ended, just as marriages between local spouses ended if there was conflict or one spouse disappeared for a year or more. Both sides gained from such temporary marriages; the woman and her family acted as local liaisons for the foreigner, and thereby gained prestige through their contact with an outsider. Concepts of debt also structured marriage patterns in other ways, as in some Southeast Asian cultures where a prospective groom worked for his father-in-law for a period of time to pay off his debt for his bride. European travelers and officials, used to a system in which women brought a dowry, were often startled at this pattern of bride-service. They were more startled at men who inserted pins or balls into their penis, reportedly to increase women's sexual pleasure, which was rarely a concern of European men.

As in India, some Southeast Asian cultures had ritualized religious roles which were permanently or temporarily androgynous. In the Philippines, religious leaders termed *baylans* or *catalonans* were generally married older women, regarded as to some degree androgynous because they were no longer able to have children. They were thought to be able to communicate with both male and female spirits, and this, in addition to their lack of fertility, gave them greater freedom of movement than younger women had. When men performed rituals as *baylans* or *catalonans*, they wore women's clothing or a mixture of men's and women's clothes. In South Sulawesi (part of Indonesia), individuals termed *bissu* carried out special rituals thought to enhance and preserve the power and fertility of the rulers, which was conceptualized as "white blood," a supernatural fluid that flowed in royal bodies. The *bissu* were linked to the androgynous creator deity; they could be women, but were more often men dressed in women's clothing and performing women's tasks, like the two-spirit people of the Americas.

In China, the dominant philosophical-religious system, known as Confucianism, taught that the order and harmony of the universe began with order and harmony in the smallest human unit; if human affairs were disrupted in families, they would necessarily be disrupted in the larger political realms. The universe was structured in a balanced but hierarchical relationship between the Heavens – the superior, creative element – and earth – the inferior receptive one. Proper human relationships, especially familial ones, were modeled on those of the Heavens and earth, hierarchical and orderly. Loyalty and honor were to be extended to one's living family and to one's ancestors, a quality termed "filial piety."

Sons were needed to carry out the rituals honoring family ancestors properly. As a result, various ways were devised to provide sons for a man whose wife did not have one: taking second or third wives or concubines, legitimizing a son born of a woman who was not a wife or concubine, or adopting a nephew, or an unrelated boy or young man. A woman whose husband had died before she gave birth to a son might be expected to remarry his brother, so as to produce a son who was legally regarded as the child of her deceased husband. In the fifteenth century, however, widow remarriage of all types became less socially acceptable, and widows were expected to be loyal to their husbands' memories.

Even if their wives had sons, most upper-class men had one or more concubines, often poor girls whose parents had sold them to marriage brokers. (To be a wife instead of a concubine, a woman had to bring a dowry, something beyond the reach of poor families.) Until the beginning of the Qing dynasty in 1644, Chinese culture appears to have been tolerant of male same-sex relations, for male homosexual subcultures developed among imperial officials, intellectuals, and actors.

In Confucianism the roles of both women and men were essential to the cosmic order, but men were regarded as superior and women expected to be subordinate and deferential. This emphasis on hierarchy was accompanied by a stronger emphasis on the disruptive power of sexuality during the reinvigorated Confucian movement of the Song dynasty (960–1279). Sexual attraction was regarded as so powerful that individuals alone could not control it; walls, laws, and strong social sanctions were needed to keep men and women apart. In many parts of China, women of the middle and upper classes were increasingly secluded, and even peasant houses were walled; boys and girls were cheap to hire as servants for tasks that needed to be done outside the walls. Female seclusion was also accomplished through footbinding, a practice that began in the Song period among elite women and was gradually adopted by the vast majority of the female population in central and northern China.

Confucian notions of hierarchy and order found strong resonance in Japan, but Japan was religiously pluralistic, with traditional Japanese religion (later termed Shinto) mixing with Buddhism and other imported religious beliefs. Many of these belief systems held ambivalent ideas about sexuality: women carried out important religious rituals, yet were also regarded as sources of pollution through menstruation and childbirth; Buddhist monks were encouraged to abstain from all sex, yet same-sex relationships between monks and acolytes were common and sometimes celebrated in Buddhist monasteries.

As in China, male homosexuality in both Japan and Korea was largely tolerated among certain groups, such as officials and intellectuals.

From this brief survey, it is evident that norms and patterns of sexuality in Africa and Asia fit with those of European Christianity in some regards, but differed markedly in others. The emphasis on procreation, and particularly the birth of sons, was largely shared, as was the notion that marriage was an important matter and fundamental to social order. The very centrality of marriage and procreation also generated differences, however, for in most of the world's cultures, marriages were arranged by families and could be dissolved or additional wives secured if the first marriage failed to produce children. The consent of the spouses – especially that of the wife or wives – was not a major concern. Many cultures also allowed a range of sexual relationships rather than a strict dichotomy between married and unmarried, with the children of these unions often able to inherit, but normally disadvantaged in some way compared with the children of the primary wife or wives. In cultures with text-based religions, sexual desire was generally regarded as powerful and dangerous if it was socially disruptive, but not in itself evil. Thus there was no censure of any type of sexual activity between spouses, and little censure of men's sexual relationships, whether heterosexual or homosexual, unless they interfered with marriage. Women's sexuality was often feared or regarded ambiguously; women were accused of seducing men from their true religious and political duties – a point of agreement with Christianity – but the actual treatment of sexually active unmarried women varied tremendously by class, location, and specific situation. The treatment of married women who had sex with men not their husbands was uniformly harsh, however, but except in Muslim areas, such cases were handled by the family or political authorities, not religious courts.

Christian institutions

As noted in the last chapter, European exploration and the establishment of trading outposts in Africa and Asia began in the mid-fifteenth century, with Portuguese ventures on the Atlantic islands and the west coast of Africa. In 1505 the Portuguese established a colony on Ceylon, and in 1510, another at Goa on the west coast of India. Over the next decades they set up other colonies at Melaka (Malacca), Cochin, Macao and a number of other ports. In 1565, traveling from Mexico, the Spanish established a permanent colony on the island of Cebu in the Philippines, and in 1571 on the island of Luzon. During the seventeenth century, the Dutch East India Company (VOC) began both to take over Portuguese centers and to establish their own, founding a colony on Ceylon and at Batavia on the island of Java in the early seventeenth century, and in many other parts of Asia, along with South Africa, in the mid-seventeenth century. In all of these colonies and trading centers, religious personnel were part of the European presence. In addition, first Catholic and then (a few) Protestant missionaries traveled to countries not under European control such as China, Japan, and Vietnam in order to gain converts. Adding to this complex picture were indigenous Christian groups in southwest India and Ethiopia. In each of these situations, the institutions established and operated by religious authorities for the control of sexuality were quite different.

Portuguese colonies and mission areas

The first Portuguese colonies were established on many of the Atlantic islands, including the Azores, Cape Verdes, Madeira, and São Tomé. Most of these were uninhabited before Portuguese colonization, so that Catholicism was the only official religion, with the church under the control of the Portuguese crown. The Cape Verdes and São Tomé became independent dioceses in the 1530s, and the crown hoped to use them as a springboard for further missionary work on the African continent. Their populations quickly became a mixture of Portuguese and African, and some Africans or men of mixed race traveled to Portugal for clerical training. A seminary was opened on São Tomé in 1571, but it operated only fitfully, and the total number of Africans or Eurafricans who received priestly ordination there was small. Nevertheless, the Atlantic islands themselves were one of the few places where institutions such as episcopal courts and the Inquisition were not staffed totally by Europeans.

From their island bases, Portuguese traders set up permanent fortified trading posts along the coast of West Africa. The kings of Portugal made treaties with the rulers of coastal African states such as Benin, Oyo, and Kongo, supplying them with wool cloth, tools, and weapons, in return for gold, cotton cloth, ivory, and slaves. A few missionaries ventured inland from the coast, working to convert people. They had the greatest success in the Kingdom of the Kongo, a powerful state including parts of what is now the Republic of Congo, Zaire, and Angola.

Kongo was ruled by the *manikongo*, or king, who had both religious and political power and appointed governors for its six provinces. In the 1490s, priests began the first official Catholic mission to the Kongo, and interpreted a dream that two local nobles had simultaneously as apparition of the Virgin Mary. Other revelations followed, and there were many converts, including the manikongo Nzinga Nkuwu (ruled to 1506), who took the Christian name João I, the same name as the king of Portugal. The next manikongo, Nzinga Mbemba, whose Christian name was Afonso I (ruled 1506–43), was raised as a Christian, and worked to convert his subjects to Christianity. He wrote a series of letters to the king of Portugal complaining about the priests sent to him, and also about merchants who traded European goods for slaves. "We need from your kingdom no more than some priests and a few people to teach in schools," Afonso wrote, but not priests "who fill their houses with women of ill repute" such as one who "took a woman into his house who bore him a mixed-race child."[2] The King of Portugal did nothing about the slave trade, though the quality of priests apparently improved later in the century.

Many of the ideas of Christianity — an unseen realm of divine figures and spirits that revealed itself through visions, priests with special powers, an initiation ritual involving water and signifying rebirth — paralleled religious ideas already present in the Kongo area, and many people were baptized as Christians. Churches and chapels were built in all Kongolese provinces in the sixteenth century, each dedicated to a saint who was often chosen through revelation and linked to an otherworldly being already venerated in the area. Capuchin and later Jesuit missionaries gradually learned KiKongo, so that they could hear confessions and preach in the local vernacular; the first book printed in a Bantu language was a bilingual catechism in Portuguese and KiKongo, written in 1556 and printed in 1624. In the early seventeenth century the Jesuits opened a college in Kongo, and established confraternities for men and women. Other religious orders also established their own lay confraternities, designed to enhance Christian practice; those who kept concubines or who practiced non-Christian rituals were formally banned from these groups. Although many converts did not have a Christian wedding, as this would have required identifying only one woman as the wife, those that did occur were celebrated in grand style; as one report from 1645 noted, "even slaves dress up as if great lords, with a great escort they go to church where they hear mass, take communion and contract marriage according to the form of the Roman Church, then go back with a great escort."[3]

In India and the Portuguese colonies in the islands of Southeast Asia, conversion was a slow process for the first several decades, and the Portuguese clergy were often quite lax, living with local women just like the soldiers and merchants did. As one visitor reported in 1522, "the clergy and the friars are . . . for the most part very corrupt, and through their bad example the piety of the Christians of the country is gravely destroyed."[4] With the arrival of clergy inspired by the Catholic Reformation in the 1540s, more rigorous standards were demanded of the clergy, and more intense efforts against existing religious practices began. Zealous clergy were particularly offended by Hindu ideas that the gods engaged in sex and created through procreation; they destroyed statues and images and tore down temples, building Christian churches on the same sites. In a few places there were mass forced conversions, leading Hindus to emigrate and build temples right outside the boundaries of European colonies. Most conversions were of individuals and small groups, however, generally from the lower and middle castes.

People were particularly attracted by the many representations of the Virgin Mary, who exhibited qualities similar to those of Hindu goddesses or Buddhist divine beings and whose churches were often built on places already viewed as holy. Statues and paintings showing her carrying the infant Jesus provided evidence of Christian compassion, as well as the close link between parent and child that was part of Confucian notions of filial piety and Southeast Asian notions of debt to one's family.

Hindu and Buddhist ceremonies, including marriage, were prohibited within the boundaries of Portuguese colonies. Existing marriages between converts were blessed by a priest if they were found acceptable according to Christian rules about consanguinity and other matters. In many cases dispensations were needed and there was some question about whether authorities had been given adequate authority to grant them or whether such cases needed to be referred back to Portugal, a slow and arduous process.

Given the difficulties of relying on the Portuguese church for decisions, independent higher institutions were established locally. Goa became a bishopric in 1534, and an archbishopric in 1558; there were additional bishoprics at Cochin and Melaka. The first church council held in Asia was at Goa in 1567; among its many decrees, polygamy was forbidden, and men were ordered to live only with their first wife or to take one of their concubines as a wife. Subsequent councils passed resolutions against *sati* – though the practice was rare in the Goa area – and offered widows who converted inheritance and property rights. Clergy frequently noted that women who converted were more enthusiastic in their devotion than were men, and this improvement in their social standing may be one of the reasons.

Asian bishops and councils were under the authority of both the Portuguese monarch and the pope, and Portuguese religious officials became increasingly unhappy with the fact that the St. Thomas Christians were not. In 1599, Aleixo da Menezes, the archbishop of Goa, arranged for a meeting with representatives of the St. Thomas church, and maneuvered them into agreeing to unite with the Catholic Church, swear allegiance to Rome, and affirm the decrees of the Council of Trent. They were allowed to conduct their services in Syriac instead of Latin, but otherwise were ordered to follow Roman practices; archdeacons were expected to be celibate, although some continued to pass on their titles, but to nephews instead of sons. (In 1652 some St. Thomas Christians renounced their ties to Rome, creating two separate Christian communities.)

The Ethiopian Christian Church was also independent of Rome and followed its own patterns. In the early sixteenth century, Ethiopian envoys asked for Portuguese aid against Muslim forces, and Catholic missionaries accompanied the small force that responded. They had little success in converting Ethiopian Christians or Muslims to Catholicism. In the late sixteenth century, Jesuit missionaries were sent from Goa to Ethiopia with orders to convert the king to loyalty to Rome. Interested in Catholicism and hoping for Portuguese military assistance, King Susenyos converted in 1622, dismissing all of his wives except one as a sign of his new allegiance. Conversions never went much beyond the court, however, and attempts to introduce Catholic practices more widely led to rebellion. Susenyos allowed the Ethiopian Church free worship again, and in 1634 the Jesuits were expelled from the kingdom.

Once bishoprics were established, the Inquisition began to operate in Portuguese colonies; it was set up in Goa in 1560 and held its first *auto-da-fé* there in 1563. All European Christians were under its jurisdiction, as was anyone who had converted and been baptized, and it frequently investigated and tried those who had returned to practices regarded as non-Christian. This group often included "New Christians" – Portuguese whose families had been Jewish or Muslim but had converted – as well as former Hindus and animists. In some areas, such as the Atlantic islands, local men became officials in the Inquisition along with the Portuguese, but they had a somewhat lesser status because they were barred from taking part in cases that involved Jews, Muslims, or members of the clergy.

In the earliest decades of Portuguese colonialism, there was an expectation that an indigenous clergy would develop, and there were occasional attempts to provide for the training of local priests. A seminary was opened in Portuguese Goa in 1541; it was soon taken over by the Jesuits, who also brought the first printing press there in 1556. Though most seminarians were members of high-caste groups such as Brahmins or had European fathers, Portuguese authorities wanted them kept in subordinate positions, and they even refused to recognize the pope's appointment of Matthaeus de Castro, a Brahmin from Goa, as a bishop and vicar-apostolate. Despite this hostility, the number of native clergy in India continued to grow, although it was never sufficient to meet the needs of the widely scattered converts, and non-Europeans were never accepted as full members of religious orders in any Portuguese colony.

As in Latin America, various lay religious groups were formed in the Portuguese colonies in Africa and Asia. Religious confraternities of men and women were established, such as those of the Rosary in Melaka and Ceylon and on the southeast coast of India. Confraternities carried out charity work among the poor and sick, cared for their own members, and encouraged their members to give up non-Christian religious and cultural practices. They also helped preserve Catholicism when the Portuguese colonies were taken over by the Dutch in the seventeenth century, who banished Catholic clergy and destroyed Catholic churches or transformed them into Protestant ones. In Ceylon, devout families hid priests, as had Catholic families in Protestant England, and despite sporadic persecutions by Dutch authorities, the number of Catholics grew. By the middle of the eighteenth century, Protestant Dutch authorities reported that priests "openly by day practice their seductive religious exercises with the pealing of bells and the exposition of their idolatrous images; yes, and they even baptize and marry the people in their own sheds at their meeting places."[5] Catholics were far more numerous than Protestants on Ceylon when the Dutch were driven out by the British in 1796.

The Philippines

The Spanish program in the Philippines was directly influenced by the Spanish experience in Mexico, and members of religious orders were again in the forefront of both missionary work and political control. Because there were a large number of native languages in the islands, each order was assigned a specific area, so that its members would only have to learn a few of the native languages. Tagalog, the language spoken in the area around the Spanish settlement at Manila, was the most common language learned by Europeans, and the most commonly used for printed religious materials. The first book printed in the Philippines was a statement of faith from 1593, printed in Tagalog in both the Latin and traditional Filipino alphabet. (That alphabet did not survive long after Spanish conquest; Tagalog is now written in Latin letters.) In order to hold their small groups of converts together, missionaries sought to establish compact settlements, intentionally modeling these on the *reducciones* of Latin America, but they met great resistance and most people lived near the missionary and church only on holidays. As among the Aztec and Inca, there was to be no toleration of native religion. Missionaries cut down sacred groves of trees, trained boys to find the sacred objects used in indigenous rituals in order to destroy them, and punished local shamans, as the Dominican Diego Aduarte reported in 1600:

> The little idols that they had kept hidden . . . were handed over to the Christian boys to drag through the whole village, and at last they were burned. By this means and by the punishment of a few old women who acted as priestesses and who were called *catalonans*, the idolatry of the whole region was brought to a end.[6]

Priests Christianized childbirth and funeral rituals, offering pictures of the saints and the Virgin Mary instead to assist people through difficult times.

Missionaries reported high numbers of baptisms, although they were distressed that so many people regarded the ritual as one to cure physical ailments or establish relationships of indebtedness with godparents, rather than make salvation possible. Preaching and confession were avenues of deepening Christian understanding, so missionaries learned Tagalog and translated hymns and confessional manuals.

Confessional manuals indicate that sexual sins were an important concern of clergy; desires as well as actions were to be described and confessed. One manual suggests these questions for a priest to ask: "I also suspect that every time you saw her or thought of her, you also lusted after her. Isn't this the case? And because of your lust, did you do anything to your body, any kind of lewdness? And did your body emit something dirty?"[7] A commentary on the Ten Commandments written in Tagalog by a Spanish cleric similarly railed against both acts and desires: "Everyone is burning with sexual passion and is evil in his heart towards the Lord God. Impurity has become man's favorite activity, and is engaged in without shame or fear . . . You would really be punished by the Lord God if you looked at a woman with desire, or the same would happen if a woman did a similar thing to a man, for they want to commit adultery in their hearts."[8]

Missionaries often saw sexual control as a near-miraculous sign of conversion in both men and women, relating many stories like the following:

> A certain woman, to whom God our Lord had communicated lofty purpose and sentiments of chastity and purity, was for a long time beset with gifts and importunities from wicked men. Her refuge was to confess and devoutly to receive communion, arming herself with these holy sacraments. One day, after she had received communion in our house, one of these men lay to wait to seize her when alone; and, with a bare dagger at her breast, was about to slay her if she would not consent to his evil purpose. But she, fortified with the bread of the strong and with the wine springing forth virgins, told him she was ready to die on the spot, rather than offend God. He abused her with words, and even handled her roughly, but left her, astonished and overcome by her chastity.[9]

> Another [man], giving up all thought of God and of his own salvation, had spent many years in dreadful sin, and especially in a disgraceful lust, which was so deeply rooted and fixed in his innermost heart that he regarded our priest, who strove to lead his away from this vile

manner of life, as only less than a fool. So completely had he plunged himself into the filth of these pollutions of his soul, that, like a sow in a wallow, he seemed to take pleasure in nothing else. Yet at last this obstinate man yielded to argument and persuasion, and not only gave up visiting his harlot, but tore all lust from his heart by the roots as completely as if he had no knowledge of it; for by a general confession of the lapses of his past life he so corrected his morals that all those who knew him were amazed at the sudden change in his life.[10]

Filipino converts sometimes used more extreme measures than confession and communion to maintain themselves in "chastity and purity." In the late sixteenth century, missionaries introduced the practice of self-flagellation as a form of penance, and public rituals in which men scourged themselves became a common feature during Lent and on Fridays throughout the year. (These continue in some areas of the Philippines today, and have become a tourist attraction, although the Filipino Catholic Church has recommended more interior forms of penance instead.) Flagellants were often members of lay confraternities, with women's confraternities organized to support their actions and for other charitable and devotional purposes.

Given the reports of great numbers of enthusiastic converts, the Crown urged the ordination of more Filipino clergy. The members of religious orders in the Philippines, most of whom were from Spain, refused to do this, however, and by 1750 there were still only a few Filipino clergy, most in subordinate positions. As in Latin America, the arguments against training indigenous clergy in the Philippines emphasized Filipinos' supposed inability to maintain a celibate life, or as Archbishop Filipe Pardo put it in 1680, because of "their evil customs, their vices, and their preconceived ideas . . . the sloth produced by the climate, effeminacy, and levity of disposition. Even the sons of Spaniards, born in the islands, [are] unsuitable for priests, since they were reared by Indian or slave women."[11]

Religious authorities were also wary about religious houses for indigenous women. The first convent for Spanish women was founded in 1620, but not until 1697 did they admit a Filipino woman, and that only as a result of a royal order. The Jesuits sponsored the establishment of several small *beaterios*, uncloistered communities where women spent their time in prayer, care of the poor, and other charitable activities. Only in 1721 was an actual convent especially for indigenous women opened, and even after this most of the Filipino women who lived in religious communities continued to be servants or lay sisters rather than professed nuns.

Despite these limitations, by 1750 a large proportion of the Filipino population identified themselves as Christians. They were married in Christian ceremonies, and at least occasionally relied on a priest for advice on moral and sexual matters.

Dutch VOC colonies

As we saw in Chapter 2, the Reformed Church in the Netherlands was Calvinist in its theology and Presbyterian in its organization; social discipline was carried out by consistories, rather than by episcopal courts or the Inquisition, and was to some degree independent of state interference. This situation changed somewhat in the Dutch colonies, where the "state" was a private company, the VOC. The directors of the VOC thought it important to provide religious personnel for their own employees and to combat Catholicism in formerly Portuguese areas, but it kept these clergy strictly under VOC control. In the Dutch colonies, clergy of the Dutch Reformed Church were under the authority of VOC officials and were paid directly by the VOC, as were schoolmasters. The few who did not agree with VOC policies suffered. George Candidius, for example, was too vocal in his opposition to VOC toleration of informal marriages; he lost his post in the Moluccas in 1627, and was sent to a more challenging position in Formosa.

Not surprisingly, the VOC had difficulty finding and retaining suitable men, and in some places augmented these positions with "Comforters of the Sick" – lower-class men from the Netherlands charged with visiting the sick and holding prayer meetings – and "Proponents" – mixed-race or native laymen who were given a bit of theological training and expected to give religious instruction in local languages. Seminaries were also established at various times on Ceylon, but these were not particularly successful, and very few native clergy from anywhere in Asia were ordained. Consistories modeled on those in the Netherlands attempted to regulate sexual and moral conduct by imposing religious sanctions such as excommunication, and they could be very active. In Batavia, for example, during the period 1677–93 over 800 people were censured by the consistory, about half of them for sexual or marital matters.[12] Women predominated among those charged with sexual offenses, while men were more often charged with drunkenness, fighting, or not going to church.

Patterns of conversion varied widely in VOC colonies. In the Cape Colony of South Africa, the VOC was completely uninterested in converting either indigenous people or the slaves it imported, and very few non-Europeans became Christians. In many Asian VOC trading posts, conversion to Reformed Christianity was almost entirely the result of intermarriage, though in a few places, such as Ceylon, Amboina, and Formosa, more widespread conversion occurred, generally among those who stood to gain financially or politically from conversion. In these cases whole villages sometimes converted en masse after a Proponent or other native Christian convinced them of the spiritual and practical benefits of Christianity; baptism and church services were held in native languages whenever possible, with the sermon, rather than confession, the main method through which Christian doctrine was communicated to adults. The first translation of the New Testament into a Southeast Asian language was into high Malay by a Dutch missionary in 1688, but as literacy levels were low, conversion remained largely an oral process. In some areas, such as Ceylon, the VOC supported the opening of primary schools for local children as well as those of Dutch fathers, because it viewed children as better candidates for conversion than adults; the actual establishment of such schools was more sporadic than company officials hoped, however. Opportunities to learn about Christian doctrine were so limited that church officials debated whether baptism should be separated from participation in communion, for the reformed church held that only those who had some basic knowledge of Christian teachings and whose lives at least loosely followed Christian patterns should take communion. (Women who had children out of wedlock, for example, were denied communion.) In some colonies, such as Amboina, the separation of sacraments became the norm and facilitated conversions on a larger scale. In others, such as Batavia, it was rejected on moral as well as theological grounds; opponents argued that this policy would discourage marriage, or as one put it, "Whoremongers already openly rejoice in the separation of the sacraments, as they can easily get their concubines baptized."[13] Indigenous women in Batavia who married Dutch men had to attend confirmation classes and be examined; though it is impossible to tell how they understood Christian doctrine, expectations about behavior were apparently being communicated, as the percentage of women among individuals denied admission to communion on moral grounds steadily decreased throughout the seventeenth century.

Japan and China

In the situations described so far in this chapter, the development of Christian institutions occurred within the context of European colonialism. In Japan and China, Jesuits and other missionaries also accompanied European traders, but they operated within the spheres allowed them by the existing government.

In Japan, political disunity in the mid-sixteenth century, combined with the desire on the part of some Japanese nobles for European military technology, gave Jesuit missionaries beginning with Francis Xavier (1506–52) the opportunity for large-scale conversions, including some members of the ruling class. Jesuits presented Christianity as a unified system of faith and practice, not revealing that it was in the midst of enormous upheaval, reformation, and splintering in Europe; this unity made it particularly appealing at a time of warfare and disruption. Particularly under the leadership of Alessandro Valignano (1539–1606), Jesuits learned Japanese and produced a number of catechisms and devotional books in various Japanese scripts. They built churches, trained indigenous assistants (termed *dojuku* and *kambo*), and began to train an indigenous clergy. In the 30-year period between 1581 and 1611, nearly one hundred men were admitted into the Jesuit order, a good share of whom were ordained as priests. Some members of the nobility declared for Christianity, often ordering their subjects to receive baptism as well. For

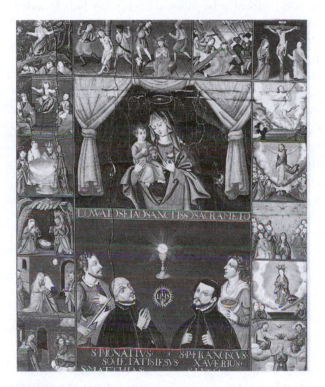

Figure 5.1

This painting depicting the Fifteen Mysteries of the Rosary was designed to be used as an aid to conversion in Japan. Painted by a Japanese convert to Catholicism, it shows the Virgin and Christ Child in the middle and Ignatius Loyola and Francis Xavier at the bottom along with two saints. The artist based his painting on images that the Jesuits brought with them from Europe. Parish priests and Jesuits often distributed such pictures to lay people, including children, to help educate them in matters of doctrine and remind them of the saints' virtues in order to encourage imitation. By permission of the Kyoto University Museum.

some nobles, the primary attraction was European trade goods and military technology, but for others the appeal included the Christian ethical code and notion of absolute obedience to an ultimate God.

Common people, especially in the southern Japanese island of Kyushu, converted as well, drawn by the Christian idea of a transcendent salvation and moral teachings. Lay converts set up confraternities that collected and distributed donations for the poor and set up hospitals. Converts included many women, who sometimes learned Latin and Portuguese in order to better study Christian literature. The women persuaded women and men to convert, disputed with Buddhist priests, translated and wrote religious works, preached sermons, baptized children and women, and taught catechism. In the early seventeenth century, a former Buddhist abbess Naito Julia founded a community of women catechists in Kyoto, whose "principal work," wrote a seventeenth-century Jesuit historian, "was teaching Christian Doctrine to pagan ladies and exhorting them to convert to the holy faith." Such work was especially needed, he commented, "because in Japan it was the custom for upper-class ladies and their daughters not to go out to see men, even clerics."[14] By 1580 there were more than 100,000 Christians in Japan, and by 1610 perhaps as many as 300,000, a higher percentage of the Japanese population at that time than during any later period.

Later in the sixteenth century the political situation changed, and leaders attempting to unify Japan became convinced – in part through the arguments of Protestant Dutch and English traders opposed to Portuguese or Jesuit influence – that Christians were intent on military conquest and overthrowing the government. Christian sexual morals provided additional grounds for suspicion; Fabian Fucan, a Japanese convert who subsequently renounced Christianity commented, "Jesus was born from a couple who had sworn chastity. What kind of a virtuous ideal is that? . . . The universal norm is that every man and every woman should marry. To go against that natural law is evil."[15] Edicts were passed in 1587 and 1614 expelling all missionaries and Japanese Christian leaders from Japan; many of these went to Manila in the Philippines, including fifteen women catechists from Kyoto. The 1614 edict was enforced by executions and gruesome torture designed to force Christians to recant. The Shimabara Revolt of 1637–38, in which peasants protested their conditions, was led by Japanese Christians in Kyushu; this resulted in a final exclusion order of 1639, banning any further visits by Portuguese ships or interaction with Catholic lands. In 1641 all contact with Europeans was limited to a small island in the Nagasaki harbor run by the Dutch East India Company. Many historians think that the perceived threat of Christianity was a central factor in Japan's decision to implement a "closed door" policy, which lasted until the 1860s.

Japanese rulers assumed they had obliterated Christianity, but despite an extensive system of surveillance with monetary rewards offered for the exposure of Christians, Christianity survived as an underground religion in remote farming and fishing villages of northern Kyushu and some smaller islands. These "hidden Christians" had no clergy, but lay leaders secretly taught, kept records, and baptized; they maintained their community by marrying within the group, and gradually developed a distinctive version of Christianity. When Japan was reopened in the 1860s, these Japanese Christians contacted Catholic priests, who were astounded to learn of their existence; half of the Catholics in Japan today are descendents of the "hidden Christians."

Christian conversion was less extensive in China than in Japan. Portuguese ships were on the Chinese coast by 1513, and a Portuguese trade mission went to Beijing in 1520, accompanied by missionaries. Most Chinese viewed the earliest missionaries as representing a variant sect of Buddhism rather than a new religion (this happened in Japan as well), and later the literary and philosophical activities of the Jesuit Matteo Ricci (1552–1610) led them to view missionaries as Confucian scholars from the west. Many of the ethical teachings of Christianity fit well with Confucian ideas, as Ricci noted in his *The True Meaning of the Lord of Heaven*, an explanation in Chinese of Catholic Christianity in terms of Confucian learning printed in Beijing in 1603. Even clerical celibacy could be understood as "a test of virtue," argued Ricci, and was not necessarily a break with filial piety and respect for ancestors:

> If it were really the case that a lack of progeny represents an unfilial attitude, then every son ought to devote himself from morning to night to the task of begetting children in order to ensure the existence of later generations. He should not interrupt his task even for a day. But does this not mean leading a man into bondage to sex? . . . The fact is that filial piety or the lack of it resides in the mind and is not something external; whether we have sons or not is determined by the Lord of Heaven.[16]

Christian sexual ideas regarding lay people were harder to accept, however, and the chief obstacle to baptism among many of the intellectuals and political leaders otherwise attracted to Christianity was the requirement that they first give up their concubines and secondary wives. The raising of children – especially sons – was central to Chinese values, and missionaries were criticized for encouraging "some girls [to] renounce marriage for ever."[17] As we will see in more detail below, some Chinese converts urged accommodation on such issues, though others collaborated with European Jesuits to produce moral tracts that criticized certain aspects of traditional Chinese sexual morality, including the acceptance of concubinage and homosexual relationships. In the later seventeenth century missionaries traveled to many parts of China beyond Beijing, so that in many cities there were significant Christian communities, for which hundreds of catechisms and devotional books were published.

As in Japan, Chinese men were admitted as members of the Jesuit order. They were (sometimes explicitly) considered honorary whites; most (though not all) European missionaries saw them as members of highly developed cultures and thus better prepared for leadership positions than darker-skinned Christians found elsewhere in Asia or Africa. The first Chinese priest, Luo Wenzao (baptized Gregorio Lopez) was ordained in 1654, and later was named as a bishop, although his appointment was fought by many in the church hierarchy. In contrast to Japan, however, the number of Chinese priests was never very high. As they had in Europe and European colonies, beginning in the 1620s Jesuits in China founded confraternities for lay men and women, generally dedicated to the Virgin Mary. The confraternities gathered together several times a year to hear Mass and take communion, and many met more often on their own without a priest to pray and worship. The primary operation of the Catholic Church in China continued to rely on European clergy, however, who were often divided by loyalties to their various religious orders and countries of origin. This situation, combined with changing politics at court, produced alternating periods of acceptance and repression. There was never a persecution campaign as severe as that in Japan, but by 1750 Christianity in China had far less influence than it had fifty or one hundred years earlier.

Other mission situations

In mainland Southeast Asia, as in East Asia, European missionaries worked within states headed by indigenous rulers. The Jesuits first came to Vietnam in 1615, and members of other orders followed. French missionaries under the supervision of the Missions étrangères de Paris established a base in Siam, and sent priests from there into Burma, Vietnam, and Cambodia. Conversions occurred among people at all social levels, and a few indigenous men were ordained as priests and appointed as lay catechists. The Jesuit missionary Alexandre de Rhodes (1591–1660) set up communities of women, termed "Amantes de la Croix" (Lovers of the Cross), who took vows of poverty, chastity, and obedience. They carried out religious devotions, and also ministered to the poor and the sick. These communities were similar in many ways to the Buddhist convents that had long been in Vietnam, although they attracted young women along with the older widows who more commonly became Buddhist nuns. Missionaries reported powerful religious zeal among the Amantes de la Croix, including one young woman who pressed a medallion of the Sacred Heart of Jesus that had been heated in the fire against her chest, "imprinting her body with this sacred image."[18] Parents who had converted sometimes supported their daughters in this choice of celibacy over marriage, though others objected, as this meant the women would not produce the sons needed to carry out rituals honoring family ancestors properly.

During the early eighteenth century, a few Protestant missionaries went to other European colonies besides those run by the VOC. Most of them were part of a movement within European Protestantism known as pietism that focused on personal holiness and spiritual commitment. The German Lutheran pastor Bartholomew Ziegenbalg, for example, went to the tiny Danish colony of Tranquebar on the southeast coast of India and translated the New Testament into Tamil in 1714; he also advocated the training of indigenous catechists and the ordination of indigenous clergy, a process that proceeded slowly.

As the British East India Company established itself as a major power in parts of India in the eighteenth century, small numbers of Protestant and Catholic missionaries worked to convert indigenous people within its territories. German Protestant missionaries were active in southern India, and Italian Catholics in northeastern India. In the state of Bettiah, for example, Italian missionaries were permitted to establish a confraternity among Indian Christians "composed of all the headmen in order to take care of observing all the religious customs . . . and in addition to judge and punish the delinquents."[19] In general the East India Company was not very supportive of missionaries, however, because it thought their activities disrupted trade. It did provide chaplains for its own employees, who were, at least in theory, under the jurisdiction of the Anglican Church and its marital and sexual regulations. In practice, company employees in the seventeenth and early eighteenth centuries rarely brought their wives with them, but developed various informal relationships with local women; chaplains rarely commented on sexual matters and even more rarely brought them to the Company's attention.

Elsewhere in Asia and the Pacific, there was little development of Christian institutions before 1750, and none that has been studied in great detail. There were women on the Spanish expeditions to the Solomon and Marquesas Islands in the 1590s. In fact, the wife of one of the expedition leaders declared herself "queen" of the South Pacific when her husband died, a claim that was never ratified by the Spanish Crown. Yet we know very little about such women or about the development and impact of Christian institutions there. There were no women on the European exploration and trading ventures along the Australian coast, a fact which occasioned comment from the aboriginal inhabitants, particularly as these men all had their bodies covered; in aboriginal eyes, such a covered-up, single-sex group must be either hostile or sacred, and there are reports that the Europeans were asked to remove their clothes and prove that they were, indeed, all men. Permanent European settlement in Australia did not begin until 1788.

Effects of Christian regulation

As one would expect, the actual impact of Christian efforts to regulate sexuality varied widely and is often very difficult to trace. Some matters cut across geographic and denominational lines, however, for Christian authorities were faced with certain issues in nearly every colonial context. The two most important issues were the blending of existing marital and sexual practices with those of Christianity – often understood from the Christian side as "accommodation" – and the treatment of interracial sexual relationships, including marriage. Both of these were linked to wider concerns shared by religious and secular authorities, and had implications for colonial social and economic policy, as well as Christian teachings.

Accommodation to existing practices

The blending of Christian and local practices in terms of sexual issues was part of the wider cultural negotiation and creolization that occurred in every colonial context. Some historians lay greater stress on elements of the original cultures that were different from one another and so resisted creolization; for example, they view African religions and Christianity as parallel systems that maintained significant continuities over long eras despite the diaspora caused by the slave trade. Others highlight similarities and adaptations; in their opinion, Africans, in this example, developed a distinct form of Christianity through the creative blending of many elements, which they carried with them in the diaspora. This scholarly debate – which ranges over other areas as well as Africa – incorporates many topics, including cosmology, theology, and ceremonies. Changes and continuities in marriage and other sexual relationships provide evidence for both sides of the debate.

In many parts of Africa and Asia, the prominent men who missionaries most hoped to convert had multiple wives and sometimes concubines, an issue that proved especially challenging. In a royal court of West Africa, the Dutchman Willem Bosman reported that a Portuguese Catholic missionary was trying "to convert the Blacks to Christianity, but in vain. Polygamy is an obstacle which they cannot get over. As for all other Points they might have got Footing here, but the Confinement to one Wife is an insuperable Difficulty." When the priest threatened damnation, an advisor to the king defended the practice, noting that "Our Fathers, Grandfathers, to an endless Number,

Liv'd as we do, and Worship'd the same Gods as we do, and they must burn therefore. Patience, we are not better than our Ancestors, and shall comfort ourselves [in hell] with them."[20] The repudiation of wives was not an easy matter, especially for powerful men whose marriages cemented political alliances; in India, the family of one displaced wife killed the missionary who had inspired this action. The requirement of marital monogamy was also often difficult for men who were otherwise intellectually and spiritually prepared to convert. The Chinese intellectual Yang T'ing-yün, for example, delayed his own baptism for years, commenting: "The western fathers are really strange . . . Can they not allow me to have just one concubine?"[21]

Some missionaries took a hard line about this, refusing to baptize men until they gave up all but one of their wives or married one of their concubines; anything else would be, in the word some of them used, both a real and meta-phorical "bastardization" of true Christianity. Diogo Gonçalves, a Portuguese Jesuit working in India in the early seventeenth century, linked polygyny among the Hindu population directly to other issues, noting "Not only is it false, the sect of these pagans, in what they teach about God, as we saw; but it is false in what they teach about the ultimate goal [of life] since they locate it in carnal pleasure with many women."[22] Other missionaries were more moderate, and viewed the accommodation of multiple wives as a tactical move. They justified their leniency by arguing that people needed to grow into Christian under-standing and that Christian practice would eventually follow from baptism and teaching. Many of these arguments, particularly those justifying mass baptisms, are both racist and paternalistic, because they assume that the people concerned are too simple to understand the complexities of Christianity but nonetheless could be baptized because they have agreed to believe whatever the missionaries tell them and would eventually change their ways.

In Japan, divorce was a bigger issue than polygyny. François Caron, who worked for twenty years for the VOC in Japan and had five children with a Japanese woman, noted that "One Man hath but one Wife, though as many Concubines as he can keep; and if that Wife do not please him, he may put her away, provided he dismiss her in a civil and honorable way."[23] Valignano, the head of the Jesuit mission, recognized that Christian opposition to divorce kept many Japanese from converting (especially prominent men, whose conversions would have brought political benefits) and tried unsuccessfully to obtain at least a temporary relaxation of the Tridentine legislation on marriage. The prohibition of divorce also created problems for female converts. Chinese merchants often lived in temporary marriages with Japanese women, and then returned to China, leaving the women and their children behind. If the Japanese woman was a Christian, there may have been a Christian wedding, a ceremony that was unimportant to the Chinese merchant, but of great importance in the eyes of the church. Valignano tried to gain some flexibility from his superiors on this issue, but this was not forthcoming, and the abandoned women thus were not allowed to remarry in a Christian ceremony. Traditional marital patterns ultimately asserted themselves among Japan's "hidden Christians," who freely divorced and remarried. (This, plus their intermarriage within a small circle, would pose problems in the nineteenth century when European missionaries returned and attempted to convince them to rejoin Catholicism.)

Missionaries operating within cultures with a strong textual tradition, such as Confucianism, Buddhism, or Hinduism, viewed accommodation as an intellectual as well as practical issue, and they debated the degree to which certain practices were not merely tolerable, but spiritually and philosophically compatible with Christianity. The debate over accommodation emerged first in China, where it came to be known as the "Chinese Rites controversy." The dispute centered on ancestor worship, funeral customs, and the words used for God. Those missionaries who regarded ancestor worship as compatible with Christianity – generally Jesuit followers of Matteo Ricci – argued that these were civic rituals designed to promote family cohesion, essentially veneration rather than worship and hence similar to the veneration of the saints. Those who opposed ancestor worship – generally Spanish Dominicans who had come to China from the Philippines – argued that it constituted paganism, and they opposed any adaptation to Chinese customs. A similar dispute (often termed the "Malabar Rites controversy") erupted in India; it centered on the policy of adaptation to Hindu customs begun in the early seventeenth century by the Italian Jesuit Roberto de Nobili. Nobili dressed and ate like a Hindu holy man, demonstrating his purity by refusing to look at a woman or talk with a European. He argued that accepting the caste system was the only way to attract upper-caste Hindus to Christianity, and that many Hindu practices were more cultural than religious.

Though most of the scholarship on the Chinese Rites controversy and similar debates elsewhere in Asia has focused on the intellectual issues involved, it is clear that sexual norms were also a key area of disagreement. For instance, Catholic baptism at the time involved more than the use of water; the priest also touched the converts' bare skin with salt, oil, and the priest's saliva, and breathed into their nostrils. Such close physical contact between an unrelated man and woman was unacceptable in many Asian cultures, as an anti-Christian book written in the early seventeenth century by the Chinese scholar Hsü Ta-Shou makes clear:

> But in their [the Christian missionaries'] residences they themselves
> invite ignorant women at night to come in front of (instead of
> staying behind) the scarlet curtains (the teacher's seat). They close

the doors and mark the women with holy oil, give them holy
water and even commit the crime of secretly lusting after them
by placing their hands on five places of their bodies. What more
can they add to the disorder between men and women?[24]

Hsü Ta-Shou also objected to male and female converts mixing at services:
"As for the wives and daughters of their followers, however, they let them
mingle with the crowd in order to receive the secret teachings of the barbarians
. . . all this in the dark night and [men and women] intermingling."[25]

   Because of such sentiments, those who advocated accommodation modified
their baptism rituals, as well as procedures at confession and other church
ceremonies. Confession was held in a large room, with a mat suspended between
the priest and his female confessant; a prominent male convert stood at the
other end of the room, so that he could observe, but not hear. (This was
certainly as private as most European confessions at the time; they often took
place in the open in a crowded church, for the confessional box did not become
widely used until the eighteenth century.) Jesuits were instructed to "seek to
create a few oratories in the homes of some Christians where women can be
baptized, mass can be said, and talks can be given to them."[26] These separate
women's chapels were established in some Chinese cities by wealthy female
converts. Prayers and services were so common in one of these, wrote a Jesuit
missionary in 1660, that the household "appeared more a convent of nuns and
religious than the family and household of a noble, secular lady."[27] In India,
Nobili also made modifications, allowing a woman who converted to wear the
tali around her neck instead of a wedding ring as a sign of her marital status,
and to receive gifts on the day of her first menstrual period after her marriage.
   The Protestants also adapted to local practices. In Dutch Amboina, men
and women did not eat together, and women were unwilling to attend church
if it meant they would have to take communion alongside men. The Reformed
Church in this case allowed them to wear a veil, though it would not allow
separate communions. Similar considerations of sexual propriety shaped
Lutheran practice in Tranquebar, where men and women (as well as persons
of different castes) were allowed to sit separately at church.
   Yet there were certain aspects of existing sexual practice which missionaries
and church authorities refused to accommodate. One of these was male same-
sex activities. On seeing male prostitutes in Beijing, the generally tolerant
Matteo Ricci severely regretted how "these miserable men are initiated in to
this terrible vice."[28] A Jesuit moral tract published in 1604 in China by Diego
de Pantoja (with the assistance of Yang T'ing-yün, the convert-to-be who
could not give up his concubine), invokes both Christian and traditional Chinese
arguments against homosexuality:

The sin of lust has many manifestations, but male homosexuality is the greatest. In my Western country, all sins have a name. Only this is the sin that dares not speak its name. As for this sin, those who commit it pollute their hearts, and those who speak of it pollute their mouths . . . The male is *ch'ien* and the female is *k'un*. This is the principle of generation. [And thus linked to cosmic generation, which was seen as binary.] A man and a woman, this is the way of humankind.[29]

As in Europe, certain groups in Asia and Africa were viewed as particularly likely to be sodomites – Arabs in North Africa, Turks in West Asia, Chinese in the Philippines – as male homosexuality was linked to developing notions of racial and ethnic difference.

Opposition to same-sex relations translated into repression. In Portuguese Goa, the Inquisition investigated a number of sodomy cases, and secular authorities publicly burned men found guilty of sodomy, including both native converts and Europeans. In 1599, royal authorities in the Philippines ordered that all who "commit or practice the said abomination against nature, or try to commit it . . . shall incur the penalty of being burned alive by fire, beside having all his goods confiscated to the treasury of his Majesty."[30] They particularly singled out Chinese merchants and posted notices in Chinese parts of Manila warning of the consequences of homosexual acts. These merchants countered that they were not converts and that such activities were acceptable in their own country, but Spanish authorities charged them with spreading the "abominable sin against nature" to native "Moro and Indian boys of these islands, by which God, our Lord, is greatly disserved," and punished those found guilty by flogging, galley service, and even execution.[31] (Flogging was also the standard punishment for any man in the Philippines found wearing a penis pin, as Spanish authorities attempted to end this practice.) In Japan, Jesuits referred to same-sex relations in Buddhist monasteries in arguments against Buddhism, and Valignano's catechism for Japanese converts specifically warns against these.

During the seventeenth century, on issues other than homosexuality, adaptation was widely accepted among both Catholics and Protestants, but in the first half of the eighteenth century this policy was reversed, especially among Catholics. Already in the seventeenth century Dominicans had complained to the papacy, and charged the Jesuits with illegitimate practices. The papal legate Charles Maillard de Tournon condemned any distinctive Indian or Chinese rites in 1704 and 1707, and ordered all missionaries to follow Roman practice; this decision was reinforced by a papal bull in 1744. Not surprisingly, the pace of conversion slowed, and some converts gave up their allegiance to Christianity.

Despite all attempts at enforcing uniformity and official condemnation of "accommodationism," however, in actual practice African and Asian Christians retained many distinctive marital and sexual practices. Christian girls in India continued to marry at a very young age (though in one celebrated case this led to a very young girl's being forcibly taken from her older husband) and Christian widows in India, even very young ones, did not remarry. Caste still largely determined marital choice for Indian Christians, as well as who they ate or socialized with and which confraternity they joined. (Only in the small northern province of Bettiah did Catholic Christians decide to form themselves into a single caste that ate together and intermarried, a tradition they have maintained to today.) Converts in Dutch Amboina continued to perform rituals that celebrated sexual maturity, such as circumcision or incision of the foreskin for boys and ritual cleaning after the first menstruation for girls. Christians on Mozambique celebrated a girl's first menstruation by invoking the "Most Holy Name of Jesus," despite the Inquisition's denunciation of such "rites, ceremonies, and superstitious abuses."[32] Filipino Catholics continued to begin sexual relations once the initial stages of marital agreements had been concluded and to petition for annulments with great frequency; European clergy working among them viewed such practices as a demonstration that sexual desire continued to be their "prince and master vice" and "so general that . . . it kept these regions aflame with an infernal and inextinguishable vice."[33] This assessment of the power of sexual desire among "tropical" peoples was communicated to the Protestant missionaries who began coming to Africa and Asia in much greater numbers after 1800. They, too, regarded indigenous marital and sexual practices as "vice" rather than social and cultural tradition.

Interracial heterosexual relationships

European authorities, both secular and clerical, brought with them a categorization of heterosexual relationships that was largely dichotomous: there was monogamous marriage, and there was everything else. As we have seen, they encountered societies with more complicated categories, and they were also confronted with additional complexities because of the colonial situation. Given the fact that almost all Europeans were men, interracial sexual relationships developed immediately, and colonial authorities were confronted with a physically "creolized" population for which they were required to balance a variety of contradictory aims and norms. All of them wanted stable and peaceful colonies and realized that controlling sexuality was a key part of this, but they differed widely in their ideas about the best sort of regulation. Policy and its implementation were often determined by the personal opinions of governors, church leaders, and company officials, and so swung wildly. Church support of monogamous marriage often collided with secular political and economic aims, and with existing or newly developing racial and ethnic hierarchies.

Some authorities hoped to avoid the problems of inter-racial relationships, and favored the importation of more women from Europe. Beginning in the mid-sixteenth century, the Portuguese crown sent white orphan girls and reformed prostitutes (who had often been housed in the same institution in Portugal) to its colonies in Goa, Brazil, and West Africa. It provided them with dowries in the form of an office or a piece of land for their future husbands, and ordered them to marry. In 1586, Spanish residents in the Philippines petitioned the royal council for transport and dowry funds so that "ten, fifteen, or twenty women [be] brought from Spain, to be married to the common people of these islands, such as soldiers and others, that this country may secure an increase of population – which it has not at present, for lack of women and marriages."[34] In the early seventeenth century, VOC officials arranged for orphan girls, whom they termed "Company daughters," to be brought from the Netherlands to the East Indies, giving them clothing and a dowry. The numbers of such girls was never very great, however, and in general, the unmarried girls and women who were willing to leave Europe were not the sort that authorities favored. Peter Both, the first Dutch Governor-General of the East Indies, suggested that the VOC ban further female immigration, since the "light [meaning frivolous, not light-skinned] women" who had come were a "great shame to our nation," and in 1632 the VOC stopped sponsoring women as immigrants to any Dutch settlement east of Africa.[35]

Other authorities were realistic about the number of European women who could be encouraged to immigrate, and viewed interracial marriage as the best way to create stable colonies. The Duke of Albuquerque – the leader of the Portuguese forces that conquered Goa – hoped that his men would marry the widows of the Muslim defenders of Goa and never return to Portugal. He allowed soldiers who married to retire from the army, and gave them subsidies to set up a household. A similar policy was adopted by the directors of the VOC, who gave soldiers, sailors, and minor officials bonuses if they agreed to marry local women and stay in the VOC colonies as "free-burghers." This policy was opposed by some Dutch missionaries, but accepted by others such as George Candidius in the Dutch colony on Formosa, who hoped marriage with local women would not only win converts but give missionaries access to female religious rituals. He was unmarried himself, and suggested that he should model the practice, but the governors of the VOC thought this was going too far. The petition by Filipino citizens asking for woman from Spain quoted above also requested dowries for native women to enable them to marry soldiers and sailors of lower ranks. The Directors of the British East India Company gave additional encouragement in 1687, decreeing:

> The marriage of our soldiers to the native women of Fort St. George is a matter of such consequence to posterity that we shall be content to encourage it with some expense, and are thinking for the future to appoint a Pagoda [4 rupees of Indian currency] to be paid to the mother of any child that shall hereafter be born of any such future marriage upon the day the child is Christened.[36]

There were limits to this acceptance of intermarriage, however, often explicitly along racial lines. Albuquerque encouraged marriage to higher-caste Indian women who were "white and beautiful," but discouraged unions with the darker-skinned "black women" of the Malabar coast.[37] Rijkloff von Goens, one of the VOC governors of Ceylon, supported mixed marriages, but then wanted the daughters of those marriages married to Dutchmen "so that our race may degenerate as little as possible."[38] (By "our race" von Goens probably meant the "Dutch race" because he worried about mixed marriages with Portuguese-heritage women as well.) In the Dutch colony of the Cape of Good Hope (South Africa), though the races were not segregated and there was much sexual contact between European men and African women, this color hierarchy was so strong that it largely prevented interracial marriage. Until 1823, slaves in Cape Colony could not marry in a Christian ceremony; a man wanting to marry a slave had to baptize and free her first. Slaves marrying among themselves often devised their own ceremonies, or married in Muslim ceremonies even though Islam was not a recognized religion.

Hesitation about intermarriage came not only from the European side, however. In the patrilineal societies of West Africa, such as the Mandinka and Wolof, Portuguese men and their mixed-race children were not allowed to marry local people of free standing, as this could give them claims to land use; their children could not inherit or join the kin and age-grade associations that shaped political power structures. Asian families of high social standing were generally not eager to marry their daughters to the type of European men usually found in the colonies, especially as wives and children were required to adopt their husband's religion. This reluctance was clear to European colonists. In the 1640s, for example, the Goa municipal council wrote to the king, suggesting he pass a decree ordering all upper-class Indian families to marry their daughters to Portuguese men born in Portugal and to give all their property to these daughters. They argued this policy would create more Christians, soldiers, and wealth for Portugal, which it no doubt would have; it would also have led to revolt, a fact which the Portuguese crown recognized and so paid no attention to the request. Those women who were willing to marry Europeans were either lower-class or already separated from their families and place of origin. Thus in Goa, in contrast to Albuquerque's hopes, a visitor noted in 1524 that "all or the great majority [of Portuguese men] are married to Negresses, whom they take to Church on horseback."[39] (By "Negresses" the commentator means lower-caste Indians with dark skins, not women from Africa.) Some of these were slaves, and by the second and third generation many of them were women of mixed race. In Dutch and English areas, some of these women were Catholic, the children of marriages between Portuguese men and local women; Protestant church authorities worried about the women retaining their loyalty to Catholicism, raising their children as Catholics and perhaps even converting their husbands. Thus although they often tolerated Catholicism in general, they required marriages between a Protestant and a Catholic to be celebrated in a Protestant church and demanded a promise from the spouses that the children would be raised Protestant.

European and local notions about acceptable marriage partners combined in some places to create distinctive patterns. For example, in the Portuguese colonies and trading posts of West Africa, marriages between Portuguese men and African women were often not recognized as such by the Portuguese Crown; often the men involved also had a wife and children in Portugal, so the Crown defined their African marriage as concubinage and periodically ordered the men to return to their original family in Portugal. As we saw above, many West African societies also did not view the children of these unions as high-status partners and they could not inherit land. This meant that they generally went into trade, and in some places women became the major traders, with large households, extensive networks of trade, and many servants and slaves. Because these wealthy female traders – termed *nharas* in Criulo and *signares* in French – had connections with both the African and European worlds, they were valued as both trade and marriage partners by the French and English traders who moved into this area in the eighteenth century. "Some of these women were married in church," reported one French commentator, "others in the style of the land, which in general consists of the consent of both parties and the relatives."[40] In the latter form of marriage, the women's European husbands would have paid bridewealth to their new in-laws (instead of receiving a dowry as was the custom in Europe), provided a large feast, and been expected to be sexually faithful. If the husband returned to Europe, the *signare* was free to marry again.

Despite doubts about intermarriage from both sides, colonial governments also recognized this was a way to build up stable colonies, and adopted various policies to make sure that interracial families remained where they were. In VOC colonies in Asia, men were not allowed to take their Asian wives or children back to Europe with them, nor to return to Europe without them, a Catch-22 policy to which very few exceptions were made. European widows were obliged to stay in the colonies and find a new spouse there, and the daughters of European families to stay at least five years after they married, virtually assuring that they would marry someone willing to remain in the colonies.

Marriage was, of course, only one type of interracial sexual relationship, and perhaps the least common in most European colonies. At times government policy explicitly encouraged relations outside of marriage, especially in the earliest years of any colony. On São Tomé, the Portuguese Crown apparently provided each European man with either a deportee from Europe – including newly baptized Jewish girls and women – or a slave from Africa explicitly to increase the population, and did not require a marriage ceremony. Though some clergy there and elsewhere in the Portuguese empire objected to such toleration of extra-marital sex, their views were moderated if the woman was baptized, and they could at least pretend a marriage might eventually result. Carmelites who visited São Tomé in the 1580s, for example, commented that both the European and African men there had "a wife or two as concubines" who had "a baby each year"; they approved of the formation of families, though weakly recommended that it would be better if Christian marriage ceremonies could be celebrated.[41] Most Portuguese men paid little attention to clerical opinion in any case, and many had households that had not only one or two, but a number of women. Nicolas Lancilotto, a Jesuit writing to Ignatius Loyola from Malaka in 1550, astutely linked this with the easy availability of slaves, commenting, "There are innumerable Portuguese who buy droves of girls and sleep with all of them, and subsequently sell them. There are innumerable married settlers who have four, eight, or ten female slaves and sleep with all of them, and this is known publicly."[42] In port cities, both Portuguese and indigenous pimps often bought and sold girls for sexual purposes, with the money going to the girl's family or the pimp; a small portion might go to the girl herself, through which she accumulated a dowry for her eventual marriage.

There were sporadic attempts to control extramarital sex, particularly once a colony was established. By 1559 the Portuguese Crown declared itself shocked at the situation in São Tomé where "many women give themselves publicly for money. They live irregularly in the town alongside married householders and other people who lead regular lives, from which arise many scandals and bad examples and things which are a disservice to Our Lord." Such women were ordered to move outside the towns and serve only local customers; married men and clergy who maintained mistresses were also ordered to give them up or pay a fine, with a penalty of deportation for the third offense. The local bishop was to implement these measures, but he was less than enthusiastic; he reported to the Crown that the penalties set were far too harsh, and that punishments should take into account "the quality of the person concerned and the scandal of the offense. I am very merciful with those who confess their fault and promise amendment."[43] VOC governors periodically tried to ban the maintenance of female slaves and concubines and to order all Christians living together to marry. Such prohibitions were generally ineffective, for even high-ranking VOC officials and Protestant schoolmasters maintained concubines or lived together with women without an official church ceremony.

The fate of children from extramarital, interracial unions varied enormously. Some of them were legitimated by their fathers through adoption or the purchase of certificates of legitimacy, and could assume prominent positions in colonial society. For example, two of the sons of François Caron, whose views on Japanese customs are quoted above, later became well-known ministers in the Dutch Church. On the Portuguese Atlantic islands and on Mozambique, mixed-race children from the first generations came to form a local aristocracy, dominating both land ownership and the slave trade. On the other hand, many children of lower-class European men did not get much support from their fathers, and in some colonies survived by begging and petty crime. This situation led to the opening of orphanages in many colonies, which in theory were to take in only legitimate children, but in practice did not look too closely at family background. In Goa, for example, an orphanage called "Our Lady of the Mountain" was opened ostensibly for the legitimate, white, "good-looking" daughters of soldiers who had died fighting, but in actuality most of the residents were mixed-race, and some were born out of wedlock. (The records do not reveal whether requirements about appearance were similarly ignored.) The VOC Council in Batavia tried to solve the issue of mixed-race children born out of wedlock by banning their fathers from returning to Europe, a policy that was counter-productive as it simply discouraged European men from recognizing or supporting their children.

Like state and company policies, church policies regarding marriage and morality were often counter-productive. In VOC colonies, for example, marriages could only be solemnized when a pastor visited, which in remote areas might be only every several years. This did not keep people from marrying, however, but instead encouraged them to maintain traditional patterns of marriage, in which cohabitation and sexual relations began with the exchange of gifts, rather than a church wedding. Protestant missionaries advocated frequent church attendance, viewing sermons as a key way to communicate Protestant doctrine; the Asian wives of European men took this very much to heart and attended church so frequently and in such great style that sumptuary laws were soon passed restricting extravagant clothing and expenditures for church ceremonies. In Lutheran Tranquebar, children of European men and local women born out of wedlock were denied baptism, but they were simply taken down the road and baptized in Portuguese Catholic churches, clearly not the intent of the Danish authorities.

Other issues

Along with issues peculiar to the colonial situation, such as creolization and interracial relationships, the Christian churches also faced many of the same problems they did in Europe, and their solutions were largely similar. Individual clergy were charged with concubinage, soliciting sex during confession, and otherwise not living up to the moral standards which church officials expected of them; the most frequent charges against priests handled by the Inquisition in the Philippines were for sexual lapses. Consequences could range from nothing to removal from office to imprisonment; members of religious orders such as the Jesuits were generally dismissed from their positions and sometimes from the order itself. In some of these cases the church may have been more upset than the local population, for whom clerical chastity was not a long tradition and who saw advantages in allying themselves with clergy through sexual relationships involving their daughters.

Asylums for repentant prostitutes and other women charged with sexual crimes were opened in some European colonies, including Goa, Batavia, and Manila. These sometimes housed the young unmarried women brought in as possible marriage partners, local orphans or other poor girls thought to be in danger of becoming prostitutes, and also women who had been abandoned or mistreated by their husbands. Though in the ordinances establishing these houses, the different groups of women were to be separated, in practice the houses were often very small, and all the women lived together. As in Europe, life in these asylums was a mixture of punishment and penitence, with work and strict discipline intended to "reclaim . . . such debauched women . . . from their ill course of life."[44] As with similar institutions in Latin America, these houses reflected and reinforced racial hierarchies; as the initial statutes of one such house in Goa stated, "no native woman, however demoralized she may be, shall be admitted in this house, but only white women."[45]

Examples of sexual magic similar to those in Spain and Latin America emerge occasionally in the colonial secular and church courts, of women like Catrina Casembroot in 1639 Batavia who, "by various impermissible and ghastly means of witchcraft, charms, and administered potions has constrained and tried to force persons to her uncouth desires." Casembroot bought her poisons from indigenous women, and all of them were sentenced to be executed, "for their godless demeanor, fornication, thieving, devilish practices, and empoisonments."[46] As in this example, love magic was often termed "witchcraft" or "devilish practices," terms also applied, as they were in the Americas, to the rituals of indigenous religious practitioners. Accommodation to existing beliefs and practices was never supposed to include those judged demonic, but the boundaries of this were highly subjective. Educated members of the clergy deplored the use of charms and fetishes for any purpose as "heathen," but individuals who understood themselves to be good Christians – sometimes including clergy themselves – believed in their power, and so purchased and used them.

* * *

Examining the history of any aspect of Christianity in most of Asia and Africa before 1750 is in many ways examining a prehistory, for the major mass missionary efforts did not begin until after this date. The mid-eighteenth century did mark a significant break, however. In 1759 the Jesuits were expelled from Portugal and its colonies, in 1767 from Spanish areas, and in 1773 were disbanded as an order. The Iberian colonies thus lost their most energetic missionaries, and both conversion and regulation efforts slowed; when the Jesuits were reestablished in 1814, the colonial political scene was very different. At the same time, the British East India Company was becoming more important than the Dutch VOC in Asian trade and colonization, and, outside of Dutch and German colonies, subsequent Protestant missionary efforts would be largely a British story. Those later missionary efforts would come to involve people with European backgrounds from what in 1750 were still colonies – that is, from the former British and French colonies of North America, later the United States and Canada. It was North America in the centuries before 1750 that gave European Christians their best opportunities to create moral and sexual utopias, whether among native converts or immigrants. It was in North America that the various experiments in how best to do this were most extreme.

Selected further reading

A good overview of many issues relating to gender and sexuality, along with extensive bibliographies, may be found in the Restoring Women to History series, published in 1999 by Indiana University Press, which has separate volumes on sub-Saharan Africa, the Middle East and North Africa, Latin America and the Caribbean, and Asia. André Burguière *et al.*, eds, *A History of the Family: Volume One: Distant Worlds, Ancient Worlds* and *Volume Two, The Impact of Modernity* (Cambridge, Mass.: Harvard University Press, 1996) contains essays on the family in China, Japan, India, Africa, and the Arab world. Arvind Sharma's two books, *Women in World Religions* and *Religion and Women* (Albany: SUNY Press, 1987 and 1994) cover women's role and attitudes toward sexuality in many of the world's religions. Don S. Browning, M. Christian Green, and John Witte Jr., *Sex, Marriage, and Family in World Religions* (New York: Columbia University Press, 2006) contains excellent original sources from Judaism, Christianity, Islam, Hinduism, Buddhism, and Confucianism, while Koschorke, *History of Christianity* (note 2 of Chapter 5 in "Notes") contains sources on Christianity in these areas.

Both gender and religion in Africa during this period are often discussed in broader studies of political and social developments. See, for example: Tamrat Taddesse, *Church and State in Ethiopia, 1270–1527* (Oxford: Clarendon Press, 1977); Iris Berger, *Religion and Resistance: East African Kingdoms in the Pre-Colonial Period* (Tervuren, Belgium: Musée royal de l'Afrique central, 1981); Anne Hilton, *The Kingdom of Kongo* (Oxford: Clarendon Press, 1985); Wyatt MacGaffey, *Religion and Society in Central Africa: The BaKonga of Lower Zaire* (Chicago: University of Chicago, 1986); John Thornton, *Africa and Africans* (note 41); Linda M. Heywood and John K. Thornton, *Central Africans* (note 3). John Thornton has been especially influential in examining the syncretic process of creolization in the African diaspora, while James Sweet, *Recreating Africa* (note 1), emphasizes continuities in African religions. Isabel P. B. Fêo Rodrigues, "Islands of Sexuality: Theories and Histories of Creolization in Cape Verde," *The International Journal of African Historical Studies* 36(1) (2003): 83–103 provides a useful introduction to theories of creolization.

For studies that focus specifically on gender in sub-Saharan Africa in the pre-colonial period, see: Onaiwa W. Ogbomo, *When Men and Women Mattered: A History of Gender Relations among the Owan of Nigeria* (Rochester: University of Rochester Press, 1997); David Schoenbrun, *A Green Place, A Good Place: Agrarian Change, Gender, and Social Identity Between the Great Lakes to the Fifteenth Century* (Portsmouth, N.H.: Heinemann, 1998); Sandra E. Greene, "Family Concerns: Gender and Ethnicity in Pre-Colonial West Africa," *International Review of Social History* 44, supplement 7 (1999): 15–31; "In the Mix: Women and Ethnicity among the Anlo-Ewe," in Carola Lentz and Paul Nugent, eds, *Ethnicity in Ghana: The Limits of Invention* (London: Palgrave Macmillan, 2000), 29–48 and *Sacred Sites and the Colonial Encounter: A History of Meaning and Memory in Ghana* (Bloomington: Indiana University Press, 2002); Shane Doyle, "The Cwezi-Kubandwa Debate: Gender, Hegemony, and Pre-colonial Religion in Bunyoro, Western Uganda," in *Africa* 77(4) (2007): 559–81.

There are a number of studies that focus specifically on women or sexuality in Islam. See: Basim Musallam, *Sex and Society in Islamic Civilization* (Cambridge: Cambridge University Press, 1983); Leila Ahmed, *Women and Gender in Islam: Historical Roots of a Modern Debate* (New Haven, Conn.: Yale, 1992); Judith Tucker, *Gender in Islamic History* (Washington, DC: American Historical Association, 1990) and *In the House of the Law: Gender and Islamic Law in Ottoman Syria and Palestine* (Berkeley: University of California Press, 1998); Gavin Hambly, ed., *Women in the Medieval Islamic World* (New York: St. Martin's Press, 1998); Dror Ze'evi, *Producing Desire: Changing Sexual Discourse in the Ottoman Middle East* (Berkeley: University of California Press, 2006); Nikki R. Keddie, *Women in the Middle East: Past and Present* (Princeton, N.J.: Princeton University Press, 2007).

Of all of the parts of Asia covered in this chapter, China has received the most attention. For works that discuss traditional Chinese norms and structures, see: David Buxbaum, *Chinese Family Law and Social Change: In Historical and Comparative Perspective* (Seattle: University of Washington Press, 1978); Rubie S. Watson and Patricia Buckley Ebrey, *Marriage and Inequality in Chinese Society* (Berkeley: University of California Press, 1991) and *The Inner Quarters: Marriage and the Lives of Chinese Women in the Sung Period* (Berkeley: University of California Press, 1993); Harriet T. Zurndorfer, ed., *Chinese Women in the Imperial Past* (Leiden: Brill, 1999); Bettine Birge, *Women, Property, and Confucian Reaction in Sung and Yuan China (960–1368)* (Cambridge: Cambridge University Press, 2002). For Japan, see: Osamu Saito, "Marriage, Family Labour and the Stem Family Household: Traditional Japan in a Comparative Perspective," *Continuity & Change* 15(1) (2000): 17–45; Haruko Wakita, *Women in Medieval Japan: Motherhood, Household Management and Sexuality,* trans. Alison Tokita (Tokyo: Tokyo University Press, 2006); William R. Lindsey, *Fertility and Pleasure: Ritual and Sexual Values in Tokugawa Japan* (Honolulu: University of Hawai'i Press, 2006); Janet R. Goodwin, *Selling Songs and Smiles: The Sex Trade in Heian and Kamakura Japan* (Honolulu: University of Hawai'i Press, 2007).

For works that discuss gender relations in other parts of Asia, see: Susan Bayly, *Saints, Goddesses and Kings: Muslims and Christians in South Indian Society* (Cambridge: Cambridge University Press, 1989); Neil Jamieson, "The Traditional Family in Vietnam," *Vietnam Forum* 8 (Summer–Fall 1986): 91–150; Anthony Reid, *Southeast Asia in the Age of Commerce 1450–1680, Volume One, The Lands Below the Winds* (New Haven, Conn.: Yale University Press, 1988), especially 146–72 and *Volume Two: Expansion and Crisis* (New Haven, Conn.: Yale University Press, 1993), esp. 132–73; José Ignacio Cabezón, ed., *Buddhism, Sexuality and Gender* (Albany, N.Y.: SUNY Press, 1992); Sangkuk Lee and Hyunjoon Park, "Marriage, Social Status, and Family Succession in Medieval

Korea (Thirteenth–Fifteenth Centuries)," *Journal of Family History* 33(2) (April 2008): 123–38; Andaya, *Flaming Womb* (note 18).

Many general studies of the spread of Christianity in Africa and Asia, particularly older studies written from a clearly confessional viewpoint, make no mention of sex and very little mention even of marriage. Some that do, and which are useful in presenting the broader story, are: Horacio de la Costa, *The Jesuits in the Philippines* (Madison: University of Wisconsin Press, 1961); George H. Dunne, S.J., *Generation of Giants: The Story of the Jesuits in China in the Last Decades of the Ming Dynasty* (South Bend, Ind.: Notre Dame University Press, 1962); S.D. Franciscus, *Faith of Our Fathers: History of the Dutch Reformed Church in Sri Lanka* (Colombo (Sri Lanka): Pragna Publishers, 1983); Elizabeth Isichei, *A History of Christianity in Africa: From Antiquity to the Present* (Grand Rapids, Mich.: William Eerdmans, 1995); Dauril Alden, *The Making of an Enterprise: The Society of Jesus in Portugal, Its Empire, and Beyond 1540–1750* (Stanford, Calif.: Stanford University Press, 1996); Pete C. Phan, *Mission and Catechesis in Seventeenth-Century Vietnam: Alexandre de Rhodes and Inculturation in Seventeenth-Century Vietnam* (New York: Orbis Books, 1998); Ines G. Zupanov, *Diputed Mission: Jesuit Experiments and Brahmanical Knowledge in 17th Century India* (Delhi: Oxford University Press, 1999) and *Missionary Tropics: The Catholic Frontier in India (16th–17th Centuries)* (Ann Arbor: University of Michigan Press, 2005); Tanya Storch, ed., *Religions and Missionaries around the Pacific, 1500–1900* (Aldershot: Ashgate, 2006); Brockey, *Journey to the East* (note 26); Rafael, *Contracting Colonialism* (note 7); Gernet, *China and the Christian Impact* (note 17); Neill, *Christianity in India* (note 36). More specialized articles include Isabel Pina, "The Jesuit Missions in Japan and in China: Two Distinct Realities. Cultural Adaptation and the Assimilation of Natives," *Bulletin of Portuguese/Japanese Studies* 2 (2001): 59–76; Pratima Kamat, "The Tail Wags the Dog? Colonial Policies of Conversion and Hindu Resistance through Syncretism and Collaboration in Goa, 1510–1755," *Indian Historical Review* 30(1) (2003): 21–39; Angela Barreto Xavier, "Disquiet on the Island: Conversion, Conflicts and Conformity in Sixteenth-Century Goa," *Indian Economic & Social History Review* 44(3) (2007): 269–95.

Christianity in Japan has been particularly well studied. See: C.R. Boxer, *The Christian Century in Japan, 1549–1650* (Berkeley: University of California Press, 1967); Richard H. Drummond, *A History of Christianity in Japan* (Grand Rapids, Mich.: William Eerdmans, 1971); Ann M. Harrington, *Japan's Hidden Christians* (Chicago: Loyola University Press, 1993); John Nelson, "Myths, Missions, and Mistrust: The Fate of Christianity in 16th and 17th Century Japan," *History & Anthropology* 13(2) (2002): 93–111; João Paulo Oliveira e Costa, "The 'Misericordias' among Japanese Christian Communities in the 16th and 17th Centuries," *Bulletin of Portuguese/Japanese Studies* 5 (2002): 67–79.

Most of the scholarship on the VOC colonies is, not surprisingly, in Dutch, though there are increasing numbers of works in English that address the issues discussed in this chapter. These include: J. van Goor, *Jan Kompenie as Schoolmaster: Dutch Education in Ceylon 1690–1795* (Groningen: Wolters-Noordhoff, 1978); Jean Gelman Taylor, *The Social World of Batavia: European and Eurasian in Dutch Asia* (Madison: University of Wisconsin Press, 2nd edn, 2009); Robert C.-H. Shell, *Children of Bondage: A Social History of the Slave Society at the Cape of Good Hope, 1652–1838* (Hanover: Wesleyan University Press, 1994); Leonard Blussé, "Retribution and Remorse: The Interaction between the Administration and the Protestant Mission in Early Colonial Formosa," in Gyan Prakash, ed., *After Colonialism: Imperial Histories and Postcolonial Displacements* (Princeton, N.J.: Princeton University Press, 1995), 153–82 and *Bitter Bonds: A Colonial Divorce Drama of the Seventeenth Century*, translated by Diane Webb (Princeton, N.J.: Markus Wiener, 2002); Patricia W. Romero, "Some Aspects of Family and Social History among the French Huguenot Refugees at the Cape," *Historia* 48(2) (2003): 31–47; Kerry Ward, *Networks of Empire: Forced Migration in the Dutch East India Company* (Cambridge: Cambridge University Press, 2008); Laura J. Mitchell, *Belongings: Property, Family, and Identity in Colonial South Africa, An Exploration of Frontiers, 1725–c. 1830* (New York: Columbia University Press, 2009); Blussé, *Strange Company* (note 13); Boxer, *Dutch Seaborne Empire* (note 35).

The issues discussed in this chapter are often framed in terms of Iberian colonialism as well as the spread of Christianity. For works that take this approach, see: John Leddy Phelan, *The Hispanization of the Philippines: Spanish Aims and Filipino Responses 1565–1700* (Madison: University of Wisconsin Press, 1967); C.R. Boxer, *The Church Militant and Iberian Expansion, 1440–1770* (Baltimore, Md.: Johns Hopkins, 1978); Ann Pescatello, *Power and Pawn: The Female in Iberian Families, Societies and Cultures* (Westport, Conn.: Greenwood, 1976); Albert Chan, "Chinese–Philippine Relations in the Late Sixteenth Century and to 1603," *Philippine Studies* 26 (1978): 63–86; M.V. Pearson, *The Portuguese in India* (Cambridge: Cambridge University Press, 1987); Francisco Bethencourt and Diogo Ramada Curto, eds, *Portuguese Oceanic Expansion* (Cambridge: Cambridge University Press, 2005); Boxer, *Race Relations* (note 32).

Studies that focus specifically on gender and religion in the early modern period are increasing. For Africa, these include: Ivana Elbl, "Sexual Arrangements in the Portuguese Expansion in West Africa," in Jacqueline Murray and Konrad Eisenbichler, eds, *Desire and Discipline: Sex and Sexuality in the Pre-Modern West* (Toronto: University of Toronto Press, 1996), 60–86; John K. Thornton, *The Kongolese Saint Anthony: Dona Beatriz Kimpa Vita and the Antonian Movement, 1684–1706* (New York: Cambridge University Press,

1998); Richard Gray, "A Kongo Princess, the Kongo Ambassadors and the Papacy," in *Christianity and the African Imagination: Essays in Honour of Adrian Hastings* (Leiden: Brill, 2002), 25–40; Brooks, *Eurafricans in Western Africa* (note 40). For Asia, these include: Barbara Watson Andaya, "The Changing Religious Role of Women in Pre-modern South East Asia," *Southeast Asian Research* 2(2) (1994): 99–116; Mary John Mananzan, "The Filipino Woman: Before and After the Spanish Conquest of the Philippines," *Essays on Women* (Manila: Institute of Women's Studies, St. Scholastica's College, 1989), 1–17. For a fascinating analysis of European accounts of the Indian practice of *sati* that connects these to European constructions of womanhood, see Pompa Banerjee, *Burning Women: Widows, Witches and Early Modern European Travellers in India* (London: Palgrave, 2003). The most significant work on gender and religion in the colonial Philippines has been done by Carolyn Brewer, including "From 'Baylan' to 'Bruha': Hispanic Impact on the Animist Priestess in the Philippines," *Journal of South Asia Women Studies: 1995–1997* (Milan: Asiatica Association, 1997), 99–117 and *Shamanism, Catholicism, and Gender Relations in Colonial Philippines, 1521–1685* (Aldershot: Ashgate, 2004). The most important work on gender issues involving Christianity in Japan has been done by Haruko Nawata Ward, including: "The 'Christian Nuns' of Early Modern Japan," *Portuguese Studies Review* 13(1–2) (2005): 411–48, "Jesuits, Too" (note 14) and especially her wonderful *Women Religious Leaders in Japan's Christian Century, 1549–1650* (Aldershot: Ashgate, 2009).

Studies of same-sex relations and gender reversals in Africa and Asia are beginning to appear, although most of these are anthropological rather than historical. The works that include historical materials generally focus on Asia, including: Bret Hinsch, *Passions of the Cut Sleeve: The Male Homosexual Tradition in China* (Berkeley: University of California Press, 1990); Gary Leupp, *Male Colors: The Construction of Homosexuality in Tokugawa Japan* (Berkeley: University of California Press, 1995); Serena Nanda, *Neither Man nor Woman: The Hijras of India* (Belmont, Calif.: Wadsworth Publishing Co., 1990); Stephen O. Murray, ed., *Oceanic Homosexualities* (New York: Garland Publishing, 1992); Gregory M. Pflugfelder, *Cartographies of Desire: Male-Male Sexuality in Japanese Discourse, 1600–1950* (Berkeley: University of California Press, 1999); Sophie Volpp, "Classifying Lust: The Seventeenth-Century Vogue for Male Love," *Harvard Journal of Asiatic Studies* 61(1) (2001): 77–117; Evelyn Blackwood, "Gender Transgression in Colonial and Postcolonial Indonesia," *Journal of Asian Studies* 64(4) (2005): 849–79; Matthew H. Sommer, "Was China Part of a Global Eighteenth-Century Homosexuality?" *Historical Reflections* 33(1) (2007): 117–33. On Africa, see James H. Sweet, "Male Homosexuality and Spiritism in the African Diaspora: The Legacies of a Link," *Journal of the History of Sexuality* 7(2) (1996): 184–202.

Chapter 6

NORTH AMERICA

T HE INTRODUCTION OF CHRISTIANITY into North America began in the Spanish-held areas of the southwest and Florida in the early sixteenth century. There was regular trade between Spanish areas and the rest of North America, which came to include goods such as rosaries or objects decorated with Christian symbols, but not Christian ideas or institutions. These were thus not established until the seventeenth century brought permanent colonists from northern Europe.

Colonial development in America north of the Spanish- and Portuguese-held territories is generally seen as falling into three major patterns. In the far north beginning in the early seventeenth century, French explorers and fur traders established small colonies and traded with the indigenous population. This trading zone gradually extended westward to the Great Lakes and into the Mississippi Valley all the way to Louisiana, but the overall French population remained very small throughout the seventeenth century, and the vast majority of French immigrants were men. By the early eighteenth century this had changed somewhat in the eastern areas of what would become Canada; in Acadia (present-day Nova Scotia, New Brunswick, and Prince Edward Island) and Quebec French farmers and fishermen settled in families. The west remained a frontier area in which most Europeans were male fur-traders, for European women were banned from most fur-trading areas until the 1820s. The fur-trade companies were virtual rulers in many areas in the seventeenth and eighteenth centuries, and missionaries worked under their shadow in a relationship marked by both conflict and cooperation. Intermarriage between French traders and Indian women was far more common than in the English colonies, and marriage often tied traders to Indian communities.

England also claimed parts of what would become Canada, and the seventeenth and early eighteenth century saw intermittent conflicts between French and English, with each side allying itself with different Indian groups and territories switching from one power to the other. These wars were part of French–English conflicts taking place throughout the world and resulted in part of Canada going to England in 1713, and the rest in 1763, after what Americans call the French and Indian War.

Despite eventual English dominance in Canada and the Mississippi Valley, in religious terms French Catholicism was far more important than English Protestantism. French Catholic missionaries, primarily Jesuits, began work among the indigenous residents of eastern Canada in the early seventeenth century, and they accompanied the fur traders further west and south shortly afterward. Many Jesuit missionaries were killed during periods of inter-tribal war, providing the church in New France with its first martyrs and saints. In some places, missionaries established separate communities for Indian converts, loosely based on the Latin American mission model. The first of these was at Sillery outside Quebec in 1637, where the male missionaries were joined by several Augustinian nursing nuns two years later. In the same year, Marie de l'Incarnation and several others established an Ursuline house in Quebec, which soon took in both native women and European immigrants. In 1674 a French bishop, François Xavier de Laval (1623–1708), was installed at Quebec; he vigorously promoted missionary work, sometimes in opposition to the wishes of the French royal governor.

By contrast, English Protestant missionaries were far fewer in number than French Catholics, for Protestant clergy concerned themselves primarily with European immigrants. There was no institution for women corresponding to convents in Protestantism, and no Anglican bishoprics were established anywhere in North America in the colonial period. Thus Christian influence on sexuality in northern and western North America in the colonial period is primarily the story of French missionaries' attempts to introduce European patterns of marriage and sexual relations among indigenous peoples, and to maintain some semblance of sexual "morality" among the largely male European population whose own conduct was far from ideal.

A second pattern of immigration and colonialism developed in New England. Here, beginning with the Pilgrims at Plymouth in 1620 and the Puritans in the Boston area in 1630, family groups of religiously inspired English Protestants were interested in permanent settlement rather than simply the extraction of natural resources such as furs. Immigration continued throughout the rest of the seventeenth century, and this, combined with a high birth rate and early marriage, meant a rapidly expanding European population. The early New England colonies were regarded by their founders as religious communities bound to God by a special contract or "covenant." Political participation was limited to men who had undergone a personal conversion experience and were church members. Women became church members independently through their own conversion experiences, and were regarded as part of the religious covenant, though this did not give them political rights. The Puritans had left England seeking a place to practice their religious faith without encumbrance, but this did not make their leadership willing to give others the same freedom. Religious dissenters were whipped, expelled, or even executed; though each church gradually became more independent – an organizational pattern called congregationalism – in the earliest years clergy in prominent churches were able to assert their control over doctrine and discipline.

In the first decades after settlement, adults had to make a confession to the whole congregation describing their personal conversion experience in order to be full church members. Children were regarded as sharing in their parents' covenant, however, and by the 1660s most congregations decided that people whose family background was within the church, but who had not personally confessed, should also be admitted to church membership in what came to be termed the "Half-Way Covenant." Many historians regard this as an indication that the spiritual vigor in many congregations had begun to wane, and track this through changes in conduct as well as membership rules.

Because the European population of New England grew so quickly, the main story of native–immigrant relations is one of European appropriation of native land for new settlements, made easier by the dramatic drop in Indian populations from introduced diseases. This expansion was accompanied, in the seventeenth century, by a number of wars with various native peoples; these led to the eventual expulsion of Indians from many parts of New England. Even while this was going on, there was some missionary activity among the Indians. Separate settlements for Native American Christians, "praying towns" in which converts were expected to follow European Christian marital and sexual practices, were established, but the number of such towns was never very great in comparison with white settlements. In contrast to French Catholic missionaries, the main focus of most Puritan clergy was on European immigrants and their descendants, not on Indian converts. Tracing Christian regulation of sexuality in New England thus involves a primary focus on Puritan attempts to make their ideals a reality among white immigrants and a secondary focus on Indian–European encounters.

Many cultural historians view the experience of Puritan New England as central in the shaping of American culture, particularly in terms of American attitudes toward morality, the body, and sexuality. Suspicion of sexual pleasure or attempts to avoid discussion of sexuality are often termed "puritanical," with common ideas about the Puritans summed up by the author and critic

H.L. Mencken, who defined Puritanism as "the haunting fear that someone, somewhere, may be happy." Defenders of the Puritans have argued that this is only part of the picture, for it overlooks Puritan ideals of companionate marriage and stable family life, but the debate goes on.

No one contends that the immigrants to the Chesapeake area of Virginia and Maryland, the third pattern of settlement in North America, were in any way puritanical. English settlers began to arrive there in the early seventeenth century, though, as in Canada, most of these were men, and many of them were indentured servants. The first Africans came in 1619 in a ship named the *Jesus*, and though in the early decades some Africans were indentured servants, most of them became permanent slaves. By 1720, 30 percent of the Virginia and 70 percent of the South Carolina population was black; by 1776, 20 percent of the total United States population was black, of which 96 percent were slaves. Native Americans were also enslaved in many parts of the south, but their numbers were soon dwarfed by those of Africans.

A year after the first Africans came to Virginia, the Virginia Company began to import women from England as brides for men to purchase, hoping to encourage the growth of families and population. These occurred very slowly, however, and throughout the seventeenth century the gender balance among both whites and blacks in Virginia and Maryland was very skewed in favor of men. Many of the white women who did come were indentured servants rather than wives or daughters, and, like male indentured servants, were prohibited from marrying during the term of their service.

In theory the early settlers to Virginia and the Carolinas were part of the Anglican Church, with the clergy under the control of a bishop in England. However, clergy were financially supported by the local laity, and because the population was widely scattered on plantations rather than in compact settlements like New England, pastors often traveled rather than having a permanent parish church. There were very few churches for immigrants, so worship was often in people's houses and did not necessarily follow Anglican forms. As in Puritan New England, men who were not members of the official church were politically disadvantaged, but despite this levels of church membership were low. There was very little missionary activity among Indians in the south when compared with French areas or even with New England.

As slavery rather than indentured servitude became the more common condition for people of African descent, slave owners often chose not to baptize their slaves, for they feared this might mean they would have to free them. Some slaves had become Christians in Africa, but their religious allegiance was generally unrecognized. In 1667, the Virginia House of Burgesses passed a law stating that baptism did not change one's condition of servitude, but many owners still refused to allow their slaves to be baptized. This also occurred in other British North American colonies and in the British-held islands of the Caribbean such as Jamaica, Barbados, and the Leeward Islands, where vast numbers of African slaves were imported to work on sugar plantations. Catholic slave owners in the French and Spanish Caribbean islands were more likely to baptize their slaves than were British Protestants. Catholicism also appears to have been more appealing to slaves than Protestantism in the Caribbean, and Catholic saints, rituals, and images often became elements in the New World religions such as *vodun* that built on African traditions.

These three patterns of settlement and three types of religious structure – Catholic, Puritan, Anglican – were joined somewhat later in the seventeenth century by a fourth. Puritan intolerance led Roger Williams, Anne Hutchinson and others to found communities in what became Rhode Island which offered religious freedom and toleration; in 1681 William Penn, a Quaker, founded a colony in what became Pennsylvania which also had no single official church. Catholics founded Maryland in 1634, with the understanding that this colony would also offer religious freedom. The diversity of settlers in the other colonies, some of which had originally been held by the Dutch, Swedish, or Danish – New York, New Jersey, Delaware and later Georgia – meant that these areas also never established a single strong state church the way the southern or New England colonies did and it is difficult to make generalizations about them.

By the later seventeenth century, religious diversity was joined by disinterest in many parts of North America. People chose to be part of Baptist, Quaker, Presbyterian, Anglican, Catholic, Congregationalist, or other communities, or – more likely – chose to join no denomination at all. In 1691, Massachusetts made property ownership rather than church membership the pre-requisite for voting rights. In contrast to the popular view of church-going Americans, most historians estimate that by 1700 the majority of colonial residents were not church members and rarely attended a service. Disinterest in religion changed somewhat in the 1730s and 1740s with the religious revival movement known as the Great Awakening. The Great Awakening was a movement of personal religious conversion that spread throughout all of the colonies, especially in frontier areas away from the coast where state churches were the weakest. It emphasized emotion, the spoken word, personal experience, and leadership based on a sense of calling, and attracted Indians and Africans as well as Europeans. People were encouraged to discipline their own conduct, but there was less focus on sexual sins than on those of pride, anger, and a lack of trust in God.

Ideas and patterns before the arrival of the Europeans

The cautionary words at the beginning of the chapter on Latin America about the difficulties in learning about or understanding indigenous patterns apply even more strongly to the North American situation. In contrast to the Aztecs and Mayas, no North American group north of Mexico had a written language, so the words of indigenous people from the colonial period come largely through a European filter. In addition, the archeological record is sparser than it is for groups such as the Aztecs or Inca, and there are few stone structures or monuments that might reveal information about religious or social structures. Added to this is the fact that disease and war completely eradicated many of the peoples of eastern North America; diseases such as smallpox often preceded actual contact with Europeans in the interior of the continent, so that the first European traders and explorers encountered villages and settlements whose population levels were already much lower than they had been before 1600. For many groups, oral tradition, a central means of conveying Native American history, was lost, disrupted or diminished.

Difficulties with sources have led to debate among historians and anthropologists about many aspects of North American society in the seventeenth century, but there are some things on which most scholars agree. The peoples of the eastern woodlands were divided into a number of nations (what Europeans would term "tribes"), which can themselves be loosely divided into large linguistic groups, primarily the Algonkian (which includes the Delaware, Penobscot, Montagnais-Abenaki, Micmac, Ojibwa, Algonquin, and most of the other nations in the eastern woodlands), Iroquoian (which includes the Huron, Mohawk, Seneca, and Iroquois), Siouan (which includes the Catawba and Winnebago), and Muskogean (which includes Choctaw, Chicasaw, Creek, and Seminole). They combined agriculture, gathering, and hunting activities in different degrees, and developed various types of political systems.

Despite linguistic differences and frequent warfare, certain characteristics were widely shared. Society was often organized matrilineally into family and clan groups, with marriage generally occurring outside of the clan, although the families of political leaders – whom the English called "sachems" – frequently married kin. Marriage was a way to link villages and clans and to assimilate outsiders, thus bringing them into the group. This pattern would be very important in French-speaking areas where traders were encouraged to marry local women to facilitate peaceful relations. Adoption was another way to assimilate outsiders, and women often decided the fate of prisoners, who could either be executed or adopted to make up for lost relatives. Many groups were matrilocal, which meant that husbands came to live with their wives' clans and related women lived together. Matrilineal ties were thus important in many aspects of life, although formal political leadership was often passed down patrilineally.

Marriages in some groups were suggested or arranged by older women, including the mothers of the couple, although in others the parents had little say in the matter and the consent of the couple was all that mattered. Women apparently had more control over whom they married than was common among Europeans; a Protestant missionary among Mohawks in 1716 commented that "the Women court the men when they design Marriage."[1] Weddings generally involved a feast and an exchange of goods between the spouses to signify their complementary roles; she gave him corn bread, for example, while he gave her venison. Among some groups, there appears to have been a sort of "trial marriage," which could easily be broken if there were no children or the spouses proved incompatible. Most couples were monogamous, although, as in many other parts of the world, tribal leaders sometimes had more than one wife, occasionally marrying sisters in what is termed "sororal polygyny." Such polygyny may have resulted in part from a shortage of men, for there was no institutional role for women (or men, for that matter) who did not marry.

Individuals abstained from sexual relations at different times for ritual purposes, but life-long chastity was regarded as bizarre and most people married at some point in their lives. French Jesuit priests noted they were frequently teased about their lack of wives or offered women to marry, and one of the first sisters at the Quebec hospital reported that Hurons and Algonquins who met them were astonished "when they were told that we had no men at all and that we were virgins."[2] Attitudes toward pre-marital sexuality varied, with some groups regarding it as a normal precursor to marriage and others less accepting. Punishment for sex outside of marriage also varied; some groups set it at death or mutilation, while others did not punish it at all.

Among some groups divorce was frowned upon after children had been born, but among many, it was quite easy for either spouse to initiate. A man who wished to leave his wife simply left her house, while a woman put her husband's belongings outside her family's house, indicating that she wished him to leave; the children in both cases stayed with the mother and her family. The ease with which this happened was noted by early missionaries, such as the Jesuit superior Father Barthelemy Vimont, who commented in 1639 that Indians had "a complete brutal liberty, changing wives when they pleased – taking only one or several, according to their inclination."[3]

As in Latin America, there were two-spirit people among some Indian groups in North America, who were usually morphologically male but combined what were regarded as masculine and feminine clothing, tasks, and behavior. Two-spirit people often had special religious and ceremonial roles because they were regarded as having both a male and female spirit rather than the one spirit which most people had; they could thus mediate between the male and female world and the divine and human world. Two-spirit people in the eastern half of North America were found primarily in Florida and the western

Great Lakes, where French traders and missionaries encountered them later in the seventeenth century. Many groups honored and accepted such individuals, although among others they were ridiculed and exploited; the reasons for this diversity of treatment are not yet clear, and scholars differ widely about whether they should primarily be celebrated or pitied.

Most individuals with religious and ceremonial authority among Native Americans were not two-spirit people, but men or women who gained their power through connections with either the spiritual realm in general or with a single special spirit. Such individuals, termed "pau-waus" in Algonkian – a word that Europeans came to use for a gathering of native people for spiritual purposes, and spelled "powwow" – had personal supernatural power achieved through dreams and visions rather than power that came through their positions in an institution as Christian clergy did. Connections with the spirit world were reinforced through ceremonies in which the entire nation participated. Such ceremonies emphasized both success in hunting and agricultural fertility, viewed respectively as part of the male and female realms; many of these ceremonies involved specific rituals designed to promote individual and group health and vitality. Religious practices also included sexual taboos: women who were menstruating or giving birth often separated themselves from the rest of the village, reflecting their status as simultaneously powerful and vulnerable; men preparing to hunt or engage in warfare remained sexually continent.

Some aspects of native spiritual life, such as prayer, visions, and guardian spirits, appeared familiar to European observers, while others seemed very alien. The lack of understanding worked both ways, however, for just as Europeans regarded Indians as irreligious because they lacked churches and clergy (and Christ), Indians regarded Europeans as irreligious because they did not have rituals or taboos regarding the central events of life, such as birth, hunting, or warfare.

Although many aspects of native beliefs and traditions were shared across large areas and appear to have been maintained for a long time, significant changes occurred in the sixteenth and seventeenth centuries that were only tangentially related to the coming of the Europeans. During the seventeenth century, the Hurons, Montagnais-Abenaki, and Algonquins of Ontario were repeatedly attacked by Iroquois coming from the south, who by mid-century were equipped with firearms provided by the Dutch. In Virginia, the Algonkian-speaking chief Powhatan began building a military and economic alliance with other groups before the English arrived, cemented these alliances by collecting tribute and marrying women from dominated villages, and then sent them back once they had borne him a child. Such chiefdom-building tactics were a sharp break from earlier traditions, but they influenced the way in which Europeans assessed indigenous practices and mores.

Christian norms and institutions

The pace of change in Native American culture speeded up dramatically with the coming of Europeans. Even those groups not directly in contact with Europeans were affected by their diseases, trading intentions, and political and religious structures, though the institutions established to spread and maintain Christianity, and to regulate sexuality, were quite different in each of the patterns of colonization noted above.

French North America

The first systematic missionary work was begun among the Micmacs, an Algonkian-speaking people on Nova Scotia in 1610, and during the following decade both Jesuits and the smaller religious order of the Recollects began to proselytize among other nations in various parts of eastern Canada, initially preferring the settled groups such as the Hurons over the more nomadic Algonquins and Montagnais. As French traders and trappers moved into the Great Lakes areas and the Mississippi Valley, missionaries moved with them. As in the Spanish colonies, many of these missionaries were sponsored by the monarchy, because the French kings viewed missionary work as an exercise of their royal power.

Jesuits in particular learned local languages and lived with potential converts, traveling with the more nomadic peoples. They used every occasion to preach and catechize, including funerals, councils, and visits to the sick, and employed imagery that fit with local traditions, often acting like shamans by curing illnesses and interpreting dreams. The conversion process was not simply an oral one, for missionaries also used pictures, chants, plays, music, bells, and holy objects such as amulets, crucifixes, and altar vessels. Jesuits tended to have a more positive view of indigenous culture, or at least of indigenous capacity for true conversion, than members of other orders did, although less positive than that of Jesuit missionaries in China. Though native converts became "prayer-captains" (*dogiques*) and a few native women became nuns, no Native American man became a priest, and most Indian women in convents were lay sisters rather than professed nuns.

The number of converts in French North America grew slowly during the seventeenth century, as conversion generally cut one off from the family and kin networks that were essential to survival; many of the early converts were war-captives, already separated from their home people. Adults often waited until they were near death to be baptized, and missionaries recognized that it would be important to organize mission communities for those who converted earlier. Such communities, beginning with Sillery near Quebec, were closely supervised by a priest, with residents subject to strict discipline, administered by the priest himself or by the native *dogiques*. Such discipline included punishment for sexual and moral offenses, and for having contacts with non-Christians among one's own nation, or contacts with Europeans other than those approved by the priest. In these communities, churches were built with elaborate decorations, schools were opened, and confraternities were established. Indians often came to missions for protection during times of warfare or for recuperation after epidemics, for the priests offered material aid along with spiritual advice to those who converted. In some places, such as Kahnawake near Montreal, Indians formed Christian communities on their own as refuges from war and the alcohol-induced violence that was destroying many native communities.

After 1700 the number and vigor of missions declined in much of French North America, as the Jesuit order lost dynamism. There were also increasing conflicts between Protestants and Catholics, because Protestant missionaries from the British colonies began working among Native Americans in French or disputed areas. Religion came to be seen as a way of holding Indians and Europeans to French or British loyalty, with each side prizing conversions, both from the "wrong" type of Christianity and from native belief systems.

Along with churches, schools, and religious institutions for Indians in French North America, there were also churches and institutions for European residents. Churches were found predominantly in the towns and cities of the east, and were much fewer in number than those in the English colonies of New England, for the European population of New France grew very slowly in the colonial period. (Historians estimate that at the time Britain took over Canada in 1763, there were only 75,000 French people in the entire area, compared with perhaps two million in the British colonies.) Upper-class families in French Canada did attempt to follow French marriage norms as much as possible, requiring parental and familial consent for marriage and intermarrying with each other.

The first confraternities were founded for men and women in New France in 1652, and the first schools, run by members of religious orders, at about the same time. The original women's houses of Ursulines and Augustinians grew to seven, which meant there were more religious orders for women, both European and Indian, than for men. By 1725, one out of every hundred European residents in New France was a nun. In 1665, enclosed convents were joined by another type of religious community for women, when Marguerite Bourgeoys (1620–1700) established a teaching congregation modeled on those being founded in Europe in the frontier town of Montreal. Bourgeoys, who described the Virgin Mary's uncloistered life as her model, took in Canadian-born and immigrant French girls. Later Native American

Figure 6.1
Mohawk women taking vows of perpetual virginity in front of a statue of the Virgin
Mary at the Jesuit mission of Kahnawake near Montreal during the 1670s. This drawing
appears in the annual report to his superiors of Claude Chauchetière, one of the Jesuit
priests at the mission. A group of female converts at the mission followed severe ascetic
practices, including long exposure to cold, but for the Jesuits the women's choice to
remain virgins was the most important aspect of their piety. By permission of the
Archives départementales de la Gironde, Bordeaux.

and mixed-race girls were admitted as well, both as temporary residents before
marriage and full members. In New Orleans, a group of French Ursulines
also took the Virgin Mary as their patron when they established a community
and school in 1727 and a women's lay confraternity in 1730. As in Europe,
the members of the Marian confraternity in New Orleans, which soon included
more than a third of the free women and girls in the city, vowed "to serve
the Blessed Virgin, to honor her not by their prayers alone, but also by their
morals, and by all the conduct of their lives."[4]

Christianity in French North America was shaped by changing government
policy about how best to increase the colony's population and strength. Most
immigrants in the seventeenth century were unemployed young men from
urban environments, who stayed briefly and then either died or went back
to France. For a brief period in the 1660s the French Crown directly recruited

young women to go to New France, mostly poor women from charity hospitals, and paid for their passage; about eight hundred of these *filles du roi* (daughters of the king) did immigrate, more than doubling the number of European women who were not nuns. They were matched to prospective husbands by Bourgeoys and other heads of Quebec's religious communities for women, but their numbers were never great enough to have a significant effect on the population. French finance minister Jean-Baptiste Colbert decided not to expand the program, however, stating explicitly in 1667 that "it would not be wise to depopulate the kingdom in order to populate Canada." Instead he recommended that "the most useful way to achieve it would be to try to civilize the Algonquins, the Hurons, and the other Savages who have embraced Christianity; and to persuade them to come to settle in a commune with the French, to live with them, and educate their children in our mores and our customs . . . after some time, having one law and one master, they may form one people and one blood."[5] Thus official policy in New France in the seventeenth century was one of the assimilation of Native Americans through *Fransication*, through which they would be "made French."

The policy of *Fransication* included intermarriage between French men and indigenous women, for the French hoped that such marriages would help the fur trade and strengthen ties between French and Native American communities and families. In a few cases, this policy had exactly the effect that the government hoped it would: couples married in Christian ceremonies and Indian women adopted the clothing, work patterns, and language of French women. In many more cases the opposite happened, however. Marriages, if they occurred at all, were "in the custom of the land," and French men adopted "savage" customs. Official opinion changed. "One should never mix a bad blood with a good one," wrote the governor of New France in 1709, "Our experience of [intermarriage] in this country ought to prevent us from permitting marriages of this kind, for all the French men who have married savage women have been licentious, lazy and have become intolerably independent; and the children they have had are even lazier than the savages themselves. Such marriages should thus be prohibited."[6] Prohibition of intermarriage became official policy in New France in 1716, and Indian–French marriages were discouraged by secular officials elsewhere in French North America, although the Jesuits who lived far from colonial governments in Montreal and New Orleans ignored this. They recognized that sexual relations between French traders and Native American women would continue, and regarded Catholic marriage as preferable to concubinage or marriage according to local customs. In 1724, French colonial Louisiana (which included a large part of the Mississippi Valley) also forbade the "King's white subjects" to "contract a marriage or live in concubinage with Blacks."[7] (There were very few African slaves in the northern parts of

French North America, mostly household servants in wealthy urban households, so black–white relations were not a matter of great concern there.)

Officials in Louisiana tried positive measures as well as prohibitions. They succeeded in convincing the king to again pay for the transport of women from France, and from 1704 to 1728 several hundred French women came to Louisiana. The administrators wanted "hard-working girls . . . daughters of farmers and the like," but the young women were often recruited from houses of detention in France, so instead turned out to be "women and girls of bad life" who were also "extremely ugly." Male settlers refused to marry the new arrivals, and in 1727 the governor of Louisiana recommended building a "house of correction here in order to put in the women and girls of bad lives who cause a public scandal."[8] The program was stopped in the following year.

New England

The norms of conduct in New England were derived originally from English Puritanism, and continually promulgated in sermons and printed tracts by New England clergy. They generally held that sexual relations within marriage were a positive good, as long as they were not excessive. John Robinson, the pastor of the Pilgrim settlers in Plymouth, warned:

> Marriage is a medicine against uncleanness . . . [but] As a man may surfeit at his own table or be drunken with his own drink; so may he play the adulterer with his own wife, both by inordinate affection and action. For howsoever the marriage bed cover much inordinateness this way: yet must modesty be observed by the married, lest the bed which is honourable and undefiled (Hebrews 13.4) in its right use, become by abuse hateful, and filthy in God's sight.[9]

All sexual relations outside of marriage were unacceptable; the Puritan pastor Samuel Danforth argued that, "Uncleanness pollutes the body, and turns the temple of the holy ghost into a hog-sty and a dog's kennel."[10] Certain types of sexual acts were worse than others. Those between men and women – defined as "natural" – were deemed less polluting than those between persons of the same sex or persons and animals. These were described repeatedly as "unnatural" or, in the Puritan preacher Cotton Mather's words, "vile . . . unutterable abominations and confusions."[11]

Sexual deviancy and religious heresy were often linked in the minds of religious leaders. In the trials of Anne Hutchinson and several Quaker women for heresy and sedition, Puritan clergy charged that their teachings would lead, in the words of John Cotton, to "all promiscuous and filthie cominge together of men and Woemen without distinction or relation of Marriage . . . and soe more dayngerous Evells and filthie Unclenes and other sines will follow than you doe now Imagine or conceave."[12] Clerics referred to England as "Sodom," a society meriting punishment for its sexual sins, and worried that New England was also becoming lax. Such harsh opinions about sexual activities were not limited to clergy; a New Haven magistrate warned a suspected couple that fornication was:

> a sin which shutts [them] out of the kingdome of heaven, without repentance, and a sinn which layes them open to shame and punishment in this court. It is that which the Holy Ghost brands with the name of folly, it is that wherein men show their brutishness, therfore as the whip is for the horse and asse so a rod is for the fooles back.[13]

A range of institutions were charged with enforcing standards of sexual behavior. The earliest law codes of New England, based on the Old Testament and English statutes, provided capital punishment for a number of sexual offenses. Included in these were adultery, defined as intercourse with a married or engaged woman, and rape, defined as forced sexual relations with a married or engaged woman, or with a single woman under the age of ten. Forced intercourse with an unmarried woman over age ten was excluded from definitions of rape in some colonies, as was any intercourse that resulted in pregnancy. Along with their European counterparts, colonial authorities accepted the notion that conception required female orgasm and would not occur if the woman truly objected to the intercourse; as a 1655 manual for justices of the peace stated, if the women was pregnant, "consent must be inferred."[14] Bestiality was also a capital crime, as was sodomy, though its definition varied; in most colonies it included only male–male relations, though in New Haven it also covered female–female relations, heterosexual anal intercourse (described as "carnall knowledge of another vessel then God in nature hath appointed to become one flesh"), and male masturbation "in the sight of others . . . by example, or counsel, or both, corrupting and tempting others to doe the like."[15]

Law codes set lesser punishments for other types of sexual offenses, including fornication, "lewd and lascivious carriage" (overly flirtatious behavior in women or men), spouse abuse, "wanton dalliance" (appearing to give one's attention to several suitors), living apart from one's spouse, and courting a woman without first obtaining approval from her parents or the local magistrate.

Punishments included fines, whipping, branding, loss of voting rights, and various shaming rituals.

Marriage was considered a civil contract, and, until the 1690s, all marriages were conducted by a secular magistrate, not a pastor. Because of its civil nature, and also because Puritans regarded harmony between spouses to be essential in a marriage, most New England colonies allowed divorce for a variety of reasons, including desertion, impotence, adultery, cruelty, and bigamy. In some areas the remarriage of divorced spouses was limited, but in others, especially in New Haven, innocent spouses were given the blanket right to remarry. This relative ease of divorce stood in sharp contrast to practice in England, where after 1660, divorce was only possible by act of Parliament. In establishing such laws the colonies were, in fact, disobeying English laws and colonial mandates.

Laws regarding sexual acts were enforced by secular courts, which heard all of the types of cases that in England were handled by ecclesiastical courts. County courts heard the less serious cases, such as fornication, and circuit courts the more serious, such as divorce, adultery, rape, and infanticide. Courts ordered midwives to examine women accused of fornication, pregnancy out of wedlock, or infanticide, and charged neighbors to keep an eye on their neighbors, lest they be accused of being accessories in sexual crimes.

Courts were not the preferred avenue of enforcement, however, for Puritan communities favored informal mechanisms of control whenever possible. Clergy and concerned neighbors privately admonished families to control their unruly members, viewing the male head of household as the first line of defense. This was one reason that unmarried adults in New England were officially required to live with a married or widowed male head of household. Another was a suspicion of those who lived alone, which made one, in the words of an Essex County, Massachusetts, court, "subject to much sin and iniquity, which ordinarily are the consequences of a solitary life"; the convicted man in this case was ordered to "settle in some orderly family in the town, and be subject to the orderly rules of family government."[16] Though in this instance it was a man who was ordered to submit to "family government," women were the more common recipients of such admonitions. Wives were ordered to obey their husbands and authorities were often slow to interfere in cases of wife-beating, particularly if the wife was viewed as provoking her husband.

If family and neighborhood pressure did not work, church discipline was the next step. Members were admonished to confront individuals they suspected of moral infractions, and ask them for repentance. If this appeal was unsuccessful, they were to report the actions to the pastor, who was to handle the matter privately. If this still did not have the desired effect, suspected offenders were investigated by a church committee, and if the suspicions appeared to be warranted, they were asked to appear before the congregation and make a public, oral confession. If they did, and the congregations judged them properly penitent, they were reintegrated into the community, for the congregation was more interested in reclaiming sinners than in punishing them. Such confessions might be very dramatic, such as that of a Massachusetts woman accused of fornication in 1681 who, "being put to it to speak by way of acknowledgment of the sin, she gave noe answer but weept whether for the shame or the sin that was not known."[17]

If the sinner did not or would not confess, however, sterner punishments were available. Church records contain many cases similar to this one from the First Church in Boston in 1638:

> Anne Walker, the wife of one Richard Walker and sometime [i.e., previously] the wife and widow of our brother Robert Houlton having before this day been often privately admonished of sundry scandals, as of drunkenish, intemperate, and unclean or wantonish behavior, and likewise of cruelty towards her children and also of manifold lies and still to this day persisting impenitently therein, was therefore now with joint consent of the Congregation cast out of the Church.[18]

Excommunication had to be voted on by a majority of the adult male church members and was the strongest punishment the church could impose; excommunicates could nevertheless be liable for secular punishments for the same acts, as there was no notion of double jeopardy.

The early involvement of the entire congregation in discipline changed somewhat beginning in the 1660s, when ministers were given a stronger voice in church deliberations and women became more numerous than men as church members. First women and then men were allowed to write their confessions for the minister to read, thereby reducing their dramatic effect. Slightly later the audience at such confessions was limited to full church members, so the whole community no longer listened in. With the acceptance of the Half-Way Covenant in 1662, the number of people required to make confessions increased, however, for now everyone who had been baptized was open to church discipline.

The disciplinary institutions described so far primarily involved the European population of New England. The African population in New England was relatively small in the colonial period – historians estimate there were 11,000 Africans in New England by 1750, most of them slaves – and only a few blacks were accepted as full church members. This was also true for Dutch Reformed congregations in New Amsterdam/New York, but German Lutherans, who began establishing congregations in the mid-seventeenth century, were more open. Lutherans admitted African Americans as full church members and supported both the marriage of slaves and interracial marriage among free people. Many free blacks in colonial New York became Lutheran, although this trend ended in the mid-eighteenth century when Lutheran churches absorbed the growing racism around them and became less welcoming. African Americans then moved into Methodism, and, after the American Revolution, began founding their own churches.

Although the original English colonial charters listed the conversion of Indians as an aim, missionary work among the Indians began slowly in New England. In the 1640s Thomas Mayhew, Jr. began to preach to the Wampanoags on Martha's Vineyard, and John Eliot began work among the Massachusetts near Boston. In 1649, the New England Company was founded to support Eliot's work. He and one of his converts, Job Nesuton, prepared a Bible in Massachusetts, the first Bible translation into a North American language; it was printed in 1661 with only Eliot's name on the title page.

Like some of the early French officials in Canada, Eliot thought it essential that Indians adopt European dress, housing styles, economic organization, patriarchal family structure – what he termed "visible civility" – along with Christianity. He thus established "praying towns" for converts beginning with Natick, where Indians were to learn European agriculture along with Scripture and to form covenanted congregations modeled on those of their Puritan neighbors. Native sexual and marriage practices such as "trial marriage" and easy separations were defined as sin. Missionaries were most interested in winning male converts, who were to instruct their families, so schools for Indian boys were an essential part of these praying towns, and many native converts became schoolmasters. Fourteen praying towns were established before 1675, and Eliot estimated that he and others had 2,300 converts, 300–400 of them baptized. Eliot worked with the Massachusetts secular authorities to also set up a separate system of Indian courts, with Indian judges that would hear cases involving native converts. Indians from Natick served as missionaries to other groups, confronting pau-waus with medical treatments, preaching, prayer, and psalm singing, and also served as preachers and catechists within their own congregations.

The armed conflict led by the Wampanoag sachem Matacom in 1675–76 – known as King Philip's War – devastated many New England towns; hundreds of colonists and thousands of Native Americans died. Many Indians, both converts and non-converts, were taken from their homes; some were forced to live on an island in Boston Harbor and others deported to Bermuda. Many were placed as indentured servants in English homes, where they were to be taught Christianity as well as English ways, but now by a white male household head, not by a schoolmaster or catechist from their own people. Missionaries no longer hoped to transform Indian society, but simply make more modest changes; in achieving this lesser goal even women could assist, and missionaries increasingly advised female converts to promote family prayers and good household order. Despite restrictions on their freedom, however, native Christians themselves continued to develop a distinctive religious culture that combined Christian and Indian rituals and devotional practices. Healing and funeral rituals included elements from both English and Indian traditions, and even English settlers sometimes turned to native ritual practitioners when they sought cures or supernatural assistance.

Outside of Massachusetts there were fewer converts in the seventeenth century, for the few English missionaries in frontier areas such as Maine or New York were less successful than the French Jesuits who were also working in these areas. This situation changed somewhat in the early eighteenth century as the Anglican Church began more intensive missionary efforts; it formed the Anglican Society for the Propagation of the Gospel in 1701 and sponsored translations of Scripture and the Book of Common Prayer into Mohawk. These frontier converts, however, were not organized into missions or praying towns. Conversion among Indians in southern New England also increased during the Great Awakening, when, as among the whites around them, many native individuals saw visions or experienced a sense of "calling."

Southern colonies

Colonization in the south (north of the Spanish colonies in Florida) began in Virginia and the Chesapeake, where the original authorities, although institutionally Anglican, were just as interested in establishing order as were the Puritan leaders in Massachusetts. In 1619, the Virginia Assembly ordered ministers and other religious officials to report all "ungodly disorders," including "suspicions of whoredomes, dishonest company keeping with weomen and suche like," to the county courts so that such actions could be punished.[19] As in New England, religious and secular authority were intertwined. Ministers were ordered to read all new laws and ordinances from the pulpit, and lay church officials, termed "vestrymen" or "church wardens," often served as sheriffs and justices of the peace. Conversely, punishments set by secular courts for sexual and moral offenses included rituals of penance, such as wearing a white sheet in the local parish church.

Yet there were also some significant institutional differences between the two areas. The Church of England (Anglicanism) was the official state religion in the south throughout the colonial period, and Anglican churches had no system which paralleled the Puritan congregation's public confession. Thus matters of sexual and moral conduct were handled either informally through the family, or formally through the secular courts, which explicitly enforced the laws of the Church of England. In 1690, James Blair, the commissary of the Bishop of London and one of the most powerful men in Virginia, attempted to introduce church courts to that colony, but his plan failed. Anglican clergy were generally less powerful and less outspoken than their Puritan counterparts in New England, with laymen taking the lead in disciplinary matters. Because marriage did not carry as much ideological weight in Anglicanism as it did in Puritanism, adultery was not regarded quite as seriously – it was not a capital crime in the south; on the other hand, divorce was prohibited, for bad marriages were to be tolerated, not dissolved.

The settlement pattern of the Chesapeake area resulted in steady business for secular courts. As noted above, early gender ratios were highly skewed in favor of men, and three-fourths of the women who immigrated to the Chesapeake area in the early decades were indentured servants, generally traveling without their families and forbidden to marry during their term of servitude. These factors led to an incidence of pregnancy out of wedlock that was far higher than elsewhere in the English-speaking world; one out of five female servants bore a child outside of marriage. The punishment was originally set at a fine and an extra year or two of service, until authorities discovered that masters were intentionally impregnating their female servants to gain this extra time, in the same way that Spanish Christian men forced sex on Muslim women under their jurisdiction in order to receive them as slaves. The law was revised, and a servant who became pregnant by her master, "shall, after her time by indenture or custom is expired be by the churchwardens of the parish where she lived when she was brought to bed of such bastard, sold for two years, and the tobacco [which served as money in Virginia] to be imployed by the vestry for the use of the parish."[20] Only the servant and not the master was to be punished, for her original period of service with him was not shortened. Servants were also prohibited from engaging in secret marriages or promising themselves to one another, though this was impossible to stop.

Clandestine or extra-legal marriages were not limited to servants in the colonial south; because people often lived great distances from a church, visits by pastors were infrequent, and marriage licenses cost money (or tobacco). Thus although English marriage customs were supposed to be followed, in actuality people often married themselves and began living together in what became known as "common-law" marriages, accepting, in the words of one Maryland man in 1665, that "his marriage was as good as possible it could be made by the Protestants he being one because before that time and ever since there has not been a Protestant minister in the province and that to matrimony it is only necessary the parties consent."[21] Most people were probably comfortable with this situation, though occasionally the more pious petitioned the government for support for more pastors "to suppress the vice and immorality now greatly prevailing in those parts of this province."[22] Such pleas rarely led to actual appointments, however.

The first laws regarding marriage and sexual relationships in the south made no distinctions among Africans, Europeans, and native peoples. In 1638, the Dutch colony of New Amsterdam explicitly forbade sex outside of marriage between "Christians" and "Negroes." This dichotomy was common in other European colonies as well, and appeared in a 1662 law of the Virginia Assembly declaring that the children of slave women would be slaves:

> Whereas some doubts have arrisen whether children got by any Englishman upon a negro woman should be slave or free, *Be it therefore enacted and declared by this present grand assembly*, that all children borne in this country shalbe held bond or free only according to the condition of the mother, *and* that if any christian shall committ fornication with a negro man or woman, hee or shee soe offending shall pay double the fines imposed by the former act.[23]

By making paternity irrelevant for the children of slave women, the law reversed normal English practice, in which legal status followed the father. Its Christian/Negro dichotomy suggests that lawmakers did not recognize that some Africans were Christians, though of course they did, as only a few years later they would pass another law stating that being or becoming Christian would not free "slaves by birth." Similar laws regarding the heritability of slave status were passed in other colonies. The piously titled "Act to Incourage the Baptizing of Negro, Indian, and Mullato Slaves" passed in New York in 1706, for example, noted that the legal status of any "Negro, Indian, Mullato, and Mestee Bastard Child or Children" would follow "ye state of the Mother," and would not be affected by baptism.[24]

At the end of the seventeenth century, "Christian" completely disappeared as a way of categorizing individuals in marital and sexual relationships, and distinctions based on skin color were extended to other groups. The first use of the word "white" as an official category was in a 1661 census in the British West Indies, a usage picked up in a 1691 Virginia statute regulating sex: "Whatsoever English or other white man or woman being free shall intermarry with a negroe, mulatto, or Indian man or woman bond or free shall within three months after such marriage be banished and removed from this dominion forever." Though the basic law is gender neutral, the preamble is gender specific, warning of the "abominable mixture and spurious issue which hereafter may encrease in this dominion, as well by negroes, mulattoes, and Indians intermarrying with English, or other white women."[25] Further clauses in the law set severe punishments, including imprisonment, fines, involuntary servitude, and banishment, for white women who gave birth to mixed-race children even if they did not marry the father, reinforcing the message of the preamble. Between 1700 and 1750, all of the southern states, and also Pennsylvania and Massachusetts, passed laws prohibiting all interracial sexual relationships, with steep fines set for any minister who performed an interracial marriage. Most abhorrent in the eyes of authorities was the rape of a white woman by a non-white man; punishment for attempted rape was set at castration in Virginia, Pennsylvania, and New Jersey, and punishment for a completed rape brought death.

As the 1691 Virginia and the 1706 New York laws make clear, in contrast to the complex hierarchy of *castas* that developed in Latin America, all persons of Indian and mixed heritage in the British North American colonies were regarded as black, including those whose proportion of "white blood" vastly outweighed their proportion of "black blood." This polarization was accompanied by a steady stream of rhetoric describing non-whites as sexually dissipated, as both animalistic and barbaric in their sexual practices.

Once it was stipulated that children of slave women would be slaves, sexual relations among slaves themselves were rarely the concern of secular authorities. As a Maryland judge put it, "we do not consider them as the objects of such laws as relate to the commerce between the sexes. A slave has never maintained an action against the violator of his bed. A slave is not admonished for incontinence, or punished for fornication or adultery."[26] Only in New England were marriages between slaves legally recognized, and the churches in the southern colonies made little effort to get slaves the right to marry. There were some marriages on the larger plantations in the south, but because the gender balance among slaves was highly skewed in favor of men before 1750, there was little possibility of marriage or permanent relationships for many slaves, which provided further evidence, to white eyes, of their lack of sexual restraint.

There were no southern counterparts to the New England praying towns for Indian converts, and the few schools for Native Americans that were established were short-lived and had little impact. Boys who attended them seldom acted as missionaries when they returned to their home villages, and white missionaries were rare in the southern colonies. After 1701 there were a few missionaries sponsored by the Society for the Propagation of the Gospel and later, especially in Georgia, by the Moravians and the Methodists, but most of these ministered only to Indians who lived near white settlements or who came to them. The French Jesuit practice of living in Indian villages or with nomadic groups was not emulated in the southern colonies, whose governors and political leaders regarded the primary task of the limited number of clergy to be ministering to white residents.

Effects

Given the widely varying levels of institutional development among the various Christian denominations in North America, it is not surprising that there was also wide variation in the actual effects of attempts to regulate sexual behavior.

French North America

There is no debate about the devastating effects of European diseases on the indigenous population of French North America, but historians do disagree about the effects of Christian teachings on marital patterns, sexual norms, and other aspects of gender structures. Some historians see Catholic teachings as imposed largely by force, particularly on Indian women, and as very disruptive to native traditions. They find that women were often the strongest opponents of the Jesuits, noting instances in which women recognized conversion would bring a loss of status, refused to convert, or urged male converts to renounce their faith. According to Jesuit reports, male converts placed in positions of authority as *dogiques* attempted to force women to comply with Christian norms, commenting "it is you women . . . who are the cause of all our misfortunes – it is you who keep the demons among us . . . You are lazy about going to prayers; when you pass the cross, you never salute it; you wish to be independent. Now know that you will obey your husbands; and you young people, you will obey your parents and our Captains; and, if any fail to do so, we have concluded to give them nothing to eat."[27] *Dogiques* enforced Catholic rules about the permanence of marriage, ordering women who had left their husbands to return to them or face imprisonment, and punished those who were otherwise disobedient. They were successful to some degree, for divorce was rare in missions, polygamy became increasingly unusual, and many mission residents chose to marry (or remarry, if they had been married earlier in Indian ceremonies) in Christian ceremonies.

Other historians point out that some women accepted Catholic ideas enthusiastically. Marie Rouensa, for example, the daughter of a prominent leader of the Kaskaskia, refused to marry the French trader her father wanted her to marry because he was a known opponent of church aims. The Jesuit missionary Jacques Gravier supported her refusal, noting that "God did not command her not to marry, but also that she could not be forced into doing so; that she alone was mistress to do the one or the other."[28] She was also supported by a group of at least fifty women and girls, who barricaded themselves in a church in defiance of the male leaders of the Kaskaskias. The situation was resolved when Marie Rouensa agreed to the marriage providing both her father and the French trader agreed to become Christian, and their child was the first to be baptized in what later became Illinois (in 1695, at Peoria). This marriage became the model for subsequent marriages between French men and native women in the Illinois area. Christian spouses chose godparents for their children from among other converts, creating Catholic kin networks cemented together by both French and Indian traditions.

Native women effected conversion through catechizing and preaching as well as through their marital choices. The Sisters of the Quebec Hospital reported that Cécile Gannendaris, a Huron, "was so solidly instructed in our mysteries and so eloquent in explaining them that she was sent new arrivals among the Savages who were asking to embrace the faith. In a few days she had them ready for baptism . . ."[29]

Some converts adopted more extreme Catholic practices, including grueling asceticism and self-mortification. A group of Mohawk young women in the Jesuit community of Kahnawake near Montreal, for example, refused to marry, carried out long fasts, whipped themselves with branches, and burned themselves with glowing coals. "In the depth of winter," reported the Jesuit Claude Chauchetière, a missionary at Kahnawake, "two of them made a hole in the ice and threw themselves into the water, where they remained during the time that it would take to say the rosary slowly and deliberately."[30] Fasting and flagellation were penitential practices that were well known among European Christians, but voluntary exposure to cold and burning were not; the young women may have adopted these from earlier Iroquois rituals of healing and war preparation, a good example of the creolization of Christian practices.

One of the women, Catherine (or Kateri) Tekakwitha (1656–80), died at a young age perhaps in part because of her austerities, and Chauchetière became convinced that she was a saint whose rosary and grave had healing properties. He and Pierre Cholenec, another Jesuit colleague who had been Tekakwitha's confessor, wrote long texts describing her virtues and the many miracles that occurred as a result of prayers asking for her assistance or visits to her grave. A local cult developed among French Catholics, although both native Christians and the higher-ups in the Jesuit order were not persuaded about her miraculous healing powers or sanctity. Recognizing how important virginity was to ideals of female saintliness, Cholenec increasingly emphasized this aspect of her life, declaring, "What made our Catherine more blessed than all the rest and placed her in a higher rank, not only than the other Indians of the Sault, but than all the Indians who have embraced the faith throughout New France, was this great and glorious title of virgin. It was to have been the first in this new world who, by a special inspiration of the Holy Ghost, consecrated her virginity to Our Lord."[31] Cholenec's biography was published in 1717, with "first virgin of the Iroquois" as part of the title, and several years later a Spanish translation was published in Mexico City as part of a campaign to open a convent specifically for Indian nuns. Tekakwitha's life was proof, said the translator, that native women could be sexually chaste. Her Jesuit hagiographers hoped to make her an official as well as local saint, but the campaign for this was not powerful or sustained enough in Rome and it did not happen. (In the twentieth century US bishops began a process to have her beatified, the first step on the path to sanctity, and in 1980 Pope John Paul II agreed to this; the Tekakwitha Conference, an organization of Native American Catholics, and other groups continue to press for her canonization.)

The debate about whether the conversion of Native Americans was primarily forced or voluntary is part of the larger rethinking of just what "conversion" means and how we measure it. Do practices that brought together indigenous and Catholic traditions indicate a shallow conversion, or a very deep one? Are Jesuit and later Protestant descriptions of conversions to be believed, or are they simply plugging Indians in to narrative models already in their heads? Some scholars take a firm stance on one side or the other of such questions, but others have concluded that these set up false dichotomies; conversion is a *process* in which new beliefs and practices are selectively adopted, blended with existing ones, and openly, unknowingly, or surreptitiously rejected.

In terms of sexual practices, French missionaries noted that the most difficult Catholic teaching to accept appeared to be the indissolubility of an unsatisfactory marriage. The Jesuit Father Vimont wrote in 1642, "The stability of marriage is one of the most perplexing questions in the conversion and settlement of the Savages; we have much difficulty in obtaining and in maintaining it," and in 1644, "Of all the laws which we propound to them, there is not one that seems so hard to them as that which . . . does not allow them to break the bonds of lawful marriage."[32]

Native people were not the only ones who found certain Christian norms of sexuality difficult to follow. In western French North America, despite the fulminations of authorities about mixing blood, European men and Indian women continued to engage in sexual relations, and in areas where inter-marriage worked to the benefit of the local people, to marry. These marriages were often formalized by Native American rituals rather than Christian ones; in the standard phrase, they were "in the style of the land." Only sixty-five church marriages between French men and Indian women are listed in the records for all of New France during the whole period 1608 to 1765, out of a total of more than 27,000 marriages.

Many of the issues involving religion and sexuality that emerged in other parts of the world were largely absent from French North America, however. There was no Inquisition, and there were very few trials for witchcraft. Only three dozen witchcraft accusations made it into the records for the entire period 1645–830, most of them in larger towns, and no one was ever executed for witchcraft in French Canada. All of the witchcraft cases involved Europeans, for, in contrast to South America, the magical activities of Indians or mixed-blood people were largely ignored by the Catholic Church of New France. Both church and state authorities also appear to have ignored same-sex activities except among Europeans. A few cases of "crimes against nature" emerge in the records of secular courts, especially among soldiers, but apparently none of these resulted in an execution.

New England

Puritan concerns about moral conduct were, by some measures, vigorously enforced in the earliest decades of settlement, with heads of household, local officials, and pastors acting together. New England had few of the institutions that in old England sometimes limited godly discipline, such as craft guilds or journeymen's organizations, and no long-standing customs that people could use as a defense for engaging in behavior judged immoral or ungodly. Rates of illegitimate birth and bridal pregnancy were far lower than in England or the southern colonies, but fornication was the most frequent category of crime heard by lower courts throughout New England in the seventeenth century, and sexual crimes constituted between 20 and 40 percent of serious crimes. This concentration on sexual matters meant that women made up a larger share of those prosecuted for criminal offenses than was normally the case in early modern societies. Men were also convicted in fornication cases in the seventeenth century, for the woman's word about her child's father was often taken seriously and the putative father pressured into confession. (Women who would not name the father in cases of children out of wedlock suffered excommunication along with secular punishments such as whipping, so that most women named a father.) Men were sentenced to whipping for bastardy and "lascivious carriage" almost as often as were women, a sharp contrast to England, where customary male prerogatives were more powerful and men were rarely prosecuted for sexual crimes. Because sexual relations were part of what Puritans considered a good marriage, men were also occasionally disciplined for not having sex with their wives, for, as one 1665 case put it, "refusing to perform the marriage duty to her according to the law of God and man."[33] Sexual gossip and rumors, along with other types of slander, were prosecuted frequently, with the slanderer ordered to bring proof or take the inflammatory words back in both court and church. Authorities sometimes deferred to the wishes or rights of spouses in cases of adultery, but not always, for adultery was viewed as harmful to the community as well as the marriage.

Courts and churches extended their punishments even to those judged not guilty. People suspected of fornication or adultery but let go because of insufficient proof were forbidden to see each other alone or given more stringent sentences. Adultery was a capital crime, and required two witnesses for proof of guilt; juries knew this was difficult to obtain, but remained careful, and often grudgingly convicted the couple only on the lesser charges of "adulterous behavior" or "lascivious, gross, and foul actions tending to adultery." This still merited punishment, of course. Like the Spanish boys suspected of sodomy and so passed through the fire as a warning of what would happen if they continued their behavior, New England couples found guilty of suspected adultery were ordered to "stand upon the ladder at the place of execution with halters about their necks for one hour."[34] This might be followed by a further shaming ritual, with the couple ordered to "for ever after wear a capital A of two inches long, and proportional bigness, cut out of cloth of a contrary color to their clothes, and sewed upon their upper garments, on the outside of their arm, or on their back."[35]

Although the New England colonies allowed divorce for a much wider range of causes than did the church in England, divorce statistics indicate that the Puritan stress on the importance of the family, combined with the economic significance of the family as a unit of production, worked to keep most couples together. One count of divorces finds 128 in all of New England for the period 1620–99, and some of them were actually annulments. Most divorces were sought by women, and most of these for desertion; men seeking divorce generally charged adultery. There were no divorces for cruelty or abuse alone, though cases of verbal and physical abuse were handled in courts and churches, and there were more convictions for adultery than divorces for it, indicating that spouses (usually wives) were willing to put up with adulterous behavior. One out of six divorce petitions involved charges of male sexual incapacity – as the petitioning wife in one case put it "His yard Is as weake as a pece of flesh without bone or sinnow" – which reflected Puritan teachings that sexual performance was an essential part of a husband's proper social role.[36]

Court records indicate that many people internalized Puritan values. Couples who had resisted confessing to having sexual relations during betrothal generally gave in and confessed when they wanted to get a child baptized.

Elizabeth Dane, a married woman, replied to a seducer who told her that no one would see their actions, "but God sees if nobody [else] sees, for God sees in the dark."[37]

On the other hand, court records also provide evidence that even in the initial decades, Puritan external and internal control of morals was less stringent than popular stereotypes would lead one to believe. New England governments and churches did interfere more in personal and household behavior than did those in the southern colonies, but only in extreme cases were family heads actually punished. Neighbors reported on their neighbors in church or when questioned in support of a legal case, but despite admonitions about "mutual surveillance," almost no sexual offenses were actually brought to courts by prying neighbors. Fines for fornication or pre-marital sex could be steep – the price of a steer – but convictions did not bring permanent loss of status, as long as one confessed, and there is evidence that many New Englanders accepted the practice of sexual relations between betrothed couples. There were harsh sermons preached at sex-related executions, but very few of those executions. "Adulterous behavior" could result in punishment, but in Massachusetts Bay Colony during the period 1673–1774 there were only 38 total indictments for actual adultery and only one execution. The reduction of a capital crime to one less serious also occurred in rape cases, for there were only five executions for rape in seventeenth-century New England, and the only cases of forcible sex actually tried as "rape" were those in which the victims were under ten.

This disjuncture between rhetoric and reality is evident in the treatment of sodomy, for despite harsh denunciations of sodomy, actual prosecutions were very rare. There were about twenty sodomy prosecutions in British North America, of which two ended in hanging, both in the seventeenth century; two cases involved women, but they were termed "lewd" behavior rather than sodomy. Because sodomy convictions required proof of penetration and two witnesses, they were extremely difficult to prove, and it appears that communities were willing to tolerate a surprising amount of same-sex behavior, even among those expected to maintain higher moral standards. In one case, a Baptist minister in Connecticut was charged several times over a period of thirty years with "unchaste behavior with his fellow men when in bed with them," but the ultimate penalty was simply a brief dismissal from his position that ended quickly by congregational vote after he confessed his sins.[38] There is no evidence of a homosexual subculture in America, in part because there were few large cities, a situation which also resulted in very little organized prostitution before 1750.

However one chooses to judge New England's moral behavior in the seventeenth century, it is clear that after about 1720 – the timing differs slightly from community to community – people's conduct became more like that elsewhere in the English-speaking world. The proportion of brides who were pregnant increased, and slander and defamation suits declined. Fewer adulterers and fornicators made church confessions, but simply remained excommunicate, while those accused of lesser morals crimes joined a less stringent denomination. In large part this "decline" – for that is how many preachers interpreted it – resulted from the success of the New England colonies. Many historians estimate that the white population of New England doubled every twenty-five years throughout the colonial period, an expansion that brought greater diversity and lessened the ability of all institutions – family, church, and state – to enforce behavioral conformity.

Changes in the eighteenth century also arose from secular authorities' decreasing interest in enforcing godliness. The churches still heard confessions of fornication, but courts generally no longer handled fornication cases unless a child was involved, and shaming rituals and whippings became less frequent, even for illegitimacy. Secular authorities became more concerned with the economic issues involved in out-of-wedlock births than with the moral ones, so more of their cases involved marginal people, especially poor women. Because of this, skepticism about relying on the woman's word alone in fornication and rape cases increased, and women were punished for not resisting their rapists. Men increasingly fought paternity charges, usually successfully, and a sexual double standard developed. In Connecticut, coercive father–daughter incest became the only sexual act for which white men were always punished. Thus secular scrutiny of moral behavior was increasingly limited to the poor, with propertied men and women excluded. Puritan preachers decried this trend as a sign of moral decline, but they could do little to stop it. The prominent preacher Jonathan Edwards was, in fact, dismissed from his post by a congregational vote in 1750, in part because, as Edwards himself commented in his farewell sermon, they found his campaign "for suppressing vice among our young people" and calls to avoid "impurity, levity and extravagance," "obnoxious" and of "great offense."[39] During the last quarter of the eighteenth century, many congregations voted to end public confession, instead simply requiring those who wanted to join to confess any moral lapses to a minister in private.

This change in attitudes about the enforcement of godliness emerged most dramatically in New England in handling the two crimes most clearly associated with female sexuality, infanticide and witchcraft. Though the New England colonies did not officially adopt the Jacobean law making an unmarried woman's concealment of her infant's death presumptive evidence of murder until the 1690s, convictions and executions on such grounds began in the 1630s, and the rates of indictment for infanticide in New England far exceeded those of

England. In pamphlets, lectures, and sermons preached at executions, Puritan leaders in New England emphasized the gravity of infanticide, and linked it with moral depravity, concealment of sin, demonic actions, and women's weakness in the face of temptation. Writing about the first execution for infanticide in Massachusetts, John Winthrop noted, "she was so possessed with Satan that he persuaded her (by his delusions, which she listened to as revelations from God) to break the neck of her own child, that she might free it from future misery."[40] In *Pillars of Salt, an History of some Criminals Executed in This Land for Capital Crimes* (1699), Cotton Mather focused on the uncleanness, concealment, and disobedience involved in infanticide, and linked the fires of lust with the fires of hell. Mather's work was timely, as the 1690s were the high point of convictions for infanticide in New England. As with other types of crimes related to sexuality, however, conviction rates declined after that, and after 1740 no woman in New England was executed on the evidence of concealment alone. In 1784, punishment for concealment of the death of an illegitimate child in Massachusetts was reduced to 100 dollars or a year's imprisonment, with references to God, sin, or morality gone from the law.

The timing and tone of infanticide convictions directly parallels those for witchcraft in New England. The death penalty was set for witchcraft in 1641 in Massachusetts and 1642 in Connecticut; both laws stressed the diabolical compact discussed in Chapter 2. As in most parts of Europe, the majority of people accused of witchcraft in New England (over 300 between 1620 and 1725) were women. Trials often included issues of interference with sexual relations or birth, mothering, or harm to children. The only mass trial in North America, the Salem outbreak of 1692, began with teenage girls who attempted to use magical means to find out whom they would marry, and subsequently accused several women of bewitching them. Social, political, religious, sexual, and economic tensions in the Salem community led what might have been a minor incident to explode until almost 200 people were accused, at least fifty people confessed, and nineteen were executed (those who confessed were not executed). Puritan leaders argued that Satan had enticed women into undermining their godly commonwealth, and that only executions would cleanse the community. Their language in this directly parallels their words about infanticide, and their concerns about the godly community partially explain why 95 percent of the known witchcraft accusations and 90 percent of the executions for witchcraft in British North America happened in New England. The Salem trial turned out to be an aberration rather than a model, however, for a few years later many Puritan leaders, including those who had been judges at the trial, felt guilty about their actions, and in 1711 the Massachusetts General Court passed a bill reversing the convictions of twenty-two people.

One of the women initially accused in the Salem case was Tituba, a slave from Barbados who confessed to having helped the girls search out witches, though not to bewitching them. (She was not executed.) Her position as an outsider in a largely white society certainly made her more vulnerable, but in this, as in so much else, the Salem case was unusual, for Native Americans – Tituba was part African and part West Indian – were generally not charged with witchcraft.

Native Americans who had converted in New England were occasionally charged with sexual crimes – the first Indian was tried for adultery in Massachusetts in 1639 – and the praying towns had strict rules of conduct, forbidding idleness and drunkenness along with a range of sexual activities. Protestant ministers reported that residents of the praying towns took such rules seriously, but also found some of them difficult to follow. When describing his own conversion, the Natick convert Ponampam noted in 1653 that "my heart did love the having of two wives, and other lusts of that kind." It is not clear whether Ponampam was talking about two wives at one time, or the more common practice of a series of marriages; whatever the case, this nearly made him give up his decision to become a Christian, as "my heart was troubled, because many were my sins."[41] Enforcement of these rules was the responsibility of Indian as well as white leaders, and punishments such as fines and whippings were imposed.

Concern with unusual marriage practices among Indian converts lessened in the late seventeenth century, however, as a result of three trends operating together: the narrowing of missionary aims as the result of King Philip's War; the general decline of interest in enforcing godliness; and a particular lack of concern about marriages among the impoverished underclass, which increasingly included most Indians as well as black and mixed-race slaves and servants. Some Native American groups responded to this by first recording – or perhaps inventing – customary laws regarding marriage, which they used in colonial courts in cases involving economic issues connected to marriage such as inheritance and property ownership. Groups such as the Narragansetts asserted that their marital traditions were a central part of their cultural identity as Narragansetts. For white officials, however, anything that was not a formal Christian marriage was not a true marriage, and a two-tier system of marriage developed, the upper involving formal church weddings for most whites, and the lower a variety of folk customs for Indians, blacks, and some poor whites.

Southern colonies

In some ways the actual pattern of sexual regulation in the south parallels that of New England. Serious sexual crimes such as sodomy, bestiality, rape, or incest, were very rare, while lesser moral offenses such as fornication, sexual slander, sexual relations during betrothal, or having children out of wedlock, made up a significant share of the business before the county courts. Some actions that were officially illegal – common-law marriage or sex during betrothal, for example – were accepted by many people. Estimates of the Chesapeake area during the seventeenth century find that common-law marriages actually outnumbered church marriages among the white population and that about one-third of brides were pregnant at marriage, a rate two to three times that of England during the same period. The frequency of bridal pregnancy led some people actually punished for this infraction to object. Thomas and Eady Tooker, for example, found guilty of pre-marital sex by a Virginia County Court in 1641, were ordered to do penance at their parish church, "standing in the middle ally of said church upon a stool in a white sheet, and a white wand in their hands, all the time of the divine service and shall say after the minister such words as he shall deliver unto them before the congregation." Instead Eady, "like a most obstinate and graceless person, did cut out and mangle the sheet wherein she did penance" and was sentenced to twenty lashes and to repeat the penance "according to the tenor of the said spiritual laws and form of the Church of England in that case provided."[42]

Adultery was generally punished with whipping and penance, and could be the basis of a legal separation, though not, as in New England, a divorce with right of remarriage. Legal separations were expensive and very rare, with desertion a more common solution to marital breakdown. Although in theory children were required to obtain the consent of their parents to any marriage, in practice the lack of marriage registration and the frequency of common-law marriage meant that no law about consent could be enforced. Marriages without parental consent were punishable by a fine, but the marriage itself was not voided, which gave parents (and the extended family) far less control over the marriages of their children than in areas under French or Spanish law, including French Canada and Latin America.

The declining moral fervor noted in New England also affected the south. During the seventeenth century, sex between unmarried persons, sex between engaged persons, and bearing an illegitimate child were all tried as fornication in the secular courts and punished by fines, whipping, and shaming rituals. Court records suggest that some people internalized feelings of shame, or at least said they did to authorities; Ann Gray, a married woman, voluntarily confessed to adultery in 1667, and the records note: "Her owne guilty conscience and desire to ask her husband's forgiveness did occasion this her confession of Adultery."[43] After confession and punishment, however, most of those involved, including women who had borne a child out of wedlock, were reintegrated into their communities.

By the eighteenth century the primary concern of the courts was the financial support of children born out of wedlock; charges of fornication were added to those of illegitimacy only when the mother was white and the child of mixed race. The courts concentrated on finding and securing money from the father, not on shaming him. He rarely appeared in court along with the mother, and the women who did appear were more often poor or marginal. These women appear to have had greater difficulty in subsequently finding a husband than was the case in the seventeenth century, in part because attitudes toward them had changed, and in part because the sex ratio was becoming increasingly balanced making it easier for men to find wives. As in New England, southern courts were reluctant to punish men of property for sexual crimes; rape accusations by female servants were generally dismissed, and in one case the court ordered a seven-year-old rape victim to be "corrected by her mother for that her fault and for that there appeareth in her a signe of more grace and greife [grief] for her offence."[44]

Fornication, adultery, bastardy, and rape records in this era only concern white women. Forced sex with a slave woman was not legally defined as rape or fornication; her children were sometimes referred to as "bastards" – as in the New York law cited above – but because slaves were often prohibited from marrying, their children could not be anything else. It was their status as slaves, not as children born out of wedlock, that mattered to their owners. Slaves in the south and elsewhere in the colonies sometimes married in Catholic or Protestant ceremonies, or with rituals they devised themselves. Despite the lack of legal recognition for slave families, black residents of the south often developed strong family connections, frequently transplanting certain characteristics of African families, such as vigorous extended kin networks. Owners sometimes attempted to prohibit slave marriages, but more often simply ignored them when deciding to sell or purchase slaves. The conditional nature of slave marriage might even be officially recognized in the ceremony. One white minister in Massachusetts, for example, had marrying slaves promise fidelity to one another only "so Long as God in his Providence, shall continue your and her abode in Such Place (or Places) as that you can conveniently come together."[45]

Black membership in Christian churches grew significantly with the Great Awakening, which emphasized personal conversion experiences and revelations of the Holy Spirit. Many Methodist, Baptist, and Moravian churches took in black members, although their stress on the equal duty of all to "live soberly, righteously, and godly" put slaves in a difficult situation. Churches often regarded all extramarital sexual relations as sin, even for slaves who were prohibited from marrying or forced to live apart. Slaves were sometimes excommunicated for "living in fornication" or even simply "wanting to commit adultery."[46] In this case the secular courts' neglect was a more realistic response than the churches' regulation.

African American preachers and revivalists also established their own churches affiliated with the Methodists and Baptists in the American South and British Caribbean, traveling as free people or shipped from place to place as slaves. Both women and men developed new and distinctive patterns of worship, forms of Christian expression, and institutional structures in these churches. By the latter half of the eighteenth century some black churches were disciplining their own members for moral issues such as adultery, fornication, or attempted rape, although they rooted their handling of these issues in the situations faced by enslaved and free black people.

Other areas and groups

The discussion in this chapter has primarily focused on three areas – French North America, New England, and the southern colonies – and on three types of religious institutions – Catholicism, Puritanism, and Anglicanism – all of which operated in close cooperation with secular authorities. This is an incomplete picture of Christianity and sexuality in North America, however, for there were many other Christian groups that developed highly distinctive sexual and marital patterns. Some of these groups were localized and some found throughout the colonies; some cooperated with or even became the secular authorities, while others were hostile to secular government; some of these groups began in Europe, and some, especially those which developed in the eighteenth century or later, started in North America.

Organized sexual variation – their opponents would say deviation – began in 1625 with Thomas Morton's settlement at Merry Mount near Plymouth, where both European settlers and Indians had sexual relations outside of marriage, including with each other. Morton was deported and later died after a harsh imprisonment, but the next group confronting the Puritan leadership was not so easily dismissed. In the 1630s Roger Williams, Anne Hutchinson and others were expelled for opposing Puritan leadership, but their followers grew in numbers in Rhode Island and other colonies. Many of them became Baptists and adopted rituals of adult baptism; each congregation made its own decision on most theological and disciplinary matters. Some congregations had elaborate disciplinary procedures with public confession and penance, with both women and men serving as petitioners, defendants, and witnesses.

English Quakers began to preach in Massachusetts and other colonies in the 1650s, and, despite, harsh punishments including whipping, deportation, and execution, were not dissuaded from their mission. Quakers were more egalitarian than other Christian groups, with women as well as men serving independently as missionaries. This egalitarianism was also reflected in their structures of church governance. Quakers had no ordained clergy, but were guided by men's and women's meetings, which regulated morality along with doctrine. The first women's meetings were established in British North America in 1681, and generally oversaw marriage formation. To be allowed to marry "within the meeting" (Quakers used the words "meeting" and "meeting house" rather than "congregation" and "church") people had to produce a certificate stating that they were free to marry and that both parties were Quaker; marriage to non-Quakers was stringently opposed, with those who did so required either to repent or to face expulsion, and parents urged to cut "out-marrying" children off from inheritance.

Persecution of Quakers in Massachusetts led to the founding of Pennsylvania in 1681, where Quaker principles initially underlay the law codes and their enforcement. Quakers were pacifists and generally opposed killing, so that the only capital crime was willful homicide; sodomy, rape, and incest were to be punished by whipping and imprisonment. (Pennsylvania was forced in the early eighteenth century to reinstate the death penalty for sodomy, as the British Crown wanted to bring Pennsylvania laws in line with those in Britain.) Divorce was allowed for adultery, bigamy, sodomy, or bestiality, and in the late eighteenth century, for cruelty, although, as in New England, the actual number of cases was very small.

Religious toleration in Pennsylvania led other groups to immigrate there in the eighteenth century, many of whom had very distinctive sexual ideas and patterns. Conrad Beissel (1690–1768) established Ephrata Cloister in 1732 in Lancaster County and preached the superiority of asceticism and celibacy for both women and men. Though there was some hostility from local men when their wives left them to join the Cloister, eventually a stable community of male and female celibates along with married couples developed, sustained by specialized trades such as printing for men and medicine preparation for women. In 1741, the Moravians founded a community at Bethlehem, which quickly grew to several hundred residents and sent out scores of missionaries to Indian, European, and African communities. The members were organized into sex and age cohorts called "choirs," and were segregated by sex until marriage. Decisions on marriage partners were made by lot. A man seeking a wife came to the Elders' Conference, the group of all adult communicants, which proposed a possible spouse. Three colored ballots standing for "yes," "no," and "wait" were placed in a box, and one was drawn, which was regarded as "the Saviour's decision."[47] Prospective spouses and their families had to consent to the match, but the ultimate decision rested with the lottery.

During the Great Awakening, small groups of people elsewhere in the British colonies developed unusual ideas about the relationship between Christianity and sex. In New England, "perfectionists" argued that religious conversion had made them free from sin, and "Immortalists" held that conversion had made them bodily incorruptible. Such ideas led a few people to "deny The Civil Authoritys Power in Marriage" and "hold that the union between two Persons when rightly married together is A Spiritual Union."[48] The spiritual nature of marriage led a handful to reject sex in marriage, and others to leave their spouses and take others who had similar religious convictions. Such actions horrified more traditional Puritan and Anglican clergy, who viewed them as "criminal freedoms with the other sex under the splendid guise of spiritual love and friendship," and as proof of the continuing link between religious deviance and sexual disorder.[49] Even the Methodists were somewhat suspect along these lines, because they used vivid language of romantic love for religious devotion, and supported romantically based marriages between "soul-mates" (their words), even if these conflicted with family wishes.

Experimentation with distinctive sexual patterns and family forms continued in North America after the American Revolution with religious groups such as the Shakers and the Mormons, and in many ways continues today. All of these groups enforced their patterns primarily by expelling those members who objected or deviated, a procedure that, as we have seen, began with the earliest Puritan colonists. Because these later groups were not state churches, however, this expulsion was not reinforced by secular penalties; because expulsion occurred in areas where there were often many different active denominations, expelled members could usually find a different Christian group to join, or start their own. The same was true for Puritans in New England and Anglicans in the south by 1750, and slightly later for Catholics in Canada, as Moravians, Presbyterians, Baptists, Methodists and others all sent missionaries and established congregations.

* * *

In some ways North America offered early modern Christians the best opportunities to put their ideas about social discipline and the proper sexual order into action, either among Native Americans whom missionaries regarded as blank slates awaiting conversion or among colonists who intended to create model communities based on Christian principles. Unfortunately for the most eager souls, native people were not the blank slates nor colonists the model citizens they had anticipated, and expectations about the ease with which sexuality and other aspects of human morality could be regulated were rather quickly dashed. The intersection between Indian and European – and in the southern colonies African – cultures, and the very early mixing of a range of Christian groups and ideas meant that diversity would outweigh conformity from almost the beginning of colonial history. By 1750, the drive to establish moral communities was no longer a political one enforced by secular courts, but largely a religious one enforced by religious bodies and binding only upon church members. Although challenging one's own tradition and leaving the denomination of one's family could be a wrenching experience, the religious landscape of North America offered so many choices in most areas that most people who did choose to break with their original faith community could find an alternative acceptable to them elsewhere.

Selected further reading

John D'Emilio and Estelle B. Freedman, *Intimate Matters: A History of Sexuality in America* (New York: Harper and Row, 2nd edn 1997) provides a general overview of sexuality in American history, and both Smith, *Sex and Sexuality* (note 14) and Godbeer, *Sexual Revolution* (note 22 of Chapter 6 in "Notes") analyze sex in colonial America. General studies of gender and religion in the colonial Americas include Leslie J. Lindenauer, *Piety and Power: Gender and Religious Culture in the American Colonies* (New York: Routledge, 2001) and Susan E. Dinan and Debra Myers, eds, *Women and Religion in Old and New Worlds* (New York: Routledge, 2001). Lindman and Tarter, *Centre of Wonders* (note 46) includes essays on ideas about the body in the colonial United States.

Denise Lardner Carmody and John Tully Carmody, *Native American Religions: An Introduction* (New York: Paulist Press, 1993) is a good place to begin for a look at American religions before the coming of Christianity, and Nancy Shoemaker, ed., *Negotiators of Change: Historical Perspectives on Native American Women* (New York: Routledge, 1995) a good collection on women's roles. On men's roles, see R. Todd Romero, "'Ranging Foresters' and 'Women-Like Men': Physical Accomplishment, Spiritual Power, and Indian Masculinity in Early-Seventeenth-Century New England," *Ethnohistory* 53(2) (Spring 2006): 281–329. Sue-Ellen Jacobs, Wesley Thomas, and Sabine Lang, eds, *Two-Spirit People: Native American Gender Identity, Sexuality, and Spirituality* (Urbana: University of Illinois Press, 1997) presents a variety of perspectives on two-spirit people; see the readings at the end of Chapter 4 for further scholarship on this subject.

Many of the works that consider Native American and European history together rather than separately, such as the works of James Axtell and Colin Calloway noted in the Introduction, pay special attention to the role of religion and/or sexuality in these encounters. See: Neal Salisbury, *Manitou and Providence: Indians, Europeans, and the Making of New England 1500–1643*

(New York: Oxford University Press, 1982); Margaret Connell Szasz, *Indian Education in the American Colonies, 1607–1783* (Albuquerque: University of New Mexico Press, 1988); Richard White, *The Middle Ground: Indians, Empires, and Republics in the Great Lakes Region, 1650–1815* (Cambridge: Cambridge University Press, 1991); Daniel K. Richter, *The Ordeal of the Longhouse: The Peoples of the Iroquois League in the Era of European Colonization* (Chapel Hill: University of North Carolina Press, 1992); Matthew Dennis, *Cultivating a Landscape of Peace: Iroquois–European Encounters in Seventeenth-Century America* (Ithaca, N.Y.: Cornell University Press, 1992); Robert Grumet, *Historic Contact: Indian People and Colonists in Today's Northeast United States in the 16th–18th Centuries* (Norman: University of Oklahoma, 1995); Daniel R. Mandell, *Behind the Frontier: Indians in Eighteenth-Century Eastern Massachusetts* (Lincoln: University of Nebraska Press, 1996); James Axtell, *The Indians' New South: Cultural Change in the Colonial Southeast* (Baton Rouge: Louisiana State University, 1997); Jean M. O'Brien, *Dispossession by Degrees: Indian Land and Identity in Natick, Massachusetts, 1650–1790* (Cambridge: Cambridge University Press, 1997); Karen Ordahl Kupperman, *Indians and English: Facing off in Early America* (Ithaca, N.Y.: Cornell University Press, 2000). James Axtell, ed., *The Indian Peoples of Eastern America: A Documentary History of the Sexes* (New York: Oxford University Press, 1981) and Colin G. Calloway, ed., *Dawnland Encounters: Indians and Europeans in Northern New England* (Hanover, N.H.: University Press of New England, 1991) and *The World Turned Upside Down: Indian Voices from Early America* (Boston: Bedford Books, 1994) all provide original sources.

General works on the history of Canada that provide useful background include: Olive Patricia Dickason, *The Myth of the Savage and the Beginnings of French Colonialism in the Americas* (Edmonton: University of Alberta Press, 1984); William Eccles, *The Canadian Frontier, 1534–1760,* rev. edn (Albuquerque: University of New Mexico Press, 1984); John Webster Grant, *Moon of Wintertime: Missionaries and the Indians of Canada in Encounter since 1534* (Toronto: University of Toronto Press, 1984); Bruce G. Trigger, *Natives and Newcomers: Canada's "Heroic Age" Reconsidered* (Kingston and Montreal: McGill-Queen's University Press, 1985); Alison Prentice, *Canadian Women: A History* (Toronto: Harcourt, 1988); Allen Greer, *The People of New France* (Toronto: University of Toronto Press, 1999); Katie Pickles and Myra Rutherdale, eds, *Contact Zones: Aboriginal and Settler Women in Canada's Colonial Past* (Vancouver: UBC Press, 2005). The most important original source for the study of early Christianity in French North America is the 73-volume *Jesuit Relations and Allied Documents* (note 3); the documents in this collection are parallel translations, with both French (or occasionally Latin) and English. Nearly every volume has some comments about sexual issues, with volume 18 providing the most concentrated observations on this.

Studies that look at the ways in which European colonists and Native Americans constructed racialized differences include Nancy Shoemaker, *A Strange Likeness: Becoming Red and White in Eighteenth-Century North America* (Oxford: Oxford University Press, 2004); Thomas N. Ingersoll, *To Intermix with Our White Brothers: Indian Mixed Bloods in the United States from Earliest Times to the Indian Removal* (Albuquerque: University of New Mexico Press, 2005); Belmessous, "Assimilation and Racialism" (note 5); Aubert, "Blood of New France" (note 6). Studies that focus primarily on black/white issues in the construction of race include: Kirsten Fischer, *Suspect Relations: Sex, Race, and Resistance in Colonial North Carolina* (Ithaca, N.Y.: Cornell University Press, 2001); Elise Lemire, *"Miscegenation": Making Race in America* (Philadelphia: University of Pennsylvania Press, 2002); Colin Kidd, *The Forging of Races: Race and Scripture in the Protestant Atlantic World* (Cambridge: Cambridge University Press, 2006); Steven Martinot, "Motherhood and the Invention of Race," *Hypatia* 22(2) (Spring 2007): 79–97; Jennifer Spear, *Race, Sex, and Social Order in Early New Orleans* (Baltimore, Md.: Johns Hopkins, 2009).

There are many excellent studies of the conversion process in French North America, including Eleanor Leacock, "Montagnais Women and the Jesuit Program for Colonization," in Mona Etienne and Eleanor Leacock, eds, *Women and Colonization: Anthropological Perspectives* (New York: Praeger, 1980), 25–42; Karen Anderson, *Chain Her By One Foot: The Subjugation of Women in Seventeenth-Century New France* (London: Routledge, 1991); Carol Devens, *Countering Colonization: Native American Women and Great Lakes Missions, 1630–1900* (Berkeley: University of California Press, 1992); Annemarie Shimony, "Iroquois Religion and Women in Historical Perspective," in Yvonne Yazbeck Haddad and Ellison Banks Findly, eds, *Women, Religion and Social Change* (New York: State University of New York Press, 1985), 397–418; and "The Rise or Fall of Iroquois Women," *Journal of Women's History* 2 (1990–91): 39–57; Peter A. Goddard, "Augustine and the Amerindian in Seventeenth-Century New France," *Church History* 67 (1998): 662–81; Peter A. Goddard, "Converting the Sauvage: Jesuit and Montagnais in Seventeenth-Century New France," *The Catholic Historical Review* 84(2) (April 1998): 219–38; Susan Sleeper-Smith, *Indian Women and French Men: Rethinking Cultural Encounter in the Western Great Lakes* (Amherst: University of Massachusetts Press, 2001); Carl J. Ekberg, *Stealing Indian Women: Native Slavery in the Illinois Country* (Urbana: University of Illinois Press, 2007); Kathleen DuVal, "Indian Intermarriage and Metissage in Colonial Louisiana," *The William and Mary Quarterly* 65(2) (April 2008): 267–304; Davis, "Iroquois Women" (note 2). On Catherine Tekakwitha, see Nancy Shoemaker, "Katerina Tekakwitha's Tortuous Path to Sainthood," in Shoemaker, *Negotiators of Change*, (49–71) and especially Allan Greer, *Mohawk Saint* (note 30).

The role of convents and women's orders in Canada has been discussed in: Leslie Choquette, "'Ces Amazones du Grand Dieu': Women and Mission in Seventeenth-Century Canada," *French Historical Studies* 17 (1992): 626–55; Natalie Zemon Davis, *Women on the Margins: Three Seventeenth-Century Lives* (Cambridge, Mass.: Harvard University Press, 1995); Allan Greer, "Colonial Saints: Gender, Race, and Hagiography in New France," *The William and Mary Quarterly* 57(2) (April 2000): 323–48. Two books by Patricia Simpson look at the life of the remarkable Marguerite Bourgeoys: *Marguerite Bourgeoys and Montreal* and *Marguerite Bourgeoys and the Congregation of Notre Dame* (Montreal and Kingston, McGill-Queens University Press, 1997 and 2005). On convents in New Orleans, see Emily Clark, *Masterless Mistresses: The New Orleans Usulines and the Development of a New World Society, 1727–1834* (Chapel Hill: University of North Carolina Press, 2007) and *Voices from an Early American Convent: Marie Madeleine Hachard and the New Orleans Ursulines, 1727–1760* (Baton Rouge: Louisiana State University Press, 2007).

There are several good overviews of women's experience in the colonial United States that include discussion of marriage and sexuality. These include: Mary Beth Norton, *Founding Mothers* (note 15); Paula Treckel, *To Comfort the Heart: Women in Seventeenth-Century America* (New York: Twayne, 1996); Larry D. Eldridge, *Women and Freedom in Early America* (New York: New York University Press, 1997). Many useful sources may be found in Frey and Morton, *New World* (note 18). Several essay collections about women and religion in America include colonial materials: Rosemary Radford Ruether and Rosemary Skinner Keller, eds, *Women and Religion in America. Volume 2: The Colonial and Revolutionary Periods* (San Francisco: Harper and Row, 1981); Marilyn J. Westerkamp, *Women and Religion in Early America, 1600–1850: The Puritan and Evangelical Traditions* (New York: Routledge, 1999).

The many works on the family also contain important information about attitudes toward sexuality and sexual practices. These began with several that focused on the Puritan family, including Edmund S. Morgan, *The Puritan Family: Religion and Domestic Relations in Seventeenth-century New England* (New York: Harper and Row, 1966) and John Demos, *A Little Commonwealth: Family Life in Plymouth Colony* (New York: Oxford University Press, 1970). Works that look beyond the Puritans include: J. William Frost, *The Quaker Family in Colonial America* (New York: St. Martins, 1973); Philip Greven, *The Protestant Temperament: Patterns of Child-Rearing, Religious Experience and the Self in Early America* (New York: Knopf, 1977); Barry Levy, *Quakers and the American Family: British Settlement in the Delaware Valley* (New York: Oxford University Press, 1988); Carol Shammas, "Anglo-American Household Government in Comparative Perspective," *William and Mary Quarterly* 52 (1995): 104–50; Aaron Spencer Fogleman, *Jesus is Female: Moravians and the Challenge of Radical*

Religion in Early America (Philadelphia: University of Pennsylvania Press, 2007); Wall (note 43). For works on Native American Christian families, see Tracy Neal Leavelle, "Geographies of Encounter: Religion and Contested Spaces in Colonial North America," *American Quarterly* 56(4) (December 2004): 913–43; Douglas L. Winiarski, "Native American Popular Religion in New England's Old Colony, 1670–1770," *Religion and American Culture* 15(2) (Summer 2005): 147–86; Plane, *Colonial Intimacies* (note 41).

Puritan attitudes toward sex and their effects continue to be debated. For two largely opposing viewpoints, see Edmund S. Morgan, "The Puritans and Sex," *New England Quarterly* 15 (1942): 591–607 and Kathleen Verduin, "'Our Cursed Natures': Sexuality and the Puritan Conscience," *New England Quarterly* 56 (1983): 220–37; for a study that brings in other aspects of Puritan thought, see James T. Johnson, "The Covenant Idea and the Puritan View of Marriage," *Journal of the History of Ideas* 32 (1971): 107–18. For a study of the impact of Puritan attitudes, see R.W. Roetger, "The Transformation of Sexual Morality in 'Puritan' New England: Evidence from New Haven Court Records, 1639–98," *Canadian Review of American Studies* 15 (1984): 243–57. For one example of decidedly non-puritan (with a small "p") sexual activities, see Michael Zuckerman, "Pilgrims in the Wilderness: Community, Modernity, and the Maypole at Merry Mount," *New England Quarterly* 50 (1977): 255–77.

Discussion of sexuality is often included in works that focus on women. Those covering New England include: Laurel Thatcher Ulrich, *Good Wives: Image and Reality in the Lives of Women in Northern New England 1650–1750* (New York: Oxford University Press, 1980); N.E.H. Hull, *Female Felons: Women and Serious Crime in Colonial Massachusetts* (Urbana: University of Illinois Press, 1987); Susan Juster, *Disorderly Women: Sexual Politics and Evangelicalism in Revolutionary New England* (Ithaca, N.Y.: Cornell University Press, 1994); Cornelia Hughes Dayton, *Women Before the Bar: Gender, Law and Society in Connecticut, 1639–1789* (Chapel Hill: University of North Carolina Press, 1995); Elaine Forman Crane, *Ebb Tide in New England: Women, Seaports, and Social Change, 1630–1800* (Boston: Northeastern University Press, 1998); Ruth Wallis Herndon, "Women as Symbols of Disorder in Early Rhode Island," in Tamara L. Hunt, ed., *Women and the Colonial Gaze* (New York: SUNY Press, 2002), 79–90.

The Salem trial has been the best-studied witch case anywhere in the world; there are over thirty books, exploring it from every possible angle. Those that analyze sexual and gender elements include: Carol Karlsen, *The Devil in the Shape of a Woman: Witchcraft in Colonial New England* (New York: Random House, 1987); Elaine Breslaw, *Tituba, Reluctant Witch of Salem: Devilish Indians and Puritan Fantasies* (New York: New York University Press, 1995); Elizabeth Reis, *Damned Women: Sinners and Witches in Puritan New England* (Ithaca,

N.Y.: Cornell University Press, 1997); Marilynne Roach, *The Salem Witch Trials: A Day by Day Chronicle of a Community Under Siege* (Lanham, Md.: Taylor Trade Publishing, 2004). Frances Hill, *The Salem Witch Trials Reader* (Cambridge, Mass.: Da Capo Press, 2000) includes a wide array of original sources.

Along with studies of women, those that investigate the handling of moral offenses in New England also contain information about sexual practices. See, for example, Emil Oberholzer Jr., *Delinquent Saints: Disciplinary Action in the Early Congregational Churches of Massachusetts* (New York: Columbia University Press, 1956); David H. Flaherty, "Crime and Social Control in Provincial Massachusetts," *The Historical Journal* 24 (1981): 339–60 and *Privacy in Colonial New England* (note 17); David Thomas Konig, *Law and Society in Puritan Massachusetts: Essex County, 1629–1692* (Chapel Hill: University of North Carolina Press, 1979); Roger Thompson, "'Holy Watchfulness' and Communal Conformism: The Functions of Defamation in Early New England Communities," *New England Quarterly* 56 (1983): 504–22; Roger Thompsen, *Sex in Middlesex: Popular Mores in a Massachusetts County, 1649–1699* (Amherst: University of Massachusetts Press, 1986); Erik R. Seeman, "'It is Better to Marry than to Burn': Anglo-American Attitudes Toward Celibacy, 1600–1800," *Journal of Family History* 24(4) (October 1999): 397–419; Dwight Bozeman, *The Precisionist Strain: Disciplinary Religion and Antinomian Backlash in Puritanism to 1638* (Chapel Hill: University of North Carolina, 2004); Richard J. Ross, "Puritan Godly Discipline in Comparative Perspective: Legal Pluralism and the Sources of 'Intensity,'" *American Historical Review* 113 (October 2008): 975–2002. Some studies in the growing history of masculinity also discuss sexuality; see Anne S. Lombard, *Making Manhood: Growing Up Male in Colonial New England* (Cambridge: Harvard University Press, 2003); Thomas A. Foster, *Sex and the Eighteenth-Century Man: Massachusetts and the History of Sexuality in America* (Boston: Beacon, 2006). Articles that explore the links between gender and identity include: Kathleen Brown, "Changed . . . into the fashion of man: The Politics of Sexual Difference in a Seventeenth-Century Anglo-American Settlement," *Journal of the History of Sexuality* 6 (1995):171–93; Sarah E. Yeh, "'A Sink of All Filthiness': Gender, Family, and Identity in the British Atlantic, 1688–1763," *The Historian* 68(1) (Spring 2006): 66–88.

Turning to the Chesapeake, useful studies of marriage, sexuality, and religious life include: Thad W. Tate and David L. Ammermann, eds, *The Chesapeake in the Seventeenth Century: Essays on Anglo-American Society* (Chapel Hill: University of North Carolina Press, 1979); Lois Green Carr, Philip D. Morgan, and Jean B. Russo, eds, *Colonial Chesapeake Society* (Chapel Hill: University of North Carolina Press, 1988); Mary Beth Norton, "Gender and Defamation in Seventeenth-Century Maryland," *William and Mary Quarterly*, 3rd ser., 44 (1987): 3–39, and "Gender, Crime, and Community in

Seventeenth-Century Maryland," in James Henretta *et al.*, eds, *The Transformation of Early American History* (New York: Knopf, 1991), 126–50; Janet Moore Lindman, "Acting the Manly Christian: White Evangelical Masculinity in Revolutionary Virginia," *William and Mary Quarterly* 57(2) (April 2000): 393–416; and Horn, *Adapting* (note 42). On women in Chesapeake and the south, see: Linda l. Sturz, *Within Her Power: Propertied Women in Colonial Virginia* (New York: Routledge, 2002); Cara Anzilotti, *In the Affairs of the World: Women, Patriarchy, and Power in Colonial South Carolina* (Westport, Conn.: Greenwood Press, 2002); Terri L. Snyder, *Brabbling Women: Disorderly Speech and the Law in Early Virginia* (Ithaca, N.Y.: Cornell University Press, 2003); Debra Meyers, *Common Whores, Vertuous Women, and Loveing Wives: Free Will Christian Women in Colonial Maryland* (Bloomington: Indiana University Press, 2003); Brown, *Good Wives* (note 44).

Analyses of African Christianity in the Americas in the colonial period include: Mechal Sobel, *Trabelin' On: The Slave Journey to an Afro-Baptist Faith* (Princeton, N.J.: Princeton University Press, 1979); Sylvia Frey and Betty Wood, eds, *Come Shouting to Zion: African-American Protestantism in the American South and British Caribbean to 1830* (Durham, N.C.: University of North Carolina Press, 1998); Jon F. Sensbach, *Rebecca's Revival: Creating Black Christianity in the Atlantic World* (Cambridge, Mass.: Harvard University Press, 2006). More general studies of African culture include Donald R. Wright, *African Americans in the Colonial Era: From African Origins Through the American Revolution* (Arlington Heights, Ill.: Harlan Davidson, 1990); John Thornton, *Africa and Africans in the Making of the Atlantic World, 1400–1680* (Cambridge: Cambridge University Press, 1992). Works on the role of African women include David Barry Gaspar and Darlene Clark Hine, *More than Chattel: Black Women and Slavery in the Americas* (Bloomington: Indiana University Press, 1996) and Jennifer Morgan, *Laboring Women: Reproduction and Gender in New World Slavery* (Philadelphia: University of Pennsylvania Press, 2004).

Studies that address specific issue include the following.

On divorce: Merril D. Smith, *Breaking the Bonds: Marital Discord in Pennsylvania, 1730–1830* (New York: New York University Press, 1991); Nancy F. Cott, "Divorce and the Changing Status of Women in Eighteenth-century Massachusetts," *William and Mary Quarterly*, 3rd ser., 33 (1976): 586–614; Sheldon S. Cohen, "What Man Hath Put Asunder: Divorce in New Hampshire, 1681–1784," *Historical New Hampshire* 41 (1986): 118–45; D. Kelly Weisberg, " 'Under Greet Temptations Heer': Women and Divorce in Puritan Massachusetts," *Feminist Studies* 2 (1975): 183–93: Phillips, *Putting Asunder* (note 16).

On rape: Barbara Lindemann, " 'To Ravish and Carnally Know': Rape in Eighteenth-century Massachusetts," *Signs* 10 (1984): 63–82; Sharon Block, *Rape and Sexual Power in Early America* (Chapel Hill: University of North Carolina Press, 2006).

On same-sex relations: Louis Crompton, "Homosexuals and the Death Penalty in Colonial America," *Journal of Homsexuality* 1 (1976): 277–93; Robert F. Oaks, "'Things Fearful to Name': Sodomy and Buggery in Seventeenth-Century New England," *Journal of Social History* 12 (1978): 268–81 and "Defining Sodomy in Seventeenth-Century Massachusetts," in Salvatore J. Licata and Robert P. Peterson, eds, *Historical Perspectives on Homosexuality* (New York: Haworth Press, 1981), 79–83; Roger Thompson, "Attitudes Towards Homosexuality in the Seventeenth Century New England Colonies," *Journal of American Studies* 23 (1980): 27–40; Colin Talley, "Gender and Male Same-Sex Erotic Behavior in British North America in the Seventeenth Century," *Journal of the History of Sexuality* 6 (1996): 385–408; Godbeer, "Cry of Sodom" (note 10); Foster, *Long Before Stonewall* (note 12).

CONCLUSIONS

THE HUNDREDS OF AUTHORS WHOSE research has informed my study
would no doubt have different answers to its central question: How did
Christian ideas and institutions shape or attempt to shape sexual norms and
conduct in the early modern world? The spectrum of scholarly opinions initially
tempted me (invoking a vocabulary familiar to the discourses of Christianity
and sexuality) to abstain from writing a conclusion, to bridle my desire to
make grand sweeping statements in favor of the moderate chapter conclusions,
and instead to allow readers to exercise their free will and rational capacities
in making their own final judgements. I do not allow my students to avoid
pulling material together, however, and further reflection convinced me that
a final chapter was necessary. Though the preceding chapters have separated
ideas, institutions, and effects – into what might be thought of as principle,
policy, and practice – this one brings them back together in a final conversation.

    Much of the current scholarship on sexuality and cross-cultural encounters
has concentrated on questions of identity and difference, and such questions
were also of great concern in early modern Christianity. "Christian" and its
denominational subheadings – Catholic, Orthodox, Lutheran, Anglican, and
so on – were primary identities, established not only by matters of belief,
but also by outward behavior. The desired identity needed to be maintained
through both external agents of control, such as courts and officials, and
internalized agents of control, such as a sense of guilt or shame created
through education, preaching, and confession. Together or in combination,
these agents worked to control and minimize doctrinal deviance, a process
that has been traced extensively in studies of the various Inquisitions, heresy
trials, and religious wars of the early modern period. As we have seen, they

also worked to curb moral and sexual deviance, by creating and maintaining boundaries between what was acceptable and unacceptable for Christian groups and individuals.

The notion of boundaries is a helpful way to think about many of the developments we have traced in this book. There are many different types of boundaries – between nations, languages, social classes, families, religions, ethnic groups – and they serve different functions. Some boundaries define spheres of influence, others set out permissible realms for action, others create or perpetuate ideological categories of difference. Some boundaries are sharp, while others are fuzzy and have liminal border areas; some are permeable, while others are impermeable; some are long-lasting, while others are constantly contested, modified, and revalued. Boundaries are defended through war, diplomacy, propaganda campaigns, or a variety of other means; these campaigns make up much of what we usually call "history." They are also maintained by regulating sexual activity. This may be done through laws prohibiting inter-group marriage or sexual contacts, but it is done more effectively through the establishment and fostering of traditions and other forms of internalized mechanisms of control. If children are taught very early who is unthinkable as a marriage partner, and unattractive as a sexual partner, the preservation of boundaries will not depend on laws or force alone.

The centrality of sex to the preservation of boundaries is something that nearly all human societies have recognized. They have developed laws and norms regarding marriage and other sexual contacts, both to keep their group distinct from others and to preserve hierarchies within the group. Societies sometimes allow elite men to marry or (more often) to have non-marital sexual relationships with non-elite women, and place various restrictions on the children of those unions. The reverse case is much rarer, because the sexual activities of elite women are the most closely monitored in nearly all societies. Thus socially defined categories of difference such as race, nation, and class are maintained by sexual restrictions, and these restrictions are gendered, with women's experience different from that of men.

Christian authorities recognized the importance of regulating sexual activity through external controls and internal norms long before the early modern period. Though conversion did not bring the right to divorce a non-believing spouse, unmarried converts were encouraged to marry other converts, and eventually, Christians were prohibited from marrying Jews and Muslims. Such prohibitions appear to have been effective even in areas with significant Jewish and Muslim populations such as medieval Spain, though there were other types of sexual contacts between persons of different faiths, such as prostitution. Christian groups outside of Europe, such as the Malabar Christians in India and later the "Hidden Christians" in Japan, were also endogamous – marrying within the group – and missionaries throughout the New World and Asia enforced religious endogamy by refusing to marry Christians to non-Christians.

After the Protestant Reformation, secular and religious authorities in both Europe and colonial areas attempted to prohibit marriages between members of different denominations, or when they occurred, to ensure that the children were raised within the "correct" faith. (This practice continues in some denominations today, with a spouse from outside that tradition required to promise that any children will be raised within it, whether or not the outside spouse also converts.) As in many cultures, such rules sometimes involved a sexual double standard that prohibited women from marrying outside the group while allowing men to do so. Whether gender-specific or not, these regulations varied in their effectiveness. People sometimes crossed not only denominational boundaries to marry and start families, but also physical boundaries, traveling to a different area to find a religious authority who would marry them or baptize their children. Small radical Protestant groups were the most effective at policing intermarriage, as they made out-marriage grounds for expulsion. In such cases, the group itself (or a subset of its members) was the ultimate authority, but the marriage did not bring with it civil penalties as it might in areas where secular authorities enforced prohibitions on inter-marriage.

Religious affiliation is a particularly tricky boundary to maintain as it is to some degree volitional – that is, people can change from one religion to another more easily than they can change their mother tongue or skin color. Most early modern Christian denominations were, of course, actively seeking conversions among both non-Christians and other types of Christians, but these very conversions challenged their categories of self and other. Though on one level conversion was desired, on another it was suspect precisely because it was volitional, and the convert could always revert, particularly because conversion is a process, not an event. Converts always selectively adopted new beliefs and practices, and blended these with existing ones, but in doing so they were often suspected of retaining some loyalties to their original religious affiliation.

As we have seen, religious beliefs were often conceptualized physically as blood, with people regarded as having Jewish, Muslim, or Christian blood, and after the Reformation, Protestant or Catholic blood. "Blood" was also a way of talking about class differences in many parts of the world, with those of "noble blood" prohibited from marrying commoners and taught to be protective of their lineage. Blood was also used to describe national boundaries; those having "French blood" were distinguished from those with "German blood," "English blood," or "Spanish blood." Conceptualizing class status and national identity as "blood" naturalized these and made them appear God-given and innate; sexual contacts across such fundamental dividing lines could thus be made to appear threatening and dangerous.

As Europeans developed colonial empires, blood became a way to describe racial distinctions as well as those of religion, class, and nation. In the case of Jews or Jewish converts in Spain and its empire, or the Gaelic Irish in Ireland, religious and racial differences were linked, with religious traditions being viewed as signs of barbarity and inferiority. Initially, in colonial areas outside Europe, the spread of Christianity was used to justify the conquest and enslavement of indigenous peoples. As they converted, however, religion became a less persuasive means of differentiation, and skin color took its place. Virginia laws regarding fornication distinguished between "christian" and "negroe" in 1662, but by 1691 between "white" men and women and those who were "negroe, mulatto, or Indian." "One drop of [black] blood" made one black in the binary racial classification developing in North America, whether or not one was Christian. Religious affiliation also played an increasingly small role in the more complex ethno-racial hierarchies that developed in Latin America and the European colonies in Asia, where Crown, church, and company policies about intermarriage vacillated between promotion and prohibition. Churches were important agents in the creation and maintenance of those hierarchies, however. Church officials had the authority to affirm (or alter) one's racial classification for the purposes of marriage, entering a convent, or becoming a priest by assessing the level of European, creole, Native American, Asian, or African blood in one's veins.

Religious affiliation and race were not the only significant boundaries for early modern Christians. Religious and secular authorities drew (or attempted to draw) a sharp boundary between marriage and other types of sexual relationships, and endeavored to limit sexual activity to married people. These efforts began during the Roman Empire in Europe, as the Church preached against concubinage and other non-marital sexual arrangements, and in favor of allowing individuals of any social status, including slaves, to marry. The sharp divide between married and unmarried was accepted only slowly in Europe, and even more slowly when Christianity was exported outside of Europe into cultures in which there was a range of approved sexual relationships, but it was still there. In some situations certain population groups came to be regarded as exempt from the requirement of marriage or were actually prohibited from marrying, and their sexual activities were rarely the concern of church or state authorities. These groups, such as slaves in the southern British colonies of North America or mixed-race people in the Spanish colonies, were thus further marginalized by their exclusion from marriage and the legitimacy it conferred; this in turn was taken as a sign of their moral depravity. In these areas, race became a marker of marital status, with slave or *mestizo* children simply assumed to be illegitimate.

In all early modern societies, marriage was a matter of concern for families and communities as well as religious and secular authorities, for marriage was closely linked with familial and individual honor. At times familial and community interests conflicted with Christian doctrine. At least in theory, the consent of the parties was required for marriage and that of the individual for a vow of celibacy; these conditions put a greater emphasis on individual choice and what some historians have termed "sexual agency." The power of kin and community over these choices was never completely relinquished, however, and at certain times and locations it made a resurgence in law as well as practice. On the other hand, some individuals were able to defy family wishes in their choices about marriage, and occasionally enlisted religious authorities as their supporters.

Conflicts between individuals and their families over marital choice could be dramatic and protracted, and they have left a historical record no doubt out of proportion to their frequency. In many more cases, familial, community, and church aims supported one another, and young people were socialized effectively enough to choose appropriate marital partners. This pattern in marital choice has often been described as marriage for convenience in contrast to a more modern pattern of marriage for love. In many ways this sets up a false dichotomy, for harmony and companionship – both viewed as aspects of love – were widely regarded among early modern Christians as more easily achieved between spouses whose family backgrounds were similar. Letters and diaries reveal that both men and women expected affection from their spouses and were disappointed when it was lacking.

Christian authors frequently addressed the sexual and emotional elements of marriage in sermons, treatises, and advice manuals as well as private letters, precisely because sex was to be limited to marriage. The glorification of heterosexual married love began in medieval sermons, but it was intensified after the Reformation by Protestants and later by Catholics. Only a handful of Christian authors after 1500, such as a few Orthodox writers from Russia, envisioned the possibility of marriage without sex, for a "chaste marriage" was increasingly defined by both Protestants and Catholics as one in which spouses were sexually faithful to each other and moderate in their sexual activity, not one in which they renounced sex. Marital sexuality still carried with it the taint of sin for many Catholic authors, but most Protestants and some Catholics such as Tomás Sánchez regarded it as morally neutral or even morally good because it increased spousal affection. The inability to have sex in marriage was grounds for annulment, a practice that continues in many states in the United States today, where consummation along with a legal ceremony is required for a marriage to be complete.

The restriction of sexual activity to marriage made a range of sexual activities morally unacceptable, and in many cases illegal, as church and state authorities first in Europe and then elsewhere sought to "criminalize sin." The criminalization of certain sexual activities was not new in the early modern period in Europe; nor was it limited to Christianity. Medieval Christians and non-Christians set punishments for adultery (usually defined as sex with a married women), marrying someone within a prohibited degree or type of relationship, and engaging in sexual activities which broke religious taboos. After 1500 such sexual crimes were joined by others, and the mechanisms of investigation and punishment were expanded, in part through technical innovations such as the printing press and institutional innovations such as birth and marriage registers. All sides in the religious controversies that engulfed western and central Europe during the sixteenth and early seventeenth centuries regarded the control of sexual activities as extremely important, for to religious and political authorities order, morality, discipline, hierarchy, propriety, and stable families were all linked and a mark of divine favor. In both Europe and beyond, authorities established and supported institutions which attempted to control the sexual activities of their adherents or subjects, and tried to instill attitudes which would encourage discipline and decorum. Control of language was an important part of these efforts, and individuals were punished for denying church doctrines about sex, reciting love charms, using sexual blasphemy, or defaming their neighbors with sexual slander. The most rigorous authorities hoped to shape thoughts along with words and actions, haranguing people in confession or sermons about lascivious thoughts and dreams. Secular courts adopted procedures and punishments developed by religious bodies, imposing sentences that involved public confession and shaming rituals. As sins were made crimes, crimes were also made sins.

Efforts to control sin generally had a greater effect on elites and urban residents than they did on non-elites and rural dwellers, but they also often excluded those very elite people whose moral and sexual conduct were not subject to the same rules as the rest of the population. Because the consequences of heterosexual activity were visible in the bodies of women, the criminalization of non-marital sexuality was discriminated by gender as well as class, and the ones who suffered most were often non-elite women who became pregnant. Undisciplined sexuality in both men and women was portrayed from the pulpit and press as a threat to Christian order, but it was women's lack of discipline that was most often punished, even in cases which authorities recognized as involving coercion or force. Penalties for abortion and infanticide increased; women were required to report all pregnancies, and unmarried women were occasionally subject to bodily searches. Only in cases of purported impotence were male bodies subjected to similar public scrutiny.

The desire to draw a sharp boundary between honorable and dishonorable conduct and character led to stricter controls on women whose sexual lives were in some way irregular. Authorities defined them all as "whores" and attempted to punish or incarcerate them in convents or prisons. Gender shaped the handling of clerical sexuality among Catholics as well. Priests and monks were encouraged to abstain from sex and occasionally incarcerated if their sexual activities led to scandal; nuns and other female religious were physically enclosed to keep them from the temptations of the world as pure "Brides of Christ." In Orthodox Russia, elite lay women were similarly enclosed in special women's quarters to keep them pure, though for an earthly, rather than heavenly, bridegroom.

Race along with gender and social class shaped the enforcement of sexual regulations, and the discourse of racial difference was sexualized and gendered. In Europe, the oppositional pair white woman/non-white man was used in literature and art to represent the contrast between purity and evil, while that of white man/non-white woman was used to represent domination and submission. Sexualized conceptualizations of race were more obvious in colonial areas, where in the initial years of conquest, indigenous peoples were often feminized, described or portrayed visually as weak and passive in contrast to their virile and masculine conquerors. Sexual violation was not simply a metaphor in colonial areas, however, for conquest also involved the actual rape of indigenous women and the demands for sexual as well as other types of labor or services. After the immigration of more European women, new discursive elements emerged, and racial hierarchies became linked with those of sexual virtue and purity, especially for women. Again, this was not a matter of language alone; unmarried white women who bore mixed-race children were more harshly treated than those who bore white children, while pregnancy out of wedlock was often ignored or even encouraged among non-white women, who were not pressured to name the father the way their white counterparts were.

The boundaries established by religion, race, and marital status were undergirded by an even more fundamental opposition, that between "natural" – which often shaded into godly – and "unnatural" – which shaded into demonic. Sodomy in all its forms – homosexual, bestial, heterosexual anal – was first defined as a "crime against nature" in about 1250, and viewed by some authorities as heresy and a violation of God's commandments. Causality more often moved in the other direction, however, with persons accused of heresy, such as the Knights Templars in France or New Christian officials in Spain, also charged as sodomites. Racial and ethnic classifications were also a factor in sodomy accusations; the Chinese, Turks, Arabs, and Italians, for example, were seen as particularly likely to engage in sodomy and certain Indian tribes to engage in sodomy and other "unnatural" practices such as cannibalism.

The "unnaturalness" of certain activities linked them firmly to the demonic. In the eyes of their neighbors, only the devil could lead men in Sweden to have sex with animals, or women in Belgium who were pregnant out of wedlock to kill their own children. Contraception was both "unnatural" and "demonic" in the eyes of some authors, as were coital positions other than man-on-top because they overturned the "natural" gender hierarchy and might have contraceptive effects. In Mexico and the Andes, practitioners of indigenous religions were accused of unnatural sexual practices as well as idolatry. In New England, Anne Hutchinson and Mary Dyer, a Quaker woman, were charged with giving birth to monstrous children as well as monstrous ideas. The link between unnatural sexuality and demons was particularly evident in witchcraft accusations; demonologists were often obsessed with how witches copulated with the devil, while less educated people were more concerned with the practical effects of witchcraft on fertility, such as making men impotent or women miscarry.

The actual ability of religious authorities to maintain boundaries through the control of sexuality varied widely, but nowhere were they as successful as they hoped they would be. Though agents of control in the early modern period were certainly more numerous and powerful than they had been in the Middle Ages, they did not approach the policing possibilities of twenty-first-century democratic states, to say nothing of totalitarian regimes. Thus there is an enormous – and sometimes misleading – gap between rhetoric and reality in almost all aspects of sexual regulation.

The gap between learned ideal and lived reality was especially evident in issues surrounding marriage. Particularly in rural areas, people refused to accept the idea that sex between engaged persons was wrong, for it did not upset the marital household as long as the wedding actually took place as planned; thus they continued to engage in it, defend it verbally, and hold fancy weddings despite the obvious pregnancy of the bride. "Trial marriages" continued among the Basques and North American Indian converts, for these practices, too, were viewed as reinforcing the stability of marriage. Despite post-Tridentine demands that weddings be conducted in public, Catholics in Italy continued to hold weddings in secret to ward off evil spells cast by envious neighbors. Christian wedding ceremonies were thought to bring luck and fertility to converts in Africa and Latin America, and they were sometimes added to existing rituals, especially for the first marriage, but they were also avoided so that restrictions on divorce could be ignored. Those restrictions were also less cumbersome in actuality than in theory: abandonment served the function of divorce for many poor people; annulments were frequently possible for the elite; divorces were occasionally granted in Protestant areas on grounds such as severe incompatibility that were socially, though not legally, acceptable. In some places Christians avoided the need for such measures by simply avoiding marriage in the first place. Despite the praise for marriage and the legal advantages which it brought, high rates of births out of wedlock continued in Latin America, for instance, where "concubinage" and other non-marital arrangements were socially useful.

Marriage was not the only sexual matter with a demonstrable gap between theory and practice. In a few cases, such as adultery in Geneva or sodomy in Scotland, punishments were harsher than those set by legal statute, but in most cases the reverse was true. In colonial North America, there were harsh denunciations and stringent laws against adultery and same-sex activity, but

Figure 7.1
Men being burned and hanged for sodomy on the city square in Amsterdam during the Dutch persecution campaign of 1730–31. This engraving appeared as part of a set titled "Temporal Punishments Depicted as a Warning to Godless and Damnable Sinners," published in Amsterdam shortly after the events. This crackdown, apparently begun because of secret denunciations, involved interrogations with torture and led to the execution of perhaps one hundred men and boys. Such "moral panics" were sporadic, and became less common in the eighteenth century. From *The Gay Academic*, by permission of ETC Publications, Palm Springs, California.

almost no cases. Fornication was prohibited, but it was almost never prosecuted in most parts of the world unless it resulted in the birth of a child. Consanguinity – defined differently in various denominations – was forbidden, but the lack of records in Catholic and Orthodox Europe and the colonies made consanguinity rules impossible to enforce except among the elites whose family connections were known. Those elites could generally obtain dispensations to marry their relatives in any case. Brothels were closed, but prostitution continued; popular rituals celebrating or condemning sexual activity, such as Maypoles or charivaris, were prohibited, but went on; clerical concubinage and solicitation were condemned and punished and probably declined, but did not disappear.

Religious and political authorities recognized the limitations on their abilities actually to shape behavior and to maintain boundaries, and so relied upon other individuals and institutions to assist them, including heads of families, volunteer or paid investigatory agents such as the *familiares*, and even concerned and watchful neighbors. To describe such individuals and groups as "assisting" authorities is, in many cases, misleading, for often they, and not higher authorities, took the lead in policing, denouncing, and investigating sexual conduct. Guilds, confraternities, and neighborhood groups might even be more rigorous than church or state authorities, for they often had more to lose if marriages broke down or their members or neighbors were tainted with dishonor. On a day-to-day basis this informal control of sexuality had more of an impact than written laws or formal courts; the actual policing of boundaries was thus very much a shared task, rather than simply imposed from above. Informal policing was done by women as well as men; women arranged marriages, shaped sexual reputations through conversations with their neighbors, accused other women of witchcraft, or reported people who said fornication was not a sin. In colonial areas, control was also exerted by indigenous or mixed-race Christians – *dogiques* in Canada, *fiscales* in Mexico, or Proponents in the VOC colonies – as well as Europeans, who catechized, investigated cases, punished those found guilty of moral lapses, examined candidates for marriage, and sometimes even heard confessions.

Individuals also policed their own activities through the internalization of Christian norms communicated to them in sermons, printed materials, schools, and confession. Confession, either to a priest or to a congregation, encouraged people to talk about their sexual sins, with the ultimate goal of repressing the activity deemed sinful. Confession to a priest may have worked more to disseminate sexual information in some areas than to restrict activity, but it is clear many people developed a sense of guilt that was stronger than simply a fear of being discovered or receiving punishment in this world. It is, of course, impossible to measure something as subjective as a sense of guilt, and those who felt most guilty left the most records, for their feelings led them to indict themselves to their neighbors, legal authorities, or religious personnel, or leave behind private writings like diaries. In some cases these self-indictments were undoubtedly duplicitous, as individuals recognized that expressing contrition was a way to avoid or lessen sentences for such offenses as prostitution or sodomy, but in many cases the sense of guilt appears to have been genuine.

Of all the issues covered in this book, historians disagree the most on how to interpret local and internalized control of sexual norms and activities. Some ignore these aspects, and focus primarily on formal religious institutions such as the Inquisitions, episcopal courts, consistories, or missions, noting the ways in which such institutions narrowed the range of acceptable sexual behavior and promoted hierarchical gender structures. Others view popular control and self-discipline as examples of "false consciousness," and argue that people were deluded into working against their own self-interest and repressing their sexual desires. Others apply Gramsci's idea of hegemony, in which some individuals and groups become convinced through education or other forms of socialization that agreeing with authorities is preferable; they then gain special privileges through their association with the dominant group and its ideas.

These largely negative or dismissive views of internalized and popular control of sexuality are countered by other scholars who point out that in many instances, including colonial ones, the norms of authorities and those of local families and communities actually meshed to a great degree. Yes, families and groups were disciplined, they argue, but they were also disciplining. When the goals of higher authorities did not fit with community standards, they were generally not accomplished, because groups adapted Catholic or Protestant norms to their own situations. This selective adoption and in the colonial world creolization of Christian values and practices was not an example of "false consciousness," but of actual religious conversion in which people chose to shape their behavior and thoughts in order to follow Orthodox, Catholic, or Protestant norms. These scholars assert that though Christianity introduced a language of repression, it also provided ideas and models that individuals and groups found appealing or liberating, and for which they created their own meanings.

As the preceding chapters have shown, there are examples to support all sides of this debate, and historians' positions are determined to a large degree by their general philosophical views on the ability of people to determine their own history. Their arguments are also shaped by the particular situation with which they are most familiar, for the common concerns with boundary setting shared across the early modern Christian world were accompanied by significant local differences in the exact definitions of those boundaries and the ways sex was regulated to establish and preserve them.

First, though I have identified certain ideas and approaches as Catholic, Protestant, or Orthodox, there was wide variation within each of these traditions. Even official theology was not univocal: some Catholics openly doubted the value of celibacy while some Protestants thought it had merit; the morality of sexual enjoyment in marriage was debated in both Protestant and Catholic circles; Jesuits and Jansenists fought over the importance of sexual activities to salvation. Lay people were similarly split: lay Catholics in some places tolerated clerical concubinage, while in others they took the lead in combating it; lay Calvinists in some places reported their neighbors to authorities but not in others; some lay Orthodox celebrated fertility rituals that were pagan in origin, while others killed themselves as Old Believers in defense of traditional Orthodox doctrines. Uniformity in belief was often invented or pretended when one denomination came into conflict with another or was threatened from the outside, but differences emerged again when the threat had passed.

"Protestant" covers a particularly large spectrum of belief and practice, from state-church Lutherans who emphasized the patriarchal family to radical groups who wanted no connection to a secular government and experimented with family forms. Divorce was possible only by act of Parliament in Anglican England, but was available on grounds which went far beyond the traditional Biblical ones in Calvinist Neuchâtel and Lutheran Sweden. Though a few radical groups were sexually freer than magisterial Protestants or Catholics, most of them were more moralistic, using exclusion and excommunication to shape sexual conduct and create a small "sacralized society" within the larger and more sinful society. Groups such as the Quakers and Moravians, in which the entire body made disciplinary decisions, were more egalitarian in their policing of boundaries than those that relied on authorities such as pastors, judges, or inquisitors, but they were also more rigorous and effective.

In some instances, the differences within Protestantism, Catholicism, and Orthodoxy were caused by factors outside the realm of religion. In some parts of Europe and its colonies, royal or municipal courts gained power over marriage, beginning a process of secularization that would speed up in the eighteenth century as the regulation of sexuality was tied to state-building. When monarchical interests conflicted with those of the church, as in Peter the Great's Russia or post-Tridentine France, monarchs often won. In both Russia and France, for example, parental consent was required for a marriage to be valid, despite church doctrine about the primacy of spousal consent.

Second, though there are striking similarities among all early modern Christian denominations and, as just noted, striking differences of opinion within them, there are also some basic distinctions between them. Despite doubts about the value of forced celibacy among Catholics and Orthodox, voluntary celibacy and virginity continued to be highly prized and praised. For some Russian Orthodox writers, this included marital virginity, a practice that Luther and other Protestants regarded as grounds for divorce as well as unnatural. Their rejection of celibacy meant Protestants saw stronger links between marriage, honor, and adulthood than did adherents of other denominations. Both Orthodox and Catholic authorities were suspicious of unmarried women who lived on their own and enforced stricter enclosure on female religious, but Protestants were also suspicious of unmarried adult men, ordering them in some places to move in with married couples. The ability of an adult to reject a life that included sexual activity was denied by most Protestants, for whom celibacy also meant an abdication of his or her basic nature as a man or woman. Protestants thus set up a uniform ideal of sexual life, with marriage and parenthood as essential for both sexes, while Catholicism and Orthodoxy endorsed a range of options.

A third line of difference is that between Europe and the colonies. In some colonial settings, such as the Puritan towns of Massachusetts or the Jesuit missions of New France and Latin America, religious authorities attempted to create disciplined moral and sexual utopias where God's law, as they interpreted it, would be the basis of all social and legal institutions in ways that were impossible in the more decadent Europe. They gathered their co-religionists or converts tightly together in order to supervise their lives and encourage mutual surveillance. For brief periods such places may have been the most sexually disciplined communities in the Christian world, but their isolation was difficult to maintain for long, and those who objected to discipline went elsewhere.

In most parts of the colonial world, opportunities for Christian discipline were less rather than more intense than those in Europe. Christian authorities were generally few in number and widely scattered geographically, so that their ability to shape actual behavior was more limited than it was in Europe where courts and churches were more numerous. Settlements were widely dispersed in many colonial areas, and the opportunities for neighborly surveillance were minimal, as were the opportunities to reinforce one's internal controls by listening to sermons or attending confession. There were more institutions of moral control in colonial cities than in the countryside, but also more opportunities for activities judged immoral, such as prostitution or same-sex relationships. (This is also true of European cities.)

In all parts of the colonial world, whether mission utopia or urban fleshpot, Christian notions were redefined in the face of pre-existing values and norms. This redefinition had also occurred in Europe as Christianity accommodated itself to existing Roman and Germanic practices, but by 1500 it was largely in the past. Accommodation was ongoing in colonial settings: in Asia, for example, ideas about moral debt shaped confessional practices and the development of a sense of guilt; in Latin America, ideas about balance shaped notions of the value of celibacy. Catholicism, Protestantism, and Orthodoxy in Europe were not static in this period, but the range of possibilities was greater in the colonial world.

It was not infinite, however, and although indigenous people developed their own patterns and served as religious officials, the ultimate authority in most colonial settings was in European hands. Other than in Malabar and Ethiopia, Christianity was initially foreign and imported in the colonial world in ways that it was not, of course, in Europe by 1500. It was also part of a structure of dominance that went primarily in one direction, for the attitudes and expectations of European Christians about the peoples they encountered ultimately had a much greater impact on those peoples than the reverse. Colonization had some impact on the regulation of sexuality in Europe, both in terms of demographic changes such as male out-migration and intellectual changes such as new notions of racial difference, but these cannot compare with the changes in colonial areas. In some parts of the world, colonization also brought European diseases and demographic catastrophe along with Christianity, which influenced family relations and sexual activities far more than any courts or clergy.

A fourth line of difference occurs among the colonies. Creolization not only made the situation in Europe different from the colonies, but it also made each colony distinct. Such distinctions in Christian forms were added to many other differences: whether the ultimate purpose of the colony was trade, exploitation, or settlement; how many people immigrated; how many of those people were free or slave women; what Christian authorities thought about the local culture; whether clergy saw their most important function as conversion of indigenous peoples or ministering to immigrants. Each of these and many other factors not only made the experience of colonies different from one another, but also created great differences within a single colony.

A final line of difference is one that intersects all of the others: change over time. As we have seen, in each geographic area there were "moral panics," high points of concern with morality and sexual conduct, followed by periods of less intense scrutiny. There was also a slow tendency toward fewer cases and milder punishments of sexual offenses after a high point sometime in the late sixteenth or early seventeenth century in Europe, and the late seventeenth century in the colonies. Executions for sodomy and witchcraft ended; fornication was no longer prosecuted unless a child needed to be supported, and even then often not if the father was a member of the elite; infanticide was no longer assumed if a child born out of wedlock died. By 1750, new ideas were beginning to develop about the sexual natures of women and men, the importance of personal and familial privacy, and the proper boundaries between religion and the state. All of these ideas would play a role in the development of "modern" sexuality and create a world where Christianity played a lesser role in its definition and regulation than that we have traced here.

Our modern world has not shaken this history as much as some theorists of sexuality have posited, however. The reactions of my friends and neighbors when I began working on the first edition of this book reinforced my sense of its continuing importance. As that edition was published, a sex scandal had just led to the impeachment of the American president, and phrases that appear often in these pages — "criminalization of sin," "puritanical zeal," "public confessions," and even "witch hunt" — were used regularly on the evening news. Commentators from outside the United States trying to understand and explain the situation referred often to the distinctive religious history of Britain's North American colonies and their attempts to create sacralized societies by disciplining sexuality. As I finish work on this second edition, a mixed-race man has just been elected the American president, with a different set of phrases that appear in these pages used throughout the campaign, though only on certain channels of the evening news — "racial mixing," "unnatural," "false convert," "black blood." Any lingering doubts I might have had about the enduring significance of Christianity to contemporary sexual and political discourse are gone.

NOTES

Introduction

1   Vern Bullough, "Sex in History: A Redux," in Jacqueline Murray and Konrad Eisenbichler, eds, *Desire and Discipline: Sex and Sexuality in the Premodern West* (Toronto: University of Toronto Press, 1996), 4; Edith Hamilton, *The Greek Way* (New York: Norton, 1942 and many reprints).

2   Eve Kosofsky Sedgwick, *Epistemology of the Closet* (Durham, N.C.: Duke University Press, 1993), 44.

3   Michel Foucault, *The History of Sexuality I: An Introduction*. trans. Robert Hurley (New York: Random House, 1990), 33 (orig. *L'Histoire de la sexualité 1: La Volonté de savoir* [Paris: Gallimard, 1976]).

4   M.M. Bakhtin, *The Dialogic Imagination: Four Essays*, ed. Michael Holquist, trans. Caryl Emerson and Michael Holquist (Austin: University of Texas Press, 1981), 324.

Chapter 1

1   Alfonso X, *Siete partidas*, and St. Vincent Ferrer, *Sermons*, translated and quoted in David Nirenberg, "Conversion, Sex, and Segregation: Jews and Christians in Medieval Spain," *The American Historical Review* 107(4) (October 2002): 1067–68.

2   Clement of Alexandria, *Stromateis*, trans. John Ferguson (Washington, DC: Catholic University of America Press, 1991), 251, 253.

3   Tertullian, "On Exhortation to Chasitity" and "On the Apparel of Women," trans. S. Thelwall, in Alexander Roberts and James Donaldson, eds, *The Ante-Nicene Fathers* (Grand Rapids, Mich.: Wm. B. Eerdmans, 1951), Vol. 2, 55, 23.

4   "The Life of Saint Pelagia the Harlot," in Ross S. Kraemer, *Maenads, Martyrs, Matrons, Monastics: A Sourcebook on Women's Religions in the Greco-Roman World* (Philadelphia: Fortress Press, 1988), 317, 323, 324.

5   Saint Jerome, *Commentaries on the Letter to the Ephesians*, book 16, cited in Vern Bullough, *Sexual Variance in Society and History* (Chicago: University of Chicago Press, 1976), 365.

6 Saint Jerome, *The Letters of St.Jerome*, trans C. Mierow, *Ancient Christian Writers* (Westminster, Md.: Newman Press, 1946), Vol. 1, letter 22, 162.

7 Augustine, *City of God*, 22. 24, 30, quoted in Margaret R. Miles, "Sex and the City (of God): Is Sex Forfeited or Fulfilled in Augustine's Resurrection of Body?" *Journal of the American Academy of Religion* 73(2) (June 2005), 320–21.

8 Augustine, *Contra Mendacium*, 7.10, quoted in John Boswell, *Christianity, Social Tolerance and Homosexuality: Gay People in Western Europe from the Beginning of the Christian Era to the Fourteenth Century* (Chicago: University of Chicago Press, 1981), 157.

9 Jerome, *Adversus Jovinianum* 1.49, quoted in James A. Brundage, *Law, Sex, and Christian Society in Medieval Europe* (Chicago: University of Chicago Press, 1987), 90–91.

10 Hrosvit of Gandersheim, *Dulcitius*, translated and quoted in Katharina M. Wilson, *Medieval Women Writers* (Athens: University of Georgia Press, 1984), 56.

11 Mark D. Jordan, *The Invention of Sodomy in Christian Theology* (Chicago: University of Chicago Press, 1997), 112.

12 St. Vincent Ferrer, *Sermons*, translated and quoted in David Nirenberg, *Communities of Violence: Persecution of Minorities in the Middle Ages* (Princeton, N.J.: Princeton University Press, 1996), 142.

13 Thomas Aquinas, *Summa theologica*, Part 2 of Part 2, Question 154, Article 1, quoted in James A. Schultz, "Heterosexuality as a Threat to Medieval Studies," *Journal of the History of Sexuality* 15(1) (2006), 18.

14 Thomas Aquinas, *Summa Theologica*, trans. Fathers of the English Dominican Province (London: Burns, Oates and Washbourne, Ltd., 1914) Part 1, Question 96, Article 3 and Part 1, Question 92, Article 1, reprinted in Elizabeth Clark and Herbert Richardson, eds, *Women and Religion: A Feminist Sourcebook of Christian Thought* (New York: Harper and Row, 1977), 87, 88.

15 Bridget of Sweden, *Revelationes* 7.22, translated and quoted in Katharina M. Wilson, *Medieval Women Writers* (Athens: University of Georgia Press, 1984), 345.

16 *The Book of Margery Kempe*, ed. William Butler-Bowdon (New York, Devin-Adair, 1944), 42.

17 The three quotations are from St. John Chrysostom, Commentary on Romans, Homily 4, translated in Boswell, *Christianity*, 359–62.

Chapter 2

1 The motto of the consistory at Nîmes, translated and quoted in Raymond A. Mentzer, "*Disciplina nervus ecclesiae*: The Calvinist Reform of Morals at Nîmes," *Sixteenth Century Journal* 18 (1987): 89–115.

2 *Luther's Works*, ed. Walter Brandt, vol. 45: *The Estate of Marriage* (Philadelphia: Muhlenberg Press, 1955), 36.

3 Martin Luther, "Vom ehelichen Leben, 1522," *D. Martin Luthers Werke* (Weimar: 1883) vol. 10/2, 296.

4 *Luther's Works*, ed. Walter Brandt, vol. 45: *The Estate of Marriage* (Philadelphia: Muhlenberg Press, 1955), 40.

5 Martin Luther, "Vom ehelichen Leben, 1522," *D. Martin Luthers Werke* (Weimar: 1883) vol. 10/2, 296.

6 *Luther's Works*, ed. Jaroslav Pelikan, vol. 7: *Lectures on Genesis* (St. Louis: Concordia, 1965), 76.

7 The quotations in this paragraph are all taken from Kathleen Crowther-Heyck, "'Be fruitful and multiply': Genesis and Generation in Reformation Germany," *Renaissance Quarterly* 55(3) (Autumn 2002): 904–35.

8 Quoted and translated in Bridget Heal, *The Cult of the Virgin Mary in Early Modern Germany: Protestant and Catholic Piety, 1500–1648* (Cambridge: Cambridge University Press, 2007), 286.

9 The quotation from Calvin is from the Institutes 2.8.44, ed. John T. McNeill, trans. Ford Lewis Battles, 2 vols., *Library of Christian Classics*, vol. 20–21 (Philadelphia: Westminster Press, 1960), 1:408.

10 Robert Cleaver, *A Godley Form of Household Government* (1603), quoted in Daniel Doriani, "The Puritans, Sex, and Pleasure," in Elizabeth Stuart and Adrian Thatcher, eds, *Christian Perspectives on Sexuality and Gender* (Leominster: Gracewing, 1996), 42.

11 Quoted in James Strayer, "Vielweiberei als 'innerweltliche Askese': Neue Eheauffassungen in der Reformationszeit," *Mennonitische Geschichtsblätter* 37 (1980): 34. Strayer's translation.

12 Lawrence Clarkson quoted in Christopher Hill, *The World Turned Upside Down: Radical Ideas during the English Revolution* (London: Penguin, 1972), 215.

13 Translated and quoted in Richard Greaves, "Church Courts," in *Oxford Encyclopedia of the Reformation*, ed. Hans Hillerbrand (New York: Oxford University Press, 1996), 1:437.

14 Quotations in this paragraph taken from Faramerz Dabhoiwala, "Sex and Societies for Moral Reform, 1688–1800," *Journal of British Studies* 46(2) (April 2007): 290–319.

15 Quoted in Richard L. Greaves, *God's Other Children: Protestant Nonconformists and the Emergence of Denominational Churches in Ireland, 1660–1700* (Stanford: Stanford University Press, 1997), 293.

16 1533 ordinance of a girls' school in Wittenberg, translated and quoted in Gerald Strass, *Luther's House of Learning: Indoctrination of the Young in Luther's Germany* (Baltimore: Johns Hopkins University Press, 1978), 197.

17 Quoted in Peter Sherlock, "Monuments, Reputation and Clerical Marriage in Reformation England: Bishop Barlow's Daughters," *Gender & History* 16(1) (April 2004), 65.

18 1562 Eheordnung and 1563 *Ehegerichtsordnung*, quoted and translated in Joel F. Harrington, *Reordering Marriage and Society in Reformation Germany* (Cambridge: Cambridge University Press, 1995), 188, 189.

19 German church ordinances, quoted in Dagmar Freist, "One Body, Two Confessions: Mixed Marriages in Germany," in Ulinka Rublack, ed., *Gender in Early Modern German History* (Cambridge: Cambridge University Press, 2002), 282, 285.

20 Records of the Strasbourg XXI, translated and quoted in Merry E. Wiesner, *Working Women in Renaissance Germany* (New Brunswick: Rutgers University Press, 1986), 20.

21 London Consistory Court Deposition Books, quoted in Laura Gowing, *Domestic Dangers: Women, Words and Sex in Early Modern London* (Oxford: Clarendon Press, 1996), 221–22. Spelling and orthography modernized.

22 Quoted in Mary Fissell, "The Politics of Reproduction in the English Reformation," *Representations* 87 (Summer 2004), 65.

23 Quoted in David Cressy, *Birth, Marriage and Death: Ritual, Religion, and the Life Cycle in Tudor and Stuart England* (Oxford: Oxford University Press, 1997), 227.

24 Marriage court records of Zurich, quoted and translated in C. Arnold Snyder and Linda A. Heubert Hecht, eds, *Profiles of Anabaptist Women: Sixteenth-Century Reforming Pioneers* (Waterloo, Ontario: Wilfried Laurier University Press, 1996), 41.

25 Quoted in Roderick Phillips, *Putting Asunder: A History of Divorce in Western Society* (Cambridge: Cambridge University Press, 1988), 290.

26 Notary's record from Neuchâtel, quoted and translated in Jeffrey R. Watt, *The Making of Modern Marriage: Matrimonial Control and the Rise of Sentiment in Neuchâtel, 1550–1800* (Ithaca: Cornell University Press, 1992), 103.

27 Prussian court record from 1746, quoted in Ulrike Gleixner, *"Das Mensch" und "der Kerl": Die Konstruktion von Geschlecht in Unzuchtsverfahren der Frühen Neuzeit* (Frankfurt: Campus, 1994), 158. My translation.

28 1578 Memmingen ordinance, quoted in Wiesner, *Working Women*, 62.

29 Statute of the city of Strasbourg, translated and quoted in Merry E. Wiesner, "Having Their Own Smoke: Employment and Independence for Singlewomen in Germany, 1400–1750," in Amy Froide and Judith M. Bennett, eds, *Singlewomen in the European Past, 1300–1800* (Philadelphia: University of Pennsylvania Press, 1999), 201.

30 Quotation from Beate Schuster, *Die freien Frauen: Dirnen und Frauenhäuser im 15. und 16. Jahrhundert* (Frankfurt: Campus, 1995), 399; my translation.

31 Melchior Ambach, *Von Tantzen . . .*, Frankfurt, 1564, fo. B iv v, quoted and translated in Lyndal Roper, *Oedipus and the Devil: Witchcraft, Sexuality and Religion in Early Modern Europe* (London: Routledge, 1994), 155.

32 A. Rulman, Harangues, quoted and translated in Philippe Chareyre, "'The Great Difficulties One Must Bear to Follow Jesus Christ': Morality at Sixteenth-Century Nîmes," in Raymond A. Mentzer, ed., *Sin and the Calvinists: Morals Control and the Consistory in the Reformed Tradition*, Sixteenth Century Essays and Studies, vol. 32 (Kirksville, Mo.: Sixteenth Century Journal Publishers, 1994), 88.

33 Quoted in Patricia Crawford, *Women and Religion in England, 1500–1720* (London: Routledge, 1993), 16.

34 Quoted and translated in E. William Monter, *Ritual, Myth and Magic in Early Modern Europe* (Athens, Ohio: Ohio University Press, 1983), 118.

35 Quoted and translated in Helmut Puff, *Sodomy in Reformation Germany and Switzerland, 1400–1600* (Chicago: University of Chicago Press, 2003), 146.

36 Quoted in Susan C. Karant-Nunn and Merry E. Wiesner-Hanks, ed. and trans., *Luther on Women: A Sourcebook* (Cambridge: Cambridge University Press, 2003), 167.

37 Quotations in this paragraph from Silke R. Falkner, "'Having it Off' with Fish, Camels, and Lads: Sodomitic Pleasures in German-Language *Turcica*," *Journal of the History of Sexuality* 13(4) (2004): 401–27.

38 Quoted and translated in Theo van der Meer, "Sodomy and the Pursuit of a Third Sex in the Early Modern Period," in Gilbert Herdt, ed., *Third Sex, Third Gender: Beyond Sexual Dimorphism in Culture and History* (New York: Zone Books, 1994), 141.

39 Quotations from Swedish court records, translated and quoted in Jonas Liliequist, "Peasants Against Nature: Crossing the Boundaries between Man and Animal in Seventeenth- and Eighteenth-Century Sweden," *Journal of the History of Sexuality* 1(3) (1991): 407, 401.

40 *Malleus Maleficarum*, translated and quoted in Alan C. Kors and Edward Peters, eds, *Witchcraft in Europe 1100–1700: Documentary History* (Philadelphia: University of Pennsylvania Press, 1972), 127.

41 *De sagis*, translated and quoted in Gerhild Scholz Williams, "On Finding Words: Witchcraft and the Discourses of Dissidence and Discovery," in Lynne Tatlock and Christiane Bohnert, eds, *The Graph of Sex and the German Text: Gendered Culture in Early Modern Germany 1500–1700*, Chloe: Beihefte zum Daphnis, 19 (Amsterdam: Rodopi, 1994), 55.

42 Quoted in Christina Larner, *Witchcraft and Religion: The Politics of Popular Belief* (London: Basil Blackwell, 1984), 85.

43 *The wonderful discoverie of the witchcrafts of Margaret and Philippa Flower*, 1619, printed in Barbara Rosen, *Witchcraft in England 1558–1618* (Amherst: University of Massachusetts Press, 1991), 379.

Chapter 3

1 John Major, *In quartum Sententiarum* (Paris, 1519) translated and quoted in John Noonan, *Contraception: A History of Its Treatment by the Catholic Theologians and Canonists* (New York: Mentor-Omega, 1967), 374.

2 *Concilium Tridentinum* 8:624, translated and quoted in James A. Brundage, *Law, Sex, and Christian Society in Medieval Europe* (Chicago: University of Chicago Press, 1987) *Law, Sex*, 568.

3 *The Canons and Decrees of the Sacred and Oecumenical Council of Trent*, ed. and trans. J. Waterworth (London: Dolman, 1848), Session 25, Chapter 14, 270.

4 Ibid., Session 25, Chapter 5, 240.

5 Geminianus Monacensis, *Geistlicher Weeg-Weiser gen Himmel* (Munich 1679) translated and quoted in Ulrike Strasser, *State of Virginity: Gender, Religion, and Politics in an Early Modern Catholic State* (Ann Arbor: University of Michigan Press, 2004), 38.

6 Tomás Sánchez, *De sancto matrimonii sacramento*, translated and quoted in John T. Noonan, *Contraception: A History of Its Treatment by the Catholic Theologians and Canonists* (New York: New American Library, 1965), 391.

7   Carlo Borromeo, *Avvertenze* (1574), translated and quoted in Wietse de Boer, *The Conquest of the Soul: Confession, Discipline, and Public Order in Counter-Reformation Milan* (Leiden: Brill, 2001), 69.

8   Quoted and translated in Emlyn Eisenach, *Husbands, Wives, and Concubines: Marriage, Family, and Social Order in Sixteenth-century Verona* (Kirksville, Mo.: Truman State University Press, 2004), 31.

9   André Burguière and François Lebrun, "Priest, Prince and Family," in André Burguière, et al., eds, *A History of the Family: Volume Two – The Impact of Modernity* (Cambridge, Mass.: Harvard University Press, 1996), 129.

10 Jean Benedicti, *Somme des péchés* (Paris, 1601), translated and quoted in Pierre Hurteau, "Catholic Moral Discourse on Male Sodomy and Masturbation in the Seventeenth and Eighteenth Centuries," *Journal of the History of Sexuality* 4 (1993): 13.

11 Letter written in 1585 by the inquisitors of the provinces of Galicia and Asturias, translated and quoted in Jaime Contreras and Gustav Henningsen, "Forty-four Thousand Cases of the Spanish Inquisition (1540–1700): Analysis of a Historical Data Bank," in Gustav Henningsen and John Tedeschi, eds, *The Inquisition in Early Modern Europe: Studies on Sources and Methods* (Dekalb: Northern Illinois University Press, 1986), 120.

12 Translated and quoted in Marc R. Forster, *Catholic Revival in the Age of the Baroque: Religious Identity in Southwest Germany, 1550–1750* (Cambridge: Cambridge University Press, 2001), 142.

13 1652 visitation report, translated and quoted in Andrew Barnes, "The Social Transformation of the French Parish Clergy," in Barbara B. Diefendorf and Carla Hesse, *Culture and Identity in Early Modern Europe (1500–1800): Essays in Honor of Natalie Zemon Davis* (Ann Arbor: University of Michigan Press, 1993), 142.

14 Simone Laqua, "Concubinage and the Church in Early Modern Münster," *Past & Present* (2006), 92.

15 Quoted in Phil Kilroy, "Women and the Reformation in Seventeenth-Century Ireland," in Margaret MacCurtain and Mary O'Dowd, *Women in Early Modern Ireland* (Edinburgh: Edinburgh University Press, 1991), 189.

16 Quoted in Frances E. Dolan, *Whores of Babylon: Catholicism, Gender, and Seventeenth Century Print Culture* (Ithaca, N.Y.: Cornell University Press, 1999), 90.

17 Diego Pérez de Valdivia, *Aviso de gente recogida* (1585), translated and quoted in Stephen Haliczer, *Sexuality in the Confessional: A Sacrament Profaned* (New York: Oxford University Press, 1996), 111.

18 Baltasar Alvarez, *Escritos Espirituales*, translated and quoted in Jodi Bilinkoff, "Confessors, Penitents, and the Construction of Identities in Early Modern Avila," in Diefendorf and Hesse, *Culture*, 86.

19 Pope Urban VIII, *Annullatio*, quoted and translated in Strasser, *State of Virginity*, 159.

20 Village priest in France, 1774, translated and quoted in Nicole Castan, et al., "Community, State and Family: Trajectories and Tensions," in Roger Chartier, ed., *A History of Private Life: III: Passions of the Renaissance* (Cambridge, Mass.: Harvard University Press, 1989), 567.

21 Letter from Jean d'Arrerac, translated and quoted in Burguière and Lebrun, "Priest," 128.

22 Translated and quoted in Jutta Sperling, "Marriage at the Time of the Council of Trent (1560–70): Clandestine Marriages, Kinship Prohibitions, and Dowry Exchange in European Comparison," *Journal of Early Modern History* 8(1) (2004), 97.

23 Quoted in Edward Behrend-Martínez, *Unfit for Marriage: Impotent Spouses on Trial in the Basque Region of Spain, 1650–1750* (Reno: University of Nevada Press, 2007), 106.

24 Translated and quoted in Daniela Hacke, *Women, Sex, and Marriage in Early Modern Venice* (Aldershot: Ashgate, 2003), 124.

25 Ibid., 141.

26 Quoted in Monica Chojnacka and Merry Wiesner-Hanks, *Ages of Woman, Ages of Man: Sources in European Social History, 1400–1750* (Harlow: Pearson, 2002), 142. Translation by Allyson Poska.

27 Allyson M. Poska, *Women and Authority in Early Modern Spain: The Peasants of Galicia* (Oxford: Oxford University Press, 2005).

28 1575 Inquisition deposition, translated and quoted in Jean-Pierre DeDieu, "The Inquisition and Popular Culture in New Castile," in Stephen Haliczer, ed., *Inquisition and Society in Early Modern Europe* (Totowa, N.J.: Barnes and Noble, 1987), 139–40.

29 Inquisition records in the diocesan archives of Cuenca, translated and quoted in Sara T. Nalle, *God in La Mancha: Religious Reform and the People of Cuenca, 1500–1650* (Baltimore, Md.: Johns Hopkins, 1992), 61.

30 Legal proceedings in the Archivo della Curia Vescovile, Gallipoli, 1749, translated and quoted in David Gentilcore, *From Bishop to Witch: The System of the Sacred in Early Modern Terra d'Otranto* (Manchester: Manchester University Press, 1992), 58.

31 Chojnacka and Wiesner-Hanks, *Ages of Woman*, 52. Translation by Allyson Poska.

32 Archives of the Society of Jesus at Rome, 1593, translated and quoted in Louis Châtellier, *The Europe of the Devout: The Catholic Reformation and the Formation of a New Society* (Cambridge: Cambridge University Press, 1989), 45.

33 Madre Magdalena de San Gerónimo, *Razón, y forma* . . . (1608) translated and quoted in Mary Elizabeth Perry, "Magdalens and Jezebels in Counter-Reformation Spain," in Anne J. Cruz and Mary Elizabeth Perry, eds, *Culture and Control in Counter-Reformation Spain* (Minneapolis: University of Minnesota Press, 1992), 135–36.

34 Bavarian electoral decrees, translated and quoted in Strasser, *State of Virginity*, 103, 106.

35 Edict of Henry II, 1556, translated and quoted in Burguière and Lebrun, "Priest," 111.

36 de Boer, *Conquest*, 242.

37 Quotations from the letteres of the Valencian inquisitors, translated and quoted in Christian Berco, *Sexual Hierarchies, Public Status: Men, Sodomy, and*

Society in Spain's Golden Age (Toronto: University of Toronto Press, 2007), 4, 125, 127.

38 Translated and quoted in Michael Rey, "Police and Sodomy in Eighteenth-century Paris: From Sin to Disorder," in Kent Gerard and Gert Hekma, eds, *The Pursuit of Sodomy: Male Homosexuality in Renaissance and Enlightenment Europe* (New York: Harrington Park Press, 1989), 141.

39 1546 inquisitorial examination of Magdalena de la Cruz, translated and quoted in Alison Weber, "Saint Teresa, Demonologist," in Cruz and Perry, *Culture and Control*, 173.

40 *Potrebnik* (1651), translated and quoted in Eve Levin, *Sex and Society among the Orthodox Slavs, 900–1700* (Ithaca, N.Y.: Cornell University Press, 1989), 204.

41 Translated and quoted in Paul Bushkovitch, *Religion and Society in Russia: The Sixteenth and Seventeenth Centuries* (New York: Oxford University Press, 1992), 55–56.

42 Translated and quoted in Levin, *Sex and Society*, 99.

43 Daniel H. Kaiser: "'Whose Wife Will She be at the Resurrection?' Marriage and Remarriage in Early Modern Russia," *Slavic Review* 62(2) (Summer 2003), 312.

44 Mikhail Lomonosov, *Sochineniia*, translated and quoted in Natalie Pushkareva, *Women in Russian History from the Twelfth to the Twentieth Century*, trans. Eve Levin (Armonk, N.Y.: M.E. Sharpe, 1997), 158.

Chapter 4

1 Translated and quoted in John F. Chuchiak, "The Sins of the Fathers: Franciscan Friars, Parish Priests, and the Sexual Conquest of the Yucatec Maya, 1545–1808," *Ethnohistory* 54(1) (Winter 2007), 81.

2 Translated and quoted in Arthur J.O. Anderson, "Aztec Wives," in Susan Schroeder, Stephanie Wood, and Robert Haskett, eds, *Indian Women of Early Mexico* (Norman: University of Oklahoma Press, 1997), 60.

3 Also de la Peña Montenegro, *Itinerario para párrocos de indios* (1668), quoted and translated in Jorge Cañizares Esguerra, "New World, New Stars: Patriotic Astrology and the Invention of Indian and Creole Bodies in Colonial Spanish America, 1600–650," *American Historical Review* (February 1999), 65.

4 Lawrence A. Clayton, Vernon James Knight Jr., and Edward C, Moore, eds, *The De Soto Chronicles: The Expedition of Hernando De Soto to North America in 1539–1543*, 2 vols (Tuscaloosa: University of Alabama Press, 1993), 1:289.

5 Royal order, translated and quoted in Juan Francisco Maura, *Women of the Conquest of the Americas*, translated by John F. Deredita (New York: Peter Lang, 1997), 34.

6 1752 royal order, translated and quoted in Ramón A. Gutiérrez, *When Jesus Came, the Corn Mothers Went Away: Marriage, Sexuality, and Power in New Mexico 1500–1846* (Stanford, Calif.: Stanford University Press, 1991), 217.

7 Translated and quoted in Ramon Gutiérrez, "From Honor to Love: Transformations of the Meaning of Sexuality in Colonial New Mexico," in

Raymond T. Smith, ed., *Kinship Ideology and Practice in Latin America* (Chapel Hill: University of North Carolina Press, 1984), 244.

8 Quoted in Stephen Neill, *A History of Christian Missions* (New York: Penguin, 1964), 171.

9 Translated and quoted in Alida Metcalf, "Women as Go-Betweens? Patterns in Sixteenth-Century Brazil," in Nora E. Jaffary, *Gender, Race, and Religion in the Colonization of the Americas* (Burlington, Vt.: Ashgate, 2007), 25.

10 Barry D. Sell and Louise M. Burkhart, eds, *Nahuatl Theater, Vol. 1: Death and Life in Colonial Nahua Mexico* (Norman: University of Oklahoma Press, 2004), 207, 209.

11 Translated and quoted in Kenneth Mills, "Diego de Ocaña's Hagiography of New and Renewed Devotion in Colonial Peru," in Allen Greer and Jodi Bilinkoff, eds, *Colonial Saints: Discovering the Holy in the Americas* (New York: Routledge, 2003), 57, 61.

12 Pete Sigal, *From Moon Goddesses to Virgins: The Colonization of Yucatecan Maya Sexual Desire* (Austin: University of Texas Press, 2000), 120.

13 Chuchiak, "Sins of the Fathers," 92.

14 From Fr. Juan de la Anunciacíon, *Doctrina christiana muy cumplida donde se contiene la exposición de todo necesario para doctrinar a los indios* (Mexico City 1575) quoted and translated in Serge Gruzinski, "Individualization and Acculturation: Confession Among the Nahuas of Mexico from the Sixteenth to the Eighteenth Century," in Asuncion Lavrin, ed., *Sexuality and Marriage in Colonial Latin America* (Lincoln: University of Nebraska, 1989), 101.

15 Quoted and translated in Harry Kelsey, *The Doctrina and Confesionario of Juan Cortés* (Altadena, Calif.: Howling Coyote Press, 1979), 115.

16 Translated and quoted in Laura Fishman, "French Views of Native American Women in the Early Modern Era: The Tupinamba of Brazil," in Tamara L. Hunt and Micheline R. Lessard, eds, *Women and the Colonial Gaze* (New York: Palgrave, 2002), 73.

17 Antonio Ruiz de Montoya, *The Spiritual Conquest*, trans. C.J. McNaspy, S.J. (St. Louis: Institute of Jesuit Sources, 1993), 54.

18 Acosta, *Historia Natural y Moral de las Indias* (Seville, 1590), translated and quoted in C.R. Boxer, *Mary and Misogyny: Women in Iberian Expansion Overseas 1415–1815* (New York: Oxford University Press, 1975), 108.

19 *A Harvest of Reluctant Souls: The Memorial of Fray Alonso de Benavides, 1630*, translated and edited by Baker H. Morrow (Niwot, Colo.: University Press of Colorado, 1996), 31–2.

20 Translated and quoted in Luis Martín, *Daughters of the Conquistadores: Women of the Viceroyalty of Peru* (Albuquerque: University of New Mexico Press, 1983), 152.

21 Translated and quoted in Richard E. Boyer, *Lives of the Bigamists: Marriage, Family, and Community in Colonial Mexico* (Albuquerque: University of New Mexico Press, 1995), 103.

22 Ibid., 128.

23 Quoted in Boxer, *Mary and Misogyny*, 51.

24 Letter of Count of Lemos to Queen Regent Mariana (1669) translated and quoted in Nancy E. van Deusen, "Defining the Sacred and the Worldly: *Beatas* and *Recogidas* in Late-Seventeenth-century Lima," *Colonial Latin American Historical Review* 6 (1997): 464.

25 Archives of Chihauhau, translated and quoted in Cheryl English Martin, *Governance and Society in Colonial Mexico: Chihauhau in the Eighteenth Century* (Stanford, Calif.: Stanford University Press, 1996), 174.

26 Translated and quoted in Robert Haskett, "Activist or Adulteress? The Life and Struggle of Doña Josefa María of Tepoztlan," in Schroeder, *Indian Women*, 149.

27 Translated and quoted in Elisa Sampson Vera Tudela, "Fashioning a *Cacique* Nun: From Saints' Lives to Indian Lives in the Spanish Americas," *Gender and History* 9 (1997): 187.

28 Juan de Pérez Bocanegra, *Ritual formulario* . . . (1631) translated and quoted in Regina Harrison, "The Theology of Concupiscence: Spanish-Quechua Confessional Manuals in the Andes," in Francisco Javier Cevallos-Candau, ed., *Coded Encounters: Writing, Gender, and Ethnicity in Colonial Latin America* (Amherst: University of Massachusetts Press, 1994), 146.

29 Quoted in Serge Gruzinski, "The Ashes of Desire: Homosexuality in Mid-Seventeenth-Century New Spain," in Pete Sigal, ed., *Infamous Desire: Male Homosexuality in Colonial Latin America* (Chicago: University of Chicago Press, 2003), 198.

30 Mexican Inquisition Records, translated and quoted in Fernando Cervantes, *The Devil in the New World: The Impact of Diabolism in New Spain* (New Haven, Conn.: Yale University Press, 1994), 38–9.

31 Translated and quoted in Lisa Sousa, "The Devil and Deviance in Native Criminal Narratives from Early Mexico," *The Americas (West Bethesda, Md.)* 59.2 (October 2002), 167.

32 Jesuit report, quoted and translated in Susan Deeds, "Indian Women in Jesuit Missions," in Schroeder et al., *Indian Women*, 261.

33 Translated and quoted in Ana Mariella Bacigalupo, "The Struggle for Mapuche Shamans' Masculinity: Colonial Politics of Gender, Sexuality, and Power in Southern Chile," *Ethnohistory* 51(3) (Summer 2004), 490.

34 Translated and quoted in Martha Few, *Women Who Live Evil Lives: Gender, Religion, and the Politics of Power in Colonial Guatemala* (Austin: University of Texas Press, 2002), 38.

35 Ibid., 87.

Chapter 5

1 Translated and quoted in James Sweet, *Recreating Africa: Culture, Kinship and Religion in the African-Portuguese World, 1441–1770* (Chapel Hill: University of North Carolina Press, 2003), 37.

2 Letters of Afonso I (1514 and 1526), in Klaus Koschorke, Frieder Ludwig, and Mariano Delgado, eds, *A History of Christianity in Asia, Africa, and Latin*

America, 1450–1990: A Documentary Sourcebook (Grand Rapids, Mich.: William B. Eerdmans, 2007), 152, 153.

3 Quoted in Linda M. Heywood and John K. Thornton, *Central Africans, Atlantic Creoles, and the Foundation of the Americas, 1585–1660* (New York: Cambridge University Press, 2007), 174.

4 Dominican friar Duarte Nunes (1522), quoted in Koschorke, *History of Christianity*, 15.

5 Dutch Church Consistory of Colombo (1751), quoted in ibid., 45.

6 Quoted in Carolyn Brewer, *Shamanism, Catholicism, and Gender Relations in Colonial Philippines, 1521–1685* (Aldershot: Ashgate, 2004), 109.

7 P. Sebastien Totanes, *Manual tagalog* (1745), quoted and translated in Vicente L. Rafael, *Contracting Colonialism: Translation and Christian Conversion in Tagalog Society under early Spanish Rule* (Ithaca, N.Y.: Cornell University Press, 1988), 105.

8 Antonio Ma-Rosales, O.F.M., *A Study of a 16th-century Tagalog Manuscript on the Ten Commandments: Its Significance and Implications* (Quzon City: University of Philippines Press, 1984), 53, 55, 57.

9 Relation of Pedro Chirino (1604) in Emma Blair and James Robertson, *The Philippine Islands (1493–1898)* (Cleveland: Arthur C. Clark, 1902–) 13: 127.

10 Letter from Fr. Francisco Vaez to Rev. Fr. Claudio Aquaviva, general of the Jesuits, June 10, 1601, in Blair and Robertson, *Philippine Islands*, 11: 199.

11 Archbishop Filipe Pardo, in Blair and Robertson, *Philippine Islands*, 45: 182.

12 Statistics in H.E. Niemeijer, *Calvinisme en koloniale Stadscultuur Batavia 1619–1725* (Dissertation, Free University of Amsterdam, 1996), 222–23.

13 Quoted in Leonard Blussé, *Strange Company: Chinese Settlers, Mestizo Women and the Dutch in VOC Batavia* (Dordrecht: Foris, 1986), 170.

14 Francisco Colín, *Labor evangélica* (1663), translated and quoted in Haruko Nawata Ward, "Jesuits, Too: Jesuits, Women Catechists, and Jezebels in Christian Century Japan," in *The Jesuits II: Cultures, Sciences, and the Arts, 1540–1773*, edited by John W. O'Malley, et al. (Toronto: University of Toronto Press, 2006), 647.

15 Translated and quoted in George Elison, *Deus Destroyed: The Image of Christianity in Early Modern Japan* (Cambridge, Mass.: Harvard University Press, 1973), 279.

16 Matteo Ricci, *The True Meaning of the Lord of Heaven*, translated by Douglas Lancashire and Peter Hu Kuo-chen, S.J. (St. Louis: Institute of Jesuit Sources, 1985), 431.

17 Cited in Jacques Gernet, *China and the Christian Impact: A Conflict of Cultures* (Cambridge: Cambridge University Press, 1985), 191.

18 Translated and quoted in Barbara Andaya, *The Flaming Womb: Repositioning Women in Early Modern Southeast Asia* (Honolulu: University of Hawai'i Press, 2006), 99.

19 Father Marco della Tomba, 1763, quoted in David N. Lorenzen, "Europeans in Late Mughal South Asia: The Perceptions of Italian Missionaries," *Indian Economic & Social History Review* 40(1) (2003), 19.

20 William Bosman, *Description of Guinea Coast* (1704) in Koschorke, *History of Christianity*, 171.

21 Quoted and translated in N. Standaert, *Yang Tingyun, Confucian and Christian in Late Ming China: His Life and Thought* (Leiden: Brill, 1988), 54.
22 Quoted and translated in Ines G. Zupanov, "Lust, Marriage and Free Will: Jesuit Critique of Paganism in South India (Seventeenth Century)," *Studies in History* 16(2) (2000): 219.
23 François Caron, *A True Description of the Mighty Kingdoms of Japan and Siam*, reprinted in Michael Cooper, ed., *They Came to Japan: An Anthology of European Reports on Japan, 1543–1640* (Berkeley: University of California Press, 1965), 61–62.
24 Quoted and translated in Adrian Dudink, "The *Sheng-Ch'ao Tso-P'i* (1623) of Hsü Tu-Shou," in Leonard Blussé and Harriet Zurndorfer, eds, *Conflict and Accommodation in Early Modern East Asia; Essays in Honour of Erik Zürcher* (Leiden: Brill, 1993), 115–16.
25 Ibid., 114–15.
26 Quoted in Liam Matthew Brockey, *Journey to the East: the Jesuit Mission to China 1579–1724* (Cambridge, Mass.: Harvard University Press, 2008), 333.
27 Quoted in Liam Matthew Brockey, "Flowers of Faith in an Emporium of Vices: The 'Portuguese' Jesuit Church in Seventeenth Century Peking," *Monumenta Serica* 53 (2005): 61.
28 Jonathan D. Spence, *The Memory Palace of Matteo Ricci* (New York: Viking Penguin, 1984), 220.
29 Diego de Patoja, *Seven Victories*, quoted and translated in Ann Waltner, "Demerits and Deadly Sins: Jesuit Moral Tracts in Late Ming China," in Stuart Schwartz, ed., *Implicit Understandings: Observing, Reporting, and Reflecting on the Encounters Between Europeans and Other Peoples in the Early Modern Era* (Cambridge: Cambridge University Press, 1994), 434–5.
30 Ordinances enacted by the Audience of Manila, 1598–99, in Blair and Robertson, *Philippine Islands*, 11: 57.
31 Ibid., 56.
32 1771 Edict of the Inquisition at Goa, quoted and translated in C.R. Boxer, *Race Relations in the Portuguese Colonial Empire 1415–1825* (Oxford: Clarendon Press, 1963), 46, 45.
33 Pedro Murillo Velarde, *Historia de Philipinas*, 1749, in Blair and Robertson, *Philippine Islands*, 44: 93–94.
34 Memorial to the Council by the citizens of the Philippines, July 26, 1586 in Blair and Robertson, *Philippine Islands*, 6: 172.
35 C.R. Boxer, *The Dutch Seaborne Empire, 1600–1800* (New York: Knopf, 1965), 216.
36 Quoted in Stephen Neill, *A History of Christianity in India, The Beginnings to AD 1707* (Cambridge: Cambridge University Press, 1984), 372.
37 Quoted in Boxer, *Race Relations*, 64.
38 Quoted in Boxer, *Dutch Seaborne*, 221.
39 Quoted in Neill, *Christianity in India*, 95.
40 Quoted in George E. Brooks, *Eurafricans in Western Africa: Commerce, Social Status, Gender, and Religious Observance from the Sixteenth to the Eighteenth Century* (Athens, Ohio: Ohio University Press, 2003), 214.

41 Translated and quoted in John Thornton, *Africa and Africans in the Making of the Atlantic World, 1400–1800*, 2nd edn (Cambridge: Cambridge University Press, 1998), 170.

42 Quoted in Boxer, *Race Relations*, 61.

43 Quoted and translated in C.R. Boxer, *Mary and Misogyny: Women in Iberian Expansion Overseas, 1415–1815* (New York: Oxford University Press, 1975), 20–21.

44 Johan Nieuhof, *Voyages and Travels to the East Indies, 1653–1670*, quoted in Barbara Watson Andaya, "From Temporary Wife to Prostitute: Sexuality and Economic Change in Early Modern Southeast Asia," *Journal of Women's History* 9(4) (1998): 24.

45 Quoted in Pratima P. Kamat, "From Conversion to the Civil Code: Gender and the Colonial State in Goa, 1510–1961," *Indian Historical Review* 27(2) (2000): 71.

46 1639 resolution of Batavian Council, translated and quoted in Blussé, *Strange Company*, 166, 167.

Chapter 6

1 From Society for the Propagation of the Gospel Records, cited in Daniel K. Richter, "'Some of Them . . . Would Always Have a Minister with Them': Mohawk Protestantism, 1683–1719," *American Indian Quarterly* 16 (1992): 478.

2 Jeanne-Françoise Juchereau de St. Ignace and Marie Andrée Duplessis de Ste. Hélène, *Les Annales de l'Hôtel-Dieu de Québec, 1636–1716*, ed. Albert Jamet (Québec: Hôtel Dieu, 1939), 20, translated and quoted in Natalie Zemon Davis, "Iroquois Women, European Women," in Margo Hendricks and Patricia Parker, eds, *Women, "Race," and Writing in the Early Modern Period* (London: Routledge, 1994), 246.

3 Reuben Gold Thwaites, ed., *Jesuit Relations and Allied Documents* (Cleveland: Burrows Brothers, 1896–1901), Vol. 18: 125 (hereafter JR).

4 Register of the Congregation of the Children of Mary, quoted in Emily Clark, "'By all the Conduct of their Lives': A Laywomen's Confraternity in New Orleans, 1730–44," *William and Mary Quarterly* 54 (October 1997), 779.

5 Letter from Colbert to Intendant Jean Talon, January 5, 1666, quoted and translated in Saliha Belmessous, "Assimilation and Racialism in Seventeenth and Eighteenth-century French Colonial Policy," in *American Historical Review* 110(2) (April 2005), 325, 326.

6 Quoted in Guillame Aubert, "'The Blood of New France': Race and Purity of the Blood in the French Atlantic World," *William and Mary Quarterly* 61(3) (2004), 449.

7 Aubert, "Blood of New France," 459.

8 Quoted in Jennifer M. Spear, "'They Need Wives': Métissage and the Regulation of Sexuality in French Louisiana, 1699–1730," in Martha Hodes, ed., *Sex, Love, Race: Crossing Boundaries in North American History* (New York: New York University Press, 1999), 47, 48, 50.

9 John Robinson, *The Works of John Robinson, Pastor of the Pilgrim Fathers* (Boston: Doctrinal Tract and Book Society, 1851) cited in Rosemary Radford Ruether and Rosemary Skinner Keller, eds, *Women and Religion in America. Volume 2: The Colonial and Revolutionary Periods* (San Francisco: Harper and Row, 1981), 161–62.

10 Samuel Danforth, *The Cry of Sodom Enquired Into* (Cambridge, Mass., 1674), cited in Richard Godbeer, "'The Cry of Sodom': Discourse, Intercourse, and Desire in Colonial New England," *William and Mary Quarterly*, 3rd ser., 52 (1995), 263.

11 Cotton Mather, *An Holy Rebuke to the Unclean Spirit* (Boston, 1693) cited in Godbeer, "Cry of Sodom," 264.

12 Quoted in Anne G. Myles, "Border Crossings: The Queer Erotics of Quakerism in Seventeenth-Century New England," in Thomas A. Foster, ed., *Long before Stonewall: Histories of Same-Sex Sexuality in Early America* (New York: New York University Press, 2007), 122.

13 Quoted in Gail S. Marcus, "Criminal Procedure in New Haven," in David D. Hall, John M. Murrin, and Thad Tate, eds, *Saints and Revolutionaries* (New York: Norton, 1984), 132.

14 Quoted in Else L. Hambleton, "The Regulation of Sex in Seventeenth-Century Massachusetts: The Quarterly Courts of Essex County vs. Priscilla Willson and Mr. Samuel Appleton," in Merril D. Smith, ed., *Sex and Sexuality in Early America* (New York: New York University Press, 1998), 96.

15 Charles J. Hoadly, ed., *Records of the Colony or Jurisdiction of New Haven, 1653 to the Union* (Hartford, 1858) cited in Mary Beth Norton, *Founding Mothers and Fathers: Gendered Power and the Forming of American Society* (New York: Knopf, 1996), 349–50.

16 *Records and Files of the Quarterly Courts of Essex County, Massachusetts* (Salem, Mass., 1911–21) cited in Roderick Phillips, *Putting Asunder: A History of Divorce in Western Society* (Cambridge: Cambridge University Press, 1988), 146.

17 *Dorchester Church Records* cited in David H. Flaherty, *Privacy in Colonial New England* (Charlottesville: University Press of Virginia, 1967), 160.

18 Richard B. Pierce, ed., *Records of the First Church in Boston, 1630–1868* (Boston, 1961), cited in Sylvia R. Frey and Marian J. Morton, *New World, New Roles: A Documentary History of Women in Pre-Industrial America* (New York: Greenwood Press, 1986), 80–81.

19 Lyon Gardiner Tyler, ed., *Narratives of Early Virginia, 1606–1625* (New York, 1907), cited in Kathleen Brown, *Good Wives, Nasty Wenches and Anxious Patriarchs: Gender, Race, and Power in Colonial Virginia* (Chapel Hill: University of North Carolina Press, 1996), 91.

20 William Waller Hening, ed., *The Statutes at Large; Being a Collection of All the Laws of Virginia, from the First Session of the Legislature* (1823; facsmile reprint Charlottesville: University of Virginia Press, 1969), II: 166–67.

21 William Brown et al., eds, *Archives of Maryland* (Baltimore, 1883–1912) cited in Frey and Morton, *New World*, 10.

22 1749 South Carolina petition, quoted in Richard Godbeer, *Sexual Revolution in Early America* (Baltimore, Md.: Johns Hopkins University Press, 2002), 137.

23 Hening, *Statutes*, II:170.

24 Cited in Carl H. Nightingale, "Before Race Mattered: Geographies of the Color Line in Early Colonial Madras and New York," *American Historical Review* 113 (February 2008), 69.

25 Hening, *Statutes*, III: 86.

26 Thomas Harris and John McHenry, eds, *Maryland Reports* (New York, 1809), cited in Winthrop Jordan, *White over Black: American Attitudes toward the Negro, 1550–1813* (Chapel Hill: University of North Carolina Press, 1968), 160.

27 JR 18, 105–7.

28 JR 64: 195.

29 Jeanne-Françoise Juchereau de St. Ignace and Marie Andrée and Duplessis de Ste. Hélène, *Les Annales de Hôtel-Dieu de Quebec, 1636–1716* (Quebec, 1939), cited in Davis, "Iroquois Women," 255–56.

30 Cited in Allan Greer, *Mohawk Saint: Catherine Tekakwitha and the Jesuits* (New York: Oxford, 2005), 116.

31 Cited in Greer, *Mohawk Saint*, 176.

32 JR 24: 47; JR 25: 247.

33 Plymouth colony records, quoted in Godbeer, *Sexual Revolution*, 59.

34 John Winthrop's journal, quoted in Godbeer, *Sexual Revolution*, 103.

35 *The Charters and General Laws of the Colony and Province of Massachusetts Bay* (Boston, 1814) cited in Frey and Morton, *New World*, 20–21.

36 Essex County Court Records, quoted in Thomas A. Foster, "Deficient Husbands: Manhood, Sexual Incapacity, and Male Marital Sexuality in Seventeenth-Century New England," *William & Mary Quarterly* 56(4) (1999): 740.

37 R.R. Wheeler, *Concord: Climate for Freedom* (Concord, Mass.: Concord Antiquarian Society, 1967), 40.

38 Letter of the New London congregation to the General Meeting of Baptist Churches (1756) cited in Godbeer, "Cry of Sodom," 277.

39 Quoted in Ava Chamberlain, "Bad Books and Bad Boys: The Transformation of Gender in Eighteenth-Century Northampton, Massachusetts," *New England Quarterly* 75(2) (2002), 201.

40 John Winthrop, *Journal*, cited in Peter C. Hoffer and N.E.H. Hull, *Murdering Mothers: Infanticide in England and New England 1558–1803* (New York: New York University Press, 1981), 40.

41 Quoted in Ann Marie Plane, *Colonial Intimacies: Indian Marriage in Early New England* (Ithaca, N.Y.: Cornell University Press, 2000), 42.

42 Lower Norfolk County records, cited in James Horn, *Adapting to a New World: English Society in the Seventeenth-Century Chesapeake* (Chapel Hill: University of North Carolina Press, 1994), 214.

43 Accomack County records, cited in Helena Wall, *Fierce Communion: Family and Community in Early America* (Cambridge, Mass.: Harvard University Press, 1995), 60.

44 Cited in Brown, *Good Wives*, 194.

45 Cited in Plane, *Colonial Intimacies*, 139.

46 Quoted in Janet Moore Lindman, "The Body Baptist: Embodied Spirituality, Ritualization, and Church Discipline in Eighteenth-Century America,"

in Janet Moore Lindman and Michele Lise Tarter, eds, *A Centre of Wonders: The Body in Early America* (Ithaca, N.Y.: Cornell University Press, 2001), 182, 186.

47 Adelaide L. Fries et al., eds, *Records of the Moravians of North Carolina*, cited in Ruether and Keller, *Women and Religion*, 304.

48 *The Diary of Isaac Backus* (1751), cited in Erik R. Seeman, "Sarah Prentice and the Immortalists: Sexuality, Piety, and the Body in Eighteenth-Century New England," in Smith, *Sex and Sexuality*, 119.

49 *Diary of Ebenezer Parkman*, quoted in Godbeer, *Sexual Revolution*, 244.

INDEX